THE
PLANTATION
MISTRESS

THE
PLANTATION
MISTRESS

WOMAN'S WORLD
IN THE OLD SOUTH

CATHERINE
CLINTON

 PANTHEON BOOKS, NEW YORK

All rights reserved under International and Pan-American
Copyright Conventions. Published in the United States by
Pantheon Books, a division of Random House, Inc., New York,
and simultaneously in Canada by Random House of Canada
Limited, Toronto.

Grateful acknowledgment is made to the following for
permission to reprint previously published material:

University of Missouri Press: Excerpts from *The Family Letters
of Thomas Jefferson*, edited by Edwin Betts and James Adam
Bear, Jr. Copyright © 1966 by The Curators of the University
of Missouri. Reprinted by permission of The University of
Missouri Press.

University of North Carolina Press: Verse from *True Tales of
the South at War, 1861–65*, edited by Clarence Poe. Copyright
© 1961 by The University of North Carolina Press. Reprinted
by permission of The University of North Carolina Press.

Library of Congress Cataloging in Publication Data

Clinton, Catherine, 1952–
The plantation mistress.

Bibliography: p.
Includes index.
1. Mistresses—Southern States. 2. Plantation
life—Southern States.   3. Sex customs—Southern
States.   I. Title.
HQ806.C53   305.5'67   82-3549
ISBN 0-394-51686-9   AACR2

Designed by Naomi Osnos
Manufactured in the United States of America
First Edition

THIS BOOK IS DEDICATED
TO

CLAUDENE CLINTON

BOBBIE SIMMS

BARBARA LEVY UHLMANN

with appreciation
for their love,
encouragement,
and inspiration,
which made this volume possible.

*B*ut the effect of her being on those around her was incalculably diffusive: for the growing good of the world is partly dependent on unhistoric acts; and that things are not so ill with you and me as they might have been, is half owing to the number who lived faithfully a hidden life, and rest in unvisited tombs.

—George Eliot, *Middlemarch*

CONTENTS

PREFACE

HIDDEN LIVES

T he pageantry of days gone by—chivalrous cavaliers and belles in hoop skirts—lives in memory for many Southerners. The popular celebration of plantation legend, the Lost Cause, and the romance of Confederate lore (boy generals and seductive Rebel spies) spin a web of wonder, even today. This reverence for the Old South reveals an ironic obsession with glory as well as history. Southerners are as concerned with what might have been as with what was. The canvas of the southern past is liberally splashed with folklore, embellished by exaggeration, highlighted with pomp and spectacle. By redrawing history, in fact, the vanquished South defies defeat. Repeated and loving resurrection of the Old South's glory renovates the plantation past to a splendor that far outshines its foundation in reality.

Despite this elaborate re-examination and renewal, aspects of that past remain obscure. In this study, I focus on a character both overlaid by romantic mythologizing and considerably shortchanged by traditional historical literature—the plantation mistress. By looking through the prism of her actual experience, we transform our vision of the Old

South and, correspondingly, our understanding of the nature of slavery and sex in the American past.

This book was written first of all to tell a story. Although the final study remains continuously aware of theoretical issues, my research took me from archives to historic homes and ante-bellum plantation sites. While I cannot hope to reproduce all that I absorbed of texture as well as texts, this work tries to reflect the range and intensity of those myriad sources.

Concerned about the meaning of race in American history, I began with slavery. When I began to absorb as much literature as I could on the subject, I was overwhelmed by both the quality and the quantity of work on the topic. I greedily devoured the work of the "great men" of slave scholarship who reigned during my undergraduate years—Kenneth Stampp, Stanley Elkins, Winthrop Jordan, and Eugene Genovese—and was privileged to study with both Orlando Patterson and C. L. R. James during my years at Harvard. Yet I was most bedazzled by the rich primary literature to which I was exposed: Frederick Law Olmsted's accounts of travels in the Old South, Robert Manson Myers' editions of the Jones family correspondence (beginning with *The Children of Pride* in 1972), and finally the diary of Mary Boykin Chesnut, which has recently received some measure of the attention it deserves courtesy of C. Vann Woodward's new edition of her work. Although my interest in slavery increased over the years, my disenchantment with the secondary literature also grew. Where were the women?

This was a question that also grew out of the intellectual ferment of the sixties. After I had plowed through scores of volumes that maintained utter silence about white women in the slave South, two very valuable and essential works rescued me: Julia Cherry Spruill's *Life and Work of Women in the Southern Colonies* (1938) and especially Anne Firor Scott's *The Southern Lady: From Pedestal to Politics, 1830–1930* (1970). These two books stimulated my curiosity concerning plantation women and set me searching through the library stacks and probing the archives, even as an undergraduate.

Five years later, as I prepared to launch a doctoral dissertation, I determined to do justice to the massive and relatively unexplored documentary sources. Although I wanted to study all women throughout the southern states during the entire ante-bellum era, I was soon forced to narrow my focus. It is the aim of this work to provide a female counterpoint to the vast literature on the southern planter. In setting about to find the plantation mistress, I focused on women in residence on plantations with twenty slaves or more. Thus the majority of my subjects are elite, although a number of women who did not meet this economic or residential standard have made their way into the book. My study includes the seven seaboard states of the plantation South (excluding Florida): Virginia, North Carolina, South Carolina, Georgia, Alabama, Mississippi, and Louisiana. After surveying the large body of manuscript material available on the planter class for this region, I narrowed my chronological sights to the period 1780–1835.

This time frame is neither random nor arbitrary, for it serves scholarly as well as intellectual functions. Not only does it fit neatly between those examined in Spruill's and Scott's works, but it offers a southern counterpoint to Nancy Cott's recent study, *The Bonds of Womanhood: Woman's Sphere in New England, 1780–1835*. Furthermore, this period—known in historical circles as the "early American Republic" or "new nation" era—was not only an epoch of dynamic transformation for the country as a whole but perhaps the single most significant developmental stage in the history of the American South.

Historians have pondered the deep change of this era. During the decades following independence, political ideology, economic orientation, and social structure altered dramatically. These new developments were not wholly original, but the American nation—like the goddess Athena who sprang full grown from Zeus' head—proved a striking departure from both Britain and its other colonies. The birth of a specifically American *mentalité* was crucial; Tocqueville commented frequently in his work on the intangible *esprit* of the Americans.

These considerations focused my investigation of plantation women in this critical period of southern history. What were the lives of the mistresses of ante-bellum plantations like? How could I reconstruct their world? Literary sources and primary materials abound, and I began with the published diaries and memoirs of women of the Old South. Then I reviewed the travel literature for the southern states. By this time I was confident that the personal records of planter families during this era would afford rich and abundant source material.

The bulk of this study is based on a survey of nearly five hundred manuscript collections housed in twenty-four archives throughout the United States, but mainly in the seven states under scrutiny. At each of these archives I examined planter collections for the fifty-five years following the American Revolution, reading all letters by women, most letters by men to women, and most family correspondence between men. In addition, I examined as many personal papers as possible that were relevant to women on plantations: household inventories, the papers of female academies, commonplace books, physicians' records, a few wills, and a number of lovesick verses by self-styled poets. Unpublished diaries and memoirs were a vital part of my research. Although much can be gained by examining court cases, legislative petitions, census data, and other legal documents, I concentrate on the private and personal materials available from the era. Finding plantation mistresses an eloquent and intriguing group, I let them speak for themselves.

Using a number of accurate and detailed genealogies, I have also assembled data for 750 individuals of the planter class born between 1765 and 1815, collecting the following information for each sample member: name, sex, year of birth, year of death, place of birth (state), number of marriages, age at first marriage, age at second marriage, cousin marriage, death/death of spouse in childbirth, second marriage to dead spouse's sister/brother, number of children, number of sons, number of daughters, number of children to survive infancy (two years), number of children to reach maturity (eighteen years), state of adult residence, place of death (state), and mobility (state to state or region to region). I chose for a control group a comparable agricultural aristocracy: 100 farmers of Dutch descent located in the Hudson valley. This survey affords crude statistical indicators of patterns for the planter class during the early national era (See Appendices A and B).

After examining these primary materials on plantation mistresses' lives and vital statistics on the planter class, I further explore the question of gender in ante-bellum southern culture. As many feminists have pointed out, woman is, in part, a cultural creation; certainly femininity is an attribute that varies from one society to another. Although my study concerns itself mainly with specific women, I also examine the abstract concept of "woman" in the Old South. The image of the southern lady was more a product of fable than fact, but her real incarnation had a more vital impact on ante-bellum life than her legend. Cultural prescriptions interacted in an elaborate and contradictory manner with practical conditions. The inflated expectations of planter patriarchs with respect to their demands on women and their requisites for "womanhood" combined to create a tangled sexual ideology. These issues cannot be sorted out completely, but I address some of them to advance my argument that sex is as critical a factor for understanding social relations in the South as race.

I cover a number of themes that challenge traditional and sexist views of southern history, as well as the regional chauvinism of women's history—what I call the "New Englandization" of women's studies, which has focused interest on northern women. First, contrary to the view generated by contemporary historiography of slavery, southern women were not merely decoration on ante-bellum plantations. They performed essential and complex functions within the cotton economy as well as in the planter ideology. Women North and South had identical educational opportunities during the early years of the Republic, but because society in the North provided greater opportunities for educated women, it has wrongly been assumed that women received little or no academic training in the Old South. Because of women's special role as keepers of the culture and, as I shall show, the "conscience" of plantations, mistresses had anomalous positions within the structure of southern slavery. Although they were white and members of the planter class, they were—by necessity, in this rigidly hierarchical society—subjugated to male rule. Only men might serve effectively as masters of black slaves. The mistress could struggle to impose order and discipline, but slaves clearly recognized the division of authority along gender as well as color lines. Even if an unusual woman overcame these obstacles and managed her own affairs and slaves within the boundaries of her estate, society curtailed her participation by means of legislative restrictions that essentially prevented women's independent administration of plantations.

The New Englandization of American women's history has likewise distorted perceptions of white women's labor on cotton plantations. Their valuable contributions were increased during the post-Revolutionary cotton boom, in direct contrast with the apparent decline in importance of the household economy in the industrializing Middle Atlantic and New England states. While women's networks and reform movements blossomed in the ante-bellum North, however, southern activity within this domain was noticeably absent. Slave society aggressively censored and prohibited any agitation or organization on women's part.

Plantation mistresses had dynamic and various roles in ante-bellum society. Women's functions were essential and subject to severe scrutiny. The material offers us some notion of the average life of the ante-bellum plantation mistress, as well as information on the women who did not fit the model—the fallen women, the laudanum addicts, and the invalids. Unlike the myths and fables that have distorted our vision of plantation mistresses, my story has no moral.

Every book is a personal odyssey—one hopes, for the reader as well as the author. I should like to offer some acknowledgment of the events as well as the authors that influenced me to pursue this study.

The day before my sixteenth birthday, Martin Luther King was gunned down in Memphis. When riots broke out across the country—even in the sleepy midwestern town of Kansas City—issues of racial discrimination and violence, the unresolved riddles of American slavery, came home to roost. Burning, looting, tear gas, bomb threats, curfews, the National Guard, accompanied by outbursts of racist indignation, white liberal guilt, and black rage, brought these issues home to me. This, of course, was not the initial phase of America's postwar awareness of the significance of "the race problem." But it was my own personal awakening.

I regret that neither of my fathers lived to see the publication of this book. Both my father by blood and my stepfather gave me love and support. I hope that my brother, David, will take pride for them.

Many friends have contributed to my sanity and inspiration during the past decade; I want to thank some whose special efforts have made this book possible. The railings of a feminist have often proved trying for men friends. I want to express gratitude to Thomas Viola, Eric Rayman, Craig D'Ooge, Nick Harris, Tom Levitt, William Fitzgerald, Walter Isaacson, Kurt Andersen, and especially to Bob Chapman, whose bemused indifference prodded me onward. To list all the women who have made a difference in the quality of my life over the years would be impossible. Nevertheless, I welcome the opportunity to thank the following for their continuing friendship: Julie Charmley, Elizabeth Riopelle, Barbara Platt, Cindy Rosenwald, Beverly Haviland, Stephanie Bruno, Kate Kemper, and Patty Marx.

I wish to acknowledge my back-up: a trio of women whose investments in postage and phone bills alone have been astronomical, but who have donated what is more important, steadfast emotional support. The tough-mindedness and soft-heartedness of three special friends have created a climate that has helped my work to flourish: Carla Robbins, who contributes boundless enthusiasm and invaluable public relations; Pilar Viladas, who provides a terrific bounty of substance and style *par excellence;* and Trina Hikel, whose gift of herself affords an array of treasures.

Graduate school was an excruciating ordeal, made bearable only by the camaraderie of fellow sufferers. Thanks to those who contributed to my endurance: first and foremost, Christine Lunardini, as well as Tom Knock, Perry Blatz, Maureen Callahan, Michael Roth, Steve Ross, and one who made us all believe tomorrow was another day, Leona Halvorsen.

Paul Uhlmann is in a class by himself. No words can convey my appreciation for his unwavering devotion to my best interests.

It would be impossible to mention all the professional people who made this book possible. Although some may want their name kept out of it, I want to express a debt of gratitude to those whose time and efforts made what I feel were particular improvements in my work.

I found that the staffs of the various archives I visited provided me with constant support and enthusiasm for my research. I especially thank those at the Southern Historical Collection, the Duke University Library, and the North Carolina State Archives, who made my stay in North Carolina a delightful as well as an enlightening experience. I also wish to acknowledge the extraordinary diligence of the staff at the College of William and Mary. Everywhere I went in the South, the advice and help of archivists and librarians greatly aided the success of this project.

The South is known for its hospitality and generosity for good reason. I would like to thank the following kind and gracious hosts for opening their homes to me: Bob and Susan Lunardini, Jackson, Mississippi; Lisa Diethelm, Birmingham, Alabama; Mason and Mary Robertson, Savannah, Georgia; Luisa and E. P. Douglass, Chapel

Hill, North Carolina; the late Mr. and Mrs. Julian Kohn, Montgomery, Alabama; Pat Sullivan, Atlanta, Georgia; Elizabeth Riopelle, New Orleans, Louisiana; and Stephanie Bruno, New Orleans, Louisiana.

I pursued my graduate work in a relatively Yankee camp, deciding to become a historian of the South while marooned in central New Jersey. Without the inspiration of, and discipline imposed by, Arthur Link, I do not believe I would have accepted this challenge. He taught me a love of the South and a respect for the documents which has proved invaluable in my work. His course on editing was one of the most rigorous and challenging of my graduate career. I must confess that although I am reassured that the Lord may forgive me my errors in this book, I can only hope that He will put in a good word for me with the editor of the Wilson Papers.

Many people were liberal with advice and criticism during the course of my research and writing. The completion of this project is due in large part to James M. McPherson, whose advice and patience were forthcoming at every step of my graduate career. I would also like to thank Henry Drewry, Drew Gilpin Faust, and Douglas Greenberg for their comments. The following persons made valuable suggestions on early drafts of chapters: Richard Latner, Christine Lunardini, Duncan MacLeod, Mary Beth Norton, Jack Pole, Robert Wells, Jon Wiener, and Joel Williamson.

Ben Barker-Benfield, Eric Foner, and Peter Wood provided me with detailed and enriching criticism of the entire manuscript. I am grateful for their time and collective wisdom. I owe these men an even greater debt, for they provided me with faith in my ability to write history and their own achievements assured me of the worthiness of such an endeavor.

Halfway into my project, I became privy to the splendor of word processing. I want to thank those whose technical expertise and solid assistance greatly facilitated the preparation of this manuscript: Helen Cernik and Herman Williams.

Union College has been extraordinarily generous with support, and I thank both the college and the Humanities Faculty Development Fund for enabling me to complete this manuscript.

I am grateful to many people at Pantheon Books—above all to André Schiffrin, who first gave me hope that readers outside academe might have an interest in what I was writing. Then to Wendy Wolf, who convinced me that if I wanted anyone to read my work, I should stop looking over my shoulder and get on with the book. There are some people with whom it is worthwhile locking horns, and luckily she proved to be one of them. Her criticism and queries helped me to wrestle with my ideas and emerge with a better understanding of what I wanted to say and how best to say it. With enormous gratitude, I salute her. Sara Bershtel volunteered for hazardous editorial duty: to see me through the final stages of my first book. She, too, had a tremendous impact on this project by tirelessly imposing polish and improvements. I am grateful for her aid and enthusiasm. I would also like to thank my friend and student Anna Corti for her assistance on the index.

Finally, an acknowledgment, a debt, an appreciation: of my husband, Daniel Colbert, who defies realistic expectations in favor of romantic abandon by making me happy all the time.

Catherine Clinton
New York City
January 1982

THE
PLANTATION
MISTRESS

I

WOMEN IN THE LAND
OF COTTON

I n 1620 ninety maids landed in Virginia, a gift from the propri-
etors to the colony. They were intended as brides for members
of the planter class; only freemen could wed these available women
upon payment of 120 pounds of leaf tobacco to defray transportation
costs. Colonial authorities encouraged marriage by granting a free-
holder an increased lot of land if he had a wife. English gentlemen
who supported these tactics argued that "the plantation can never
flourish till families be planted and the respect of wives and children
fix the people on the soil."[1] The ploy was successful. Virginia shortly
received two other shipments of fifty women each from the colony's
sponsors. Thirty-eight more potential brides were supplied by private
entrepreneurs, who raised the price per wife to 150 pounds of tobacco.
By 1622 all these maids had married.

Women were an economic commodity. Much like slaves, these early
women settlers were plucked from the Old World and deposited in
the New. Shipped across the ocean like stock, they were sold off into
marriage with little regard for their human status and dignity. This

high "value" but chattel treatment put women in a complex position within plantation society. Under Colonial law, females found their political and economic situation somewhat better than it had been in England, but substantially worse than that of male colonists. And as in the Old World, women were locked into their dependent status. The Maryland assembly, for example, passed a "seven year" provision for women: females were required to marry or remarry within seven years of landholding. Daughters were subject to their fathers' will, and a married female was by law wholly under her husband's control.[2] Despite this inferior status, females in early America were highly valued by the male authorities. Much like another disadvantaged group, African slaves, women immeasurably boosted prospects of success for these southern colonies. As the Virginia House of Burgesses had declared in 1619, "in a newer plantation it is not knowen whether man or woman be the most necessary."[3]

After the Revolution, tobacco was no longer a boom crop for southern planters. Erosion and soil exhaustion combined to disfigure the tidewater countryside, and with arable land in disrepair, Virginia estates were overstocked with slaves. Land depletion was not, however, as great a problem along the Carolina-Georgia coast, where planters still prospered.

Some historians have argued that slavery was a dying institution during the third quarter of the eighteenth century, kept alive only by the development of the cotton gin in the century's last decade. But the slave population was dramatically increased during the 1780s and 1790s by slave imports. Despite any temporary short-term setbacks (panics and drops in cotton prices), slaveholders retained confidence in the cotton plantation system. Although their buoyancy might have been as misplaced as Scarlett O'Hara's—in the scene from *Gone with the Wind* when, at war's end, she remarks that "cotton will go sky high"—planters were optimistic and greedy for hard cash. They believed that cotton was a profitable crop and slave labor the most economical means to cultivate it. To expand both their "Cotton Kingdom" and the productivity of cotton plantations, planters pushed southwestwards. This geographical expansion, the increase in slave holdings, and the demand for cotton combined to accelerate settlement of the New South regions: western Georgia, Alabama, Mississippi, northern Florida and Louisiana, Arkansas, and Texas.

From the Colonial era onward, southern settlement patterns had diverged from those of the North, and in the ante-bellum era these differentials increased. While the political center in New England remained the town, plantation society revolved around the county unit. Urbanization and industrialization, which made such inroads into northern society, had little impact upon the plantation South. European immigrants avoided the region; the planters discouraged any influx of foreigners, from a xenophobic impulse to preserve their own homogeneity; and the recent arrivals shunned competition with slave labor. The economic differential between the two regions increased in these decades with the growth of manufacturing in New England and the boom in cotton in the Gulf states. Planter arrogance centered on the agricultural pre-eminence of the South; in 1858 South Carolina Senator James Hammond boasted: "What would happen if no cotton was furnished for three years. . . . England would topple headlong and carry the civilized world with her save the South. No, you dare not make war on cotton. No power on earth dares to make war on it. Cotton is King."[4]

Political economy was not the only area in which North and South diverged. The cultures that had sprung from these two regions differed radically. Both Yankee and planter accepted these incompatibilities, each arguing for his own superiority. Thomas Jefferson articulated this line of thought in his catalogue of differences between Northerners—"cool, sober, laborious, persevering, independent, jealous of their own liberties, chicaning, superstitious and hypocritical in their religion"—and Southerners—"fiery, voluptuary, indolent, unsteady, independent, zealous of their own liberties but trampling on those of others, generous, candid and without attachments or pretentions of any religion but that of the heart."[5] By the outbreak of the Civil War, Dixie ideologues had refined their racist doctrine, identifying Yankees as well as blacks as inferior. In 1861 the *Southern Literary Messenger* published an article the title of which proclaimed "The True Question: A Contest for the Supremacy of Race, as Between the Saxon Puritan of the North and the Norman of the South."[6]

In the great mass of evidence demonstrating the split between the ante-bellum North and South, one significant aspect has been repeatedly overlooked by historical scholarship: the role of women. Although the southern lady remains a staple of plantation legend, indeed an icon of the Old South, her symbolic impact seems to have overshadowed and indeed substituted for any assessment of her substantial contributions, much in the way the roles of blacks were ignored until recent scholarship.

That slavery provided for the exalted position of whites within society is a truism of southern history. What remains to be explored is how this system contributed to a parallel oppression of women, both white and black—for slavery and the plantation system imposed handicaps on the women of the owner class. The challenge in evaluating this oppression is to assess the impact of slavery on the preexisting patriarchal structure, not in the least unique to southern society.

The term "family" comes from the Latin word meaning all those included in a household—slaves, women, and children—who were subject to the master's supreme will. Each huge southern household conferred proportionate authority on the "father" of the vast plantation family. These dependents, moreover, formed a solid base of power that extended into the apparatus of the state. The more dependents, the more power, and the more power, the larger the share of influence within the state apparatus. Thus slavery, while it did not alone create women's oppression, did accentuate sex roles and perpetuated women's subordinate status.

A free woman's status within slave society was an extension of her family role; indeed, her status emphasized her dependency and inferiority. Without the oppression of *all* women, the planter class could not be assured of absolute authority. In a biracial slave society where "racial purity" was a defining characteristic of the master class, total control of the reproductive females was of paramount concern for elite males. Patriarchy was the bedrock upon which the slave society was founded, and slavery exaggerated the pattern of subjugation that patriarchy had established.*

Women's lives were also affected by plantation agriculture itself. Although northern society was slowly transformed by modernization (industrialization, urbanization, the growth of a market economy, and consumerism), southern society remained rural, provincial, and de-

---

*See discussions of female purity in Chapter V, "The Moral Bind," and of the southern racial mixture in Chapter XI, "The Sexual Dynamics of Slavery."

pendent upon staple-crop production. The household, not the marketplace, was the central focus of the southern economy.

When families on farms were the basic economic unit of society, the female portion of the population participated equally in domestic labor. Women, however, did not share equal credit for their work. Within agricultural production, chores were sex-differentiated. Women might do men's work when the male was absent, and conversely, men might fill in for women, but farm labor was ordinarily divided along gender lines. Despite this partnership, only male work was highly rewarded with economic compensation, political recognition, and social esteem.

Relatively little is actually known of women's work in the antebellum South. This leads to a fundamentally distorted view of the operation of the plantation economy. Slaves supplied the field labor, but wives generally provided the domestic labor force for southern household management. Women administered food production, purchase, and distribution not only in the planter's home but for the whole plantation. While their husbands supervised the raising of the cash crops, women managed the dairy, the garden, and the smokehouse. Although the overseer might have given some assistance in the barnyard, the critical food-production spheres were clearly those of "women's work."* The plantation mistress held the keys as the symbol of her domain.

During the early national era, rhetoric celebrated the importance of republican motherhood: the virtue and vitality of patriotic women who reared future statesmen. These lavish notions of their essential role in the building of a nation and of the nobility of their sacrifice socialized American women. New emphasis on the significance of feminine influence considerably reshaped popular ideology. Continuing in the tone of Revolutionary propaganda, men wanted women's participation to take private rather than public forms. Politicians promised status and esteem to women, but delivered only marginal improvements in women's position. At the same time, a bourgeois notion of the division of spheres—male and female as well as public and private—flourished in response to the growth of a market economy. The rise of industrial capitalism in the North stimulated this

*See Chapter II, "Slave of Slaves."

ideological split between "life" and "work" which placed household labor outside the realm of "the economy."[7]

Sexual reproduction has always been a woman's religious and cultural duty, but maternity became a patriotic obligation in the new republic. In the South, populating the frontier with whites was among the most urgent of political necessities. This ideology sought to bind up a woman's self-concept completely with her "biological destiny." A woman's primary duty to her husband was to provide him with heirs, and her primary duty to her country was to produce citizens. When one Southerner wrote to his sister that she should serve the nation and get married, she wryly responded: "You say you think it is time I was doing something for my country, but I think it is time enough to enter such business as I am not so very fond of domestic affairs and brawling affairs of children."[8]

Women over all took their new tasks with patriotic seriousness, however, and transformations followed. This era ushered in the academy, to educate girls for republican motherhood. Virtue and piety were equally important for the northern maiden and for the southern belle. Domesticity was the realm of all American women, and in both the urbanizing, industrializing North and the primarily agricultural South, the exercise of any measure of political control in the public domain became less and less possible for them. In plantation society, this rule of female exclusion was universally observed.

The same phenomena of restriction and oppression appeared in both North and South, but often took markedly different forms. For example, in the plantation South, women were firmly tied to the household, with chaperonage limiting their mobility. In New England and Middle Atlantic farming communities, women were equally subject to restrictions, but because of the relative proximity of households to each other, these women did not suffer the isolation of their southern counterparts. Chaperonage was a matter of propriety in both regions, but this "protection" of women carried more handicaps for plantation females. Planter wives constantly complained about their lack of female companionship and about their inability to travel for want of chaperones. The irony of this plight appears even more bitter when one realizes that many women were left alone by their absent husbands to manage large estates and numerous slaves—sometimes without an overseer—yet forbidden to travel because of the "dangers" involved. When a husband returned, he might arrange an excursion for his wife, but most often the devoted helpmeet was expected to remain at home with her spouse. Thus even—or especially—when acting as surrogate for the master, the plantation mistress became a prisoner of circumstance.

The biracial character of American slavery played no small part in this imprisonment. Each plantation was essentially a protectorate, a small fiefdom ruled by the planter. The lady of the manor was guaranteed safety so long as she remained within the limits of proper behavior, in the abstract, and, concretely, within the boundaries of the plantation. "Off the land" a lady was afforded no such protection. The South pictured itself as a country fraught with danger and challenge. Most threatening were runaway slaves, together with rough-necks and ruffians; farther west, even Indians lurked in the imagination, if not the woods. Poor roads and the difficulties of negotiating the backwoods presented even more intractable obstacles to female travel. The exhilaration of independence and mobility was severely tempered for southern women, who spent most of their lives in side-saddle, hemmed in by the ideal of the "lady."

The North provided women with a much more realistic model: the "notable housewife," the ideological granddaughter of Cotton Mather's "daughters of Zion." This virtuous housewife, the standard by which northern women lived their lives, was easily transformed into the "true woman" Barbara Welter discusses in her collection of essays, *Dimity Convictions*, or the "sentimental conspicuous consumer" described in Ann Douglas's *Feminization of American Culture*. New England women, especially, found their roles more tolerable during the transformations of the post-Revolutionary North.[9] Accomplished women met the demands of housewifery with a growing sense of importance within the domestic realm. They strove for attainable goals, and were assured of social recognition as their reward. No such luxury was afforded on the plantation.

Northern women during this era were busily building their own community. All across New England and the Middle Atlantic states, females transformed the liability of segregation into the asset of collective identity. This movement was so widespread and important that historian Nancy Cott has called her study of New England women from 1780 to 1835 *The Bonds of Womanhood*. The title was taken, ironically enough, from the correspondence of a southern woman, Angelina Grimké, who signed herself "thine in the bonds of woman-hood." Of course, the Grimké sisters had exiled themselves from the South; their philosophical and political bent made them pariahs within slaveowning culture. But the spirit and sorority of the North beck-oned them. Within northern society, women were able to create a successful counterculture that undermined patriarchal oppression.

The roots of this counterculture were deeply imbedded in the very impulse to separate male and female spheres that patriarchy had spawned and nourished. As early as the post-Revolutionary era, American men were rightly concerned that women might attempt to translate the egalitarian rhetoric and ideology of the rebellion into their own bid for liberty. Indeed, Abigail Adams warned of such a revolt in her correspondence with her husband John:

> I desire you would Remember the Ladies, and be more generous and favourable to them than your ancestors. Do not put such unlim-ited power into the hands of the Husbands. Remember all Men would be tyrants if they could. If perticular care and attention is not paid to the Ladies we are determined to foment a Rebelion, and will not hold ourselves bound by any Laws in which we have no voice, or Representation.[10]

Although Adams's quotation is perhaps overused, there was no lack of similar sentiment among women of her class and level of education. American historians have, during the past decade, introduced us to a wide array of accomplished and challenging women of the late eigh-teenth and early nineteenth centuries: Judith Sargent Murray, Susan-nah Rowson, Hannah Webster Foster, Mercy Otis Warren, Grace Galloway, Sarah Livingston Jay, Catherine Livingston, Esther De Berdt Reed, Sarah Franklin Bache, Eliza Lucas Pinckney, Theodosia Burr, and Elizabeth Drinker, among others. They all testify to the vigor and complexity of the debate over women's position and politi-cal responsibilities in American society.

During the early years of the Republic, national and regional changes were transforming the lives of women both North and South. The shift from "hearthside" to "marketplace" economies created a vacuum allegedly filled by women's role as "republican mothers." But perhaps more crucial was the growth and influence of a bourgeois consumer consciousness.[11]

Women's sudden preoccupation with finding "values" (bargains) as well as preserving "values" (mores) created a new American domestic model, celebrated in the tons of feminine literature churned out during the ante-bellum era. Between 1784 and 1860 almost one hundred magazines concentrating on "women's interests" were published. Also during this era, a class of women novelists sprang up to meet the demand for popular fiction. Their themes and scenarios featured both sharp and sentimental renderings of domestic life.[12]

Besides this explosion of prescription and analysis, northern women created their own female culture. This stemmed partly from young women's dynamic and disproportionate role in the Second Great Awakening during the opening decades of the nineteenth century. Designated as the active stewards of religion within the culture, women were given a moral crusade during the ante-bellum era; their roles were culturally exalted. Ministers turned their attention toward these newly significant members of dwindling congregations, as church attendance plummeted during the period following the Revolution. Religious fervor began to manifest itself outside formal denominational activities. Women throughout the country began to organize benevolent societies and reform organizations,[13] most abundant in the cities, but supported even in rural New England.

Similar reform in the South, however, definitely lacked the size and scope of the movement in northern communities. This was a consequence both of the physical isolation of southern women and of the needs of plantation society itself. Although southern planters urged their women to do good works and promote benevolence, this effort was to extend itself no farther than the boundaries of the plantation. If women's attention wandered from the welfare of their families and their husbands' slaves and other property, it might stray to a critical attack on society. Many ante-bellum evangelicals, especially Northerners, identified slavery as one of America's greatest ills. If plantation mistresses came under the influence of such propaganda, planters feared for their way of life.

Slaveowners often discouraged their wives openly from such agitation-prone activity. Virginia planter David Campbell had a close and affectionate relationship with his wife, Maria. The couple were childless, and although they adopted nieces and nephews, they relied heavily upon each other. While Campbell spent much of his career in Richmond, leaving his wife alone on their remote estate in western Virginia, he encouraged her to participate in entertainments that would make her less melancholy in his absence. But the usually indulgent Campbell became testy over the issue of his wife's interest in camp meetings. His protests cite numerous drawbacks but fail to specify what must have been his greatest objection: that his wife might be influenced by these "fanatics." He sent her a letter of disapproval in 1823:

> You mention that you had intended going to a Methodist class meeting. . . . Have you not often seen my anxiety about you at those places, and why would you be willing to go to them and run the hazard of being jostled about in a crowd of fanatics without my protecting arm?—Indeed, why go there at all? A person of your good sense must be satisfied that he who gave us being cannot delight in such worship. . . .[14]

The female academy movement swept the South as well as the North after the Revolution, creating a more critical intellectual perspective for upper-class women. Such a perspective sometimes led women to speak out against the evils of their society, and slavery became a target. Many females in the South were unable to voice their criticisms, but some attempted to enact their ideas in individual protests. The never-married Mary Telfair of Savannah hoped, with her confidante, Mary Few, to start a conversation circle like that of their idols, the British bluestockings. Soon after, Mary Telfair resolved to free herself from the toils of slavery: "I have abandoned the old fashion of having a waiting maid, the first step towards a reform. Alexander [her brother] seems to think I will be too independent for a Lady, but I already experience the salutary effects of running up and downstairs and waiting upon myself."[15] And as if these rumblings of discontent from within slaveowning society were not enough, planters were faced with the full-blown monstrosity of abolitionism in the North.

By the third decade of the nineteenth century, it was clear that educated women had become a mainstay of the abolitionist movement, assuming a role that was vital to the success of antislavery and electrifying for the participants. Indeed, much of the work on nine-teenth-century feminism reveals the significance of antislavery apprenticeships for these activists. Ellen DuBois points out in her landmark study, *Feminism and Suffrage*, that not only were northern women ideologically charged by their comparison of slaves' status with their own, but both the negative and positive aspects of their abolitionist careers inspired females to seek their own rights. Thus slaveowning planters were doubly threatened by the prospect of women's antislavery activity, for hand in hand with their oppression of slaves went their subjection of women. George Fitzhugh—always a colorful commentator, though certainly an *unrepresentative* ante-bellum ideologue—maintained in his *Sociology for the South* (1854) that either a change in the status of women or the downfall of slavery would bring about the end of southern civilization.

During the 1830s, when abolitionist agitation was on the rise in the North, southern planters responded with a series of social as well as political maneuvers to keep this movement from advancing south-ward. The women's academy movement went into decline; although schools did not close down completely, the headway made in the post-Revolutionary period was undermined. Following the failure of many educational ventures in the panic of 1837, Southerners were slow to reopen many of these women's academies. Futher, the curriculum of the institutions altered. While classical education had been the back-bone of programs for most schools North and South during the early republican era,* the slaveowning planters wanted less emphasis on intellectual faculties and more concern with social graces. This retrenchment to a preoccupation with "polite arts" was a return to the "ornamental" education of the eighteenth century. Although the 1850s saw the rise of many educational institutions in the South, this increase can actually be attributed to provincialism rather than to any progressive educational movement.

During the decades leading up to the Civil War, slaveowners expanded this "bunker mentality." The South, alarmed at sending its sons northward, wanted the planter class tutored on native ground. The prescriptive literature of the era also took a provincial turn. Southern perceptions became narrower, more defensive. Preceptors

*See Chapter VII, "Equally Their Due."

and moralists churned out texts promoting the system of slavery and deriding the "anthills" of the North. In both education and publishing, southern efforts were aimed at propagandizing. Southerners wanted their educational activities to curtail the free exchange of ideas rather than to ensure intellectual freedom. Dissemination of abolitionist literature in the South was prosecuted. Dixie politicians even introduced a gag law in Congress to stifle abolitionist opposition.

As the South closed ranks, women in plantation society lost those relative freedoms, such as improved education, that they might formerly have enjoyed. After the 1830s the ideological and practical divergence between females North and South was perhaps even greater than the split between male cultures. Women in the North forged stronger bonds, which eventually provided the underpinnings for the suffrage movement (politically launched at Seneca Falls in 1848) and other feminist activities. At the same time, however, women in the South found themselves isolated from one another, scattered across a hostile environment, and subject to the demands of an oppressive system that, ironically, they had to help maintain. The threat of antislavery locked plantation mistresses even more tightly into positions designated and guarded by planter patriarchs.

When the proslavery crusade gained momentum in the South after the Nullification controversy of 1832–1833, women as well as men were assigned roles in the new ideological campaign. Southern proslavery propagandists painted a glowing portrait of plantation society: "the sunny South." They tried to shift the image of slavery from "necessary evil" to "plantation school" by means of this picturesque fictional portrait. Literature celebrated the familial mingling of black and white on the plantation and the beneficence masters bestowed on slaves. Planters sentimentalized to the point of caricature the image of happy darkies singing in the fields—omitting all reference to whips, chains, brands, maiming, selling families apart, and rape, among the numerous atrocities slavery allotted to blacks only. The masters sought to legitimate their authority by emphasizing their benevolent paternalism, the alleged Christian motivation of the enslavement of blacks.

Women played no small part in advancing this illusion, both by means of their images and by their actual deeds. As plantation mistresses were charged with the direct care of slaves, their behavior was critical to the bolstering of planter claims to humanitarianism.* By the late ante-bellum era, the persona of the plantation mistress was an ally in the campaign to defend slavery in the public sphere, despite her litany of complaint in the private realm. In this sense, the planter had come to dictate her identity as well as her dependency. A shield that planters might hold up against attacks from the North, she indeed generally served a positive or sympathetic role in the system, to the degree that she was identified by blacks as a possible advocate, an intermediary between slaves and masters or slaves and overseers. But southern women were by no means unambivalent about slavery. Their role in the system, in practical and in ideological terms, created extreme tension; the mask might crack or even shatter under the severe pressure they endured.†

Despite the ambivalence and the suffering of plantation mistresses, it must be remembered that they were nevertheless *free* in a slave society—a precious advantage. They were accorded many privileges of their color and class, despite their gender. Stereotypes and psychological stresses were severe handicaps, but one cannot equate the plight of the plantation mistress with the brutal dehumanization of slaves. Yet the nature and extent of women's oppression is revealing for the history of whites and blacks, since white slaveowners refined systematic and sometimes similar methods of keeping blacks and women excluded from spheres of power; and often employed near-identical ideological warfare against them.

This study of plantation mistresses cannot be definitive, but by concentrating on the lives of white women on plantations, our understanding of the whole of slavery will be broadened and enriched. And in exploring plantation mistresses' contributions to the ante-bellum South, we can finally gain for them what they have so long been denied: recognition, acknowledgment—at long last, a history.

---

*See Chapter X, "The Curse of Slavery."
†See Chapter X, "The Curse of Slavery," and Chapter IX, "Every Woman Was an Island."

II

SLAVE OF SLAVES

The mistress of a plantation was the most complete slave on it.
—Susan Dabney Smedes, *Memorials of a Southern Planter*

While visiting the home of an ante-bellum southern planter, one visitor was charmed by the grace and hospitality of the mistress. She was warm, gentle, and refined in her manner. He found her a genial hostess and a model of what he expected "the southern lady" to be. Having gained the permission of his host to stroll around the plantation alone during this visit, the stranger one day spied his host's wife hard at work. The matron was considerably disarrayed; hoop removed from her skirt, she was bent over a salting barrel, up to her elbows in brine. As he was about to approach her, the gentleman realized that he faced a delicate situation. To fail to greet her might seem rude, but to acknowledge her would put the woman in an awkward position. He had essentially caught his hostess behind the scenes, accidentally violating the rules by wandering backstage. Thus he ambled by without a direct glance. This would have been an insult in the normal course of events, but as an acceptable outcome it reveals the absurdity of the myth-ridden South. A guest passes right by the mistress of the plantation, paying her less attention than he would a slave. Exalted imagery and an unwillingness to cope with reality when it conflicted with the ideal created this eccentric world.

During the ante-bellum era, labor was a subject of sore controversy throughout the nation. The southern states were convinced that slavery provided the most satisfactory and profitable economic system, especially suited for cotton plantations. In the North, although abolitionists mounted a vigorous campaign, statesmen were not particularly concerned about the moral depravity of such a system. Wage slavery in the factory was not much better than chattel slavery on southern plantations. Indeed, some historians have argued that the material conditions of slaves were better than those of their free counterparts in northern and European cities.[1] But Yankees feared that the degradation of labor in the form of slavery would damage the moral and economic pillars upon which the republic was founded.

Within the perimeters of the Cotton Kingdom, planters created their own moral and political universe, a biracial slave society whose symbols and values were vastly different from those of the North. First and foremost, manual labor and physical work were disdained. Contemporaries and historians of planters believed that this disdain bred anti-Puritanism, which resulted in "the lazy South."[2] Whether southern ante-bellum society was lazy or merely genteel, whether planters were "premodern" or "antibourgeois," the system of slave labor created separate and distinct cultural values for the ruling class in the plantation South. These values generated significant divergence from the North, not just in economic and political matters but in all aspects of social interaction. The southern lady was a symbol of gentility and refinement for plantation culture, designed to fill the requisites of chauvinist stereotype by embracing those qualities slaveowners wished to promote, even though the practical needs of plantation life cast her in quite a different role. The clash of myth and reality was monumental.

The stately, pillared mansion at the end of a winding, tree-lined road was another symbol of the plantation South. The manor house was actually one of many buildings on the property. In addition to the "Big House"—the term generally used to designate the planter's home regardless of its size—most southern estates also included extensive outbuildings: barns, stables, workshops, and warehouses. Slave cabins were built at a convenient distance from the master's home. Many planters also provided nursery and hospital facilities for their slaves. The Big House often had a detached kitchen, and on larger estates separate smokehouses and storehouses were erected. The "household" thus extending far beyond the walls of the Big House required upkeep and daily work as well as the care and feeding of all those, both black and white, who lived and worked on the plantation. This was the plantation mistress's domain.

The mansion, therefore, was merely the showpiece of the plantation. Because it was the most visible symbol of the slaveowner's wealth and status, it was usually as grand and lavish a monument as the planter could afford. The style and size of these homes varied from region to region and period to period, but generally plantation houses were substantial two- or three-story structures. Most had spacious receiving halls on the ground floor. Dining rooms, parlors, libraries, music rooms, and sitting rooms were located off the central hall; bedrooms and nurseries, on the upper floors. Many mansions had porches on both upper and lower stories. Most homes were equipped with fireplaces in every room. A handsome staircase in the center of the house was often supplemented by a back stairs for servant use. Some homes had basement storerooms.

The planter's wife was in charge not merely of the mansion but of the entire spectrum of domestic operations throughout the estate, from food and clothing to the physical and spiritual care of both her white family and her husband's slaves. The borders of her domain might extend from the mansion's locked pantry to the slave-quarter hospital and the slaughtering pen for the hogs. Very little escaped the attention of the white mistress, and most plantation problems were brought to her unless, being crop-related, they fell within the sphere of the overseer. Indeed, the mistress often served as an intermediary between slave and master, bypassing the overseer's authority. This made her role pivotal as well as productive within the realm of plantation slavery.

Contrary to popular belief, not all free women in slave societies are relieved of the drudgery of household labor. Such may well have been the case for the wives of farmers who owned few slaves during the ante-bellum era; the labor generated by the small slave-labor force was well worth the addition of a few extra mouths to feed and bodies to tend. But generally, the larger the plantation, the more extensive the household cares and responsibilities that devolved upon the mistress. Even though in a few cases a large slave force offset the disadvantages of management, the only women in the South who wholly escaped manual labor were invalids; for the rest, unpaid domestic service to their families and their husbands' slaves was the rule.

In 1794 Erasmus Darwin, in his guide to female education, deplored the fact that although men were trained to their profession from an early age, most women began their "important office with a profound ignorance."[3] As young girls, southern women were seldom trained to keep house; education at home and in academies instead emphasized intellectual and artistic accomplishments. When females were taught such rudimentary skills as sewing, they concentrated their efforts on samplers and other ornamental needlework rather than on the practical application of such ladylike accomplishments. One planter wrote to his recently married daughter: "You will have to study housekeeping. You are too young to have learnt much of it; but you have been an apt scholar in other branches and I hope will prove so in this. It is a fault in female education housekeeping is not made more a part of it; book learning is not sufficient: the kitchen and dairy must be attended to as well as the drawing room."[4]

Parents lectured daughters during their adolescent years on the necessity of being good housekeepers,[5] but gave them little preparation, and after marriage a woman suddenly found herself saddled with both marital duty and household responsibility. In 1831 a mistress wrote in despair of the transformation: "Now I have turned housekeeper for to my sorrow I know there is no romance in going from the smoke house to the store room and from there to the cellar half a dozen times a day."[6] The majority of plantation mistresses keenly felt the necessity of their presence and the simultaneous burden of their responsibilities.[7]

The storerooms were the center of the household and of the wife's operations; she held the keys and directed the distribution of supplies. A wife put her house in order by tending first to the pantry. In 1811 Ann Cocke wrote to her mother about the remodeling of her new home, Bremo: "I am as much interested in my Cellar every morning for an hour or two as I used to be in paying visits, and when I get it completely fitted to my taste I shall be still more fond of my projects. The covered way to the cellar is a great comfort to me."[8] Bremo, like many large plantations during the ante-bellum era, had a detached facility in which to store food supplies. Although storerooms were generally on the ground or basement floor of the house, many mistresses expanded the smokehouse into a general supply building. Another woman described her grandmother's plantation in Saint Landry parish, Louisiana: "There was a large store house where rows of hams and shoulders hung from beams overhead, and there were long rows of tubs holding pickled pork and corned beef, and long rows of nine pound loaves of white sugar sent by the commission merchant from New Orleans; with sundry boxes and cases, barrels of flour, cases of olive oil and wines, brandy and other things without number. . . . Where women waited with large wooden trays for the different supplies for the day."[9] Besides the early morning visit to the storeroom, the plantation mistress was constantly on call: "I keep all the keys and if anything is wanted they are obliged to come to me, so the consequence is that every now and then I have to run up and down the stairs."[10] Such duties varied from plantation to plantation, but almost every slaveowner's wife supervised the supplies and kept the keys to household locks on her person.

Most often the matron of the house was up shortly after dawn, directing the daily housekeeping and seasonal household activities. She might send breakfast upstairs to her daughters still abed, but the plantation mistress was less than any other member of the white household able to enjoy such luxury from slaveholding. One woman complained to her husband of her rigorous routine during the winter season: "As for myself I am constantly astonished that after the fatigues of the day (which are not trifling) that I am able to sleep sound and rise without a headache. For the last three or four days I have been very busy with my Hogs and all the troubles that the season brings. Now at half past 10 o'clock I am watching a corn husking in fear lest some mischief may happen."[11]

The ante-bellum plantation mistress shared common work patterns with many other women of her era. Like all married women, she was subject to the demands of her husband on her time and energies. Like all mothers, she performed long and arduous tasks connected with child care. As a housekeeper, the plantation mistress undertook numerous chores similar to those of her northern or urban or impoverished sister. Like her New England counterpart, the planter's wife managed a large household. She was responsible for food, clothing, shelter, and medical care for family and servants alike. Whether in the city or the country, southern women were gracious and conscientious homemakers. Matrons managed the household budget, dealt with local merchants, and handled all internal matters of finance. Even without the work created by their husbands' slaveowning, the numerous tasks of ante-bellum housekeeping kept plantation mistresses busy: gardening, dairy activities, salting pork, preserving fruits and vegetables, mixing medicines, the making of candles, soap, rugs, pillows, linen, bedding, and so on. Women believed that their work was never done, and their assiduous activity testified in favor of such claims. Complaints flowed freely in family letters.[12] Many women felt that plantation labors combined with family demands drove them to a state of near-collapse. One woman confessed: "I do not know if I have any positive disease, but I have my own proper share of nervousness, weakness, swimming in the head and a dull sleepy sensation. . . . My family claims untiring attention."[13] Women's only respite came on the Sabbath; for six days of the week, a ceaseless stream of household activities overwhelmed them.

The universal burdens of women notwithstanding, and beyond other factors of time and place, the institution of slavery made the domestic work of plantation mistresses difficult and forced upon them a way of life and set of duties quite different from those of other ante-bellum housewives, especially their northern counterparts. Ironically, while New England and the Middle Atlantic states moved into a new industrializing age, the South self-consciously looked to the ancient world for role models. During the Revolutionary era, patriots throughout the country embraced a "Roman revival," but Southerners especially lauded this imperial past. Ante-bellum slaveowners romanticized antiquity and generated a reverence for and a return to their version of classical values. The prevalence of slaves named after Roman statesmen is but one example of the adoption by southern culture of self-styled "ancient" patterns. The actual similarities of the two cultures are far less important than the aping of Rome by planter patriarchs. This is especially true with respect to the ideal of the Roman matron, held up again and again as the standard for the plantation mistress.

Indeed, just as planter statesmen elevated their rhetoric with grandiose references to Roman senators, so the Roman matron became the model wife for members of the plantation aristocracy. The contrived parallel in cultural styles between these two slaveowning societies is striking, especially in light of the centuries between the Roman Empire and the Cotton Kingdom. Roman traffic laws denied women the use of certain vehicles, which limited the matrons' mobility. This could be seen as a precedent for prohibitive aspects of southern chaperonage: even married women were forbidden to travel without a male escort. In legal matters, Roman matrons and southern mistresses suffered similar disabilities: both were prevented from independently administering their own affairs. Responsibilities and restrictions for elite women in the Old South were legitimated in terms of their seeming conformity to analogous patterns in the prestigious and authoritative slave society of imperial Rome. Classical scholar J. P. V. D. Balsdon notes:

> The Romans being for the first centuries of their existence an agricultural people, their houses, large or small, were country houses, and while the husband took care of the land, his wife took care of the household. She held the keys of the store cupboard, she brought up the children. The larger the establishment the greater the number of slaves, both in the house and on the land.

Even in its further detail, this portrait offers an illustrative example to the plantation mistress; Balsdon continues: "She never joined the guests after a meal until she had seen the silver locked up and given the slaves their supper."[14]

Care of slaves was the plantation mistress's constant chore. She distributed dairy foods and grain produced under her direction, often supervising the fields that supplied the Big House pantry and the storeroom for slave food. Even if the overseer supervised these plots, the final responsibility for feeding all those on the plantation still rested with the plantation mistress. Gardens were a major source of food for white and black, and women worked the family plots of fruits and vegetables diligently.[15] Even though slaves tended their own gardens on many plantations, the planters were responsible for staples, their wives doling out milk, pork, and corn to slaves in much the same way that they parceled out their own daily household supplies from the family storeroom.[16]

Most plantations supported an extensive dairy operation. The mistress supervised all stock kept for food (as opposed to work animals). An industrious mother of five reported to her sister in 1820: "I have 42 chickens to feed and nine cows to help with. I made 40 wt of butter last month."[17] As few plantations boasted an ice house, the processing of dairy products was a constant and delicate operation.[18]

Many women kept detailed records of their planting. Eliza Person Mitchell's gardening diary for 1834 contains fifty-one entries. Her listing for May gives some idea of the plantation mistress's agenda: "May 4th planted out cabbage plants, 6th Strawberries for tea, 16th at night a killing frost, corn, cimbelines, cotton, snaps and everything killed, 17th planted early snaps, planted salsafa planted cimbelines, 22nd planted sugar beets planted snaps, 23rd Manured the Black Raspberry vines with Woodpile Manure, 23rd Strawberries dressed over grass and weeds taken out, 23rd the weather very dry indeed, everything burning up in Garden." In addition to growing the food, plantation mistresses were preoccupied during summer and fall with preserving and pickling their garden's yield.[19]

The winter months were equally taxing. As one woman lamented in January 1833: "I will not weary you by recounting all my solitary troubles, you can well imagine them if you will but recall that hateful season to all housekeepers (the putting up of Pork)."[20] December was the month set aside for hog killing. The mistress supervised the long and complicated series of jobs that the process entailed and actually performed certain tasks herself. First the animal was hit over the head with an ax to stun it, and its throat was slit. The hog was then hoisted up and dipped into a kettle of scalding water, after which the bristles were scraped off and saved for making brushes, and the carcass hung head down from a tree, to be disemboweled and halved. Male slaves did the dirty work of the slaughter; the mistress would take little part in these preliminary activities. Once the carcass was prepared, however, the mistress took over. She emptied and scraped clean the small intestines, which were later stuffed with sausage. She processed the fat into lard, and chopped and seasoned the back meat, funneling it into skins for smoking. The ham shoulders and bacon flanks went into a barrel of brine to be corned. Thus the mistress processed each portion of the hog, down to the chitlings (intestines), into food. One plantation mistress complained that after salting meat for hours "all the skin was nearly off my hands"[21]—a far cry from the privileged "lily-white hands" celebrated in plantation legend. Another woman reported that her husband's two thousand weight of pork would keep her "up to her eyes in business" for a week.[22] It was grueling, repetitive work for planters' wives, and but one of their numerous unromantic duties.

Candlemaking and soapmaking were time-consuming chores for the southern housekeeper. Although slaves occasionally participated in the soapmaking, plantation mistresses thought the dipping of candles was too complex to trust to anyone but themselves. A skillful woman could produce in a day's work thirty dozen candles, which would provide a month's supply of candlelight.[23] Virginia women collected bayberries to make wax, as well as using animal fat (more common throughout the rest of the South). Mistresses spun the down from milkweed pods into wicks. Frugality led women to store their candles in boxes kept under lock and key.

Ante-bellum homes were filled with furnishings. Although many planters were able to purchase goods such as furniture, crystal, cutlery, and lamps, many of the necessities for the household were handmade by the plantation mistress. A young wife commented in 1829: "Two years ago I commenced the mighty job of making a carpet—a rag carpet, without being at all aware of the difficulties of the task. It is the most unseemly object imaginable."[24] Another homemaker exulted to a friend: "I have made an excellent Mattress which I am proud of, as being so much the work of my own hands, also made all my Pickles and catsup, preserves and different kinds and drying Peaches in different ways and such like things."[25] In early autumn, geese were killed and plucked. Women sorted the feathers—large ones for beds and small ones for pillows—then fashioned the quills into pens and the birds into Sunday dinners.

Though it surprises us to think of "sheltered" women grappling with such heavy burdens, women in agricultural societies throughout time have generally been charged with food production. The plantation may have been an expanded, near-industrial operation, but planters still expected women to fulfill this role. Despite wealth and status, plantation mistresses followed the tradition of their Colonial fore-bears; almost all females isolated on rural farms learned to be inventive and thrifty, developing uses for everything and seeing that nothing was wasted. Planters constantly voiced their financial worries and looked to women to reduce them through efficient and innovative management. Although women in commercial society were able to become "conspicuous consumers," plantation mistresses were far likelier to be inconspicuous producers.

With so many duties to perform and a multiplicity of roles to fulfill, the plantation mistress could easily be overwhelmed by responsibilities when she took up housekeeping. Mother and sisters often supplied goods as well as advice to the novice homemaker. A matron wrote to her newlywed sister: "I believe I forgot to tell you that I should give you two pairs of my linen pillowcases. You will find them with the beds. Supposing that a trunk might be useful to you I put the blankets up in one. Phill will give you the key. I put a dimity counterpane in it too. You will receive a box of candles, a box of hard soap, twelve hams, half a dozen brooms, and one of my low posted bedsteads. . . . You will find put up loosely in one of your pails nineteen balls of soap and six small pieces of hard soap. I have sewed up in a matt your chair."[26]

It was common for parents on both sides to supply newlywed couples with furnishings. Mothers especially concerned themselves with their daughters' new households.[27] Inventories indicate that new homes were well stocked with all the essentials and luxuries—besides the supplies of soap, candles, bedding, preserves, and other necessities, brides and grooms were usually the proud possessors of dining tables, chairs, sideboards, settees, rockers, four-poster beds, necessary chairs (with chamber pots hidden beneath the seat bottoms), chests of drawers (sets of drawers with handles, which fitted on top of one another for easy transport), silver, china, pots and pans, and sometimes family portraits and heirlooms.[28]

Most young plantation mistresses depended upon their female relatives for actual assistance, as well. Mothers and aunts, more experienced housekeepers, paid visits to novice plantation mistresses to help them "settle in." Their help and encouragement proved invaluable. Friends and neighbors might also give aid, but an aunt's visit during the summer months when jars needed filling for the winter ahead, or a mother's help during the hog killing, rescued many a young house-keeper from dreadful straits.

Housecleaning was an unpleasant series of tasks. Although she had a staff of house slaves, sometimes headed by a black steward or house-keeper, the plantation mistress regularly inspected all activities that she did not herself supervise or perform. Wives of southern planters did not participate in such basic tasks as laundering or dishwashing, but they took on other menial chores. One planter described his sister's tackling of the yard: "You should have seen with a large shovel she commenced digging away in real earnest. She made the dust fly, the chickens, too."[29] Besides the minimum daily and weekly routine of housecleaning, there were numerous seasonal tasks. In early March beds needed "scalding" to prevent bedbugs, part of the mistress's spring-cleaning ritual.[30] Most plantation kitchens were filled with copper pots and utensils; cleaning these items required careful attention on the mistress's part to prevent verdigris poisoning. In addition to the home and yard, wives with husbands in business supervised the care of their husbands' offices in town. An exasperated housekeeper reported: "It was a hard day's work for myself and three servants, the dusting and sweeping of books, papers, inkstands, etc., etc."[31]

In addition to furnishing and maintaining their homes, women supplied their own families and others on the plantation with clothing. Although mothers taught their daughters ornamental sewing as girls, few brides were accomplished seamstresses. Matrons soon learned from female relatives to knit and sew for their husbands and children, as well as their family of slaves. A married lady confessed to a friend: "I make all the Dr.'s clothes now excepting his coats, and when I was married I scarcely knew how to make a shirt."[32] The production of linen, counterpanes, and quilts was women's responsibility. Although the quilting bee afforded an entertaining diversion for the plantation mistress, it was but one of her many sewing activities in the midst of numerous domestic projects. The lament of the overworked seam-stress was a common theme in letters; a North Carolina woman confided to her sister in 1837: "I have about two months sewing to do. I never was so tired of sewing in my life. My fingers are worn out."[33]

The plantation mistress found the production of cloth and the man-ufacture of clothing to be her most demanding tasks. The ever-indus-trious Ann Cocke wrote from Bremo plantation: "The sewing of the

clothes is worse than weaving them, we have nearly a hundred shirts
to make besides other parts of dress—these I am teaching some women
of the crop to make. We shall have our weaving house, a perfect work
shop all next month, and a part of the month after."[34] Another mistress
of a large Virginia plantation wrote in 1813: "I have undertaken with
only my house servants for spinners (you know their number) to
cloathe all our Negroes, somehow I despair of accomplishing it."[35]
Mothers put unmarried daughters living at home to work at the spin-
ning wheel—hence the term "spinster"—or at the task of making
slave wardrobes.[36]

Each slave required a winter and a summer set of clothing. Southern women were also in charge of supplying blankets and clothing to
slave families; their account books are full of the details of their purchase
and distribution of goods.[37] Women bought Dutch blanketing for
slave use during the Colonial era, but following the Revolution, most
plantations attempted to produce all their own cloth. Without spinsters at home or trained slave spinners, a plantation mistress such as
Virginian Maria Campbell was forced to make her cloth herself. She
wrote in 1801: "I have turned my attention this spring to manufacturing, but find great difficulty in carrying it on, as I would wish, having
all my Cotton and Flax to purchase, and then can hardly procure any.
I shall shortly have several little webs finished."[38]

If they had money or lacked the slave labor to weave and spin, some
mistresses simply purchased cheap material for both blanketing and
clothing. On smaller plantations women distributed this cloth and
expected slave women to do the cutting and sewing for slave family
wardrobes. But on the larger plantations, turning cloth (bought or
homespun) into clothing consumed endless hours of the mistress's
time. Mary Telfair wrote in 1833: "My mind dwells upon the one
subject that I find it necessary to be actively engaged—I have been
making up clothes for the Negroes and assisted by Margaret packing
boxes to send to the plantations which for the time occupied me."[39]
Upon rare occasions mistresses were able to escape the drudgery of
clothing production by farming out these duties to the overseer's wife,
if he had one.[40]

Shoes and socks were less troublesome to produce than clothing. If
slave artisans did not make shoes on the plantation, mistresses ordered
footwear from local merchants for their husbands' slaves.[41] Mistresses

rarely purchased stockings, and instead knit them themselves. Virginia mistress Ann Cocke described her activities to her mother in 1811: "My hands are as full as possible. We have completed 25 out of the number of 40 pair of socks which are necessary for the crop hands. . . ."[42] The southern woman most often carried on her knitting at intervals during her many daily activities. A stocking took 185 stitches per row, on the average, and most plantation mistresses could manage to fit in 150 rows per day when knitting at a steady pace.[43] At that rate, a single sock took six days; a housewife could complete a pair of stockings every two weeks. At the very least, each slave required one pair of stockings per year. If a woman was mistress of a plantation with thirty slaves, she was able to manage all the knitting for her family and slaves herself, working at a relaxed pace. But if her husband owned in excess of thirty slaves, the mistress had to concentrate on knitting for prolonged periods of time, or train the black women in the house to knit their own stockings and those of other slaves. Ann Cocke reported in 1811: "Those about the house always furnish themselves, as far as the business of knitting goes—they are always furnished with the wool."[44]

The recipe books left by southern women reflect the industriousness of their lives. The record of Martha B. Eppes demonstrates her varied activities: included are how to make scarlet dye, the number of blankets distributed to slaves, and recipes for grape wine and "instantaneous beer."[45] Eliza Person Mitchell's housekeeping book contains twenty pages of recipes, notes on pickling and preserving, a record of soapmaking, a formula for furniture polish, and instructions on the making of paint.[46] But even more striking, all recipe books included, side by side with directions for mixing cakes and puddings, medical remedies.[47]

On large plantations, certain areas were designated as hospitals and nurseries. Elderly slave women served as nurses and attendants. As their recipe books tell us, the plantation mistress had to assume responsibility as ministering physician as well as housekeeper. She made daily rounds either to the cabins of sick slaves or to the buildings set aside for the invalid and infant members of the slave community. Women frequently commented on and complained about the trouble of slave illnesses in their correspondence.[48] They doctored the slaves both as humane plantation mistresses, seeing to the needs of their black charges, and in their capacity as slaveowners' wives, looking out for their husbands' property interests.

The problems of coping alone had faced women in this country since the American Revolution. Mary Beth Norton has described in her illuminating study, *Liberty's Daughters*, the transformation women's role underwent during the Revolutionary era. The war years provided a catalytic experience for females North and South. With their husbands away at war, women struggled against the fear of invading British troops.[49] In addition, they continued the planting, brought in the harvest, and supplied the militia with clothing as part of an enormous contribution to the war effort. These lessons stood southern women in good stead after the war, when they were swept away from the coast onto frontier plantations and forced to use their management skills. In 1796 a slaveowner could confidently write to his wife: "In respect to our private affairs, I need say nothing—You will do for the best, and to your descretion I leave the management of everything."[50] One planter blithely assured his wife in 1790: "I presume you have planted all the crop. I have only to add that I wish you good luck and good speed."[51]

Indeed, many of the lessons learned by southern women during the American Revolution have been incorrectly attributed to the Civil War. Some scholars have suggested that before the War Between the States, plantation mistresses led sheltered lives, unsullied by the business of plantation operation, and that the soldiers marching off in gray left behind women with little knowledge or experience. Their management of southern plantations, despite the men's absence, has been lauded as remarkable. In reality, when the American colonies severed connection with the British, the southern plantations lost important sources of goods and services; for the first time, women were forced to manufacture their own cloth, and plantations had to become self-sufficient. The South, like the rest of the country, began to adapt itself to an export economy during the early national era. Despite the bulk of evidence to the contrary, many historians have neglected or fundamentally distorted the importance of the mistress in plantation management.

Robert Fogel and Stanley Engerman, in *Time on the Cross*, present a case in point. In arguing for the crucial contribution of slaves to plantation management, their inability to filter out sexism in their analysis is disturbing. They note that "only 30 percent of plantations with one hundred or more slaves employed white overseers. On smaller plantations the proportion was even lower." Yet these scholars refer only to overseers when they describe and assess the supervision of slaves with respect to food, shelter, clothing, and medical care. The lack of a single reference to the plantation mistress in this section represents not merely a gross oversight but a major distortion. Further, when they scrupulously examine the census schedules to see if planter sons could have served as surrogate overseers, they find that "for 75 percent of the plantations without overseers, there were no sons or other males who could have assumed the duties of the overseer." They then assert: "The conclusion indicated by these findings is startling: on a majority of the large plantations the top nonownership management was black. The question that begs to be explained is how so many scholars could have been so badly misled on this issue?"[52] Considering that these historians make no mention of women's role on the plantation, their own question remains to be answered—with reference to the badly misleading assumptions of their own scholarly work.

During the post-Revolutionary era, many planters elected to political office or forced to travel extensively on business confidently left the management of their estates to wives, as well as to overseers. Although they continued to supervise plantation finances—at home or from abroad—many planters allowed their wives total discretion in business affairs during their absence. Even when masters maintained control over planting, crops, and other concerns through postal directives, the daily decisions and business of farming were of necessity left in capable women's hands when planters were called away. Managing the plantation either in a husband's absence or during widowhood did, however, inevitably pose difficulties.

A variety of sources suggest that plantation mistresses were familiar with all facets of farm management. Bolling Hall, an Alabama politician, depended on reports from his daughter Polly during his tenure in Washington: "The next time you write let me know how much corn and cotton is made at Fort Creek, how much is at Kings and how much at home."[53] Another woman frequently described plantation activities in correspondence with her husband, who traveled on the circuit court: "Sam and Moses are Coulturing the large field and I can see the dust rise in clouds as the ploughs move along. . . . Yesterday I gave an order in Mr. Johnson's favour for 3 bushells. I suppose when he comes home I must give him one for the remaining odd twenty. . . . I believe you have the farming business set before you."[54] Planters just as often sent home details about agricultural affairs to wives immersed in planting chores. Without the interim management by females, southern plantations would have suffered irreparable damage. Men expected and depended upon women's capabilities.

Money management was a significant part of the wife's household role, and the plantation mistress generally kept her own books—to account for cash spent for slaves' supplies, to detail expenditures at the local store, and to provide a record of frugality for the planter's inspection. Most husbands kept wives on informal allowances, doling out cash upon request rather than on a regular or specified basis. Husbands expected their wives to keep them informed of housekeeping expenses. A matron wrote to her husband in 1836 of her financial needs: "My dear husband, I spend as little as I can. I sometimes spent 75 cts sometimes 50, but there are so many little extras that it generally comes to a dollar a day."[55] When ready cash was unavailable on the plantation itself, many mistresses depended on their family network to provide desired goods and to clear debts.

A few women resisted the responsibilities shifted onto them by their absent husbands. Subjected to long periods of isolation on her husband's Louisiana plantation, Diana Dunbar made her own decisions about farming operations but did not shy away from expressing her complaints: "I am sorry you do not find my letters so pretty as they used to be; but if you knew, my love, how I am vex and plagu'd with a set of worthless servents you wou'd not be surprised at it, but I will make you uneasy with my complaints: I have told you already about the plantation & the Tobacco. Indeed my love there is too much to do for the few people you left. As I thought it wou'd be too long before I could get an answer from you, concerning hiring a hand to help in making up the Tobacco, I have hired one today." Diana Dunbar vacillated between anger at her husband's demands and the desire to please him with an efficient job: "You seem, my Dear, to expect we have a great deal of time upon our hands, to do everything necessary about the plantation. I would not have you expect too much for fear you may be disappointed; tho' my love, if you will consider everything rightly I don't think you will complain. . . . I would willingly follow your advice and not go in the sun if I could avoid it, but there is many things to do about a place that you men don't think of."[56] The plantation mistress was often burdened by a husband's numerous directives, while being admonished not to exert herself. Most women accepted the inherent tensions of their role and struggled when necessary to manage successfully both the household and the plantation over all.[57]

During the master's absence, financial concerns added to the burdens of planting and often posed a more serious threat to the mistress's ability to cope. Most wives sent a list of questions as well as a flurry of complaints to their absent husbands, and it is clear that despite their varying degrees of ability many suffered a lack of confidence in their business acumen, particularly when questions involved areas outside the perimeters of the plantation itself. As we shall see, law and social custom reinforced these psychological constraints. Socialization from birth trained women to defer to males; decision making outside the domestic sphere proved difficult for plantation mistresses. Some dealt masterfully, such as a matron who won her husband's approval in 1806: "What you mention concerning the purchase of pork and other matters meets with my approbation as indeed your transactions have always done."[58] Another able manager wrote to her son in 1838: "The Bargain is not closed yet, for my wheat and I begin to be very uneasy about it—10 days more to keep it, often—I thought, I had got 10/ but the bargain was not such as I expected. Mr. Haxall did not allow the difference of white over red wheat—I am sorry for it—but I still hope for the best."[59] But more often the strain provoked husbands to discourage their wives from financial transactions during the master's absences.[60]

If forced by circumstances, women could manage internal plantation affairs without the advice or consent of males. Daughters who inherited estates from their fathers or widows who were left to run plantations alone seemed to survive on the land without male intervention. These independent women, called female planters, favorably impressed Anne Royall during her celebrated travels in the South.[61] Sarah G. Haig prepared a book of direction for overseers on her Thorn

Island plantation in 1837: "You perceive that the land of this plantation is rapidly wearing out and that there is no more land to be cleared. The only possible way therefore to prevent its going to ruin is to follow a strict and diligent system of managing."[62] She provided her overseers with explicit directions concerning how many acres to plant, slave discipline, and other vital principles.

Rachel O'Conner of Louisiana was a woman planter of indefatigable energy. She chronicled her activities in a steady stream of correspondence to relatives. In November of 1823, she reported to her brother: "I have seventy bales of Cotton Prep'd and hauling them as fast as possible to the river to ship for N. Orleans—I answered my dear little Niece's last letter on saturday which I am afraid she cannot read easily. It rained and they were preparing cotton and I had to stop very often to get whatever they wanted which put me out of sorts."[63] When her sister-in-law requested directions for planting leeks, Rachel O'Conner sent her a detailed set of instructions testifying to her planting expertise. She wrote to her brother David frequently about the trials of plantation business, bemoaning faulty machinery and the falling price of cotton.[64] Many women kept detailed business records to safeguard themselves in the complex process of plantation management.[65]

Such management, either in a husband's absence or during widowhood, was problematic for reasons that had nothing to do with a woman's personal experience or expertise. Wives who took little or no interest in farming accounts often regretted their neglect after their husbands' death, and were forced to call upon male relatives for assistance. But even a mistress who demonstrated a clear ability to manage her plantation as a discrete economic unit and make it pay was not permitted by law to handle personal or business affairs in the public sphere. Women's inadequacies, real or perceived, were a direct result of the "sheltering" system that designated women as dependents, under the protection—and at the mercy—of men. While this system failed to keep women from exercising authority and demonstrating capability in daily routines, it effectively shackled them in any external dealing beyond plantation boundaries. Ready to make full use of her talents as household manager and domestic laborer, the society—ruled by males in the legislature and in the courts—deprived the plantation mistress of her own legal identity.

As a result, women rightly felt vulnerable in the world of legal finance. They held no power before the law, which provided for man's total control over woman: her property, her behavior, her very person. This was a logical development in an extended patriarchy, built upon racial and sexual differentiation and bolstered by a hierarchy of fixed roles and duties.

Moral and legal arguments quickly developed to guarantee a husband's domination of his wife, including, of course, the critical issue of reproduction. Women often referred to a girl's marrying as "resigning her liberty."[66] One Virginia matron confessed to her journal: "Our mother Eve when she transgress'd was told her husband should rule over her—then how dare any of her daughters to dispute the point."[67] But once widows had lost their husbands, they faced the reality that they had never had true freedom. Their "liberty" was not restored by widowhood, for despite a woman's substantial inheritance, females lacked legal personality, and stewardships were established for widowed or otherwise abandoned women.

A maze of financial complications faced the widow after a planter's death. Virginia plantation mistress Frances Bland Randolph Tucker wrote about this to her brother, Theodorick Bland, from Bizarre in 1781. She had remarried St. George Tucker following Randolph's death, and was concerned about her three Randolph sons: "I wish it was in my power to give a satisfactory answer about their finances, as to my utter astonishment there is not an account of any kind relative to the crops, payment of taxes, or any else—But as I am on this plantation I shall take care there shall be no more embezzlements whether here or at Roanoke."[68]

Society expected a widow's sons to render assistance and advice. At the very least, mothers could pour out their problems to sympathetic offspring. Admittedly, most sons ministered to the planting and the financial needs of their widowed mothers, when wealth permitted. But some plantation mistresses were unable to count on their male offspring. Dolley Madison's son was a notorious ne'er-do-well who caused his mother no end of worry and grief. The crop was solely the product of her own labors and expense.[69] Many women were able to manage their own plantations and affairs through the legal assistance and advice of friends of their late husbands, such as widowed Delia Bryan, who depended heavily on John Randolph of Roanoke following her husband's death.[70] Most women, however, fell back on their families for support. For the most part, fathers, brothers, and sons provided women with the supplemental guidance necessary in order for women to prosper as planters. Numerous testimonies demonstrate widows' dependence upon male advisers and their gratitude for men's protection and profit maximization.[71]

All women in southern society recognized the important financial and legal handicap under which they lived, and most accepted the limitations imposed by society as unalterable. Women did not resist as much as resent dependency. The psychological tensions—exacerbated by the enormous strain of physical chores—created depression, melancholy, and a whole range of debilities for women, discussed at length in later chapters. These women did not inhabit mythical estates, but rather productive working plantations: the routine was grueling, life was harsh. No wonder they complained of being themselves enslaved. The plantation mistress found herself trapped within a system over which she had no control, one from which she had no means of escape. Cotton was King, white men ruled, and both white women and slaves served the same master.

III

CIRCLE OF KIN

*T*he family was an institution of paramount importance in the ante-bellum South. Only slavery surpassed it in cultural influence and social significance. Paternalism, so striking in southern political culture and a significant element in slave relations, grew out of family structures and roles. Kinship provided crucial links within both economic and political systems throughout the South, and in contrast to the North, this situation lasted long past the Revolution. The primacy of family might have held sway in New England commerce during its infancy, but by the early nineteenth century expansion in industrial areas undercut family power in northern business circles. The plantocracy promoted an opposite phenomenon. As territorial settlement expanded and business relations grew ever more complex, an extended kinship network increased rather than decreased in importance in the post-Revolutionary southern states. The growth of cotton culture demanded more and more land for profitable cultivation, and extending the family was seen as the best method to secure territory.

Serious demand for land was matched by an enduring faith in old and established social patterns in the South. In coastal areas, commercial traffic introduced new and more secular ideas from the urban centers of the Northeast and Europe, but southern society on the whole remained a conservative, tightly knit, hierarchical, and closed system. In it, an established family equaled political and economic power. Without connections, businesses languished. Without family ties, politicians could not count on successful bids for office. Without intermarriage, planter dynasties failed to prosper.

Thus family structures provided the network through which land, wealth, and power were channeled. Many lines were crossed to weave the network closer and tighter. Cousin marriages and marriages to the siblings of dead spouses helped keep wealth "within the family."* Slaveowning planters bestowed on their offspring the most generous portions of land and slaves they could afford. As a rule, sons received land and daughters, slaves; sons, of course, almost always received the larger shares. This pattern changed with the availability of heirs, but patriarchs attempted to keep their property on the increase, as well as secure from one generation to the next; for this reason, planters on adjoining plantations often encouraged their children to marry each other.

These firmly patriarchal attitudes were entrenched within the framework of southern political economy by the end of the eighteenth century.[1] The centrality of kinship struck Timothy Ford, a traveler in the South, on a visit to Beaufort, South Carolina, in 1785: "It consists of about thirty houses—stands on an arm of the sea very pleasantly and is stiled a very healthy place. The inhabitants are almost all connected by some family relation which makes them sociable and friendly."[2]

To nearly all women, marriage meant the acquisition of an entirely new network of kin, but many southern girls dreaded the consequent loss of their own families. When they wed, southern women were obliged to follow their husbands—to the next plantation, the next county, the next state, or even the unexplored territories of the frontier. Many wives resisted their husbands' wanderlust and counseled settling nearer their own relatives. Thomas N. Holmes of Alabama wrote to his sister in Mississippi in 1835: "I am now sittling my

*See Chapter IV, "The Day to Fix My Fate."

business and expect to move about the last month over in Sumpter county about 60 miles from here where I have bought land. I should have bought some near you if my dear little Margarit had not been so much opposed to leaving her relations."[3] Perhaps the fact that Margaret Holmes had been married less than a year and was expecting her first child influenced her husband to heed her wishes. Many husbands were not so indulgent.[4] In 1821 a woman wrote to her brother of the distress of their cousin's wife, isolated on a plantation in the wilderness: "They are living near Salem, Georgia in the frontiers of the state and perfectly uncivilized place. Cousin W. gets a good practice—but she is almost crazy to get to Alabama where one of her sisters is living."[5]

For women, kinship assumed special importance. Men could escape into the public realm: to town, to business, to the outside world. Females spent their lives confined to the domestic sphere, and therefore their happiness was more closely connected with family relations. For this reason, daughters generally suffered the separation from parents more keenly than sons did; sisters, aunts—indeed, all the women of the household—were more tightly bound to it than were the men. Males were prepared from childhood for the public sphere, females for the private household, so their sense of self-esteem and fulfillment was localized in separate, gender-differentiated realms. Anne Steele wrote rhapsodically of an eagerly awaited homecoming: "I anticipate my return in a few short weeks to the arms of a small circle of valued and beloved friends and there testifying by every action of my life how nearly allied their happiness is to my own and in being a dutiful and affectionate daughter, niece and sister insuring (with the mediation of Jesus) felicity both in this and the world to come."[6] The dependence of a woman on her family continued throughout a lifetime.

Equally important, families depended upon their women to supply crucial domestic labor. The wife headed this working force, its ranks filled with daughters, sisters, and other unmarried females.[7] David Campbell, a childless husband, complained to his sister that his wife's illnesses presented him with real hardship, since they had no female relative living with them.[8] Although spinsters were subject to as great a demand on their time as the mothers of families, they reaped few social and psychological rewards. Expected to repress personal wishes that would interfere with family duty, the husbandless sister had no recourse but to devote her time and energies to "other women's families" if a nurse or an extra pair of hands was required.[9] The spinster represented a potential source of labor that the family circle often could, without hesitation, exploit "for the family's sake."

Kinship extended beyond traditional linear relations. Planters customarily adopted the orphaned offspring of brothers or sisters, while grandparents might supervise the rearing of motherless grandchildren. A southern gentleman described his situation upon the death of his mother in 1777: "I was carried home by my maternal grandmother, to be taken care of by her; and my sister was taken for the same purpose by some of my father's relations."[10] Parental death created households with a variety of stepbrothers and sisters as well as half brothers and sisters. In addition, many planters engendered overlapping generations.[11] This extended the crowded cast of characters within the southern household. The plantation home was a flexible unit which included but was not limited to parents and children. The male head of the household was responsible for the financial support of the entire retinue of relatives. Thus the plantation mistress provided care and comfort for her own family and any of their connection who needed material assistance.

Southern sons carried maternal devotion to an extreme. Tributes, stories, and anecdotes exalting the "tender and pious" mother were a staple of plantation folklore.[12] The other side of the coin, the mother as a formidable force within the home, is illustrated in the following recollection by a southern gentleman: "My grandmother Holcombe was a lady of fine physique and strongly marked character. She was a grand old-fashioned Virginia housekeeper, and that means a great deal to those acquainted with the social customs and immense hospitalities of that period. She was a superb manager of her servants, of her children, and we may add, *sotto voce*, of her husband. She was such a strict disciplinarian that she is said to have horsewhipped one of her sons for some act of disobedience when he was eighteen years of age."[13] In either case, recognition of the mother's central role in the socialization and supervision of children within the family was testified to by the popular and pervasive mother cult.

The paternal role was predominantly that of a distant "figurehead" rather than a direct influence on children, at least until they approached maturity. The rearing of children was a maternal function, and fathers exercised disciplinary or developmental control over their young sons and daughters indirectly, paying closer attention to their offspring only when they reached adolescence. The paternal influence clearly gained significance and stature for children with the onset of adulthood.

Within plantation society, as in most patriarchal cultures, the father represented "real," the mother "false" power. Although a mother had direct, daily supervision of her children, the father clearly ruled the household. Once sons and daughters grew to the age of reason, they could see that their mother was merely carrying out the wishes of the patriarch; no matter what the strength of her will or influence might be, male authority was dominant. The fact that some women wheedled, cajoled, or otherwise manipulated men to get their own way only reinforced the reality that men were the "legitimate" powers within society, and that women's influence was domestic, limited, and subordinate to paternal authority.

Although children keenly felt the loss of either parent, the death of a mother was traumatizing as well as disruptive. Women had a higher rate of mortality than men in the ante-bellum South;[14] death in childbirth increased during the post-Revolutionary era. In a sample study of planter women, death in childbirth doubled (from three percent to six percent) from the Revolutionary to the ante-bellum eras. The death of a mother was thus not rare. If a father died, his sons and daughters could remain with their mother—perhaps in the house of an uncle or a grandfather, but nonetheless together. If a mother died, however, children not only lost a parent but might also be separated and put into the households of assorted relatives unless their father shortly remarried. A planter whose mother died when he was five wrote: "The loss of a parent is at all times the most afflictive and severe that can befall a child, but the loss of a tender and pious mother at such a tender age is always irreparable."[15] If able, an elder daughter might take over the family duties of the mother, but this put a tremendous burden on any young girl.[16] The mother clearly held a family together.

Just as the cult of southern motherhood created competing myths of strength and weakness, so too was the paternal image contradictory. Fathers autocratically ruled offspring and state alike, but the manner in which they exercised their authority varied from family to family.

Many planters subscribed to one of two extreme schools and were either stern patriarchs or indulgent papas, though most did not conform exclusively to one model, but borrowed from each. Sketches of two post-Revolutionary southern fathers, Robert Beverley and Thomas Jefferson, illustrate these contrasting images of planter paterfamilias.

Virginia planter Robert Beverley was an archetype of the stern patriarch. His story well illustrates both the variety of obligations a family network might pose and the unyielding manner in which they might be met. Born in 1769, Beverley was one of sixteen children. He was the wealthiest of the eight sons in his family, and his relatives constantly solicited his financial aid. The women of the Beverley clan were especially dependent upon Robert Beverley's charitability. In April 1796, Lucy Beverley Randolph wrote to her brother Robert to beg him to help remedy her husband Brett's financial plight. In response to her brother's monetary assistance, Lucy Randolph wrote: "My mind is so overpowered with gratitude that my face is covered with tears before I can recollect myself." In 1798, after the Randolphs moved to a smaller farm in Henrico County, Virginia, Lucy reported that they were able to live more frugally. As to Robert Beverley's frequent advice to his unprosperous brother-in-law, Lucy Randolph confessed: "My heart accepts your generous proposals with no other sensation than that of fondest gratitude, but surely there are some considerations which a Wife that regards the delicacy of an Husband's feelings should have." Yet in 1815 Lucy Randolph was again forced to ask her brother to intervene. The sheriff had seized her slaves to settle claims against her husband. She was uncertain about Brett Randolph's financial affairs, and speculated: "Mr. R's debts are still so harassing and I fear numerous."[17]

Robert Beverley was plagued not only by his brother-in-law but by his own brother, Carter Beverley. Jane Beverley's debt-ridden husband Carter turned his land and slaves over to trustees. She wrote to Robert in January 1811, asking for two servants and any other aid he could manage to give the couple and their six children. As Robert Beverley was involved in litigation with Carter, no money was forthcoming. In July of the same year, Jane Beverley again wrote to her brother-in-law, asking him to intercede on her behalf with one of her relatives. She wanted to secure an inheritance that she thought was her due, in hopes of obtaining enough cash to prevent the sale of their house and slaves to cover her husband's outstanding loans. Apparently her scheme was unsuccessful, for she was living off her mother's charity in 1813. Settled on a small farm in Fairfax County, Virginia, Jane Beverley reported the cheerless situation of her invalid husband and seven children to Robert Beverley, signing herself, "your affectionate friend but unfortunate sister."[18]

Robert Beverley also attended to the pleas of his niece Euphrasie Beverley, the daughter of yet another sibling. While her father and brothers went off to Alabama to seek their fortune, Euphrasie and her mother were left penniless and alone on their Virginia farm. In February 1834, Euphrasie reported to her uncle that she had been unable to leave the farm from May to September of the previous year for want of proper clothes. In June 1834, Robert Beverley sent his niece ten badly needed dollars for food. The next year, Euphrasie again suffered financial embarrassment. A relative had lent her passage money to travel to her Uncle Mackenzie's. After four months she had overstayed her welcome: "I received broad hints every day that my room would be better than my company."[19] But she had no cash for her return fare. Robert Beverley sent his indigent niece the five-dollar coach fare to rescue her from her situation.

Robert Beverley resented his family's constant applications for money and displayed his discontent most callously—not in his treatment of brothers, sisters, and nieces, but in his relationship with his daughter Rebecca. After the death of his wife in 1816, Robert Beverley sent his daughters Rebecca, Jane, and Roberta to live with their married sister, Maria Clarke. Upon Maria's advice, Beverley sent his girls to school at Miss Lyman's in Philadelphia. His letters to Rebecca are filled with complaints about expense, reprimands of her conduct, and a constant flow of criticism. Rebecca Beverley suffered from her father's harshness, channeling her sense of guilt into alternating moods of angry frustration and unworthiness. She was relatively silent, however, in her reproachfulness. She most often thanked her father for his generosity, apologized for the trouble she caused him, and promised to improve according to his wishes. After receiving an especially stinging letter, Rebecca was wounded enough to reply: "You made an observation relative to me which the recollection of has more than once drawn tears from my eyes as it plainly shows me my father is anxious to be released from the trouble and perhaps I ought to add the expense of supporting and protecting me. . . . Now it is certain I am not old as I have not yet attained my nineteenth year and indeed were I several years older I should not have deserved such a rebuke."[20]

Robert Beverley continued his complaints. In 1821 she wrote in despair: "I suppose I must deserve all you say of me as you maintain you know me better than I do myself. It would be needless for me to say anything in my defense since all my feeble endeavours to obtain your approbation have been fruitless and I see you entertain as poor an opinion of me as a father could of a child. My chief study must be now to bear this misfortune as well as I can and try not to let my feelings be so much wounded or I shall soon be carried to my grave."[21] Did Robert Beverley reread this letter following his daughter's death the next year? Rebecca Beverley did not die of a broken heart, but of typhoid. Yet her father's grief could understandably have been mixed with remorse for his insensitive and constant harshness toward this daughter, dead at the age of twenty.

Robert Beverley's relationship with Rebecca contrasts with that of another Virginia patriarch, Thomas Jefferson, with his beloved eldest child, Patsy. Jefferson's daughters Martha (Patsy) and Maria (Polly) were left motherless in 1782, and Jefferson devoted himself totally to their well-being. He wrote to Patsy in 1786, counseling her to do well in school: "I need not tell you what pleasure it gives me to see you improve in everything agreeable and useful. The more you learn the more I love you, and I rest the happiness of my life on seeing you beloved by all the world, which you will be sure if to a good heart you join these accomplishments so peculiarly pleasing in your sex." A year later, Jefferson reiterated his dependence upon his daughters in another letter to Patsy: "Nobody in this world can make me so happy or so miserable as you. Retirement from public life will ere long become necessary for me. To your sister and yourself I look to render the evening of my life serene and contented."[22] Thomas Jefferson's language toward both his daughters illustrates the passionate style in which Southerners demonstrated paternal affection—if at all.

The bonds both of sentimental attachment and of the purse strings tied daughters to their fathers. Many women were torn between enjoying the financial and emotional security their fathers provided and wanting to escape the corresponding strains of dependence. Widow Elizabeth Murchison was grateful for her father's generosity to her and her two small children following her husband's death in 1820, but soon sold all but her slaves to pay her husband's debts. In April 1827 she resolved to give up all her property in order to extricate herself permanently from indebtedness to her creditors and to her father. She made this financial sacrifice to ensure her own independent integrity.

Many daughters had intense and warm relationships with their fathers and maintained strong filial dependence even after marriage. Father-husband rivalry was not uncommon in the ante-bellum South. A wife wrote to her husband during an extended visit to her parents in 1815: "If you are not very cautious he will create grounds in my heart for such is my disposition that I always love those that I stay with most. Papa, you know, is rather a dangerous rival as I have once or twice been accused of loving him more than yourself."[23] This "rivalry"— real or pretended—was part of the larger problem of conflict between family loyalties. Socialized from birth to devote herself wholly to her blood relatives, a woman experienced no small dilemma when she married and was required to shift her loyalties to her husband and an inherited family. As Thomas Jefferson warned his newly married daughter Patsy: "The happiness of your life depends now on continuing to please a single person. To this all other objects must be secondary; even your love for me, were it possible that it could ever be an obstacle."[24]

Relationships with in-laws were crucial to family harmony. Like any parents wanting the best for their children, Southerners were quick to criticize the spouse of their son or daughter. Conflict most often centered on financial matters or grandchildren. Planters openly interfered in their married children's business affairs; more often than not, the marriage contract was but one of many legal documents cementing the relations between fathers and sons-in-law. Mother-in-law problems were not unusual, as witness John Haywood's troubles with his wife's mother, Jane Williams. During the autumn of 1798 Elizabeth Haywood, in an advanced stage of pregnancy, found herself caught between pleasing her mother and pleasing her husband. The former insisted that her daughter "lie in" at her family home, because the guest rooms of the Williamses' house were preferable to the drafty quarters in Haywood's house. Haywood objected to his mother-in-law's intervention in his marital affairs, but nonetheless reluctantly agreed to let his wife visit her parents during her confinement. In

1799, after their lengthy separation, he complained that she must never again distress him by deserting their home.[25]

Despite such bickering, closeness between children and in-laws was the rule in the ante-bellum South. Planters were unusually indulgent in their relations with in-laws as the case of John Coalter illustrates. On January 11, 1816, Coalter wrote to St. George Tucker: "My mother died on the eight instant."[26] Coalter was referring, not to the mother who bore him, but to Frances Davenport, the mother of his previous wife. Since Margaret Davenport Coalter's death in childbirth in 1795, Frances Davenport had lived with Coalter as a member of his family. Despite his remarriage, Coalter generously provided for Frances Davenport, his "mother," during the twenty-one years following her daughter's death. Although Coalter's devotion to his mother-in-law was extraordinarily long in its duration, his support of family—even a relative by marriage—was not unusual. Most planters expected to provide for a large household, and as long as these family members had any blood or marriage claim on the paterfamilias, he was obliged to support them with unfailing loyalty.

The birth of children was unquestionably the most celebrated of family events; all kin joyously greeted the survival of childbirth by both the mother and the infant. In a society in which dynastic survival was paramount, however, female babies suffered from the preference for male offspring, and were discriminated against by adult women as well as men. Fathers and mothers often expressed "disappointment" and "mortification" at the birth of a daughter.[27] A recently delivered mother in Virginia wrote to her husband in Paris in 1819: "The little lock which now presents itself will first announce to my beloved husband the birth of the second pledge of our love but I fear the news will convey little pleasure to the heart of its father when told it is another daughter. I felt disappointed but it was because I had my heart set on naming it after him."[28] William Elliott reported to his mother-in-law a similar sentiment expressed by a female relative in South Carolina in 1829: "The mother is uncommonly well—and tho' disappointed in the prospect of having old maids in the family—instead of bustling sons who could take care of themselves—she seems to resign herself to the disappointment. She was so certain of calling it Ralph—that she appears quite thrown out by the necessity of finding a female name for it."[29]

Their disappointment can be rationalized. Southerners without sons were faced with genealogical extinction.[30] Only sons would continue family traditions and carry on the family name. But this preference for male offspring went deeper than genealogy and inheritance; it was part of a larger ideological framework that proclaimed men superior and women inferior. As the South expanded its hierarchical social system, gender roles became even more rigid. The function of the dynasty was to merge social and political systems within an economic unit: the family. Wealth, power, and status derived from this source. The family was not merely a mirror or microcosm of society, but an instrument; the home provided a training ground for the culture as a whole, and the favored status of males was generated as well as reinforced by domestic roles. Whatever indulgence a daughter might receive from her parents, she was never granted complete freedom of choice; her options were severely curtailed by her gender. She was granted power only to influence children in favor of the status quo. Mothers were expected to inculcate values that maintained the inferiority of women. The psychic and physical burdens of childrearing were formidable indeed.

One planter commented on the tranquillity of the domestic scene: "It certainly must be a sight highly gratifying to an affectionate husband to see his wife cheerfully performing the duties of a mother, for it must imperceptibly attach him more towards her and cement their affections beyond the power of time or chance to alter. Besides a woman so employed will not fly eagerly after every light and trifling pursuit which fashion may offer. Her mind will be too much engaged to heed the call of folly; her whole heart will be absorbed by the interesting scenes of her nursery. . . ."[31] This varies dramatically from the female perspective presented by a Virginia mother: "I received your letter of the 21st a few hours ago and read it pretty much as you say it was written, amid the bustle of half dozen children and in the intervals of attending to their wants. In this way indeed, I do everything now and my mode of locomotion is no longer a *walk*, but rather a half run a great part of my time. No admiration from Buonaparte or anybody else can console me in being claimed as a mother by so many poor scraps of humanity or support me thro' the interminable round of mill horse duties which they impose upon me. . . ."[32] William Elliott of South Carolina wrote to his wife, Ann, from Saratoga Springs,

New York, in 1828, describing parties, balls, and fashion. He closed his letter with the following confession: "Tell me of my little ones I love most at a distance. Why? Can it be because they do not plague me?"[33] Although some fathers fantasized peace and contentment at the family hearth, most men knew the demanding nature of childcare and preferred that their wives shoulder its burdens.

Because the role of motherhood was elevated and enhanced during the early republican era, women perhaps suffered more keenly from the duties imposed on them as parents. During the late eighteenth century, prescriptive tracts in both England and America lamented the evil effects of servants upon the children assigned to their care. Wet nurses and governesses were discredited as supervisors for treasured offspring. Advice literature specific to the South warned of the dangers involved in letting children come under the destructive sway of slaves tending them. Infants were considered too precious to be entrusted fully to slave women. Although the practice of employing slaves to suckle white babies was instituted and indeed encouraged during the early national era, white mothers did not regularly turn their infants over to black women as often as southern folklore suggests.

No matter how much they loved their children, mothers complained on occasion of their maternal burdens. Fanny Bland Tucker, a Virginia plantation mistress and the mother of John Randolph of Roanoke, wrote to her husband in 1787: "The children are very well but intolerably noisy and troublesome—it is a hard day's work to attend to them & the drudgery of the house—their interruptions at this moment are so frequent I scarcely know what I write."[34] Fanny Tucker's complaint was a common one. Another harassed woman wrote to her mother in 1808, begging indulgence "when you reflect that these lines are the effusions of a pen directed by the Hand of a woman whose whole life has been occupied by Domestic concerns and raising children."[35]

In addition to the tiresome details of childcare, a mother carried out the unpleasanter task of daily discipline, policing her children's behavior, interceding in quarrels among siblings, and doling out demerits, lectures, and whippings. Although the father represented final authority on the plantation, it was the mother who most often dispensed the actual punishment. One woman wrote to her brother complaining of her two-year-old son: "His father spoils him bad enough and thinks him the smartest child in the world. . . . I have all the whipping to do."[36] The supervision of young children was wholly a woman's domain. A father, left alone with his four-year-old child during his wife's visit to a relative, wrote an exasperated account of dealing with his daughter's refusal to go to bed: "I thought I would let her cry till she was tired but I found it would keep me up too long. . . . could do nothing with her till I whipped her smartly. . . . When she quit crying I was almost ready to begin. Her stubborn temper. . . ."[37] His resentment of his wife's absence led to her premature return home.

In a world where hierarchy and role definition were pre-eminent, mothers naturally believed that maintaining their proper role was crucial to the future prosperity of their offspring and thus of society as a whole. Southerners feared, however, that a mother's negligence would cause a child's deliquency.[38] Southerners preached that only a diligent effort on the mother's part would prevent children from "wandering astray." Widowed Delia Bryan wrote to her dead husband's great friend, John Randolph of Roanoke: "I am a very strict mother without being severe. I never *watch* or appear suspicious of my children, but if I *detect* them in anything becoming untruth, candour and that high independence their father was so remarkable for, it is then and only then that they have to encounter my frowns. . . . I never permit my children to be idle beyond the time which health requires."[39] Another woman warned her daughter about supervising her own child: "Be not austere with Betsy, it will make her artfull and mean, learn her also to tell you stories and you will never know what your child really is."[40] In the midst of all this advice and concern, the critical problems of motherhood remained; as one woman wrote to another in 1833: "It grieved me that you make yourself so miserable about your children— what is the use my dear child—it is certainly your duty to take care of them, but not to render your life so miserable."[41]

The mistress presumably maintained house slaves to mitigate the burdens of child supervision, but most mothers still fretted about trusting even older children to the care of black servants. One woman wrote in 1818 of her fears for her daughter: "Owing to Jules careless-ness the child has been frequently of late very much bruised and injured by falls, she let her fall this morning from the upper platform down two flights of stairs and I fear her back is injured but no visible marks have as yet appeared except her jaw and tongue are very much bruised and cut. I rarely go from home since I never have put my feet outside the door but something of the kind occurs."[42]

Mothers on plantations considered themselves doubly plagued by the "slave problem." Not only were planter wives worried about the negligence of slave servants, but their children's slave playmates, they believed, set poor examples. Warned from an early age about their contact with slaves, white children were indoctrinated with a sense of suspicion toward blacks and a demeanor of superiority. White women sought relief from the tedious daily supervision of their brood so they could carry on with their numerous domestic tasks, but they feared the results of surrogate attention. One woman worriedly wrote to her sister: "William is learning a little at home tho' but little. We have a gang of little negroes in the yard and I can't keep them apart. O how it grieves me."[43] Mothers worried about the bad influence of slaves even over grown children who had left the family for homes of their own. This concern served an important social function. The prohibition of close contacts between children and slaves taught planter offspring to maintain the distance necessary for the master-slave relationship. One concerned grandfather assured the mother of his visiting granddaughter: "She is lively and volatile, is kept as close as possible to her studies and aloof from the servants. It requires all of our care and attention to keep her straight. Your mother never fails to watch and check her every impropriety of words and actions."[44]

The plantation mistress was especially sensitive to what she had been taught to see as the debauching influence of slave women on sons who had reached puberty. "Lewd and promiscuous" behavior was always blamed on the slaves in the case of planter-concubine liaisons. Mothers feared the immoral influence of the sexual double standard but were helpless to act within the constraints of southern patriarchy. Beyond these specific hazards to morality, the plantation mistress also continually warned her children, male and female alike, to keep aloof. "Be *cautious* how you converse with Papa's Negroes," Delia Bryan wrote in 1825; "on no account familiarize with them—be *kind* and *civil* and never converse with them about family affairs of *any kind*."[45]

Mothers in the Old South bore a threefold responsibility: for their children's education, morality, and physical well-being. The plantation mistress diligently guarded the health of her offspring from the

disease and death that relentlessly threatened ante-bellum plantations.★ Mothers were responsible for early education, in order that
their sons and daughters not suffer later in life. Finally, and most
important, from society's point of view, mothers were responsible for
shaping the moral character of their offspring. Their highest priority
was to rear Christians worthy of God's grace. The moral guardianship
of children was a mother's sacred trust, in conjunction with her
nurturing role. For this reason, most plantation mistresses feared death
as much as for their children's sake as they did for their own. A
woman wrote of her five children, as she lay desperately ill: "Few
others are like them destitute of maternal connections; who, in general
guard and comfort the orphan with double kindness. I have no brother
or sister, to whom they could go with confidence, after the earth had
received me."[46] A mother's trust that her brothers and sisters would
take care of the children in case of her death gave special significance
to the role of the aunt or uncle.

In emergencies, uncles were most often valued for their financial
and family influence. Nephews and nieces could depend upon them
for monetary assistance, and maternal uncles especially were liable for
the total financial care and support of motherless children. Although
this was a traditional practice in Anglo-America, it became a strict
rule in plantation society. Men could not shirk family responsibility
and keep their good names and positions. A fatherless girl wrote to
her uncle and benefactor: "I will endeavour to do everything in my
power to gain the good will and pleasure of you and those with whom
I live. I shall always feel myself indebted to you for the care you have
taken of me. I know no other Father to apply for anything I need."[47]
Uncles could also be important for their emotional support. A young
Georgian wrote of her feelings for her beloved uncle: "You cannot
conceive how much indebted I am to him for everything. What I am
he has made me. . . . His affection I value more than anything on
earth and I would not forfeit it for my life. . . . I cannot convey to
you what my feelings are in regard to him. It is warmer than friendship as I have felt such friendship for no other and it is not so engross-
ing as love as I preferred his own happiness to mine. I persuaded him
to marry when I knew if he done so he would not love me so well as

★See Chapter VIII, "Precious and Precarious in Body and Soul."

while single, and yet I urged him to his own happiness. . . . I was once told by a Gentleman that I loved Uncle better than I thought."[48] This girl's affection was transferred to an uncle, but more often throughout the plantation South, women would develop special relationships with their aunts.

This special affection between aunt and niece was particularly characteristic of the South. As noted earlier, motherless children were sent to the home of a relative, most often a maternal aunt.[49] Even if daughters were not to be raised by relatives, the death of a mother would impel a favorite aunt into a maternal role. Maria Campbell, a Virginia plantation mistress, wrote on January 1, 1819: "My own dear Aunt, I cannot be more agreeably imployed the first day of this year than addressing the much loved friend, who has taken the place in my affections of my dear incomparable long departed mother, yes my dear aunt I always loved you but my heart has acknowledged no other mother since I was deprived of my natural one to fill the tender vacuity but yourself."[50] In "aunt adoption," these women substituted as mothers and played a crucial role in the development of young women and their sense of family. Even if a father remained as head of the family, a daughter would look to her aunt for comfort and guidance in domestic concerns. A stepmother, most daughters felt, would not supplant, as mother-substitute, a favorite aunt.

The family difficulties of Virginian Elizabeth Macmurdo illustrate certain aspects of planter family relations. When her sister died in childbirth, Martha Jones supervised the care of her niece Elizabeth. "You were the gift of a dying Mother, from her lips I received the sacred trust." She devoted herself to her charge "at a time when you required tenfold care and attention to keep you alive being deprived of your natural parent."[51] Although Elizabeth's father, Charles Macmurdo, remarried, his daughter remained attached to her Aunt Martha. In November 1812, the widower Patrick Gibson addressed himself to Macmurdo, asking for Elizabeth's hand in marriage. Martha Jones strenuously objected to the match, and upon her advice Charles Macmurdo forbade his daughter to see her suitor. The aunt believed that Patrick Gibson's several children would be a hindrance to her niece as a newlywed wife, and refused Gibson's overtures: "M. Jones returns her compliments to Mr. Gibson, begs he will decline visiting her, as it would be attended with much pain to both parties having previously made her unalterable determination from which it is impossible she can ever retract."⁵² Through the intercession of her step-mother, Elizabeth Macmurdo was able to persuade her father to consent to her marriage to Gibson, even over the objections of her aunt. When Martha Jones heard of her niece's "defection," she was hostile and adamant. A cousin wrote to her in February 1813: "You must be sensible. . . . I will not promise to comply with your request of never again mentioning her name to you."⁵³ Gibson and Elizabeth Macmurdo were married shortly thereafter. Elizabeth Gibson was assured by a cousin in April 1813 that her aunt's affection for her was as "Strong as ever, and if possible she feels more tenderly for you. . . . I do not say that she did not blame your conduct, but your good husband she thinks acted perfectly correct in every instance."⁵⁴

In March 1813, Martha Jones had forgiven her niece and blamed the break between them on Elizabeth's stepmother, "a Woman without the amiable qualities of the heart whose recommendation to the world is gayety, fashion, extravagance and folly." Yet Martha Jones's husband opposed reconciliation. The two women were forced to plot a reunion in secret. Although the aunt wished to visit her married niece, she confessed: "I most ardently wish to obtain your uncle's consent to my doing so. I must request you to write a letter to your Uncle, in an affectionate manner, expressing a wish to see him, and begging his consent to my visiting you, perhaps it may have the wished for effect, but do not let him know that I have proposed such a plan, indeed I do not wish him to know I have written this letter. If you write to him I shall know you have received this."⁵⁵ Shortly thereafter, Martha Jones was reunited with her favorite niece and family peace was finally restored.

This incident illuminates the complex layers of influence and authority within ante-bellum society. Martha Jones believed herself to be a woman of great influence, the major determinant of her niece's future. Yet she succumbed to her husband's wishes and did not see her married niece until the family patriarch could be induced to give his permission. Although Elizabeth Macmurdo had a father who finally gave his blessing to Elizabeth's proposed match with Patrick Gibson, Martha Jones's disapproval disrupted family harmony. Cousins had to intervene to effect a truce between the alienated aunt and niece. Although gender was a controlling factor in power relationships, the vicissitudes of Martha Jones and Elizabeth Gibson demonstrate that women's influence was considerable within the domestic sphere. Extenuating circumstances could and did provide for this influence to extend beyond the immediate family circle and into the kinship network. But despite an individual woman's ability to exert her own will, women were generally forced to obey patriarchal authority: daughters submitted to fathers, wives to husbands.

The high degree of attachment between nieces and their aunts was not limited to motherless daughters, but frequently existed in spite of the maternal bond. One young woman wrote to her aunt that during her child's illness she "glossed over" her fears in letters home to her mother, but that she was worried and in need of the aunt's advice.[56] It was not unusual for a childless aunt informally or legally to adopt a favorite niece. A mother with several female offspring would quite commonly send a daughter to live with a childless sister or sister-in-law. Ann Ambler Fisher—mother of seven—sent her sister Elizabeth, childless after seventeen years of marriage, her third daughter, Janetta Fisher. Elizabeth Ambler Carrington wrote on New Year's Day, 1807: "Long have I wished to have her as my own conclusively! But the dear little soul would always say I cannot leave my Ma to be aunt's child. This morning like a little cherub she came running to me with the most endearing smile says Ma has sent me a New Year's gift to you. Dear lovely child, from this moment I will devote myself to her. . . . Everything that tender love can supply shall be done by me for your child."[57] Another Virginia woman, Maria Campbell, who had been unable to conceive, took charge of the rearing of her brother's daughter Virginia, even while her sister-in-law was alive. After several years of informal guardianship, Maria's husband, David, designated his niece Virginia as one of his heirs. He advised his wife to "divide Montcalm, and give part to her and the other to my brother James' son David—Give her most of the slaves if she marries a good man—as to make their situation comfortable."[58] Virginia's natural parents were well satisfied with their daughter's happiness and prosperity after her aunt's adoption of her.

Because of the closeness of families, this process of parting was remarkably painless for both the mother by birth and the adopted offspring. An aunt was understandably elated by the opportunity to mother a favorite niece, and often proved extravagant with attention and affection. The daughter was doubly mothered by her two maternal figures; and the mother was pleased to see that her daughter received the best of maternal supervision, second only to her own. This "giving away" of a child was restricted, however, to female offspring. A son was thought too valuable to part with under any circumstances. "Extra" daughters drained family resources with little or no return; if a niece were farmed out to an aunt, parents were relieved of the high costs of education, support, and dowry. At the same time, by "loaning" this female to a blood relative, planter parents did not really lose a daughter, in that her family loyalty remained intact. Kinship ties were strengthened by this common practice.

Although most planter sons and daughters eventually went to boarding school, a younger child spent his or her life in the company of brothers and sisters, isolated on the plantation. Siblings in the South were remarkably close for this reason, and for the most part, sons and daughters cultivated enduring and affectionate relationships with each other. In young adulthood brothers might develop strong rivalries, often based on competition for property as well as paternal affection, but sisters, wholly dependent upon family networks as their sole means of support, were characteristically cautious about involving themselves in family disputes on or about the plantation. As a result, most women enjoyed satisfying relationships with brothers and sisters alike.

Sisters separated by only a few years developed a special closeness, particularly when friends of the same age were not readily available. In large families, children of the same sex often paired off according to the proximity of their ages. These intimate relationships were sometimes interrupted by boarding school. Although parents frequently sent pairs of daughters away together for their education, an older sister would equally often be sent off alone, producing emotional anguish for both parties.[59] Such a separation, however, actually prepared them for eventual parting at marriage and subsequent departure from the family circle. When sixteen-year-old Maria Bryan was left at home in Mount Zion, Georgia, after her older sibling Julia married and moved to Augusta, the younger sister wrote: "We are most truly, *truly* sorry to give you up and there was a day or two since delivered of a little dead-born wish that you might never have married but we two have been nice snug old maids living always together as 'happy as the day is long.' But this wish was too selfish to live."[60]

Sisterly devotion among southern women was deep and abiding. Virginian Anne Daniel confessed to her sister Jane in 1807: "I find my dear Jane I love you too well. It is wrong I am afraid to have favourites among sisters; but I cannot help it, you Jane, I confess are mine. . . . It is natural that our attachment to each other would be strong but I am jealous of you; I am afraid you don't love me as much as I want you; but perhaps it is selfishness that creates this jealousy. I want you to love me more than you ought." A year later the two sisters were sending each other letters written in code.[61] When Jane married William Lewis in November 1808, Anne Daniel wrote her sadly: "All the walks we used to take together I have almost forsaken; it makes me melancholy to look at them; your image rushes so strongly on my imagination it almost overpowers me. . . ."[62]

The harshness of separation was most keenly felt by daughters left unmarried at home, as in the case of a girl who wrote to her newlywed sibling Mary Owen in 1813: "I had just gone to the old quilting frame and about fixing my quilt in and thinking of my dear Sister and the many hours we had spent together over them when George handed me your letters. In vain would it be for me to attempt to describe my feeling. . . . For the first time you have given me a small hint about visiting us. The very thought of seeing my sister here again almost makes me crazy with joy."[63] A year later, even after the hoped-for visit and the advent of her own marriage, the sister was still pining for Mary: "When I reflect on the many hundred miles that separate us and the little probability of our ever meeting again in this world my heart is full and my eyes in spite of my own exertions are ready to overflow."[64] One southern woman recounted that her grandfather solved this problem for his daughters—settled in Rocktown, Virginia, in 1817—by giving each "a house so they could see and speak to each other from the front door."[65] However, most southern women were, by necessity, in residence on rural farms. During the years following the American Revolution, the cotton boom and the opening of the new South contributed to westward expansion, and the migration of families doubtless increased distances between grown siblings.

In the South's dynastic expansion, males took both a paternal interest and an active, exaggerated role in their sisters' lives. A sister's marriage could politically advance a brother; a poor match would not only eliminate the opportunity for fraternal advantage but also reflect poorly on the whole family. Men, sensitive on behalf of the family name, monitored their sisters' every move. The fraternal role anticipated the most exalted ante-bellum position: that of patriarch.

Men in the South were groomed from birth to assume this posture, just as women were trained to dependent and submissive roles. Brothers and sisters developed closeness along the gender lines dictated by slaveowning society: men made decisions, women obeyed; and men were charged with the care of family dependents, while women were solely the responsibility of males. Spinsters, for example—who often lived together on independent incomes in the North—were confined in the South; unmarried females were required to reside with parents or in the households of their siblings in plantation society. Within the family, males and females assumed the various tasks and attitudes that reflected the gender prerequisites of the culture. In a way, brothers and sisters acted out mock husband-and-wife roles—of course, without a sexual component.

But like a father or uncle, a brother rarely supplied central emotional support. On the whole, females were taught to seek comfort from women, not men. Affection was not unknown; South Carolina plantation mistress Catharine Smith, for instance, wrote to her brother John Faber in Paris, begging him to return home for a visit. She had not seen him in ten years, but claimed that her four-year-old son promised to love his uncle upon his homecoming.[66] Many brothers and sisters shared deep commitments to each other, as in the case of the various Mordecai siblings scattered throughout the South during the ante-bellum era.[67] But more commonly, brothers filled surrogate patriarchal roles for their sisters. Men were in loftier positions than women, within society as well as the family; thus the stability and reliability men afforded women was, in a sense, granted from "above." The hierarchical structure of social relations within the culture—especially those linked to gender—affected all individuals. Contact between the sexes placed the two groups on an unequal footing; just as men were proclaimed the superior sex, female inferiority was an implied if not articulated consequence. Fraternal functions were, therefore, supplemental to those of the paterfamilias and not necessarily associated with intimacy.

Brothers adopted a combative stance when it came to their sisters' reputations. As the showy and dashing honor guard of the family, they took a particular interest in the circle of acquaintance of an unmarried sister, arrogating to themselves the obligation to police her behavior and warn her of any "dangerous" company. This could be a presumptuous and self-serving role for men. A brother, away at school in 1824, wrote home to his sister: "It is possible that Caroline Lucas is going to marry that idiot John Simmons. Do pray sister keep away from such people, *for I* had rather follow you to the grave than see you, [illegible] to such a man."[68] Brothers might also take action against other gentlemen to protect a sister's honor. A woman wrote to a friend in 1822, detailing how a mutual acquaintance had broken off her engagement with a Doctor Burrell. Afterwards "her brother, who is a very fiery youth, took umbrage at some conduct of the Dr.'s on being discarded," went to Burrell's house, and "beat him severely." The doctor brought suit, and a legal battle followed the fistfight.[69]

Although brothers allegedly took up the cudgels for their sisters' sake, much evidence demonstrates that this overprotectiveness was part of a cultural ritual. Brothers could meddle in a sister's affairs with or without her expressed desire for such protection. This patrol and guard duty and any subsequent violence allowed males to flex their egos as well as their muscles, while the tradition of "honor" ensured women's further dependence upon men.

Cousins were significantly intimate within the network of planter kinship. From an early age, and even when separated geographically, cousins developed close and warm contacts that continued throughout a lifetime. Martha Randolph Triplett continued her friendship and correspondence with her cousin and childhood companion Marian Harden well into their later years. At the age of sixty-three, she was still exchanging letters with her beloved relative.[70] Female cousins near the same age formed strong relationships in much the same way that sisters cultivated intimacy within the family circle.

The southern proclivity for clannishness, with its crucial economic component, created an extraordinarily high rate of cousin marriage. Whereas cousin marriage was not found in a single case among northern planters sampled, the rate among southern planters was twelve percent.* Social geography was one contributing factor: children of the gentry, isolated on plantations, rarely met people of their own age outside of the kinship network as they were growing up. House parties, visits, and most social activities involved interconnecting family circles. Young girls, under excessive chaperonage, had few opportunities to mix with men who were not their relatives, and ladies corresponded *only* with men related to them; hence the men with whom many planter daughters developed their close relationships tended to be male cousins. Blood ties provided members of the opposite sex with one of the easiest avenues for intimacy.

In some ways, cousin marriage eased the strain of separation that a wedding imposed. Instead of being forced to reorient herself to a new kinship group—for a husband demanded that his wife leave behind her family circle and adopt his own if any conflict ensued[71]—the wife of a cousin never transferred her loyalty. In addition, the maternal father-in-law held enhanced sway over the married couple, serving as uncle to the husband as well as father of the bride. But the emotional advantage was minor in the larger scale of events; cousin marriage was not significant for its consolidation of feeling as much as for the consolidation of wealth and property that resulted from interfamily alliances. The dynasty was well served by planter daughters who were willing to marry "within the family."

Marriage and matchmaking provided social drama in southern culture. While births and deaths were part of the unknown process of life—God's will—romances and marriages were in some measure under human control. Most certainly, women were obsessed with the small segment of their lives—courtship—which put them in the limelight. Although prospective mates were available only within a certain social stratum, most females actively participated in the selection of their own husbands. Parents exercised a veto if they strongly objected to their daughter's choice—or their son's, for that matter. But generally the selection of a marriage partner was a woman's prerogative, and perhaps the decision that would most dramatically and literally determine her fate.

*See Appendix A, Table 2.

IV

THE DAY TO FIX
MY FATE

*M*atrimony determined the personal happiness of the planter wife. Parents indoctrinated daughters from birth in their marital and reproductive roles. Society expected every female to fulfill what has now been defined as sociobiological destiny—she was duty-bound to become a wife and mother. As one woman warned her daughter: "A single life has fewer troubles; but then it is not the one for which our maker designed us."[1]

The institution of marriage was much the same for northern women of the upper class as it was for planter daughters. Women North and South were apprised of the proprietary aspects of a husband's affections, as well as made aware of the consequences a bad selection could bring. Still, three significant differences are apparent in the South during the early national era: wealth was a primary factor in matchmaking, cousin marriage was prevalent, and the median age of marriage was dramatically lower for women.

Money was an obvious consideration, only resisted by the southern belle who knew, as a British author observed, that "it was fashionable to marry for money," but who "was so fashionable that she was going to marry entirely for love."[2] More often than not, wealth was as great an influence on women's decisions to marry as it was on men's choices. Again and again, mismatches of temperament were explained away by reason of fortune.[3] Men commonly described women in terms of their property value; one bridegroom detailed his wife's "excellent qualities" and added that "she is worth $2,500. She has a good piece of land he says about 10 or 12 miles from Nashville."[4] Wealth could be the hidden attraction of a popular belle, and lack of fortune an indisputable hindrance: "If she were not guilty of the unpardonable crime in Mississippi, to wit, poverty—would be a great belle. She is pretty and smart."[5]

Before marrying, a man had either to establish himself in a profession or to inherit his property. Unless he was financially secure, he could not expect a father to release his daughter to him.[6] This drove the age of marriage up for men, and proved worrisome for the young lover of slender financial means.[7] In some cases men initiated marriages to gain their inheritances; a young man dependent upon his guardian for money could often achieve financial independence by marrying, because trusts provided for a son's legacies to be bestowed either at the age of maturity or upon marriage.

The onset of adulthood—at least as signaled by marriage—was much earlier for women than for men in southern culture. The median age of marriage for southern women (taken from a sample of planters born from 1765 to 1815) was twenty, whereas the median age for men was twenty-eight. This contrasts dramatically with statistics on northern planters, for whom the median age of marriage for women was twenty-four, for men, twenty-six.*

Prior to the development of modern birth-control methods, early marriages for women contributed to higher female mortality, and youthful childbearing caused premature aging. John Bernard, a British traveler, commented concerning southern women: "The one thing I did not approve of was the juvenile period at which they bloomed and decayed. A lady here was in the habit of marrying ten years earlier than a European, so that at twenty, if she had proved a fruitful olive, her husband's table was surrounded with tall shoots sufficient to sup-

*See Appendix A, Table 3.

ply him with shade for the remainder of his days. At thirty—the glowing summer of an English dame—she had fallen into 'the sere leaf. . . .' "[8] Daughters of fifteen and sixteen were frequently married off by anxious parents, or at an impatient bridegroom's insistence.[9] There was no stigma attached to having a child bride, although planters were aware of the disadvantages young wives suffered.

Some historians have linked the youthful age of brides to a semifeudal heritage or an aristocratic matrimonial pattern. To uphold this argument, however, data on both women and men should have displayed the early age of marriage befitting a manorial model, or at least the median age of brides should have been close to that of grooms. The age of upper-class brides had been steadily rising during the same period in both England and France.

Contrary to the popular myth of women's higher status in plantation society, women of the planter class were treated as reproductive units, replaceable if necessary. This is not to say that individual planters believed their wives were dispensable. But the evidence of premature marriage, regardless of the negative effects on women, and the number of multiple marriages for men indicate that the priorities of the plantocracy were male rather than female.

Other considerations besides children contributed to the early age of marriage for females. Planters believed that daughters were more easily managed at a younger age and less likely to balk at having their fathers choose their mates. Cousin marriage, frequent for planter offspring, had as much to do with the limited social contacts of a planter daughter previous to betrothal as it did with financial consolidation. Some girls preferred to marry suitable cousins with whom they were familiar, rather than wed wealthy strangers picked out by their fathers. There was an additional factor: while males, married or single, consorted freely with female slaves, planter daughters were strictly forbidden social and sexual contact with male slaves; not content to trust in taboo, southern planters chose to marry their daughters off as shortly after puberty as a proper match could be arranged. Although these were not overriding concerns for all planters, they established a trend in marital custom in the plantation South.

Many of our images of southern women come from the stereotyped picture of the courtship of the southern belle, celebrated in fact and fiction. Women did see this brief yet bright stage of their lives as never to be forgotten. These few years between puberty and marriage were the closest that most women came to freedom. The great decision of their lives—the choice of when and whom to marry—lay ahead, and their time to choose was filled with fun and frivolity. This period—when women were most carefree, most hopeful—was therefore cherished by planter-class females. Young girls anticipated being a belle. Belles themselves conveyed a sense of exhilaration. And plantation mistresses often longed to recapture the flair of that too-brief time; most women commenced their careers as matrons when barely out of their teens.

Schoolgirls in the South as elsewhere gossiped ceaselessly about flirtations and amorous intrigues. A young girl wrote her friend: "I will not have a widower. I will have a very handsome young man or none but I flatter myself you and me can get the very best but I expect Nancy and Esther will never get any body. Esther has got but one ill-looking sweetheart. . . ."[10] Most female friends spent as much of their time writing to each other about marital speculations as they did about family concerns, especially if they were young and unmarried.[11] Almost all this matchmaking activity revolved around town life and dancing parties.[12] Matrons and men alike were bemused by the "spark and spurn" syndrome of the courtship ritual. A mother wrote to a friend about her daughter's season in Richmond: "Indeed I should be afraid; one or other of the charming fellows would steal her heart, if I did not observe that they are only like meteors with her; they blaze for a short time but leave no impression and are quickly forgotten."[13]

Families carefully supervised daughters' social contacts during these years. While at parties and other public affairs, girls had to be constantly chaperoned. In the home, parents were able to determine with whom their daughters kept company; in some cases, mothers selected suitors for them.[14] The most common cause for disapproval was a man's lack of fortune.[15] Perhaps to defend themselves against this scrutiny—and to avoid neighborhood gossip—planters' sons often called in numbers. Two or more gentlemen callers were unexceptionable on plantations with eligible belles; a single or frequent visitor to a belle's home provoked speculation: "You know yourself a Gentleman can't visit a House unless it is said directly that he intends to address the Lady, and if he should go two or three times they are going to be married directly."[16]

Courtship customs in the South varied from northern practices. Although spare beds were in short supply during plantation house parties, bundling (the New England custom of wrapping a courting couple in covers and allowing them to sleep in the same bed) was considered both odd and improper among the planter aristocracy. Chaperones were ever-present. Courting couples were left alone in northern parlors, whereas "in the South it is deemed indecorous for them to be left alone . . . and the mother or some member of the family is always in the room; and if none of these, a female slave is seated on the rug at the door." One ante-bellum planter complained "that his wife never took his arm till she took it to be led to church on her wedding day; and that he never had an opportunity of kissing her but twice while he was addressing her (they were six months engaged!) and in both cases by means of a strategem he resorted to of drugging a peach with laudanum which he gave to the attending servant and thereby put her into a sound sleep."[17] Such machinations were not necessary for northern suitors, who were given the opportunity of private audiences with their sweethearts.

Because of the excessive chaperonage and limited social contact, a young man had little opportunity to ascertain a belle's affection for him, and most southern gentlemen employed go-betweens in the early stages of courting.[18] A man would often try out his suit on a close friend or cousin to see if the object of his attentions would be receptive.[19] Belles could also indicate their preferences by using romantic intermediaries and carry out flirtations through third parties.[20]

Coquetry was a staple of the southern social scene. Men contended with the fickleness of women in a variety of ways.[21] Many responded with the kind of desperation that forced one gentleman to declare himself in 1835 to a young woman: "The tumult occasioned in my troubled breast by hearing of Mr. Nelson's pursuing you to Frederick causes me thus importunely to address you. . . . I doubt not by my conduct to you that you have been made acquainted by some of my friends with my ardent passion ever since I last saw you dear Harriet (excuse familiarity). . . . nothing will afford me more pleasure than to devote the remainder of my life to you."[22] Most men met with at least one rebuff during their romantic careers. Ladies, as a matter of propriety, discouraged proposals, and most females had spurned several suitors before they settled on a fiancé.

Men did not propose lightly, but women, so it would seem, easily rejected suits. Most women would, as a matter of course, refuse a man's first marriage offer, an action that did not necessarily signal defeat or reflect on the man's character. T. W. Brevard, in letters to his brother Alexander, described the ups and downs of his courtship with a certain Caroline, who rebuffed him twice before finally accepting his proposal.[23] A rejection could be mere form, or a signal for more time—or simply inexplicable. Although women did not always confide their reasons for rejecting men to the men themselves, they often revealed them to confidantes. Maria Bryan wrote to her sister, Julia Cumming, about the repeated proposals of Thomas F. Foster, a local politician: "He begs me to 'lay aside my peculiar and *romantic* notions,' and deliberate on the matter. I am sure that I am sufficiently averse to the thing without, deliberating would only increase this aversion: But I wonder if he does not think that his being a Congressman will batter down all my prejudices. Glorious prospects he presents, to visit the metropolis the ensuing season—and with a companion I could be so proud of, too. Love, heard from most lips is to me the most disgusting word in the world."[24]

Rejection was, however, all too clear to some suitors. One North Carolina gentleman was rebuffed by a belle in 1817. A friend reported: "She was studying Latin and it would take her two years to finish the study after which time if she had not seen any person she liked better and if he still paid her that attention a lover ought to pay his mistress she might marry him. Oh, all ye powers above what encouragement was this to the panting lover!"[25] Men, however, were not the only sufferers in romantic entanglements. An exchange of letters in 1794 between Jenny Stuart and John Coalter reveals a woman scorned. Jenny Stuart wanted to marry Coalter, a widower, but he did not love her; indeed, he repulsed her affections and ridiculed her in public. Enraged, Jenny Stuart wrote to Coalter that his late wife had been ugly and that he was lucky to be rid of her. When Coalter threatened to take her to court for these allegations, she returned his letters and they settled their differences out of court.[26] This episode was unusual in that females rarely voiced such emotions without the promise of betrothal.

Planter patriarchs clearly defined the formal steps of courtship. A man might declare himself in person, but he was encouraged instead to submit written declarations of love to his "intended." Before proceeding to the parent, he ascertained from his sweetheart whether or not his suit was welcome. Most "declarations of honorable intentions" were extremely florid.[27] Following the girl's acceptance of a gentleman's proposal, her father expected the young man to make a formal declaration to him as head of the household, stating in writing the gentleman's affections for the planter's daughter, his ability to maintain a family, and his hopes for a favorable reception.[28] This declaration was as crucial to the marital outcome as was the girl's acceptance of the gentleman's proposal. Many hopeful beaux supported their suits with letters from their parents or mutual family friends. These testimonials often assured a father of the sincerity and suitability of his daughter's prospective bridegroom. In 1820, a planter assured James Chesnut that his son would make Chesnut's daughter a fine husband. He vouched for his son's earnestness, his own enthusiasm for the union, and finally confided: "the pecuniary considerations which this topic sometimes give rise to, I shall not touch, further than to say, that the Major is now worth at least one hundred thousand dollars clear of debt."[29]

Sometimes sweethearts kept their courtship secret. In 1815, John Fraser courted Anne Couper, a Sea Island heiress. She replied to his romantic entreaties: "If you are the amiable and noble being you appear to be, the sentiment of friendship which I now feel may be changed into reciprocal affection—and rest assured that it will be the first time that the passion of love has been a guest in this house." She received his gifts and responded favorably to his courting. But during the early months of wooing, she kept Fraser's attentions a secret: "I am sorry I cannot deliver any of your compliments and excuses, for excepting my parents and brother, no one has any suspicion of our corresponding."[30] Lovers sometimes maintained secret courtships to prevent parents from interfering in what they might consider an ill-advised match.

Elopements and ensuing fracases were frequently reported among members of the planter class.[31] Jane Bruce married Samuel Jones on November 15, 1786, without her parents' permission and indeed against their express wishes. Jane Bruce had responded warmly to Jones's advances. She gave her consent to marry him while denying this fact to her parents. They forbade her to see Jones in August 1786; she wrote to him: "all correspondence between us must now be at an end and we must endeavor to forget each other." But the unhappy couple continued to correspond secretly. By early November Jane Bruce had decided to marry Jones, for "no doubt my parents will be reconciled to us one day."[32] Parents rarely carried out their threats of disinheritance, especially in cases where an errant daughter simply chose a gentleman of whom her parents were not fond, but who met certain criteria of class and wealth. Nevertheless, these elopements created dissension and crisis among planter families.[33]

Elopement almost always involved scandal. A woman reported to her sister their cousin Nancy Barclay's marriage in 1815. When a Mr. Parsons formed an attachment to Nancy, her sister begged their mother to forbid the romance. But Mrs. Barclay was unable to deny her daughter, and the courtship flourished until Mr. Barclay finally told Parsons that he was no longer welcome in his house. The young couple then revealed their secret marriage. Nancy's sister reported: "My poor Mother fainted, my Brothers were violent. . . ." After two weeks consoling her family, Nancy Parsons left home to join her husband and travel to England. A cousin found the entire episode steeped in mystery: "How this poor girl could make up her mind to take a step so contrary to nature and reason, to leave her Mother and all her family for ever, for this man who is several years younger than herself and whose family she knows nothing of. However we cannot know her reasons; perhaps the little god has blinded her! We don't know any of their objections to the young man!"[34] Within the context of southern courtship, passions were to be curbed rather than cultivated. One belle expressed this sentiment in poetry:

> *The passions are a numerous crowd*
> *Imperious positive and loud.*
> *Curb these licentious sons of strife*
> *Hence chiefly rise the storms of life*
> *If they grow wild and rave*
> *They are thy masters, thou their slaves.*[35]

Elopement signaled that a woman had enslaved herself to passion, contrary to nature and reason. Parents wanted practicality rather than love to rule a daughter's heart. If a belle forgot herself, parental reins substituted for self-restraint.

After sweethearts and parents were both certain of the advisability of a match, the betrothed couple could release their pent-up emotions—within the bounds of "acceptable" behavior.[36] Mississippian John Quitman wrote to his fiancée about his daydreams of her: "The parting kiss still warm upon my lips and I thought I still embraced you."[37] Engagements varied from couple to couple. Although custom required a grace period of two months following the formal announcement, many couples married in less time with no controversy. On the other hand, if a couple postponed their wedding for up to two years, plantation society refrained from comment.

Weddings were great social occasions that elicited enormous interest among the planter class. Every family member, from parents to distant cousins, attended the marriage ceremony. Friends were also expected to demonstrate their devotion. One confidante wrote a friend: "Tomorrow is my wedding day/ And you will then repair/ Unto the house upon the *marsh*/ All in your *looks* so *fair*. Now for the plain matter of fact, Augusta, I am to be spliced tomorrow evening & shall expect you to shed the light of your countenance on me at this important moment, remember I take no denial, for come you must."[38]

Most nuptials were elaborate, attended by large and convivial crowds. A woman wrote to her brother about such a wedding: "One friend was invited and then another untill it grew into a formidable party of young and old. A *professional* woman from Charleston came up some days previous to the marriage, with her two assistants, and turned everything in the house upside down. . . . at eleven, between forty and fifty persons sat down to a splendid dinner."[39] She reports an exotic touch: the wedding cake was topped by a "mimic bride in full dress." In addition to the hectic atmosphere of the wedding day, the bride contended with her own feelings about marriage.[40] Reactions varied from bride to bride, but certainly each woman entering into the state of matrimony saw this step as a turning point in her life.[41]

In February 1799, Nelly Parke Custis wrote to her childhood friend Elizabeth Gibson about her recent transformation: "I had made the sage and prudent resolve of passing through life as a *prim, starched spinster* to the great edification of my friends in particular and the public in general . . . at last was obliged to submit and bind myself to become that old fashioned thing called a *Wife* and now, *strange* as it may seem, I am perfectly reconciled." Some months later she confessed: "The *writer* is the once rattlepated, lazy Eleanor P. Custis who was generally stiled a thoughtless, giddy mortal fond of going to Balls— now a sedate matron attending to domestic duties and providing for a young stripling who will call her Mother . . . she is by the late circumstances *exalted* and converted into a rational being."[42]

After the honeymoon, which was traditional but not essential, the planter wife settled into the difficult routine of domestic economy on her own plantation.[43] The plantation mistress's primary duty was to care for her husband. The male role of "lord and master"[44] was doubly important in the ante-bellum South, where the planter was ruler of both his family and his slave household. The newlywed wife's concern was, above all, to please her husband. A father advised his eighteen-year-old daughter, following her marriage: "You are now in the most interesting and critical period of life—a young married lady—your own welfare and happiness and that of your husband depend much upon yourself and your early adoption of those rules of conduct that are suited to your situation. . . . kindness and gentleness are the natural and proper means of the wife—There are those among them who seek to *rule*—who make points with their husbands and who complain— cry—scold, etc. etc. To love such a woman long is more than mortal man can do."[45] Maternal advice was nearly identical: "Your amiability is calculated to increase the esteem and affections of your companion. . . . I hope you may be one of those wives whose price is far above rubies."[46]

Purity, piety, and propriety were, of course, a matron's as well as a maiden's domain. When looking for wives, men took spiritual as well as secular matters into consideration. An unmarried gentleman wrote to his sister of his disappointment in town belles: "They are represented to me as being poorly educated, excessively fond of dress and very extravagant and which if true, I suppose, I must live a life of single blessedness."[47] One woman described a female friend who had indeed fulfilled patriarchal prerogatives: "Mrs. Morris was certainly my 'beau ideal' of a perfect woman. So much sweetness and gentleness and yet firmness. So much industry and attention to her duties without noise or confusion, so much religion without parade and with all

the beauty of an angel. She was a model for a wife and mother."
Ironically, "such is the ingratitude of men her husband [an alcoholic]
could in sight of such a heaven kill himself (in a moral point of view!)
And he killed her, too, I sincerely believe."[48] Yet most women did not
suffer so unenviable a fate as Mrs. Morris's. Husbands and fathers,
more often than not, commended those wives who struggled to conform
to planter ideals.

So conscientious was one plantation mistress that she wrote from
her father's house in Charleston to her husband, away in New York:
"Papa says if a woman gets married she must expect to follow her
husband where ever he goes and that if you go to Kanschatka I must
follow so you see you have only to form the plan and I am obedient
and I shall try my best to make things agreeable. If you can't return
by the beginning of November I can go to Cambahee with Papa and
stay there until you come but you must tell me what you wish done."[49]
Society expected a wife to cleave to her husband's bosom. It was
common among planters for a wife to be referred to as a "Rib," an
allusion to the Biblical story of the creation of woman.[50]

Planters and their wives expressed devotion to each other quite
openly. Diaries and letters are filled with tender expressions of love
and longing. St. George Tucker wrote to his wife, Fanny, in 1790: "A
good night to you my Love: May we reciprocally dream of that happiness which I hope we shall enjoy in the course of the next week, by
meeting in mutual health and spirits."[51] In some extreme cases, even
intimacy and sexual ardor were conveyed in letters from husbands to
wives. A planter wrote to his wife in 1819: "It is in the bosom of
retirement all the sympathies of friendship and love are awakened.
Then our souls commune and our hearts beat together."[52] Another
husband deeply regretted his absences from his wife, and wrote: "We
must talk over those things the next time I take you in my arms in
our good, good bed."[53] Most planter couples, however, were loath to
discuss sexual matters in correspondence.*

Husbands were usually unhappy at the prospect of being away from
home, and many men conveyed a sense of sexual deprivation during
such separations from their wives. William Dunbar, who spend
extraordinarily long periods of time away, promised to return to his wife

*See Chapter XI, "The Sexual Dynamics of Slavery."

in June 1792: "I shall soon be up my Love when we shall endeavour to enjoy every pleasure and satisfaction that a good husband and wife can confer upon each other."[54] Another planter forced to spend much time absent from home wrote to his wife in 1814: "I have this morning the agreeable treat of receiving your letter of the 26th before I arose. I imagined how exquisite it would have been, had fortune at the same time placed the writer within my grasp."[55] Sentimentality and romantic notions were common; one man confessed to his wife: "I love you more now than I ever did from the first time I ever saw you and were my anxieties to see and be with you not satisfied as much as possible I should be in such a state of mind as to be unfit for anything. . . ."[56]

Women appear to have shied away from expressing their intimate feelings directly in letters to lovers or husbands, lest they appear indelicate. One plantation mistress confided to her journal: "I knew that Mr. Gayle loved me better than most men loved their wives—he had that sort of love that drew him to my presence constantly, and it seems to me that I cannot remember any time that his eyes were not seeking me, and that the expression I met there did not create and keep alive sunshine in my bosom. There is a pulse from my head to my feet and every throb is full of love for him."[57] Nelly Custis asserted to her confidante Elizabeth Gibson: "I know it is a received opinion that a married woman can have no secrets from her Husband and therefore female friends are afraid to make any communications lest *Caro Sposo* should be the wiser for them; but in the first place, we were always Honest hearted females who had no secrets to disclose. In the second, if we should perchance stumble upon a subject improper for vulgar eyes, we will recollect that it is proper to keep a Friend's counsel when we are in truth, and this settles the business at once."[58]

The happiness of married couples was both a critical concern for women and a matter they felt was out of their hands. As Martha Richardson complained to her nephew in 1821: "Marriages are said to be made in Heaven—it may be so but surely they are so jumbled together they get terribly mismatched by the time they reach us."[59] One plantation mistress keenly observed in 1809 "that wives generally become more tenderly attached to their Husbands as they grow old together and Husbands more indifferent to their wives (I speak of good wives and husbands) men even of the best principles and tempers though they continue to act with decent attention and even kindness lose that tender interest and affection. . . ."[60] Most weddings signaled a beginning filled with hope and promise; Eleanor Custis wrote to Elizabeth Gibson in 1796 about her own sister's recent marriage: "She has every chance for happiness—a goodhearted affectionate husband—one most sincerely attached to her and she is the same to him."[61] Some, of course, did not bode as well.[62] Complaints about mismatches varied in their seriousness and degree. Charles Rinaldo Floyd mused in his diary about an unsuited pair: "Rose is a Scotchman, about 46 years old, and is *not handsome*. Mary Turner is a blooming girl about 19. She is above the common size and is quite a desirable wench in cold weather, but is rather too fat for July, and too amorous, I suspect, for a lover of 46. . . ."[63] Women themselves sometimes felt disappointment in their own matches. A mistress who was twice wed, once to her cousin and once to a suitor of her own choice, confessed: "I married twice, once to please my friends and once to please myself. I was a fool both times."[64]

External as well as internal factors contributed to the breakdown of domestic happiness.[65] A husband's profession could adversely affect a married couple, taking him out of the home too often. Impoverishment always took its toll. While many husbands complained of their wives' extravagance, it was male irresponsibility or poor management, more often than not, that led to a couple's financial ruin. Whoever was at fault, the wife shared the hardships of sudden poverty equally with her spouse, even when the origin or extent of their dilemma was unknown to her. Husbands claimed that they were sheltering their wives from the "grimy details" of plantation business, but generally a woman's ignorance of aspects of plantation management was due to a planter's reluctance to reveal his own shortcomings. Such holding back could lead to tragic results for planter wives. In 1815 Lucy Randolph wrote to her brother Robert Beverley, asking him to intercede on her behalf, as the sheriff had seized her slaves to pay her husband's debts. She was not aware of how much her husband owed or how he planned to cope with insolvency.[66] Lucy Randolph was not alone in her plight. One plantation mistress complained: "I have had a trial of temper in seeing Mr. H. with a new pair of boots—we are destitute of even one blanket and I do believe Mr. H. has 20 pairs of boots. . . ."[67]

A husband's misconduct toward his wife might range from neglect to physical abuse. Timothy Ford, a traveler in South Carolina, was appalled by the love of drink in the South. He commented: "Another consequence of this intemperance is the disorder which it frequently occasions in private families. . . . I hear of more family troubles and especially of the conjugal kind than in any other place. I every day hear of unhappy marriages both in time past and present. . . ."[68] Violence toward women was taboo, but that did not stop some husbands from threatening or abusing their wives. A plantation mistress reported to a friend: "Capt. Hunter and his wife sailed for England. *He has already* used her Mother extremely ill, abusing them both dreadfully and drawing a knife on Sarah—I think she has great courage to go with him—Poor thing, I pity her."[69] Elizabeth Coltart wrote to her cousin St. George Tucker, begging him to advise her about her failed marriage:

> The Doctor has repeatedly beat me and abused in the most cruel manner he could and oblig'd me to go to different Gentlemen's Houses to Shelter me from the wheather, at last I swore the peace of him and was determined not to live with him again. . . .Give me the advice you can in what manner to proceed with the Doctor and how I shall get home to Mother and Father be kind enough to write me by the very first opportunity as court day will soon come. . . ."[70]

Even when husbands were attentive and sweet-tempered, wives worried about male infidelity. Many couples teased each other, playing on jealous suspicions.[71] Some husbands wrote home in jest about their adventures in town,[72] and at times wives responded with agitation. Diana Dunbar wrote to her spouse during one of his frequent absences: "Can my Dearest be constant and faithfull in such a wild place as Orleans where there is so many temptations, don't be angry with me, my love, for expressing my doubts tho' in my heart I am persuaded I have little cause, for I think if there can be a husband true to his wife, it must be mine."[73] Actual infidelity was a serious issue involving love and honor, but its delicacy as a topic created such anxiety for women that it was rarely discussed openly by the two sexes, even when they were on the most intimate of terms.

Men kept a close watch on their women. Planter wives were so carefully guarded in southern society that infidelity was rare in plantation mistresses. A planter rationalized to his wife: "The hardness of heart in our sex not infrequently paves the way for infidelity but your sex is blessed with sensibility, generosity and gratitude."[74] A more practical explanation is that sexual misconduct by wives was punished with disgrace and even divorce. Husbands, on the other hand, could indulge themselves in extramarital affairs—especially with slaves—with no social repercussions. Discretion assured a husband immunity within ante-bellum society. But the double standard, as plantation mistress Sarah Gayle pointed out, produced "double victims"—"his paramour" and "the wretch who bears his name."[75] A traveler in the South in 1812 reported tension in a North Carolina family: "The people appear clever but the woman is unhappy. She seems to feel that she has lost the affection of her husband. She may be jealous of a wench."[76] Another southern woman reported on the scandalous behavior of a millionaire planter in Louisiana in the 1830s: "He has seduced two sisters, one he had as his housekeeper, the youngest one he at last made his wife. He had children by both of them. . . ."[77] The nature and tolerance of sexual misconduct will be explored in depth below.*

The discovery of male infidelity could—despite the double standard—result in unpleasantness and recriminations between husband and wife, especially when the "other woman" was white. When planter James Iredell was unfaithful to his wife Hannah in 1779, many months of marital tension followed. His required absences compounded the couple's difficulties. He wrote long, penitent letters from Wilmington, North Carolina, to his wife at home in Edenton. Shortly after her discovery of his behavior, James Iredell wrote his wife: "The Injustice and Folly of my Conduct Appear in too glaring Colours. . . ." The next week he reiterated: "I have dwelt most deeply on the unhappy situation in which my Imprudence has involved you, and deliberately and most solemnly resolved to do all in my power to repair it." Four months later, Hannah Iredell remained wary of her husband's protestations of reform. He wrote while away on a visit in April: "My Affection, I can dare say, shall be yours alone. If after all, I cannot

*See Chapter V, "The Moral Bind," and Chapter XI, "The Sexual Dynamics of Slavery."

avoid an ill-founded suspicion I will try hard as it will be to submit to the consequences without murmuring." A few days later he complained: "Am I to be perpetually exposed to a most painful suspicion because I once deserved it and no allowance is to be made for any circumstance in my Conduct at a distance. . . ." The next month, James Iredell pleaded with his wife: "May your goodness still be extended to a Man sincerely sensible of its great value, who has erred, but not with an ill heart, who deserves, however, severe punishment for a conduct much too injurious to be defended, but he trusts in God, does not in his present state of penitence and contrition (which is the source of extreme misery to him) deserve as dreadful, so fatal a one as the loss of your affection."[78]

Although life on the plantation did not readily afford a planter easy access to extramarital affairs with white women, business frequently obliged him to travel. Unlike that of women in the rural South, men's physical mobility was usually restricted only by the poor quality of roads and the distance between settlements. But frequent or lengthy periods of travel away from home put serious strain on marriages. Marital separations, so much a part of plantation society, were a constant source of discontent. War and military service meant compulsory absences for men. Fanny Bland Tucker wrote to her second husband, away at war: "Pray, my love, return as soon as possible as I cannot help feeling myself allmost in a widowed state again."[79] The uncertainty of military maneuvers left husbands unable to set their schedules, and soldiering kept men away from home for indefinite periods of time. Military service was perhaps a necessary evil, but one patriotic duty led to another. Robert Beverley's wife wrote him about his sister's husband: "She informs me that the People below are so much pleased with his Military conduct that they talk of electing him a Senator for that district, but that she had much rather he should be at home, as their Negroes are becoming very ungovernable and she is miserably solitary there."[80]

Though most political widows learned to live with the situation, they constantly expressed discontent with their solitary lot.[81] Eliza Quitman wrote to her husband John in 1836: "I hope you may never again be tempted to become a candidate for any political office whatever, there is everything else—I am sick and tired of living alone."[82] These absences not only made women lonely but also imposed on them heavier responsibilities.* A Virginian plantation mistress had harsh words for her husband in the state legislature: "It appears to me that you take more pleasure in doing publik business than you do in the company of your Family. . . ."[83] But men refused to be swayed by their wives' complaints. In 1793 John Steele wrote to his wife, who was pregnant and in poor health on their isolated plantation: "The President today asked me to drink a glass of wine with him, this is considered here a great honor; It may be so, but I would have been more highly gratified in drinking a glass with my dear little Polly." Three years later he was still in Washington, however, and his wife continued to shoulder the burdens of the family farm. Steele depended on his wife's indulgence of their lengthy separations: "In the mean time, my love, I know you will live disagreeably, the negroes will be disobedient, the overseer drunken and foolish, but I must rely upon your good management. . . ."[84]

Not only political office kept men away from home; some planters were involved in business beyond the management of their plantations. The married life of William and Diana Dunbar of Louisiana was dominated by his peripatetic work pattern. In addition to owning several plantations, Dunbar conducted geological surveys. His business kept him away from his wife most of the year. Both husband and wife lamented their separations. Diana Dunbar was constantly critical of the situation: "A pretty husband indeed that does not stay with his wife above two months in the year. Is it possible that he can be such a rover and faithful at the same time. Yes, my dearest if you love me as I have no reason to doubt but you do, that will keep you so." Two years later she pleaded with her husband for some time together: "If you only stay four or five days with me when you come I shall be happy. I long much for the time when we shall have but one Plantation to look after."[85] But separations continued to be the rule in the Dunbar marriage.[86]

Correspondence provided an important link between couples forced apart. Maria Campbell expressed her dependence upon her husband's letters: "After sitting up till one o'clock last night watching for the mail how painful was my disappointment this morning when I found there was no letter from you. . . . my dear Husband how can your

*See Chapter II, "Slave of Slaves."

ready hand neglect the desolate orphan you have nurtured in your bosom who has no earthly prop but you, and when deprived of your society finds no real pleasure except in reading your letter and dwelling with inthusiastical delite on the mutual love we have for each other."[87] Men as well as women were concerned about maintaining emotional intimacy.[88] A husband wrote his wife on their first anniversary that there existed "only one drawback on my happiness and that is *our frequent separations.*"[89] Another ardent husband confessed to his wife: "If I could clasp you to my bosom at this moment how happy should I be?"[90] Homesickness was a recurrent theme for husbands, but heartache and insomnia were the lot of plantation mistresses left alone on the land.* Most women, like Charlestonian Mary Manigault, never adjusted to these strains: "You cannot imagine what gloomy ideas took possession of my brain last night. I could not get to sleep. . . . it will be a week tomorrow since we parted—and two more may yet pass before. *We* shall not get accustomed to it. I did not long more to see you when you used to leave me at the Elms for a day or two than I now do—yet my Mother used to tell me then that in a year or two I should support your absence with more composure."[91]

Upon occasion, a husband would insist that his wife join him on his sojourn. In the autumn of 1815, a planter who held national political office forced his wife against her wishes to come to live in the District of Columbia. In January 1816 she reported to family and friends that she was miserable in Washington except in her husband's company.[92] Unhappy left alone on plantations, yet often miserable if husbands forced them to live away from home, southern wives found no clear solution to the problem of marital separation.

The ultimate separation—at a husband's death—held a special dimension of loss for the plantation mistress. For a variety of legal and social reasons, widowhood was an especially unpleasant prospect for a southern woman. It often meant the breakup of the home and breakdown within the family. God could offer the plantation mistress spiritual support, but a southern widow found small secular comfort. Prayers did not keep the plantation running.

Bereaved widows might find their grief compounded by financial

---

*See Chapter IX, "Every Woman Was an Island."

pressures. Planters kept their economic affairs in notorious disorder. Many slaveowners were cash-poor, their capital tied up in land and slaves. Upon a planter's death, his wife might be besieged by claims of unpaid debts, and was frequently unable to determine exactly what wealth her husband's estate afforded. Sheltered from the "dirty" financial side of plantation operation, widows found themselves ill-prepared to cope with financial problems. Judith Randolph, widow of Richard Randolph, found her suddenly reduced circumstances a trial: "My children are at most expensive schools, I do not believe my yearly income will do more than support them. I will stay at home and spin and weave and spend nothing in order to keep out of debt, that most horrid of evils."[93]

Lacking a political voice or clearly defined legal rights, unprepared widows usually found themselves at the financial mercy of men. Not all acquiesced quietly. Lawsuits figured prominently in the widow's quest for economic stability. One widow lamented: "My only recourse will be a lawsuit. I have authorized him [the lawyer] to act according to his own judgement and I have left everything for him to do and make the best of. Alas! *two* lawsuits already! What is to become of me! and I with only *one quarter of a dollar in my purse!*"[94] Plantation mistress Martha Richardson took up a combative attitude toward her adversaries: "I know that every plan will be pursued to cross and vex me, but my resolution is equal to the contest, and they shall find that a woman is their equal—not one cent will I recede—no delicacy has been observed towards my feelings—my rights have been invaded—and they have endeavored to make me an outcast in my family." She later confessed to her nephew her pride in her embattled position: "As things turned out—I am glad that I received no help—I have been the carver of my own fortune."[95]

Hard work and hardy spirits helped some widows overcome economic reversals. The daughter of one such woman wrote to her aunt: "Mama has paid off the heavy land debt which has been due for several years. She has been decreasing the amount ever since Papa's death—this year she has paid off every cent—and is now intirely out of debt—she makes fine crops. Every year has something of all most everything to sell such as corn fodder, bacon, wheat, oats, etc., etc. She is now building an excellent house will have it completed this fall.''[96] This woman's mother was extremely fortunate in her financial renaissance. Most widows did not fare so well, unless they remarried.

A second marriage was not uncommon for widow or widower, especially one in reduced circumstances. As a Frenchman reported: "American women generally remarry. In reality, what could a widow do whose fortune consists of land and Negroes who cultivate it? If she is young, having a manager will give rise to gossip or will offend custom. . . . She must marry someone in order to take care of the fortune of her children.''[97] While she might be fully capable of running the farming of the plantation, she could not publicly execute plantation affairs without a man's assistance; no woman could transact business without a male surrogate for court and legal proceedings. Fathers, brothers, or sons who were of age could help, but the southern planter's widow suffered an unenviable plight. Widows with children were also sensitive to the problems of their fatherless offspring. Although money was certainly a factor in a widow's decision to remarry, mothers were as concerned with the welfare of their children as they were with financial security. Planters had a higher rate of multiple marriage than plantation mistresses; 20 percent of planter widowers remarried, but only 7 percent of widowed plantation mistresses.* When a widower married, he almost always chose a new wife younger than he was, and most often, younger than his late wife. A matron wrote in 1832 disdaining a widower's recent marriage: "The excellent woman he lost about 18 months ago, had the misfortune to be forty, or perhaps a few years more, of age—and lest he should be suspected of such bad taste, as to prefer a wife of that age, she had not been dead long enough for the mourning hatband to need changing, before a blooming girl of fifteen, set fire, with her eyes to the tinder box of his heart.''[98] Such a young bride, even for a widower, was not exceptional in the South.

One observer commented on another southern phenomenon: "An old gentleman 48 years of age was to marry his wife's sister only fifteen. . . . tho Virginians were famous for marrying their cousins.''[99] The Anglican church forbade both cousin marriages and marriage to a relation of a dead spouse; the latter was, in fact, illegal in England

*See Appendix A, Table 1.

until the 1907 Deceased Wife's Sister Marriage Act. Yet the practice was common in America among the planter aristocracy.*

Such an alliance was convenient for a variety of reasons. A woman noted in 1819: "He certainly has made a wise choice. She will undoubtedly make the best mother for his children." A wife might indeed expect her husband to marry her sister in case of her death. Sometimes a woman late in pregnancy feared death in childbirth and pledged her children to her sister's care. Planter Bennet Barrow reported his wife's wishes in his diary: "Emily quite unwell [she was 6 months pregnant] very low spirits seems to think of Death in fact thinks she's not to survive this year out—made our solemn pledge never to marry—she made an exception, unless I would marry or wished to marry Mrs. Haile because she knows Mrs. H. will be kind to her children."[100] Mrs. Haile, Emily's widowed sister, did not marry Bennet Barrow following his wife's death four months later. But she did come to live with the Barrow family, to care for his six motherless children.

Childcare, however, was not the only rationale for men's remarriage. Widowers sought new mistresses for their households: "He must suffer without a wife—a good housekeeper is not to be had and he is as unfit as a child to take care of that fort."[101] As men, planters might consider their world incomplete without women—but as slave-owners, they realized that their wives were as indispensable to the well-being of their domestic economy as slaves. Few plantation owners ran their estates without a wife by choice.

Life in the slaveowning South put pressure on couples that created an easy climate for marital disintegration. Yet unhappy marriages seldom resulted in official separation, and even more rarely ended in divorce. Until the 1830s, divorces were granted only by petition through the state legislature, and were difficult to obtain throughout the ante-bellum period. Since there were no specific divorce laws during the post-Revolutionary era, no explicit grounds existed for divorce. Instead, the state legislature committees reviewed the details of each individual petition and ruled on a case-by-case basis. The letter of a Virginia legislator to his wife reflects the attitude of elected officials to

*Although the statistical differential is not significant (which is why I have not included a table in Appendix A on the rate of marriage to dead wife's sister), a large number of widowers in the South nevertheless practiced this custom.

the issue of divorce: "I have great hopes that three weeks more will finish the business of the session, a great part which has been taken up by application for divorces. The applications have in every instance, but one came from the male sex. Can it be that yours are the most faulty of the two or are we more turbulent and restless. Some general law it is said will be passed upon this subject, whether it will extend so far as a man to put away his wife as soon as he is tired of her or whether more limited is yet uncertain, but as we have the power in our own hands, surely we shall carry it far enough to ensure us all the ease and pleasure we could wish."[102]

A wife's inability to coexist peacefully with her husband was no legal ground for divorce; rather, Southerners censured women for acting on such inability. A wife confided to her husband that a newlywed female acquaintance had taken leave of her husband—and perhaps her senses: "She has taken it into her head that she cannot live with him, and has been at her mother's since the spring, notwithstanding all his kind letters, refuses to go home! . . . I expect she must be somewhat deranged."[103] A southern doctor wrote in his diary of a friend's marital problems: "The next visitor was our immediate neighbour, Mrs. Paulina Moss, a living widow, being separated from her maniacal husband. She could have made a good housewife to a more rational companion. . . . Is a woman justified to live separate from her husband when the latter's aberation of mind is of a more melancholy musing species than actually pregnant with danger to attendants?"[104]

Southern custom expected a woman to stay with her husband in spite of maltreatment. The case of Virginian Sopha Septwick Dobyns was not an unusual pattern for broken marriages. She was married at the age of sixteen. After two years of married life her husband, Jonah, began to beat her without cause, and she escaped to the protection of her father. But upon Jonah Dobyns's promise to reform, Septwick released his daughter to her husband's care; in spite of his wifebeating, Dobyns had marital rights to his wife, and her father maintained this principle. After returning to her husband's home, Sopha Dobyns was again subjected to physical abuse. When her father came to intercede, Dobyns beat his father-in-law as well—only at this point did Septwick assent to his daughter's separation from her husband. But when her father died, Sopha Dobyns tried to have her marriage dissolved to protect her financial position. She petitioned the Virginia legislature in 1817, pleading that her husband had already "dissipated the liberal marriage portion of your Petitioner, as well as his own fortune," and that she feared for the money left in trust for her children by her own father.[105]

The daughter of another Virginia planter petitioned the legislature in 1806 for a divorce from her wife-beating husband. She had returned to her father's home to support herself and her children without any assistance from this husband, following his repeated brutality. But she requested the divorce not only on the ground of his beatings, for she further confided, "Ball did frequently tell me that he had carnal knowledge of different women after he was married, both black and white."[106] Infidelity, abuse, and cruelty were often cited in divorce petitions from women.[107]

A survey of the divorce petitions submitted in one year to the North Carolina State Legislature provides insight into this complex subject.[108] In 1813, forty-one petitions were submitted. Twenty-eight came from women, twelve from men, and one was jointly submitted by a husband and wife. Of the thirty-five petitions endorsed by committee, twenty-one divorces were granted, twelve were rejected, and two were carried over to the next assembly. Women generally fared better than men: of the twenty-one petitions approved, twenty were submitted by women. Of the twelve rejected by the legislature, five were submitted by women.

The reasons these husbands and wives listed for divorce included bigamy, wife-beating, desertion, infidelity, insanity, and irreconcilable differences. Only one of the twelve men petitioning for divorce failed to complain of his wife's sexual behavior; interestingly, he was the only male petitioner granted a divorce. The other eleven complained of misconduct ranging from bigamy to bearing a black child. Although some of these men merely suggested "lewd conduct," others produced sworn affidavits by men who would testify to a wife's prostitution of herself. Nonetheless, these petitions were rejected or passed over. Women most commonly claimed desertion or abandonment. Of the seventeen wives who reported that their husbands had left them, fourteen were granted divorces. In four of these cases, the women were clearly from the planter class.

In one case where an upper-class woman claimed that her husband beat and abused her, a divorce was granted; in two other cases where similar claims of maltreatment were made, wives had their petitions rejected. Their class status was not specified in the records. Clearly class standing and the number of corroborating witnesses could influence the success or defeat of an appeal to the legislature. One wife reported that her husband had deserted her and married another woman; her claim was rejected. Another wife complained of her husband's violation of the marriage covenant; her divorce was granted. One woman was granted a divorce after her husband raped another woman; another wife was given permission to divorce when she cited irreconcilable differences. Yet a wife who reported that her husband had three bastards by another woman was given no legislative relief, and a woman who documented her husband's insanity was forced to stay married, despite her pleas for divorce. Clearly, legislators made their decisions on a case-by-case basis, and no prescribed formula determined the outcomes.

The demand for divorce was relatively high in North Carolina; in sharp contrast, only *eight* divorce petitions appear in the state legislative records of South Carolina *before 1830*—three from women, four from men, and one joint petition. Although several "articles of separation" were filed annually by incompatible couples, and merchants and their wives sometimes filed agreements called "deeds of sole tradership," one can safely assume that divorce was indeed rare in South Carolina. The eight petitions were varied in nature and detail. In 1788 Fielding Woodruff petitioned for divorce, naming a correspondent, after his wife ran off with her lover and a good deal of cash. In 1791, one John C. Smith filed for divorce. In 1802, Rachel Teakle petitioned the legislature for an annulment, claiming she "never knew the above named Richard Teakle as a man and he absented himself from me." In 1810, Henry and Nancy Gambell jointly requested that their marriage end; they confessed having "never been able to live together in that harmony and Union which is indispensable to the happiness of the married state." But the Committee on Grievances replied after careful examination: "Their case is much to be lamented yet your committee are fearful that were the Legislature of this state to interfere between husband and Wife the Consequences would be dangerous in the extreme—your committee think it impolitick to interfere in this or any other like case and are of opinion that the prayer of said petitioner not be granted."[109] In 1813, Elizabeth Hamilton complained to the legislature that her husband had deserted her two years previously, then turned up living in Savannah, and that he refused either to acknowledge his wife or return home to South Carolina. In 1819, William Click's father petitioned on his son's behalf, requesting an annulment of the son's marriage to Drucilla Evans. The elder Click pleaded that his son was under age—not yet eighteen—and that at the time of the marriage ceremony, the groom had been in a state of complete intoxication; the younger Click had deserted his bride the morning after the wedding. In 1821, Mary Wilson requested a divorce; not only had her husband deserted her, he had left another wife in Kentucky in similar circumstances. Although Wilson was a proven bigamist, his second wife was well "aware of the reluctance with which the legislature interposes in business of this character."[110] Finally, in 1830 Curtis Winget wished to divorce Elizabeth Sledge. His petition lodged multiple complaints: "She openly and avowedly violated the marriage contract in taking to her bed a young man by the name of Mitchell" and "she boasted of constantly bedding with a young man living with us named Bailis." After her elopement with Mitchell, Winget had taken his wife back. But when she claimed that her newborn child was fathered by Bailis, Winget abandoned home, wife, and illegitimate child and asked the legislature to free him so he could marry again. A wife's adultery was in this case concrete and irrefutable grounds for divorce.[111] But a husband's desertion of his wife was not as clear-cut in its sequel. Although some women were granted divorces on such grounds, men enjoyed a certain measure of reverse discrimination.[112]

Further studies of divorce in the ante-bellum South are needed; no broad conclusions can be drawn from this limited survey of records from so few states. Preliminary indicators show, however, that authorities had few precedents to provide them with guidelines. This inevitably created erratic and unpredictable patterns in the disposition of divorce petitions.

Most of the relatively rare divorces in this period were accepted by the plantation aristocracy; Southerners were sympathetic to marital incompatibility once the legislature had legitimated such a claim. Ann Cocke wrote in 1815 to a friend: "The melancholy situation of our Cousin Eyre and her husband must be lamented by us all—you indeed have more cause for distress in the event of their dissolution than most of us—your sister will lose her best friend—Heaven I trust my Cousin will give her another as valuable—Let us at least hope it will be more charitable—and the hope will afford us comfort."[113]

Divorces involved not only the separating couples, however, but their families as well. Sometimes a lawsuit was necessary to settle the inevitable disputes following a marital dissolution.[114] In other cases, family intervention kept the disagreement out of the courts. But opposing and often embittered camps frequently arose. Nelly Parke Custis reported her sister's case to a friend: "I was always opposed their separation and endeavoured to reconcile them for their child's sake." Once the couple had dissolved the bonds of matrimony, the Custis family "could not see the propriety of becoming his enemies merely because my sister and himself could not be happy together, when difference of dispositions induced them to separate." Yet Nelly Custis became alarmed at the ensuing gossip: "When the *Divorce* was concluded . . . and she was *in eyes of many* free to make a new choice, I thought it more necessary to attend to those reports as they might be supposed to be justified by circumstances. They became too, more serious and more injurious . . . and I cannot believe that Mr. Law her sister's husband or his sons are entirely innocent of their origin."[115] Mrs. Law never remarried and raised her child alone.

The Law case is interesting for another reason: a woman actually had no legal right to her children. The courts did not rule on the basis of the fitness of the parent; fathers were given a clear preference. A woman who had left her husband could claim her offspring only if he saw fit to bestow them on their mother. When Julia Ellis fled to New Orleans in 1818, she wrote to her husband, Richard, in Natchez: "Be careful in having my things pack't up well, as it is my intention never to return to a place where I have spent so many unhappy hours. Happiness is to be found in my Father's House. . . ." But Julia Ellis was not prepared to seek a divorce, for she expressed hope that her husband would reform and join her. Her children remained behind; she begged him to "kiss the little ones for me."[116] Ellis had apparently fallen in with bad company, and "he and his companions," one observer reported to a family member, "are carrying on a high hand at the plantations much to the injury of the negroes. . . . They are in a constant riot, drinking, carousing, and many of the evil [illegible] attending such behavior on a plantation. It perhaps would be well to have him removed from the Plantation. I fear he is gone without redemption."[117] Even though Ellis was "gone without redemption," his wife had no claim to their children, and this prevented her from demanding a dissolution of the marriage.

Some women did not bow to the cultural pressures to marry. They saw the social reality behind the romantic idyll of marriage—that it was a contract whereby a woman abandoned one man's protection for another man's authority, trading the shared attentions of a male parent for the single attentions of a husband. Taking a husband was participation in a great gamble: "Marriage is such a lottery, there are so many blanks to a prize."[118] One woman wrote teasingly to a male relation: "We of the 'Sisterhood' unfettered by the matrimonial chains can rove wherever our inclinations lead, and can form our plans, and carry them into effect without being obliged to consult any one else."[119] But this was patent satire on her part. All women were subjected to the control of men, and spinsters had low social status and no opportunity for sexual fulfillment. The stereotype of the "old maid" ("always in an ill humour with herself and every person she meets"[120]) was explicitly negative in southern ante-bellum culture: "forlorn damsels who make the midnight air echo with the plaintive bewailings, for only bats and owls return their melancholy strains."[121] The marital status of a young girl was of such vital concern that one southern woman wrote: "Cousin Sarah is well, but not married."[122]

The culture provided no primary role for unmarried daughters. Spinsters devoted themselves to their parents, their nieces and nephews, and in general provided supplemental care wherever required within the kinship network. These women received a smaller share of their parents' material wealth; instead of surviving economically by means of paternal generosity, these unattached females most often depended on their brothers' charity. Unlike their counterparts in the North, southern spinsters were not settled with an independent income by planter parents, but were farmed out to sibling households and expected to sacrifice themselves for the needs of their reproductive kin.[123]

Unmarried women often suffered from envy and self-pity on account of their position on the fringe of southern society. Even those who generally expressed contentment occasionally felt their social instability: "There is very little medium in unmarried women—they are apt to sink into entire listlessness or be too busy in the concerns of others."[124] Some women chose not to marry because they could not find a man worth "risking their happiness."[125] These women voluntarily withdrew from the lottery. In a handful of cases, they interpreted their rejection of the married state as political—spinsterhood occasionally led to feminism, but this was clearly rare and aberrant behavior in plantation culture.[126] The majority of women necessarily accepted the wedding day as "the day that is to fix my fate."[127]

V

THE MORAL BIND

The idealized image of the southern lady had numerous sources. Men were virtually obsessed with female innocence. The notion of white women as virginal precipitated a whole series of associations: delicate as lilies, spotless as doves, polished as alabaster, fragile as porcelain—but above all, pure as the driven snow (with its inherent connotation of coldness). The vocabulary of ideologues and preceptors conveyed sentimentalized yet severe prescriptions for women.

Using this vocabulary, slaveholders created a fantasy world in an attempt to transform the harsher aspects of life around them, to insulate themselves against those elements that would eventually bring about the downfall of the plantation system. The exalted image of the lady, like the portrait of the happy-go-lucky "Sambo," was not merely a figment of planter imaginations but a powerful coercive force within plantation society.

Southern men portrayed white women as unsullied and frail, perhaps as an unconscious counterpoint to their own option of rowdy debauchery. Because the system of slavery could and did allow for the sordid exploitation of black women by white masters, male slaveowners were by implication morally tainted. The ban on sexual relations between white women and black men and the southern lady's elevation to a pedestal were socially enforced and strictly observed to counter male corruption: a balance of requisite evil and hyperbolic good. The character and nature of this double standard will be developed later, but its existence serves to remind us not only that southern slaveowners struggled with ambivalence, but that moral persuasion and economic necessity were in constant and racking conflict within plantation culture.

In the southern plantation system, relief from the burdens of physical labor allegedly offset, for the others, the moral taxation of slaveowning. Whites freed themselves from drudgery by using slaves as manual laborers—so the more indolent their lives appeared, the greater the wealth (in slaves) implied. Elite males in many societies have used women, too, as living proof of their wealth and status, testimonies of their worth. Planters necessarily chose for their women the role that would most flatter the image of plantation life that southern slaveowners were striving to project; hence the formulation of the mythical ideal of the southern lady.

The path to this ideal was long and arduous for planter daughters. The children of slaveowners were taught from an early age that their actions reflected the honor and virtue of the planter patriarchs. Southern society prided itself on a rigorous code of behavior. The female preoccupation with the "niceties," a rigid pattern of manners and politeness, contrasted with the obvious indifference of men to much of what they preached. Male authorities subjected everyone but themselves to a strict regimen. Women, children, and slaves followed rules laid down by white men; these rules ostensibly governed male activities as well, but society excused men as long as they conducted their illicit affairs discreetly.

Because a double standard was so completely integrated into southern ethical conduct, men could dedicate themselves to the maintenance of high standards—for women. Female purity became a practical crusade for a society in which the wives and mothers of the ruling class had to be above suspicion. The masters of a biracial slave system were understandably concerned with the sexual continence of those women who bore their heirs and held some sway as keepers of the culture; thus planters required their wives to be living examples of

Christian virtue. If plantation mistresses could live above reproach, their husbands, fathers, sons, and brothers could boast of the superiority of their civilization. The vessels to which these men trusted their reproductive potential and cultural values must, of necessity, be unblemished, alabaster representations of the plantation idyll. The sullying influence of slavery must not touch the women of the upper class lest the entire structure crumble.[1]

As cultivators of the land, planters were concerned with the growth and prosperity of all their holdings, human and otherwise. While they carefully supervised both real estate and chattels, nothing surpassed the patriarchs' preoccupation with their offspring. Children were plants to be tended; sons were the sturdy vines and daughters the fragile blossoms in the southern moral garden. Especially during the formative years after infancy, sons and daughters were safeguarded by pious and protective parental guidance. Bolling Hall, an Alabama politician, wrote to his daughter in 1813: "Look at the cedars in the potters' garden, they are the same with those which grow in the forest and would only have assumed their shape and form had it not been for the care and attention of a skillful hand."[2] Hall goes on to describe the evils of temper and vanity and the positive need for pruning, finally counseling his daughter that "as the cedars you will become the ornament of society." David Campbell wrote to his niece Margaret along similar lines in 1831. Concerned with her intellectual cultivation, he advised Margaret to recognize her own ignorance and imperfection, for "the ground is then prepared for the seed and nothing which is sown will be lost."[3]

The moral training of the young was a complex and continuous task for ante-bellum parents, most of whom believed, as a southern gentleman explained in his commonplace book, that "man is a compound creature made up of three distinct parts, viz. the body, which is the earthly or mortal part of him; the soul which is the animal or sensitive part; and the spirit or mind which is the rational and immortal part."[4] They saw individuals as constantly at war with themselves: spirit against flesh, reason battling emotion, mortality at odds with the immortal soul. Christians, in conscience and deed, were called upon to mediate perpetually between these claims. The goal of planter parents was to instill in their children this sense of values, for virtue was "that which can make every station happy, and without which every station must be wretched."[5]

Woman, as a function of her exalted status as guardian of the culture and her isolation from the "outside world," was assigned the role of moral exemplar and counselor. Women's purity and spirituality were believed to be vital assets in assuming the sacred charge of motherhood, which included the burden of religious training. Thus the patriarch imagined his family as a domestic haven sheltered from the pernicious influences of the world and guided by the saintly precepts of his untainted wife.

Not surprisingly, women held different views. Their ideas on moral nature were not philosophical opinions culled from texts, but rather lessons learned from personal contact. Mothers generally conceived of the battle against sin in their offspring as an internal affair, waged against the evil side of human nature, not that of society, which was, after all, merely the magnified reflection of individual nature. The plantation mistress took small comfort from her family circle's seclusion, and believed that evil lay within as well as without.[6]

The practical extension of the household added another dimension. Slaves surrounded the planter family, and their behavior especially preoccupied the majority of plantation mistresses. Most complained constantly of the lying, cheating, and disobedience of their house slaves. The task of supervising black as well as white overwhelmed many mistresses.* Few were aware of the irony involved in trying to convince a class held in bondage to follow the moral example of their masters, but all struggled to impose literal, if not Christian, order on every member of the plantation household.

The overt sexual double standard further complicated for plantation mistresses the task of imposing Christian morality on their charges, whether children or slaves. It was next to impossible to enforce ethical precepts while male planters consistently defied them. One concerned mother wrote in her diary: "My children, beloved parts of my being! dear boys, especially, whose life will expose you most, set no wicked thing before you."[7] Plantation life constantly exposed children to illicit

---

*See Chapter IX, "Every Woman Was an Island," and Chapter X, "The Curse of Slavery."

sex, venereal diseases, and other harsh aspects of sexuality. Many planter sons ignored their mothers' warnings and explored the forbidden yet beckoning world of interracial sex. Nights in slave cabins were an acceptable adolescent sexual outlet—for males only.[8]

Plantation mistresses attempted to exert an "uplifting" influence on black women—to little avail. One white woman confided in 1829: "I had much solemn talk with our cook Maria, who has now resided with us three years and whose habits in respect to personal purity are a continual violation of the seventh commandment. I hoped an impression was made, but at night she was again absent." This matron interpreted her cook's behavior in typical planter fashion, discounting the idea that Maria might have been exercising her own judgment, doing what she wanted instead of obeying the hypocritical dictates of her racist owners. Instead, this white woman viewed her slave's immorality as a genetic defect: "How truly does it illustrate that the Ethiopian cannot change his skin nor the leopard his spots."[9] Sexual debauchery, interracial or other, was never blamed on men—where surely the guilt partially rested. Planter women pretended—or indeed believed—that the "Ethiopians" were at the root of the problem, not their own husbands, brothers, sons, and fathers.

The very fact of slavery posed an obstacle to the establishment of a sound and integral moral order. Mothers feared for children exposed from so early and impressionable an age to a system ripe for abuse and characterized by tyranny, cruelty, and exploitation. They believed in the negative influence of slavery, but rationalized that this was not inevitable; they cast the issue in terms of contamination and insisted that strict segregation could shield the young by minimizing their opportunities to sin. Virginia Cary warned in her advice book of 1830: "The most deadly of all pernicious habits is that of putting young slaves to be companions of young children. The infant despot enforces his lawless authority over his allotted victim and thus encourages all the most malignant vices of his nature."[10] Although this "lawless" authority was the backbone of the slave system, mothers imagined that this bent should initially be tempered. They believed that adults, but not children, should be allowed such sway; when the individual was old enough, he would somehow rightly assume the responsibilities of the slaveowner's power. The truly Christian mother was powerless against the potent moral imperatives of slavery.

No matter how benevolently protected their childhood had been, most young men eventually succumbed to the arrogance cultivated by a slaveowning society. One girl complained: "You slaveholders have lived so long on your plantations with no one to gainsay or contradict you that you expect to govern everybody and have it all your own way. I can see it in Father—in Brother John—in Brother Patrick."[11] It was at this point that the moral universes of male and female separated; slavery, the most significant economic and political influence in southern society, was in opposition to the central value of the religious and social order, Christian virtue. Although both men and women of the master class resisted the notion that the possession of slaves was the real sin undermining virtue, planters and especially their wives were disturbed by the numerous vices that stemmed from slaveholding. Women, the guardians of virtue, had to achieve a balance between these values, and the deception, self-deception, and contradiction involved imposed considerable strain on their emotional lives.

The tombstone of Milly Jones reads: "In the various characters of wife, mother, sister, friend and mistress she was ever affectionate and truly exemplary."[12] The model woman in the plantation South was able in myriad roles, possessing "sentiments that would do honor to a Roman matron in the best times of that republic."[13] To fulfill these expectations, southern belles not only underwent long and careful tutorship beneath their domestic role-models, but also extensive formal education outside the family circle. Plantation mistresses drew on both British advice literature and American texts, including Virginia Cary's work, *Letters on Female Character*, and Mrs. Taylor's volume, *Practical Hints to Young Females*, which contained such useful chapters as Conduct to the Husband, Domestic Economy, Servants, Education, Sickness, Visitors, Keeping a Home, Recreation, and The Step Mother. The urgent need for this domestic guidance was clear to planters, despite the relative undervaluing of practical training for women. John Campbell wrote to his sister in 1827: "Some men have said that (even in our enlightened day) females need not to be taken as much pains with as to their education as the males; for the Creator has not given them as strong powers for their mind as he has given the males. What a pitiful and unfounded excuse. . . . I am of the opinion that females have equally as strong powers given to their minds as the males and if either have the strongest it is the female."[14] But planters trusted their wives to instill in daughters a sense of feminine values which would counter any "masculine" effects an education might produce.

Without proper supervision, a woman's education could lead her to the unattractive plight which Southerners believed beset the "masculine" Queen Elizabeth I. As a gentleman wrote to his sister, another Elizabeth, regarding the British monarch: "She reigned over her people with distinguished ability, yet perhaps in private life she would have been harsh and unamiable. She might not have professed those tender sensibilities, those soft feminine and engaging manners which throw such a charm around the female character in her intercourse with society."[15] Even a bluestocking like Georgian Mary Telfair wrote to her confidante and fellow spinster, Mary Few: "Superiority of intellect is no safeguard to domestic happiness—Sweetness of temper, ingenuousness, and disinterestedness are the qualities which throw a charm around the domestic circle."[16] "Throwing charm" was the paramount duty of the female sex.

Ante-bellum attitudes toward women reveal deep and pervasive conflicts within plantation culture. The cult of virtue was all the more fervent because men believed that the opposite sex possessed a dual and dangerous essence; femininity was rooted in vice, but women could be raised to a state of virtue. This process of redemption was the sacred duty of planter parents. Daughters were rescued from their sinful natures by stiff doses of discipline and the improving examples of Christian mothers, themselves already "saved." Many of the toasts proposed by planters at celebratory gatherings during this era reveal the ambivalence aroused by the female sex. The exaggerated gallantry of southern chivalry articulated the myth of innocent purity ("Woman at such an hour as this, her spirit comes over us like the sweet South that breathes upon a bank of violets, stealing and giving ardor."[17]) and, alternately, the veiled threat of feminine influence ("The fair sex—without participation in public affairs their dominion is in the hearts of their countrymen"; "The beauty of a fine woman is the only tyranny to which a man should submit"[18]). The following verse, popular in 1814, pinpoints one aspect of sexual attitudes in plantation culture by equating females with dissipation: "Women and wine, game and deceit/ Makes the wealth small and the want great."[19] In yet another toast, females are linked with the implicit threat of evil and vice: "Woman—lovely woman; if she brought death into the world, she produced everlasting life through a Saviour."[20]

Women in a sense symbolized regeneration: death and redemption. If man is to be reborn, he must brave the jaws of death—which have psychologically been personified as female. For example, females are subjected to physical and psychic penetration in the process of reproduction, while men are threatened with engulfment. Each sex endures its own psychic vulnerability: the sexual act allows both parties to participate in mutual risk, with the individual submitting to violation in order to gain a genetically everlasting life. Women's suffering historically has been more institutionalized than men's. Patriarchy has translated male vulnerability concerning reproduction into a variety of restrictions upon female behavior from chastity belts to clitoridectomies. In a realm so sensitive as reproduction, men have been throughout history preoccupied with and severe in power over females, and ante-bellum southern planters were no exception.

Chastity was a crucial condition of female purity. Men sought partners in life who were virginal before marriage and would continue to be virtuous in wedlock. A southern planter rationalized in 1827: "The only security a husband has is found in the purity of his wife's character before her marriage. . . . Hence, I am inclined to believe by the appointment of God, a man has a greater horror of sharing the person of the woman he hopes with another man than a woman has of sharing with a woman. . . . Hence incontinence before marriage, by diminishing the security the husband should have of the fidelity of his wife after marriage, sinks her value so much in the society of which she is a member, and is in fact a greater crime in a woman than in a man."[21] Chastity—or a reputation as chaste—was so much a commodity in southern culture that the courts could place a dollar value on it: "A young lady of South Carolina got a verdict of one thousand dollars against a man (of moderate means) for imputation of unchastity."[22] Although crucial to an unmarried female, continence was no less critical for the matron; husbands extolled the value of their wives in terms of purity.[23]

Social gatherings, however, created climates ripe for immodesty. One young girl confessed her horror at the spectacle of a fashionable wedding: "Their backs and bosoms were all uncovered. My heart was

indignant at the sight, and as I saw those shameless women, surrounded by their beaux, I shrank yet farther into the recess."[24] Although this sounds like prudery, a proper unmarried female of any
age showed puritanical disdain for any but the most circumspect behavior. Wary of temptation and the punishment that might ensue,
southern women believed that men and fashion could threaten their
own purity—and fashionable men were doubly dangerous. Correspondence between female friends reveals a vigorous strain of moral
chastisement; women fortified each other against the potential treach-
ery of men, as in this letter of 1834: "I am almost glad that Robert
Walton has gone; for his manners which are certainly fascinating make
his society dangerous for any girl." The writer goes on to warn: "How
often is a woman's heart, with its spotless purity given in exchange
for one whose every thought is wicked."[25] The strongest defense against
temptation was not, however, female friendship, but an auxiliary of
purity: piety.

Women's personal moral duty went hand in hand with an evangelical mission to safeguard the souls of their society.[26] Although the
ministry remained a male bastion, the role of women in the Christian
church increased rather than decreased following the American Revolution, and religion was slowly "feminized" during the first half of
the nineteenth century.[27] Indeed, the measure of spiritual prosperity
in the culture was gauged on an index of female religiosity. One
matron wrote in 1825: "In reality, carelessness and impiety on this
sacred occasion [public worship] is not less sinful in men than in
women, but public sentiment exacts a much more strict observance of
decorous and pious conduct from *our* sex than from *yours*."[28] The
"tender and pious" mother was invaluable to the moral tenor of southern culture. Elizabeth Jaquelin Ambler wrote rapturous accounts of
her mother's spiritual example: "She considered cheerfulness a Christian virtue and when ever her health would permit, entered into all
the innocent gaieties of life provided they did not interfere with religious duties (none of which under any circumstances did she ever
omit). It was her meat and drink to do the will of God and never in
one instance do I recollect her ever to have shrunk from it. Her whole
life was a continual series of practical Christian duty. . . ."[29]

The struggle against impiety was unending; most girls felt that
temptations to sin abounded. A woman wrote her sister in 1821: "I

earnestly beseech you to beware of vain jesting, light laughing and talking, in short all frivolous conversation. It will draw your attention from study and poison your mind besides disgusting any genteel person you meet with."[30] Another woman, recently converted, confessed to a friend: "There has lately been a dance at Mrs. Jones' but I did not think it would be very consistent in one who had so lately joined the church to go to a dance for although I do not think it wrong to dance, I do not think dancing parties contribute to growth of grace."[31]

The female preoccupation with "growth of grace" was not a peculiarly southern phenomenon. Rural women throughout the country manifested a strain of religious intensity in their personal lives, a pent-up energy that had little or no public outlet; they diverged only in the external form of their crusades. Southern moralists focused on the vices that most commonly plagued planter daughters: temper, vanity, immodesty, and—the greatest threat of all—impropriety. Plantation mistresses considered temper and vanity to be rather benign flaws, requiring a program of personal vigilance and self-control. Immodesty and impropriety, on the other hand, were malignancies, demanding that the individual be put right by her family and friends before disaster rendered her unsalvageable. These four sins, although not interchangeable, were nevertheless interdependent; accordingly, southern mothers waged a war on all fronts.

Temper was a special problem for plantation women, one in which slavery proved a key factor. "But of the consequences arising from slavery, one of the most pernicious and least notified," Virginia Cary wrote in her advice book, "is its effect on the female temper. I acknowledge it is hard to bear with patience, the trials incident to domestic life in Virginia."[32] Planters would not tolerate female temper, however, demanding compliance without complaint. Fathers cautioned their daughters against any departure from a pleasant disposition: "Be watchful over your temper, nothing can be more disgusting than to see the female bosom, the seat of tenderness and virtue, agitated by anger."[33] A girl's education was liberally enhanced with lessons on female character. A teacher wrote in 1812: "I have just read a little work by Miss Edgeworth, entitled 'The Modern Griselda' . . . the heroine has talents, education, beauty, accomplishments, in short almost every requisite to inspire both love and admiration, and yet renders herself, her husband and her friends miserable by a peevish, irascible temper. It would be well, I think for all our young to read 'The Modern Griselda.' "[34] But books were not enough to guard against youthful tantrums. As Martha Richardson confided to her nephew about their mutual relative: "Elizabeth is improving and I think will turn out a fine woman—she promises to be very smart—but we shall have to watch her temper—this will require great care—we must teach her the importance of governing it entirely—and not to suppress it only to suit occasions—it will cost her some pains, but it will be worth the trial—as her own happiness as well as those she may be connected with depends on it—so much do I value an amiable temper that in my opinion no advantages of education can compensate for want of it."[35]

Many of the cautionary tales traded by plantation mistresses involved the ruin of a good woman by her temper. Having learned these supposed lessons, most women wholly subscribed to the theory that contentment could be obtained only through curtailment of their complaints to men and a seeming acceptance of the established order. At the same time, men were not only disturbed but threatened by women's anger; plantation mistresses were necessary components of slave-owning plantations, and planters required cooperation from the women of the ruling class. Myth and manipulation combined to keep females subordinated. The cult of the lady may have been in part a collaboration: southern gentlemen enshrined and adorned their females, while women were willing to exemplify these "ladylike" virtues. Oppression thus was exercised not only through sanctions against rebellion but internally, as women's compliance with the silencing stereotypes determined their own self-censuring behavior.

Another threat to feminine virtue, but a sin less practically irksome to planters, was vanity. William O. Gregory summed up the fears of many planters when he wrote: "Vanity is truly and emphatically the bane of the female heart. It is a monster of exceeding rapid growth, which requires but little food in its youth to make it grow in a short time to be master of the heart, and to expel thence every noble or virtuous feeling." When Gregory's seventeen-year-old sister Martha attended a wedding against his advice, he punished his sibling for her "vanity" by canceling a prearranged holiday visit. He warned her:

"Examine nicely and earnestly into the motives which produce every action, which you do or wish to perform; and whenever you discover vanity to be the prompting cause, forbear by all means to do it."[36]

Although they lectured against the vanity of an excessive preoccupation with grooming, fathers demanded a presentable appearance from their daughters. Bolling Hall wrote in 1813 to his daughter Polly at school: "The precepts of religion strongly injoin the duty of living cleanly in our dress and persons—nothing can be more disgusting than to see a person with dirty hands or face, and to see a girl with dirty clothes is truly shocking."[37] Cleanliness and neatness were the foundations for a ladylike appearance. Thomas Jefferson advised his elder daughter, Martha, in 1783: "Nothing is so disgusting to our sex as the want of cleanliness and delicacy in yours. I hope therefore the moment you rise from bed, your first work will be to dress yourself in such stile as that you may be seen by any gentleman without his being able to discover a pin amiss, or any other circumstances of neatness wanting." Jefferson went on to warn that "some ladies think they may be under the privileges of the dishabille be loose and negligent of their dress in the morning. But be you from the moment you rise till you go to bed as cleanly and properly dressed as at the hours of dinner or tea."[38] Because the body was a temple, and cleanliness next to godliness, an unkempt woman displayed impiety; a spotless appearance equaled a spotless heart. Girls scrubbed and attired themselves to reflect both Christian devotion and proper attention to appearance.

The question of dress raised controversial issues for the pious plantation mistress. To be a lady of fashion was socially enviable, but nonetheless wholly reviled by the moral preceptors of southern culture. Fashion, therefore, represented a serious temptation toward impropriety. Virginian Maria Campbell commented to her husband in 1822: "What can be more wretched than a woman of fashion obeying every varying and yet monotonous dictate of her capricious fancy." She continued by lamenting the "woman of fashion" as "a stranger in her family, her children, if children are so unfortunate as to belong to such a mother, committed to the mercy, the inattention, the example of menials without the benefit of a mother's tenderness, instruction and care."[39] David Campbell replied to his wife: "How true is every remark, every word you have written about fashionable life. I see it here [Richmond] daily exemplified, Madam Scott is here this win-

ter. . . . She is daily on the run—after what she does not know—
Every night at the theatre or a party."[40] Most plantation mistresses in
residence at home could not afford the luxury of fashion; their rural
isolation provided little chance to see or emulate new styles, and even
those ladies who lived in town found the expense a hindrance. A
Charleston woman wrote in 1784: "The last fashion just arrived from
London; there are baloon hats arrived, the price 18 and 20 dollars,
you may form an idea of the extravagance of fashion from that one
article."[41]

In spite of these constraints, southern women remained fascinated,
and tried to find an appropriate compromise between the evil of
becoming "slaves of fashion" and the grace of dressing in a style
reflecting position and wealth. Most ladies forged a network of female
friends and relatives, extending outward from the coastal urban centers
where European imports and sophisticated tastes dominated women's
apparel. A friend in Tennessee pleaded of Maria Campbell in Virginia:
"If you have any new fashioned dress or handkerchiefs, please send
me the patterns of them by Uncle."[42] Despite the inevitable time lag,
planter wives and daughters cherished the notion that they could copy
the latest Continental creations, even in their removed circumstances,
and women traded advice on every facet of dress, from head to toe.[43]

Fashionable ladies wore corsets throughout most of the ante-bellum
era, and considered lacing an indispensable improvement to a woman's
figure. A matron wrote her daughter in 1818: "Apropos of dress,
Margaret tells me you have made a new set of corsetts and to save you
the trouble of unlacing them you have made them large enough to
jump out of them when you take them off. If you love me, alter these
corsetts before I see you. Endeavour to make your shape look as well
as I am sure with a little ingenuity you might do. You are now too old
to have any scruples on this subject. A little art in remedying the
faults of nature is always allowable. It is unpardonable and untasteful
not to do it."[44] Tightlacing, however, became a subject of some
controversy after the beginning of the nineteenth century—a conflict
stimulated both by the corsetless styles of Napoleonic Europe and by
the medical impetus of dress reform. A girl's letter to her father in
1811 reveals an amused objection to the practice: "They were laced
up so tight that everyone of the Gentlemen in the room took notice of
it. Crawford told S. Heirkeel & myself that he thought that Miss'

conscience was in the center of her breast for she always put her hand there whenever she talked but he sayed that he would keep his knife ready to cut their strings."[45]

Constriction by corset was in fact a serious issue. Some parents recognized that whalebone was an actual danger to a girl's health. Many women suffered from respiratory difficulties due to their constrictive clothing. Indeed, some were felled by internal injuries brought on by binding themselves into wasp-waisted corsets. In 1816, a friend opined that one southern girl would have had a fashionable figure "if her father did not make her spoil it by not allowing her to wear a corset bone. This she has given up merely to please him."[46] Such a parental prohibition was not unusual by mid-century, even in the South. As early as the 1840s, southern periodicals reflected the medical wisdom of the dress reform campaign, even if the plantation mistress did not. An 1842 article in *Magnolia* chastised: "Nothing can be more absurd—nothing more detrimental to health and beauty than the system of tightlacing."[47] The magazine went on enthusiastically: "French women are about casting them aside and are beginning to allow nature, not the milliner, to mould their shapes." Despite the impracticality and discomfort, women continued to heed the dictates of fashion rather than medical literature in matters of dress.

Ante-bellum ladies also obeyed strict prohibitions against sunning themselves. Plantation mistresses took precautions against overexposure—some to the degree of no exposure at all—because beauty was measured on a standard of facial pallor. A woman wrote in 1832 of one acquaintance: "Pretty, too, in spite of her freckles."[48] Freckles were viewed as natural blemishes; tanned skin, on the other hand, was an unforgivable and unnatural departure for the southern lady. Not only were there unfavorable racial connotations associated with darker skin, but ladies preserved their complexion as testifying to their pampered status within an agrarian society. Thomas Jefferson wrote to his younger daughter, Maria, in 1786: "Remember too as a constant charge not to go out without your bonnet because it will make you very ugly and then we should not love you so much."[49] Such strong warnings were not uncommon; southern girls were alternately threatened and cajoled into submission on matters of disposition and dress. A matron wrote to her sister in 1820 of a mutual acquaintance: "Jane has grown very much a very *shamefully tanned* and every one telling her of it. I could not help thinking of you all the evening and wondering if you would neglect your bonnet, and treat your friends about you with so much contempt. For it cannot be called anything else when their friendly advice is not attended to. But I will hope better of you until I hear from you."[50]

Purity ruled appearance and piety ruled thought; the measure of a plantation mistress's propriety was thereby reflected in her every deed and word. Correct behavior laid the foundation for social order. Boys and girls alike were expected to observe the rules that parents enforced with strict adherence to form and decorum. Respect rested firmly on propriety, and as one planter confessed to his wife in 1790: "I have thought frequently that if anything could forever destroy my pride it would be to see my children devoid of Reputation."[51] Bolling Hall expressed equally strong feelings in a letter to his daughter Polly in 1813: "It would make my heart bleed within me if I was to hear of your doing anything wrong—the distress which any improper conduct of yours would occasion in the trust of your parents would be indescribable."[52]

Fathers were concerned about their daughters not only for practical reasons but with respect to their capacity as potential mothers, the spiritual advisers of future families. One planter warned his daughter that "because your father on earth cannot see and know you have a Father in Heaven who sees and knows all things and from whose censure and judgment you cannot escape."[53] Thomas Jefferson, ever mindful of his responsibility to his motherless daughters, had strong opinions on this issue, as on most others. He wrote to his elder daughter, Patsy, in 1783: "If ever you are about to say anything amiss or to do anything wrong consider before hand. You will feel something within you which will tell you it is wrong and ought not to be said or done: this is your conscience, and be sure to obey it. Our maker has given us all this faithful internal Monitor, and if you always obey it, you will always be prepared for the end of the world: or for a much more certain event which is death."[54]

Once again, planters revived Roman imagery to bolster their arguments for female virtue. David Campbell advised his niece: "Propriety is to a woman what the great Roman critic says action is to an Orator: it is the first, the second and the third requisite. A woman may be knowing, active, witty and amusing; but without propriety she cannot be amiable. Propriety is the centre in which all the lines of duty and of agreeableness meet."[55] Duty and agreeableness demanded much of the planter daughter. Traveling, visiting, and social events presented girls with opportunities to amuse themselves, but parents and daughters alike feared that such frivolity might foster a climate of impropriety. Although planter families arranged an array of social activities for marriageable girls, the latter were simultaneously burdened with excessive chaperonage and severe restrictions on their behavior. John Steele reminded his daughter Margaret in 1807 that "discretion in a female is not merely commendable but to pass well and happily through the world it is indispensable."[56]

When daughters were away from home, parents tirelessly warned and advised. A planter wrote to his daughter in 1800, during her visit with relatives: "You must conduct yourself with prudence or you cannot expect to have their esteem."[57] On these visits and during girls' attendance at balls, fathers worried about the improper advances of men. Bolling Hall cautioned his daughter Martha in 1829: "If you should be in company with Gentlemen you will be treated with politeness and respect, but if any unwarrantable liberties in actions or conversations are attempted, be on your guard against such a person, and do not for an instant permit anything which modesty or virtue can disapprove."[58] It was to avoid this eventuality that most parents insisted on chaperones. Bolling Hall instructed another daughter, Polly, about ballroom etiquette: "You should never visit such a place without being accompanied by some respectable friend much older than yourself, whose presence alone would protect you from the smallest insult or suspicion, or neglect."[59]

Traveling alone was absolutely forbidden to females. Chaperonage, ostensibly for their protection, created a system in which women became virtual wards; and the price for this "protection" was high, in isolation and limited mobility.* Society subjected even married women to the practice of male chaperonage during travel. Matrons might not be as carefully guarded at balls and while on family visits, but they were still subject to the rigid code of propriety. Husbands demanded that their wives afford not even the slightest cause for reproach. John Steele enjoined his wife, Mary, in 1796: "Whilst I am doing my best

*See Chapter IX, "Every Woman Was an Island."

to make a fortune, and support an honorable character in life, it is only reasonable, my love, that you shou'd treat me with affection and preserve for my sake, for your own sake, and for the sake of our dear little ones, a sootless and unblemished reputation . . . maintain that dignity of character which you know, I and all men adore in the female sex."[60]

Cultural prescriptions concerning behavior clearly divided along gender lines. Morality ruled in the public domain; both sexes subscribed to the same ethical standards. In the private sphere, however, men might bend or break the rules at their own discretion. Such a division resulted in strict regulation of women's activities and correspondingly lax attitudes toward male affairs. Women responded with a pronouncedly pious social posture, but some men at least indulged in a sordid subculture, while striking a pose of concern for honor and reputation. It is difficult now to ascertain which was the shadow and which the substance of southern men's lives. Official southern "morality" is fairly easy to understand, but the reality of behavior is another matter. Planters habitually cloaked their illicit impulses and activities in secrecy; a few men, however, revealed themselves in diaries or private correspondence. In one such exchange, a planter son writing to his confidant referred to women vulgarly as "meat."[61] Another gentleman confided to a friend in 1831 that his thoughts were centering on women; he even contemplated getting married. In this long letter, he relates the following incident: "I met a girl not long since going to plough barefoot riding astraddle barebacked by a crook in the Road. I got up to her before she discovered me. She had a good foot and ankle, a well turned leg up to the knee. She looked to be about 18 years old, had titties as big as your fist, as round as a butter ball and would have weighed a pound."[62] He was obviously not describing a lady—a suitable object for his matrimonial designs—but rather a female about whom he could frankly admit his carnal desires.

Licentiousness, when it came to fact rather than fantasy, was costly. The recipe books of southern plantation mistresses are full of concoctions to cure gonorrhea. Venereal disease plagued plantation society. One southern gentleman reported in distress: "When on my brother's plantation, I was informed that each of his family servants were suffering from a venereal disease, and I ascertained that each of my brother's children, girls and boys had been informed of it and knew how and from whom it had been acquired."[63] But venereal diseases did not flourish exclusively within slave quarters. Maria Bryan's correspondence recorded one incident: "That wretched Holinbec who, you know, went to Columbus as a missionary, has been preaching and administering the ordinances of the church with the venereal disease upon, until it finally became so bad that concealment was impossible."[64] Such considerations made some men careful about their activities. A young man of Petersburg, Virginia, wrote in 1827 to a friend in medical college in Philadelphia: "I am much surprised at your resolution of never getting married, make haste, and get some 'sheep skin' and come to the old Dominion and if you can resist the pouting lips and cherry cheeks of the Girls, I'll be darned and you know there is plenty of them here. There will be no danger getting the Damn's clap that you speak of being so afraid of."[65]

A look behind the doors of the brothel is rare in the annals of the closed society of the ante-bellum South. William D. Valentine offers such a glance in his diary entry for March 26, 1837. Writing in Bethel, North Carolina, Valentine confessed that he had not knowingly visited the place; rather, he was passing by a house "suspected" of ill-repute and wandered in when he overheard a friend within. Valentine recorded his reactions at length:

> Lo, men, women and cards and shocking obsenity. Several of my respectable acquaintance were here and cordially greeted me. Although shocked and indignant (for some were married men) I concealed my emotion—and to make the best of my situation—I apparently (though in reality did not) participated; this is seeming to countenance what was before me. Modesty and morals were here put to blush indeed. Low life, wretched. The head of this seraglio was in every respect a beautiful girl, a splendid girl to look at. Nature has done much for her in giving her an exquisitely beautiful person and a strong mind—but vice has warped her notions of propriety—she was deficient in one quality and that quality is it which renders the fair sex so ethereal, so much the angel—the virtue of woman. . . . to see this fairest specimen of her workman-

ship prostituted to the lowest, meanest, obscenest practices. . . . my curiosity being satiated with disgust, sorrow and sympathy (for this girl expressed her sensibility of her degradation) I retired.[66]

One presumes that the appalled Mr. Valentine "retired" to his own quarters rather than to one of the chambers of the house. His repeated protestations of innocence are almost comic, although testimony of his earnestness.

The image of southern manhood was probably as significant for plantation culture as that of the lady.[67] Although drunkeness, excessive gambling, or unbridled violence could result in social ostracism, plantation culture maintained an extremely high tolerance for these vices in men—indeed, moderate indulgence in these activities was viewed as conventional masculine recreation. Women not only refrained utterly from such behavior—which would have been seen in them as insupportable—but spent considerable effort counseling their male relatives against these evils. Martha Richardson wrote to her nephew, away at school: "Do not, my dearest James, be lead away by gay* companions to follow the vile and bad habits of men. I have great confidence in you but often fear and tremble for you as you grow and are obliged to enter the world and see all its wicked ways. . . . The more I see and know men the more I dislike them and think they are a vile set of animals."[68] A concerned mother wrote home to her son in Alabama of the evils of Washington, D.C.: "There is much poverty and crime here; yesterday a poor little infant was found under some large stones a short distance from us and in sight of my chamber window! *Crime* brought it into the world and *shame* no doubt caused it to be murdered and cast out *naked!*" She closed her letter to her son, "Beware of the first step *towards vice* and think not that you can say 'thus and no further shall my passions stray.' "[69]

Many plantation mistresses saw sin in terms of increment; they were prepared to cope with small trespasses, yet ever fearful of the uncontrollable momentum of immorality. The journal of Jane Gay Robertson Bernard testifies to her vigilance. In the summer of 1825,

---

*In this nineteenth-century context, "gay" means loose and licentious, with no suggestion of sexual preference.

her husband became overly fond of card playing. He would often stay up all night playing loo, and sometimes remained away from home two nights in a row at card parties. When Jane Bernard finally demanded that her husband stop this gambling spree, he promised her that we would no longer waste time and money away from his family. Having rescued her husband from his dissipation, she calmed her own fears of his moral disintegration.[70] Some women were not so fortunate in their proposed reforms. One bemoaned the fate of a friend whose husband gambled: "Her heart is bursting to think his love for her was all too feeble to save him from vice, and that his confidence never had been hers. She will be the martyr, he may rise again, from a long, painful probation, to the station he has sunk from, but she will never be able to forget how impotent affection was to save."[71]

Gambling was not as virulent a threat as drinking. Young and unmarried planters frequently drank to excess; drunkeness was almost rite of passage for adolescent males. A man on a visit to Tuscaloosa from his native Maine wrote home to his mother: "There is vastly more dissipation here than in N.E. [New England]. It is no disgrace to get intoxicated at public times. I have seen on public days perhaps an hundred at time all partially intoxicated who would act more like maniacs than men."[72] Another northern visitor wrote home from Milledgeville, Georgia, in 1809: "The manners of the young people in this town are corrupt beyond any idea you or I could form. . . . were I to expose myself as unnecessarily and to the extent that others do, I should lose all my money in a week and die the next."[73] Not only Yankees complained of southern dissipation. Southerner Ellen Mordecai wrote to her brother Solomon in 1823 about her visit to Warrenton, North Carolina: "The old prevailing vice predominates. . . . It is shocking to hear of young men scarcely more than boys reeling intoxicated into manhood."[74]

A drunken husband made it impossible for the wife to maintain domestic harmony. Maria Bryan reported to her sister Julia Cumming of a mutual friend: "Mr. Norton it is said (entre nous) drinks a great deal, and though not unkind is far from being the devoted husband he once was. But what is certain that instead of soothing and consoling his wife and family in their misfortunes, he yields not only to gloom, but indulges harsh repinings whose profanity is absolutely shocking."[75] Ann Mordecai wrote to her daughter about a drunkard who had turned wife-beater: "Old Jos. Hinton has whipped his wife and slapped Miss Disheel's face. It created a great excitement and young men talked of riding him on a rail through the streets for it but the old man armed himself and they thought it best to leave him alone."[76]

Men's violence against men was the commonest by-product of drinking. A Yankee observer described this aggressive behavior: "At such times they fight more or less, I saw one short fight musterday about ten steps from the store. It was excessively muddy, you have nothing like it at home. The parties grappled, fell and rolled in the mud some time. . . . In their fights they generally bite, gouge or dirk."[77] The climate of violence often resulted in death to one or more parties. Quarrels and brawling were common, as was ambush or assassination. Rachel O'Conner wrote to her brother, David Weeks, of a local murder: "Tomy Chaney's killed old Mr. Coursey's son with a club. He slipped up behind him when he was eating his supper and struck him dead and then took all his own negroes and run off. Tom was drunk at the time."[78] She also wrote to her sister-in-law, Mary, about another tragedy in her Louisiana parish: "Mrs. McDermit's second son John has been at the point of death for two or three weeks caused by getting into a quarrel at the river with a man that shot him and stabed him shockingly."[79] John Quitman reported an impromptu duel in Clinton, Mississippi, to his wife: "This morning there was a dreadful encounter on the pavement before this house between Gen. Runnels and Jas. B. Marsh in which seven pistols were discharged, both are wounded. . . ."[80] Single combat was far from rare, but the format of this duel was atypical. More commonly, dueling was a serious and ritualized affair.

Francis Bacon once described dueling as "sorcery that enchanteth young men," but southern gentlemen of all ages seemed bewitched. Americans rarely dueled in the seventeenth century, but by the mid-eighteenth century more and more men of the upper class, especially planters, "defended their honor" with pistols at ten paces. The practice was imported from England, mainly by southern planters' sons educated abroad, and gained great popularity in the post-Revolutionary South, especially in Savannah and Charleston. Dueling societies, modeled on London clubs, granted admission only to those who had participated in a duel—a self-perpetuating system in which a man's rank in the organization was based on the number of his encounters.[81]

Southern state legislatures responded to both the frequency and the threat of this personal combat with anti-dueling laws, but measures passed in Georgia in 1809 and Virginia in 1810 were generally disregarded, and duels flourished well into the mid-nineteenth century.

In the popular imagery of the Old South, duels have been mistakenly associated with chivalry. But while medieval jousts were fought to gain a lady's favor, duels centered exclusively on masculine affairs. As William O. Stevens asserts in his study of the subject: "The duel over a woman was exceedingly rare. Men shot each other for gambling, debts, for a dispute . . . almost never, however, did they fight over a woman."[82] Plantation mistresses concertedly opposed the practice, seeing in the ritual senseless violence leading to needless death. One mother lamented to her son in 1821: "How delighted I would be if duelling was done away with in this country but there has been several fought this year. . . . I hope you my dear will never be placed in a situation where you will have to resort to Pistols, horrid things."[83] Martha Richardson gave the following advice to her nephew: "Every gentleman has it in his power to avoid quarrels—he should never give an affront—there are few men so brutal as to seek an opportunity mearly for the love of shooting or being shot at. . . . Keep guard over your temper and recollect that he is the greatest Hero who has learned to conquer himself."[84]

Planters habitually, however, staked their lives on their reputations—and created reputations for themselves by risking their lives. Reckless behavior was one aspect of comradeship for men in southern culture, as the example of Arthur Middleton illustrates. A planter wrote to his brother in 1807 of Middleton's affair of honor: "He found it necessary to go to Georgia to settle a dispute with a Mr. James Pringle which happened at sea, at a card table. The business was fortunately terminated without bloodshed, though they each fired three times. Arthur and Mr. J. Pringle are upon as good terms as ever, and I have met them several times lately walking arm in arm as if they had never been at variance.[85] But not all duels ended so amicably; often one of the duelists would receive a wound, which sometimes proved fatal. One woman reported an even more tragic encounter: "Have you heard of Mrs. Pearson's misfortune in the Death of her youngest son, he was killed in a Duel—his adversary as soon as he had kill'd him blew his own brains out. . . ."[86] When a gentleman had been challenged on what he felt to be unreasonable or frivolous grounds, he might ignore the challenge and keep his good name, if the challenger dropped his suit. But in general a southern planter was honor-bound to accept the challenge of a duel, if he had no family. A gentleman was routinely excused from participation, however, if he claimed family responsibility. As a woman explained concerning her brother: "He is a husband and a Father and the laws of this much famed Code of Honour does not make it binding on him to accept the challenge of any madman or fool that may envy him, or his happiness."[87] More often than not, a family claimed the gentleman's responsibility to them, rather than the other way around.

The plight of Ann McDonald in November 1828 aptly illustrates the burden imposed by the code of honor on southern women. McDonald and his doctor fell into discord; his wife feared a duel. Ann McDonald wrote to her husband's friend J. L. Lamar, begging him to intercede to prevent bloodshed; dread and despair provoked her "perhaps unwarranted liberty" in addressing him. As a woman, even as McDonald's wife, she was helpless, "for if I introduce the subject, he either avoids answering or leaves me." Her frustration led her to repudiate the code of honor, "which might be said, truly said, to be founded in *Injustice, Revenge, Ambition, Pride*—In short it might be justly defined the opposite of Civic and Divine Law." She went on to call dueling murder, and "although the perpetrator (vainly) strives to consecrate his crime by throwing around it the imposing garb of Honor . . . such argument is only chaff against the wind." She concluded that "to be a brave man one need not be a murderer."[88]

The nature of southern morality forced women into rigid and exacting roles. They were protected, yet at the same time confined, by interlocking systems of patriarchal authority. Men further confounded women with contradictory and often hypocritical challenges: to fulfill the belle ideal, to ensure the spiritual welfare of all plantation dwellers, to turn a blind eye on male transgressions. Myth, ideal, and duty weighed heavily on plantation women.

These women were merely prisoners in disguise. However comfortable their surroundings, however elaborate the rhetoric that celebrated them, however sheltered they were from the market economy and class oppression, plantation mistresses spent much of their lives under constraint and in isolation: fettered nonetheless.

VI

THE FALLEN WOMAN

Men's ambivalence toward female sexuality had diverse psychological and practical consequences in the Old South. Clearly sexual concerns underscored much paternal advice on behavior. C. A. Hull's letters to his niece Sarah Thomas reflected such fears. In 1817, Sarah was leaving her home to become a teacher, and Hull's patriarchal role led him to send her this vivid warning about her new surroundings: "I view you on the pinnacle of an awful precipice. . . . Peculiarly delicate is the crisis, and one false step forever blasts the fame of a female. . . . malevolence is so predominantly in the human heart, that in all, it displays the devouring jaws of a mighty Malestrom ready on every touch to destroy the vessel that per chance may be cast into the whirlpool."[1] Hull's metaphor depicted the explicit and implicit concerns of the planter class: actual impropriety of any sort was inexcusable, but even a hint of sexual suspicion would ruin a woman forever.[2]

One of the important goals, therefore, of the countless constraints to which women were subjected was to render them, in effect, desexualized. The medical profession of the nineteenth century supported this impulse.[3] In 1840, George Skinner diagnosed sexual arousal in women as dangerous outside of its proper and limited sphere. Too much sexual stimulation (the degree remained unspecified) was classified as a disease: *furor uterinus*. In his *Practical Compendium of Midwifery*, Skinner suggested camphor compresses and cold-water enemas as medically appropriate for such women, for instance one patient who "had the most irresistible disposition to lasciviousness imaginable. . . . when alone she could not desist from rubbing the parts until she became exhausted and bathed in perspiration." The good doctor also counseled seaside bathing and country air for women in similar distress. He treated a lady who "had always been brought up virtuously, and had hitherto been well disposed; but now a man could not pass without her experiencing those sensations which were alone her husband's right."[4] Sexual feelings were bound up with moral prescriptions, social obligations, and biological consequences. Desire was underscored by dread for the majority of women.

Perhaps fascinated with that which hints of the forbidden, Southerners seemed to report a surprising number of sexual indiscretions. In 1779, James Iredell wrote to his wife Hannah of "a maiden about the age of 30, one of the sect called Quakers and Resident with the prim Mr. Peal and herself remarkable for the most strait-laced affection, lately offended him with the sight of a too big belly for which she was indebted to his son and has since been expelled from the Father's house." Iredell added, with easy scorn: "They say it is only a repetition of an old disorder of which her conversion never thoroughly cured her."[5] Bridal pregnancy, common throughout the eighteenth century, declined during the nineteenth. Although the mishap was frowned upon, plantation mistresses seemed to withhold condemnation of pregnant brides,[6] even though such activity before marriage could lead to disaster—a break between the couple rather than the legalization of their union.[7] A wet nurse in the Randolph family in 1819 was involved in a scandal of more tragic dimensions: "Your suspicions about Susan have all been verified. The week before Sister P. came away she had a child which was undoubtedly Emerie's. She had it one night without any assistance at all and they supposed Killed it for they found it stuffed in the cock loft the next morning and it breathed after they found it. Did you ever hear of anything so horrible?"[8] Although men might be condemned for sexual misconduct, males rarely suffered the utter social ostracism to which "fallen" women were irrevocably condemned.

Only if a man seduced a female "under his protection" did the southern moral code shift the burden of guilt onto the male transgressor. Seduction was a threat of which women were constantly warned; young girls were urged to be on the lookout for these vile betrayers, referred to in popular literature as serpents in the dove's nest. But young women also put their trust in gentlemen, especially those within their domestic orbit. It was unusual but not unheard of for men to seduce their wards. A schoolgirl wrote to her aunt in 1824 of an illicit affair: "Betsy Throckmorton of N. Orleans originally from Natches has a child, Mr. Cose, her *sister's* husband is the Father of it. . . . I believe I shall form the same resolution you have never to be surprised at anything that happens, especially if a man has anything to do with it. What do you think ought to be done with Cose and he wants killing as Miss Bird used to say and that is too good for him. She was under his protection, but he is *man* and *that is* enough."[9] The Lees of Virginia were similarly subjected to scandal when Robert E. Lee's half brother, Henry—known as "Black Horse Harry Lee"—seduced his wife's sister. Gossip erupted when this sister-in-law gave birth to a child, whom Henry had presumably fathered, while she was living in the Lees' home. Social pressures as well as financial troubles forced Henry Lee to abandon his estate at Westmoreland. He died abroad, an exile in disgrace. The Cose and Lee scandals were unusual in that the men suffered at least as much as the women compromised by the sexual liaisons. But in both cases these planters were punished, not for seduction, but for the betrayal of a code and a trust—for debauching young girls who were under fatherly and honor-bound protection. Their crimes were against the patriarchal premise rather than against the women whom they had ruined.

Numerous and diverse scandals rocked the planter class during the years following the American Revolution. Specific case study of three notorious affairs will follow, because they shed light on a variety of moral problems in the ante-bellum South. These incidents were neither typical nor average, yet the details of each illustrate certain central issues of plantation culture and moral ideology. Crucial to all three incidents is the exaggerated price in suffering exacted on the women involved. As Dolley Madison wrote to her niece Mary in 1834: "Our sex are ever the losers when they stem the torrent of public opinion."[10]

The first of these affairs illustrates how common a problem seduction was, especially during wartime. The indiscretion of Rachel Warrenton, a motherless Virginia belle, had devastating results. In 1780, the Viscount Rochambeau and his ships visited the port of York. Mildred Smith wrote at the time to her childhood friend Elizabeth Ambler: "It is well for my loved Betsy that she is removed from these scenes of amusement and dissipation." She was additionally pleased that her loved Betsy Ambler was away from the negative influence of Rachel Warrenton, with her "bewitching talents" and "guileless heart."[11] Two years later, Mildred Smith's suspicions about Rachel Warrenton were proved true. Smith reported to her friend Betsy of Rachel's ruin: "She is—oh, how shall I repeat, she is indeed lost to everything that is dear to women." Contrary to her protestations, Mildred Smith was most anxious to repeat that Rachel Warrenton had given birth to a son following her liaison with the Viscount Rochambeau. Lest Betsy Ambler fail to recognize the culprit in the affair, Smith pointed out: "Why blame the Viscount had she but kept in being the dignity of her sex." Rachel Warrenton was credited with the sole excuse that she had been robbed of her mother at an early age and so perhaps had not been well enough schooled in the "heinousness of such departure from Female rectitude."

Family and friends alike were scandalized. Rachel Warrenton and her sister Camille were the nieces and wards of Susannah Riddle. Shattered by the affair, Riddle asked her nephew in England to approach the Rochambeau family in France, in order to coerce the viscount into returning to "make an honourable woman" of Rachel. But the boy grew up without a father. Miss Riddle died before being reconciled with her niece, although she had developed an affection for the illegitimate child, Louis Warrenton—whose name was later Anglicized to "Lewis."

Warrenton received a legacy from his Great-aunt Riddle, and the executor of her estate, Jaquelin Ambler, supervised his upbringing and education. Warrenton entered the navy and became a hero after his exploits in the War of 1812. He went on to be a career officer and to supervise naval operations in Virginia and Florida, married a girl from a respectable Virginia family, and successfully escaped social ostracism, in spite of his illegitimacy. As for the viscount, he never acknowledged his son. When approached in Paris by Rachel Warrenton's representatives, "he seemed rather to avoid everything that led to the subject appearing not to understand it at all." It would be safe to assume that Rochambeau endured no hardship for his part in the scandal.

This was not the case, however, for Rachel Warrenton. While sympathetic relatives pampered the son and quickly forgot the father, the mother's transgressions caused her great suffering. Elizabeth Ambler wrote to Mildred Smith of her friend's plight: "Rachel, having no pretensions to beauty or wit, had grown up that her good humor and hospitality would amply supply the deficiencies; alas what are these qualities or any other without that precious discretion which once dispensed leaves woman prey to every trifling seducer. . . ." After falling victim to Rochambeau, she had no hopes of a respectable match. Her family despised her for the scandal she had brought about; her sister scorned and ridiculed her, and her aunt disinherited her. Rachel Warrenton married a worker, had two daughters, and lived out her life in poverty and perhaps shame. Through her single act of indiscretion, she lost position, wealth, and a comforting circle of family and friends.

But seduction was not always a by-product of war. Sexual misconduct was at the core of the "Bizarre scandal," which erupted in Virginia during the winter of 1792–1793. Yet this particular affair did not remain the concern merely of a small enclave of family and friends, for the furor among the planter gentry resulted in widespread controversy, an eventual public hearing, and gossip that continued for years following the incident. This particular episode raises myriad moral issues as well as affording a historical puzzle, in that scholars still disagree on the facts in this web of conflicting accounts.[12]

On April 29, 1793, Richard Randolph was examined by the Cumberland County Court regarding reports of his murder of the illegitimate child of Ann (Nancy) Cary Randolph. Because he was rumored to be the father of the child, and because Nancy was his wife's unmarried younger sister living under his roof, the inquiry produced no small sensation among the Virginia plantation aristocracy. The incestuous aspect was compounded by the fact that Judith and Nancy were Richard's first cousins as well.

In 1791, sixteen-year-old Nancy Randolph had moved to Bizarre, the Randolph plantation, to live with her sister Judith and Judith's husband, Richard. While living at Bizarre, Nancy became romantically involved with Theodorick, Richard's brother, but before they could marry, Theodorick died of consumption in February 1792. That summer, several family members noted both a change in Nancy Randolph's shape that suggested pregnancy, and Richard Randolph's new and excessive devotion to his sister-in-law, which suggested an intrigue. When Richard, Judith, and Nancy Randolph visited their cousin Randolph Harrison in October, an incident occurred that threw family and friends into turmoil for months to come.

Sometime during the night of October 1, Nancy Randolph fell ill. Her brother-in-law Richard attended her in her chamber. After a few days in bed at the Harrisons', she had recovered and was able to travel. But on the morning of October 2, slaves at the Harrison plantation had found the remains of a newborn white child or fetus on the woodpile. Stories soon spread. Some people speculated that Nancy had miscarried; others believed she had induced an abortion. Still others suggested that Richard Randolph had committed infanticide. Most agreed that he must be the father of the child.

By January of 1793, rumors raged throughout the county, and the several branches of the Randolph clan were alarmed at the abuse of the family name. In February and March, Richard Randolph conferred with family members about the scandal. He felt that the rumors amounted to slander, and wished to face his accusers in a court of law. On March 29, 1793, he published a letter to prompt his enemies to take legal action, but the scandal still failed to subside. Exactly one month later, witnesses were called to testify to the events leading up to the incident of the previous October 1. All those present at the Harrison household that night, with the exception of Richard and Nancy, offered testimony, as did such family members as John Randolph (Richard's brother) and Martha Jefferson Randolph (Thomas Jefferson's daughter and Nancy's sister-in-law). Judith Randolph was perhaps the most persuasive figure, in that she wholly denied any wrongdoing on the part of either her husband or her sister. Although the charges were dismissed, scandal haunted the principals for the rest of their lives.

Richard remained under a cloud for his three remaining years, and died under mysterious circumstances. Although officially he succumbed to a fever, some persons held that Judith had poisoned him, while others believed Nancy had administered a fatal dose of medicine. Innuendo and gossip continued to plague the two Randolph women many years after the alleged indiscretion and infanticide. Judith was embittered. Family and friends testified to her devotion to her two sons and her loyalty to her husband, but all agreed that after a brief attempt at keeping up a good front, Judith demonstrated an unhealthy detestation of her younger sister. Nancy herself testified that she was no better than a servant in the Bizarre household; she confessed in 1803: "My employments generally consist of some species of drudgery or needlework."[13]

Nancy Randolph, much like Rachel Warrenton, lived in shame. Shunned by her own siblings, she was forced to depend upon the sullen generosity of her sister Judith and Richard's brother, John Randolph, both of whom openly blamed her for bringing dishonor and unhappiness upon the family. She endured her miserable life at Bizarre with infrequent visits to either her brother Thomas Mann Randolph at Monticello or her sister Jane. But in the spring of 1804, John Randolph accused Nancy of an illicit liaison with a slave. Accounts conflict about the exact circumstances, but Nancy Randolph, then twenty-nine, was ordered away from Bizarre. She spent the remainder of 1804 visiting family and friends. Her letters from this period indicate that either she was thrown on the mercy of persons not kindly disposed toward her or, like Edith Wharton's Lily Bart, subjected to rude advances and improper proposals. During 1805 and 1806 she was continually adrift among the Virginia plantations of her friends and relatives. John Randolph continued to harass her, and sent letters accusing her of "immodest conduct" and other transgressions. Finally, one of her brothers gave her enough money for her to be able to secure her own accommodations in Richmond in 1807. But this situation was short-lived, as John Randolph spread rumors that she had set herself up as a prostitute. His slander and her own despair drove her out of Virginia.

In the autumn of 1807, Nancy Randolph turned up in Newport, Rhode Island. Perhaps she sought refuge in the home of her third cousin, Richard K. Randolph, who resided there. In 1808, she was living in a boardinghouse in Fairfield, Connecticut. She wrote to her friend and guardian St. George Tucker, "I have long ago thrown myself on that tide of Fate which cannot be stemmed regardless whither the current may carry me." She closed the letter: "Should any Lady going in the spring to England want an attendant, I shall endeavor to procure the place."[14] But Nancy Randolph was rescued from her Connecticut boardinghouse by a pleasanter fate than a European tour as a paid companion. On a visit to New York in October of 1808, she met an old family friend, Gouverneur Morris. On this occasion, Morris "expressed a wish that some reduced gentlewoman would keep his house, as the lower class of housekeepers of his provoked the servants to a riot in his dwelling."[15] In 1809 she moved to Morisanna to serve as Morris's housekeeper, and on Christmas Day of that year, she and Morris were married. It was the first marriage for both the fifty-seven-year-old Morris and his bride of thirty-four.

Unfortunately, even a respectable marriage and motherhood (she bore Morris a son in 1813) did not shield Nancy Randolph from attacks on her character. During visits to Washington, the Morrises suffered John Randolph's ill-humor and social slights. In 1814 the entire episode was revived when Randolph, ever true to his southern moral code, circulated a letter reiterating his charges against Nancy Randolph Morris. John Randolph, who had lost both his brothers and was to remain a bachelor all his life, felt strongly that Nancy had ruined his brother Richard, wrecked his sister-in-law Judith's happiness, and impugned the honor of his dead brother Theodorick. Such a woman, Randolph believed, deserved neither a good name nor domestic contentment. When she accomplished both, twenty years after the Bizarre scandal, Randolph lashed out with accusations to stir up old memories; immodesty, lasciviousness, and fornication with a black were the charges in his diatribe against her. Whether Nancy Randolph was guilty of these sins or not, she stood condemned; because once a woman's reputation stood in doubt, she was no longer protected by the code of ethics. In 1815 she composed a reply to Randolph, which also circulated. These attacks and countercharges resurrected the whole scandal, twenty years after the actual incidents had first shocked the Virginia aristocracy.

Another Virginia woman found herself at the center of an antebellum scandal that resulted in the tragic deaths of all three of the parties involved. The Beauchamp scandal in Kentucky in 1826 revolved around the seduction of Ann Cooke by Colonel Solomon Sharp.

Once again, the facts of the case are in question. Conflicting accounts afford the historian few clues for solving the mystery, but provided rich material for poets and novelists: Edgar Allan Poe, William Gilmore Simms, and Robert Penn Warren all wrote works based on the "Kentucky tragedy."

Ann Cooke was born in 1786, the daughter of a Virginia planter. She received an excellent and liberal education. After both her sister and her father died, she and her mother moved to Kentucky to live with relatives. Sometime in 1820 she gave birth to a son, "without benefit of clergy." According to Ann Cooke and many of the local townspeople in Bowling Green, she was a victim of seduction. Cooke claimed that she had yielded to the amorous designs of Colonel Solomon Sharp, a prominent Kentucky politician. She alleged that Sharp had promised to marry her but had deserted her for a more advantageous match. Dishonored, she removed herself and her child to a secluded farm in Simpson County, Kentucky.

In 1821, Jeroboam Beauchamp, the eighteen-year-old son of a local planter, became attached to Ann Cooke, initially drawn by his sympathy for the wronged woman. He wrote in 1826 that seduction "was a species of dishonour which, from my earliest recollection, had ever excited my most violent reprobation."[16] Cooke at first rejected Beauchamp's attentions, but eventually found comfort in a romantic liaison with this suitor, seventeen years her junior and full of youthful ardor. Beauchamp was fired both with passion for Ann Cooke and with a desire for revenge upon her seducer. In 1822 the illegitimate child died, and Cooke became even more emotionally dependent upon Beauchamp. In 1824 they were married, but remained intent on punishing Sharp for his seduction and slander—Sharp had accused Cooke of loose moral character and said that her child, far from being his, was in fact a mulatto. Beauchamp, determined to murder Sharp for his villainy, plotted his vengeance and in 1826 stabbed Sharp to death. Following his trial and conviction, Beauchamp wanted to explain his actions to the world and wrote a lengthy confession: "It will teach a certain class of *heroes*, who make their glory to consist in triumphs over the virtue and the happiness of worthy unfortunate orphan females, to pause sometimes in their mad career, and reflect, that though the deluded victim of their villainy, may have no father to protect or revenge her, yet some friendly arm may sooner or later be nerved by her to avenge her blighted prospects."[17] He felt that his wife had been "buried in a living grave."

Ann's life had indeed become an obsession with honor and vengeance. Even after her wedding, she was unable to rid herself of her shame: "Can marriage erase the deep and indelible stain on my character, or make a malignant and envious world forget the folly or misfortune of a poor erring woman? Can marriage heal up the wide and yawning wounds of a lacerated and tortured heart. . . . Sorrow and pain, and mortification are my portion here. . . ."[18] She believed Sharp's seduction had made her unworthy of her husband and that only Sharp's death would free her from this unworthiness. After Beauchamp was sentenced to hang, Ann Cooke Beauchamp felt she had no reason to go on living. She visited her condemned husband in his cell, and they devised another plot: a double suicide. Sometime during their last days together, they took overdoses of laudanum, but failed to poison themselves. On the morning of his execution, Beauchamp procured a knife, stabbed his wife, and then attempted to stab himself to death. Ann Beauchamp bled to death in her husband's cell, but Beauchamp died on the gallows. Their deaths were the pathetic and gruesome consequences of "an affair of honor."

Beauchamp and his wife were both aware of the melodramatic aspects of their tragedy, and composed prose and poetry describing their emotions and motives—even planning their own epitaphs. Ann Cooke Beauchamp wrote the following verses, to be engraved on the tombstone of their double grave:

Daughter of virtue! moist thy tear,
This tomb of love and honor claim;
For thy defence the husband here,
Laid down in youth his life and fame.

His wife disdained a life forlorn,
Without her heart's lov'd honor'd Lord,
Then reader, here their fortunes mourn,
Who for their love, their life blood pour'd.[19]

Following her death, *The Letters of Ann Cooke* appeared. Although these letters may or may not be authentic, the sentiments expressed in the volume reflect the genuine concerns of the period. In the preface, the individual who "collected" these letters for publication indicates his motives: "The fate of Mrs. Beauchamp will serve as an example to those of her sex who, whatever be their cultivation or their talents, suffer themselves to be too much under the influence of feeling and passion; or, who repose too confidently on their own strength, and the honour of men."[20]

Death was the honorable sequel to seduction for a woman. Although a man might deny his role and divert attacks upon his character, a woman could not escape censure and blame when she had an illegitimate child. Later marriage failed to erase the social stigma and restore a woman to any measure of respectability. Sexual indiscretion, as men clearly warned and then proceeded to ensure, ruined a female forever. The double standard imposed sharply differentiated degrees of moral censure on the seducer and the seduced. A verse from *The Vicar of Wakefield*, found in both the correspondence of Elizabeth Jaquelin Ambler and the preface to Ann Cooke's letters, illustrates the cultural moralization of seduction:

> *When lovely woman stoops to folly*
> *And finds too late that men betray,*
> *What charm can soothe her melancholy?*
> *What art can wash her guilt away?*

Woman's despair is aptly described in that stanza, but her fate is outlined in the one that follows:

> *The only art her guilt to cover,*
> *To hide her shame from every eye,*
> *To give repentance to her Lover,*
> *And wring his bosom, is—to die.*

The southern planter shared Oliver Goldsmith's belief that once a woman lost her virtue, only death could release her from a life-sentence of shame.

In all three of these scandals, both men and women were at the mercy of gossip and rumor, yet the women suffered decidedly more than the men in the public arena of moral dispute. Females were required to be above suspicion, without a blemish: the spotless vessels of moral purity. Men were expected to transgress discreetly upon occasion. More important, men could avenge their own honor and erase any lasting social stigma in most cases, but a woman without virtue was open to public abuse of her name and private disregard of her feelings for the rest of her life. If a gentleman attached himself to a woman who had fallen from grace, he subjected himself to a variety of problems. He might have to endure the slights and jests of his peers, as did Gouverneur Morris for his marriage to Nancy Randolph. He might be forced to avenge his wife's honor, like Jeroboam Beauchamp, which could have tragic consequences. If a man was the instigator of a woman's indiscretion, he might lose his life at the hands of an avenger, as did the unfortunate Colonel Sharp. But far more commonly, the fate of seducers was mild. Most, like the Viscount Rochambeau, escaped unscathed. Society allowed these men sexual indiscretion without the censure of lifelong shame. Women were afforded no such luxury.

Public hounding and private misery shadowed these women, and their shame drove some to death, as in the frenzied example of Ann Cooke Beauchamp. Neither wealth nor family could alleviate their reduced social standing. Although men might pretend to busy themselves defending women's honor, the honor code served their own interests rather than those of women. The double standard reinforced this inequity by allowing men sexual license while preventing even the most reformed of women a restoration of her good character. Southern society could not afford compassion for the fallen woman.

Honor was a man's prerogative. Honor was his to possess, whether or not he obeyed the moral code of his culture. Honor was also his to bestow, in his denial or defense of a woman's virtue. The same swords that were drawn to protect a woman's good name could just as easily be turned against a dishonorable woman. And whereas men could survive being branded "indecent" following immoral conduct, women could not withstand the tarnish of a "fall from grace." Either a woman obeyed the rigid restrictions of her freedom, submitted to the dictates of a complex code of behavior, and fulfilled the patriarchal ideal, or she risked ruin. A woman's fall plummeted her to a position of irremedial dishonor and unmitigated regret. If morality kept southern women imprisoned, then those females who fell from grace were consigned to the lowest dungeon—to which society threw away the key.

VII

EQUALLY THEIR DUE

*I*n 1819, Maria Campbell, mistress of "Montcalm," Abingdon, Virginia, wrote her young cousin Mary Hume at Salem Academy, Salem, North Carolina:

> In the days of our forefathers it was considered only necessary to learn a female to read the Bible—the ballance of her time was spent in domestic employments. They, to be sure, were very necessary. But why should a whole life be thus spent. . . . Things are happily taking a change. Daughters as well as sons are now thought of by the fond parent. Education is considered equally their due.[1]

Maria Campbell had benefitted from the dramatic educational transition that followed the American Revolution. Born in 1785, she eventually married planter-entrepreneur David Campbell, who later served as governor of Virginia. Sent to school as a young girl, Maria Campbell cherished her education as a source of strength and comfort in her many years of isolation on her husband's plantations, childless and often alone during Campbell's long political career.

The shift in attitudes toward education did not reflect a decline in piety so much as a rising tide of republicanism that the dissemination of Enlightenment values and an outburst of patriotism during the period fostered. To build a new, liberty-loving nation, Southerners and New Englanders alike promoted female education. This was essentially a compromise, which allowed the socialization of women into "true womanhood"[2] in lieu of their participation in politics and, even more specifically, agitation for women's rights.[3] The campaign to improve women's education was linked to the heightened awareness of the importance of their reproductive role, rather than to any improvement in their political or economic status.

Until the late eighteenth century, planter daughters—like their northern counterparts—studied the Scriptures and pious texts while their brothers received rigorous, wide-ranging training in classics, philosophy, history, and mathematics. The emphasis on Bible reading led to semiliteracy. Although most plantation mistresses in the eighteenth century could read, fewer were able to write. Following the Revolution, many fathers wrote letters to their daughters away at school for mothers able only to dictate their sentiments.[4]

The rise of female education in the early national era, however, transformed the possibilities for many women. Americans knew full well that education maintains class status.[5] Upper-class women in most cultures have received special training, both moral and intellectual. While a man in ante-bellum America could achieve upward social mobility by the accumulation of wealth or political influence, such self-promotion was not possible for women. Although any woman could "marry up" into society (an avenue open equally to males), a woman's future status could be importantly determined by the nature of her education. Men of the planter class saw good sense in cultivating accomplished as well as ornamental daughters, for education gave these girls a concrete advantage on the marriage market. Parents, therefore, bought their female offspring the best possible education, even if it meant economic sacrifice, because the material reward of a successful match potentially offset any temporary financial setback. As one father described it; "A girl will be more respected with an education than with wealth."[6] During the first fifty years of American education following independence, parents turned away from the more "genteel" instruction of the Colonial period; indeed, many spoke disparagingly of the style of refinement of their forebears.[7] Although parents and educators agreed that this instruction was designed solely to improve women in their roles as wives and mothers, a reinterpretation of this role led to a virtual revolution in female education.

This revolt had its intellectual foundation in England, where, during the second half of the seventeenth century, a series of authors attacked the then-current system of British female education, proposing radical change. In the course of the eighteenth century, the education of women in England improved qualitatively and quantitatively. In the last quarter of that century, moreover, England experienced significant political and intellectual ferment, marked by a richly productive literature of reform. Out of this emerged two of the most important theorists of women's education: Hannah More and Mary Wollstonecraft. Both started out as teachers, publishing educational texts of similar substance and structure in their early careers, but while More eventually wrote *Village Politics* (1792) as an antidote to Tom Paine, Wollstonecraft's *Vindication of the Rights of Woman*—published in the same year—displays undisguised admiration of Paine. In spite of their political differences, both authors agreed that the education of women was of vital intellectual concern, and advanced identical arguments on many related issues.

Both More and Wollstonecraft celebrated "virtue." Although each had her own interpretation of the concept and its social application to women, they deplored the degradation of women that they witnessed in their society. Hannah More's *Strictures on the Modern System of Female Education* (1799) condemned the "injustice which is often exercised towards women, first to give them a very defective Education and then to expect from them the most undeviating purity of Conduct."[8] More emphasized that the education of children was woman's acknowledged power, and Wollstonecraft concurred that, after a woman's duty to herself, "the next in point of importance, as citizens, is that which includes so many, of a mother."[9] Both authors criticized the money and energy wasted on "frivolous" female training because men wanted to create companions for themselves, after a pattern of the men's own choosing.

Within a generation, educators had popularized and promoted these theories throughout the United States. Although Wollstonecraft acquired the reputation in ante-bellum America of an "immoral and dangerous" woman, her work was nevertheless widely circulated. Planter William Barry wrote to his daughter in 1826 about the infamous Beauchamp trial: "His wretched wife is a living example of the pernicious influence on the female mind of the detestable doctrines of Mary Wollstonecraft whose disciple she is."[10] Hannah More's works were best sellers in England and America, and she enjoyed a tremendous vogue, especially in the South. Southerners took particular interest in her ideas, which mirrored the educational precepts of the planter class, and discussed her work in their correspondence.

During the eighteenth century in America, the burden of educating children fell on the mother; just as the female parent was expected to nurse, feed, clothe, and minister to the health of her young, so was she entrusted with their secular and spiritual instruction. One southern gentleman wrote to an acquaintance in England of the advantage of the American system: "In our country where the fatigue and trouble of educating their children are necessarily imposed on the Mother, perhaps the pernicious effects of bad examples are not to be so much dreaded as in those countries where Nurses and Governesses who are usually uninterested in the future characters of their pupils are more common."[11] But southern women in the post-Revolutionary era— undereducated as a group, and with little time to devote themselves to the classroom—were ill-equipped to fulfill these responsibilities. One woman recounted why she had felt the necessity for a tutor for her five children: "The interruptions from housekeeping for a black family (and often for a very large white) together with sickness and the claims of society made their progress slow."[12] Even when they wanted to teach their children themselves, the increasing demands of household and plantation management denied plantation mistresses the necessary time.[13]

Mothers coped with these problems in a variety of ways. Older brothers and sisters who had been sent to boarding school were often asked to give basic instruction to their siblings during the holidays.[14] Parents encouraged their own unmarried sisters to live with them to assist with the schooling, an arrangement which strengthened kinship ties; many children became especially attached to tutor-aunts. This family home instruction was, however, very elementary; plantation women commonly limited themselves to teaching the alphabet and geography.

As more sophisticated instruction was needed, planters employed schoolmasters, who often taught on several plantations, staying with various families by rotation.[15] All tutors in this period were male, and they concentrated their efforts on the preparation of male children for further education. Planters after the turn of the nineteenth century began to hire female teachers to school both male and female pupils. These governesses were generally young, never married, and northern born and educated. Philadelphia women, especially, sought positions in planter homes; many southern families had married into wealthy Philadelphia families, which may account for the pattern. Most teachers, like Virginian Eliza Robertson, who supported her invalid mother when there was no one else to care for her, were motivated by economic necessity: "The severe change of times which our country has experienced for a considerable while render'd it necessary that I should exert myself. . . . Dr. Powell boards me and give me $500 for teaching his daughters and a few others of their connections a year."[16] Suitable instructors were a rare commodity: "I have been fortunate in getting a young lady to instruct my girls and Joseph," wrote Delia Bryan in 1819. "She is a daughter of a clergyman, and has received the first education. She understands the Latin and Greek and is the best arithmatician and grammarian for a woman I ever saw."[17] As the significance and scope of education grew during the post–Revolutionary years, home instruction for older children declined in popularity. In the South, as in New England, 1800 marked the beginning of the age of the academy.

The first boarding schools for girls started out as mere "adventure schools"; much as in England, widows and spinsters in urban centers would hang out shingles and advertise in the local papers for pupils.[18] But these day schools, with their limited curricula, fell short of the requirements of the times. Soon boarding schools were founded to provide suitable facilities for the planter daughter's education, as well as a sophisticated course of instruction. While most academies sprang up in thickly settled areas, some were located where major arteries between the coast and the backwoods formed crossroads; such establishments could draw their students from plantations throughout the South.

The earliest of these successful academies in the South were founded by refugees from Santo Domingo. Following the Haitian Revolution, both Madame Datty and Madame Talvanne (variously spelled Talvande and Talvant) established schools in Charleston, South Carolina. Although Anne Manson Talvanne outlasted her rival, maintaining her school until her death in the 1850s (Mary Boykin Chesnut was one of her pupils), Julia Datty cultivated an exclusive clientele, including the Manigaults, the Coupers, and many other wealthy lowcountry planters. In Washington County, Georgia, another refugee, Madame Dugas, founded an academy. These women primarily taught French, but also offered a standard curriculum that included reading, writing, geography, and mathematics to ensure a steady stream of pupils.

Roman Catholic schools multiplied during the ante-bellum era. The oldest ongoing institution—the Ursuline Academy of New Orleans, founded in 1727—was assured uninterrupted continuation by President Jefferson upon the American accession of Louisiana in 1803. The Nazareth and Loretta academies were founded in Kentucky in 1808. These schools earned scholarly reputations and attracted numerous non-Catholic pupils. In 1821 one student wrote to her father, politician John J. Crittenden: "The Sisters are becoming vaine, they are too sure of patronage and if they do not change they will ruin their school."[19]

Perhaps the most famous and widely praised institution during this era was the Salem Academy, located at the Moravian settlement of Salem, North Carolina. The school opened its doors to non-Moravians in 1802. By 1808, the school educated an average of forty pupils per term; by 1835, the number had grown to 120. Many ministers founded academies. These establishments were nominally nonsectarian, but all fell heavily under the influence of their founders.[20] In Georgia, the Mount Zion Academy of Hancock County, a coeducational preparatory school, was organized in 1812 by the Reverend Nathan S. Beman. In 1810, the Reverend Mr. Turner and Mrs. Turner founded a school at Fayette, North Carolina: "Near two hundred pupils of both sexes are ably instructed in every useful branch of education."[21]

The widespread interest in female education after the turn of the century provided a new market for teachers. After obtaining their education, some single men sought to support themselves by establishing a school, since tutoring within an individual family infrequently offered the economic luxury of supporting a family of one's own.[22] Widows found schools a rewarding way to supplement their income, if they were able to offer a sophisticated course of study. A Mrs. Stanley of Athens, Georgia, succeeded by teaching rhetoric, philosophy, chemistry, and arithmetic to her seventy-five scholars.[23] Equally enterprising were the men, and especially the women, who moved to the South from New England. Many well-educated Northerners established schools, rather than tutor in a family, in order to live more independently. In 1817, William Elliott of Beaufort, South Carolina, reported: "Miss Thomson—a Lady from New York is come to establish a female Academy here. Polished in her manners, from association with the first people in New York—acquainted with most modern languages, an author and professed blue-stocking—she has made quite a sensation in our little town."[24] Once individuals launched academies, many communities rallied to provide financial support for the local, yet private, institutions;[25] indeed, communities would often supply the impetus to establish them in the first place.

Community spirit was a potent force for the founding of women's academies during the early decades of the nineteenth century, both North and South. The case of Raleigh, North Carolina, provides an excellent example. In the spring of 1802, several leading citizens sponsored a subscription drive to raise funds in order to build the school by year's end. In April of 1804, the trustees advertised in Boston and Philadelphia papers for a principal. The academy set tuition and began to hire faculty in June of that year. By 1809 the Raleigh Academy was a solvent institution.[26] In Winchester, Tennessee, the West Tennessee Female Academy funded itself with a sophisticated system: "The capital necessary to put the seminary in motion was divided into shares like bank stock. . . . The stockholders elect the president and trustees who have the management of the institution. . . . The pecuniary interest of the stockholders as well as their pride induces them to see that the seminary is well managed."[27]

Community leaders in Washington, Mississippi, supported Elizabeth Academy, founded in 1818 to promote and maintain civilization in their frontier society. Within five years the school was approaching financial ruin. The trustees submitted a petition for aid to the state legislature. The five male members of the board couched their plea for funds in deferential and considered terms. They pointed out that mothers gave children their first lessons, that virtue was best guaranteed by education, and last, that Elizabeth Academy was "an institution, calculated in its nature to reflect, under proper care, so much benefit upon the state." In addition, a petition—no doubt written by the co-superintendent of the academy, Caroline Thayer—was submitted by a committee of fifty-eight ladies. This brief document offered essentially the same arguments, but with a slightly different emphasis. Concerning motherhood, it asserted: "The duties to which they [mothers] are called are no less complicated and interesting. To them is entrusted the care of rational creatures in the most important period of their existence." There was such an intense concern for female education, they insisted, "that even in these remote regions, the cultivation and mental improvement of *the other half* of the human species have become objects of considerable interest." The ladies gracefully closed with the conviction that "to use persuasion would be impeaching not only the liberality and good sense but the benevolence of the constituted authority of the state." The school was saved, and its pupils numbered fifty-five in 1826. Its handbill of the same year advertised courses in English, French, Latin, Arithmetic, Geography, Astronomy, Ancient and Modern History, Natural Philosophy and Chemistry, Moral Philosophy, and the standard fare of penmanship, epistolary composition, and Bible study. In addition, Elizabeth Academy offered its women the study of "principles of Liberty, Free government and obligations of patriotism," and in all courses pledged to "address the understanding rather than the memory."[28] The curriculum of Elizabeth Academy was not unique. By the second decade of the nineteenth century, the South was supporting dozens of reputable, popular academies which offered a classical English education. The ideological tenets of the American Revolution had found practical models in British institutions and educational theory, the latter probably most often Erasmus Darwin's detailed guide, *A Plan for the Conduct of Female Education in Boarding Schools.*[29]

Reading and writing were the primary tools of the "English education." Girls took courses in grammar and composition and were instructed in the form and style of letter writing; letters home were supervised exercises.[30] Penmanship was a skill that women particularly cultivated.[31] No doubt this emphasis arose because letter writing was a family duty; as planters moved farther and farther onto the frontier, many families were forced to communicate exclusively by means of correspondence. Letter writing became a social ritual for females, enabling women to draw attention to their talents as well as their thoughts. Literature, on the other hand, was a murky business. Most Americans condemned popular-novel reading, though from all indications the practice was widespread. Most schools did not offer courses in literature, and the few who ventured to teach it avoided controversy by concentrating on Aesop's fables, Shakespearean drama, the poetry of Milton, and other classical works.

Study of the Scriptures still had highest priority. Although Bible reading was not considered by teachers an intellectual pursuit, religion remained the indispensable core of the southern curriculum. Virginian Rebecca Beverley, at school at Miss Lyman's in Philadelphia (one of the most popular northern schools for southern daughters during this period), wrote to her wealthy planter father, Robert Beverley: "Every Friday night we read 60 pages of Milner's church history. . . . We study four chapters in the Bible regularly every Saturday so as to be able to answer any question Dr. Staughton the master may ask on Monday as he delivers a lecture on sacred history and explains Payley's Theology to us which we read over several times."[32]

Women were taught the rudiments of arithmetic to aid them in their household accounts, or to better their understanding of plantation ledgers. Also, as one planter explained: "Ladies, as well as gentlemen, should be qualified for all the business of life that is essential. . . . If not capable of business themselves [females] are ever liable to be cheated and imposed upon."[33] The fact that women were trained to take on the responsibility of keeping the books on the plantation did not mean, however, that they were expected to manage outside accounts. Their mathematical education was primarily for the incidental convenience of the planter.

Southerners prized the subject of geography, which women studied from an early age. Both ancient and modern geography were offered at academies. Schoolgirls, whose future lives as plantation mistresses were by nature unlikely to involve travel, wrote home frequently of their geographical explorations: "I have studied Europe, Asia, and I am now studying Africa."[34] The next most prescribed subject was history. Academies required their pupils to read ancient history as well as a standard southern text like Ramsay's *Life of Washington*.[35] History was consistently popular with parents and children alike, "pleasing and improving to the mind and understanding."[36] John Randolph of Roanoke drew up a reading list of essential works for his niece Elizabeth Tucker Coalter in 1822, including Rollin's *Ancient History*, Gille's *History of Greece*, Russel's *Modern Europe*, Hume's *England*, Sismondi's *France*, and Smith's *History of America;* he also recommended Herodotus, Xenophon, Thucydides, Plutarch, Livy, Tacitus, Bacon, and Voltaire.[37]

The study of languages was also important. Above all, women learned French. As one planter wrote to his granddaughter: "No lady is considered well bred who cannot converse and correspond in it."[38] Some girls even went to Paris to study; at the very least, planters expected their daughters to be able to read it.[39] This Francophilia was tied to the American sense of academic advantage: "I want you to commence the study of the French language as soon as possible. . . . I am desirous that your education should be inferior to none."[40] The penultimate accomplishment of the English education was the reading of Fénélon's *Telemachus*.[41] Contrary to popular myth, male relatives encouraged southern women to learn Latin, which, like French, was considered a mark of intellectual accomplishment.[42] Although not all planter daughters took advantage of this educational opportunity as readily as they began learning French, far rarer were girls who studied Italian and Greek, although neither of these languages was forbidden by custom.[43]

Most schools offered a variety of subjects under the heading of natural history, including chemistry, botany, and mineralogy. By the 1820s, astronomy was a popular addition to the seminary curriculum: "I have lately commenced Astronomy and find it a most fascinating study. I think it expands the ideas more than any other science, by its means we acquire a knowledge of the Heavenly bodies, trace the footsteps of the Great Creator, and learn in what manner he regulates the great machinery of the Universe."[44] According to the talents and training of the faculty, classes in rhetoric and moral philosophy were offered as well, often using Locke's essays as a standard text.

Under the influence of republican ideology, daughters were also subjected to a far more rigorous academic schedule. Compare Jefferson's advice to his daughter Patsy in 1783:

from 8 to 10 oclock	Practice music
from 10 to 1	dance one day and draw another
from 1 to 2	draw on the day you dance and write a letter the next day
from 3 to 4	read French
from 4 to 5	exercise yourself in music
from 5 till bedtime	read English, write French.[45]

with the school regimen of Mary Ann Hunt, daughter of a wealthy Mississippi planter, fifty years later:

Monday rose at five, prepared my lessons to recite. . . . We breakfasted at seven, at eight we assembled for school, during the morning recited several lessons which were very interesting, particularly Philosophy to which study I am very partial; at twelve school dismissed, we then took calisthenics in the upper hall. . . . Dined at one, at two school commenced, we attended reading, writing and French, from four to five took my music lesson. . . . Tea. . . . At seven I returned to my room to prepare my recitations for the following day, retired at eleven.[46]

As a rule, moreover, girls were given stiff doses of discipline at southern schools. Piety and propriety were as important to students and to educational institutions as to mothers. Boards of trustees outlined strict sets of rules for their pupils, such as those established by the Euphradian Academy, Rockingham, North Carolina, founded in 1824. The academy would not accept any student who had been expelled by another institution. Students observed the Sabbath, were to be moral and respectful to the faculty, rose with the sun, and retired by nine o'clock. Parental permission was required for bathing. "Tale bearing" was punishable. The trustees further admonished: "Talents in Rags is to be esteemed and respected equal with wealth in gaudy array."[47] Attendance at balls was a sensitive issue for female academies; many schools imposed a ban, but most, such as Lincolnton Academy in Lincolnton, North Carolina, were forced to repeal such prohibitions following student protest.[48]

Discipline varied from school to school.[49] Although planters liberally prescribed corporal punishment for their sons, teachers rarely spanked, strapped, or beat a planter daughter. Disobedience was usually punished by a denial of meals or a curtailment of privileges. One girl reported of a harsh schoolmistress: "She will not allow her scholars to miss a single word. If they do, they are marked down, and if that happens three times in the week, they are kept until two o'clock on Saturday and if they then fail, they remain until night and dine upon dry bread and water and if they won't eat it, they are slapped until they do."[50] In contrast, Rachel Mordecai reported to her brother Samuel of discipline at her family's academy at Warrenton, North Carolina: "We make no use of corporal punishments. Cards are given them regularly on friday evenings fully expressive of their conduct during the week, which are sent home to their parents, they are most anxiously awaited; and one word of disapprobation in the card has a greater effect than the most severe correction of any kind could possibly produce." One of Miss Mordecai's students, Charlotte Myers, was so outraged by her bad report that she set a bed on fire and nearly burned down the school.[51]

Academies operated year-round, on either a half-year or a quarter system. Most schools issued monthly reports as well as final marks.[52] Public examinations were held at the end of each term,[53] often in two parts: one for Bible study and one for regular academic subjects. An Alabama girl wrote home to her sister in 1811: "I do expect it will be the most frightening time that I ever witnessed. But I will try to have enough to support it."[54] Although children at school escaped direct parental supervision from the age of twelve or thirteen, when most children went away, until graduation, their mothers and fathers demanded letters on a regular basis and forwarded their own advice at every opportunity.[55] One Virginia planter sent his requirements to his daughter, away at school, in 1805: "It is not enough for me to know that you make as much progress in your French and Geography as you possibly can! I wish to know precisely what that progress is—I wish to know how each day is employed—what proportion is devoted to study, to writing, to cyphering, to reading, to sewing, to amusement, to idleness—a complete journal."[56]

An English-style education as described above cost approximately $150 a year during the post-Revolutionary period, although this amount varied from institution to institution and region to region, with costs steadily increasing during the ante-bellum era. Daughters attended school for two to five years. The fee for tuition usually accounted for only one-third of the boarding-school bill; boarding fees were at least equal to tuition and most often double or triple. In addition, most schools charged separately for extracurricular instruction in music, dancing, drawing, and needlework. Schools would often operate in conjunction with private boarding homes, affording parents a selection of establishments to choose from.

For all but wealthy families, the costs of educating a daughter away from home were prohibitive. In 1800, John Woolfolk of Virginia paid $30 for board and tuition for his daughter for one quarter. The Salem Academy charged $165 for annual tuition and board in 1806. In 1810, Abraham Steiner sent Alexander Brevard a quarterly bill for his daughter at Steiner's school in Salem: board and tuition $20, washing $4, music $2, needlework $2, and expenses (postage, books, medicine, and so forth) $9.76. In 1816, Charles McDonald paid $22.65 for tuition and board for his daughter Catherine's three months at Mount Zion Academy in Hancock County, Georgia.[57] To give one extreme example of the costs of education, in 1811 John Couper of Saint Simon's Island, Georgia, paid $772.52 for his daughter Anne's year of schooling at Miss Datty's in Charleston. Although the charge for French and board was a mere $220, her additional education fees were: Music $134; Dancing $40; Geography, Maps and Globes $26; Penmanship $24; Drawing and Art Supplies $67; and Embroidery $10. Her washing was $27.50, her school picture and frame $26, and her account at the local store $73.50. Her miscellaneous expenses ran the gamut from handkerchiefs to pew hire, *Telemachus* to tortoiseshell combs, and totaled $100.52. Couper also provided Anne with $2 per month pocket money.[58]

Interestingly, when a planter family fell on hard times, the education of daughters was not considered a dispensable item. Parents, however pressed, thought of boarding school as an absolute necessity for their female offspring. If planters could not afford a proper dowry or offer an illustrious family connection, the educational component of a daughter's cultivation became even more crucial to securing an advantageous match.

Mothers, more than fathers, were unhappy at having to part with their daughters for schooling away from home. One Virginian expressed her regrets at sending her eleven-year-old daughter to a distant academy: "Would to God she would have the advantage of a good school and the protection of her Parents at the same time—I have always dislike Boarding Houses for Girls—but we must often yield to circumstances."[59] Most often the father or another male relative accompanied a girl to school to inspect the boarding facilities. He would evaluate the propriety of the staff and conscientiously scrutinize the sleeping quarters to assure himself of their proper hygiene and ventilation. Once he was satisfied, his daughter would be left to fend for herself. Most schoolgirls experienced initial homesickness, occasionally exacerbated by the pain of separation from a favorite sister, as in the case of Cornelia Barksdale, parted from her beloved Frances: "After I came here I felt like a lost sheep that had wandered from the others, and like I was in the wilderness although I found all of them as kind as ever. O! sister I often think of you."[60]

Yet these years at school—not infrequently lamented by women at the time—were often the only time of their lives when southern women, encumbered by domestic and reproductive responsibilities, were able to develop personal, even intellectual interests. Shortly after school, and indeed sometimes while still schoolgirls, they would marry and start their own families.[61] One father warned his daughter at school: "Now is the time for your improvement. As you advance in life tho' your inclination may lead to reading, your situation may prevent your doing so."[62] Many plantation mistresses did look back on their schooldays as some of the happiest of their lives.[63] While still at school, some spoke of their academic training as a precious commodity: "A good education is a sufficient passport to a person no matter what part of the world their destiny may place them."[64] A few women treasured dreams of higher education: "You have heard me say it was the height of my ambition to be fitted for College, my present instructor says he will (provided I am attentive) teach me all the branches that are necessary for admission."[65] But the majority of plantation mistresses believed that the female academy was an end unto itself rather than the means to pursue further goals.

It is important to remember the differences in degree and kind between educational progress in the North and the South at this period, and what this meant in terms of the aspirations of female students. In 1786, a lecturer addressing a Savannah audience extolled the equal rank, importance, and reason of women. He chided any who would speak against learned ladies, as "there is rather a deficiency than superabundance of practice in this country, more observable than in the northern parts of the country."[66] Fifty years later, a schoolmistress justly observed that female education in the South was "far from being what it is in the North."[67] The South had made measurable improvement from the pre-Revolutionary era, but female academies and seminaries fitted women strictly for their preordained role in plantation culture: that of a well-read elite serving as wives and mothers to the master class. Unlike their northern counterparts, these women could not use their education to explore new avenues of experience. Plantation mistresses did not pioneer emerging fields like schoolteaching and social service, nor did their education provide the impetus for reform within the slaveowning culture. However equal women might be proclaimed to be in spiritual and intellectual terms, men were still the acknowledged authorities in social, political, and economic spheres. The doctrine of male dominance and female dependence was pervasive in both the North and the South, but a more urban and economically diversified northern society offered both a wider range of opportunities for women to use their education and a secular momentum for cultural transformation.

Post-Revolutionary gentry throughout the nation had embraced the notion of "republican motherhood." By the 1830s, however, celebrations of women had shifted perceptibly along regional lines; even distinctive regional vocabularies developed to convey different cultural and sexual imagery. Virtue was the most prized feminine characteristic throughout the United States, but in the North, female virtue was synonymous with industriousness and epitomized by the "frugal housewife," while in the South, the plantation aristocracy celebrated virtue in the cult of chastity. This iconography of sexual purity was an explicit ideological tool, indispensable to the ruling-class males of a biracial slave society. In this context, planters required unchallenged fidelity from their women, and therefore projected chastity as the ultimate embodiment of virtue.

Female academies notwithstanding, plantation culture severely restricted southern women and resisted at every point the impulse to "modernize" that was infiltrating from the North. If slavery were to persist as the backbone of the economy and patriarchy as the heart of social organization, the position of southern women had to remain fixed, and their education would serve only expressly limited purposes. On a visit to the North, one planter sharply observed: "I have no very high opinion of any superior advantages from these more northern schools. Besides, girls here are imbibing habits and manners not so perfectly congenial with those of the people of the South, where they are destined to live."[68]

Their brief exposure to intellectual freedom underscored for some plantation mistresses the frustration to which their own education inevitably led. A few could turn this into a most limited irony, as Maria Campbell did in a letter to her politician husband, absent on one of his many trips: "I must assure you that much the most interesting and agreeable companions I have are my books. The stream of mental pleasures, those which of course all persons of whatever condition may equally partake, flow from one to the other."[69] Although in the days of their forefathers they would have been denied "mental pleasures" altogether, in favor of Bible study and "ornamental arts," post-Revolutionary plantation mistresses, with their English-style educations, lived within domestic confines identical to those of their foremothers. And although mothers and daughters warmly greeted improvements in their education, these women of the planter class realized that their intellectual development would most likely wane with marriage, decline with housekeeping, dwindle at motherhood, and at no time result in any measure of social recognition. Women accepted this pattern as a fact of life rather than a product of culture. Yet better schooling might at least offer them the hitherto denied opportunity to improve the quality of the lives they were destined to lead. Maria Campbell, the Virginia plantation mistress, advised her niece to value her education, for "when the frosty part of life shall arrive, it will be a support for you under every vicissitude of life."[70] At the time she expressed this sentiment, Campbell was only twenty-six.

VIII

PRECIOUS
AND PRECARIOUS
IN BODY AND SOUL

*T*he mistress of a plantation survived at the mercy of her environment, subject to natural changes—from the pattern of seasons to the irregular but inevitable cycle of birth and death. Life on the plantation necessarily brought the mistress into intimate acquaintance with the unhealthy features of the southern climate. Isolation further aggravated women's fears of illness, disease, and childbearing. These factors combined to generate a preoccupation, almost obsessive for some plantation mistresses, with health.

Statistics bear out that while poor health was common in all of antebellum America, the South suffered especially seriously. Comparing two equal population regions from the 1860 United States census, mortality was higher in the South.[1] District II (Michigan, Wisconsin, Nebraska, and Minnesota), with a population of 1,725,843, lists 16,032 deaths, while District VII (South Carolina, Georgia, Florida, and Alabama), with a population of 1,504,190, records 37,094: the southern death rate was double. The particular hazards of the South come into sharper focus with a breakdown of categories: District II with 644 typhoid deaths versus District VII with 2,476; District II with 1,096 pneumonia fatalities versus District VII with 3,899; and—equally dramatic—264 deaths in childbirth for District II versus 401 deaths in childbirth for southern women from District VII. James Buckingham remarked in his 1840 volume that women seemed to suffer more than men from the southern climate. He believed that "there are consequently a much greater number of husbands who survived their wives than wives who survive their husbands."[2]

Most Southerners believed in preventive medicine. Despite the strict regulation of feminine behavior, mothers stressed the value of a steady and regular routine of physical training for their daughters from an early age. In school, girls took classes to get their exercise; some participated in gymnastics, most learned to ride, and one and all learned to dance. As Erasmus Darwin explained in his educational text: "The acquirements of literature, and of many arts makes the lives of young people too sedentary; which impairs their strength, makes their countenances pale and bloated and lays the foundation of many diseases; hence some hours should every day be appropriated to bodily exercises and to relaxation of mind."[3]

Girls took these exercises seriously. One student away from home reported to her brother: "Tell Mama I have been quite industrious and have done a good deal of work since I have been up here—I have not however missed my exercise for it, as I take a long ride every day."[4] This plan of daily activity continued throughout a woman's life unless she became an invalid; indeed, women were advised from all sides to keep up their exercise program to prevent just such a tragic advent.[5]

Riding, the most generally approved form of physical activity for women, served a practical purpose—plantations were great distances apart—but conferred less specific benefits; Maria Campbell wrote to a friend in 1809: "I have discovered that exercise in the open air and on horseback has contributed considerably towards restoring my health this summer and I wish to continue riding out in the mornings as long as the season will permit."[6] Ante-bellum travel literature celebrated the equestrian talent of southern females. One plantation visitor remarked: "The women, riding very beautiful Virginia horses, would challenge each other to a race. Since they often travel by horseback, often ride down steep mountains, cross rivers and since in their earliest years they are exposed to all the mettle of very fast horses, they are skillful and fearless riders."[7] Female riders impressed the English bride of a Southerner so much so that she vowed to take up the habit herself after she witnessed "a woman on horseback with a child *in each arm*—it was a matter of wonder to me how she could guide her horse while thus encumbered."[8] Of course, riding was not without its drawbacks; falls were common.[9] At the age of seventeen, Nelly Parke Custis wrote a friend about her injuries resulting from a collision with a low branch. She reported that her mother and grandmother "would not permit me to ride for some time. However at least I persuaded them my neck was not to be broken yet awhile and I have rode several times since. It has given me courage and more caution also."[10] This emboldening aspect of the sport stimulated some women. Caroline Howard of Savannah wrote her sister: "I have commenced riding on horseback. The first attempt I have had two falls, the relics of which linger about me in black and blue impressions even now. The second I was more successful. . . ." Once she learned to manage on horseback she confessed to having "enjoyed myself highly. There is something very independent in the feeling when one is reconciled to the situation."[11]

The stereotype promoted by Buckingham and others had, however, some basis in fact. Southern custom certainly celebrated the delicacy of planter class women, and men expected them to observe rules of decorum that included an entire range of physical restrictions, which in reality were as much for show as for safety. One southern woman wrote to a friend coyly: "I am more unhealthy than usual, I cough a good deal and make considerable pretension to being a delicate lady."[12] Heat and uncomfortable clothing were partially responsible for the frailty of plantation women that eventually led to a pattern of invalidism, real or imagined. John J. Crittenden chided his daughter in 1831: "Take care of your health—Do not sacrifice it to fashion or amusement—the lacing and bandaging now in use among the ladies will kill you. I pray you not to destroy yourself by such a petty sort of suicide."[13] Men in the marriage market, though, expected this sacrifice. As Chastellux remarked in his travel account: "Women have little share in the amusement of the men; beauty here serves only to procure them husbands; for the most wealthy planters, giving but a small fortune with their daughters, their fate is usually decided by their figure."[14]

With her arduous housekeeping tasks, the established plantation mistress could little afford the luxury of a fragile constitution, but certain debilitating conditions were unavoidable. Rachel O'Conner wrote her sister-in-law Mary Weeks about the problem of a mutual friend: "She has been sick nearly five months. She will be 59 years of age 2nd of December. Which is a great age to have her monthly discharges return and to last 4 or 5 months without intermission which has been the case with her."[15] Pregnancy and childbirth brought a variety of serious complications, magnified—as were so many other ailments—by the unrelentingly hostile climate; in this sense, the heat was not just uncomfortable—it could kill as well.[16]

The ill-health of Virginia plantation mistress Maria Campbell so worried her husband David that he sent a lengthy letter of inquiry to eminent physician Benjamin Rush of Philadelphia. The Campbells were childless, and Maria Campbell had painful and irregular menses. In 1806, after six years of marriage, David Campbell offered Rush the following list of her symptoms: "During the first year after her marriage she was much depressed in spirits and had several severe attacks of sickness. Particularly one something like cholera morbus. Now and for several years past at almost every evacuation she is pained and sometimes severely had headaches, sickness at the stomach and the blood is sometimes clotted. . . . Has them generally profusely and not regular in appearance. . . ."[17]

Although Maria Campbell had consulted several other physicians, medicine had brought her no relief. She took anti-bilious pills, Peruvian bark, and a powder described as "steel dust." But Rush replied that the Campbells should not "despair of her recovery." He designed a multifaceted program of diet, exercise, and medical remedies to restore her to health. He prohibited her from taking tea, coffee, or spirits, recommending small amounts of port on occasion. The doctor advised Maria Campbell to add oysters, cheese, chocolate, soft-boiled eggs, and vegetables to her regular diet. He urged her to spend no more than eight hours a day in bed, to rub her limbs to improve her circulation, and to ride whenever the weather permitted. In addition, Rush prescribed daily doses of an iron and ginger mixture and counseled her to employ the following vaginal douche twice daily: white oak bark, rose leaves, powdered alum, and water. A day or two before menses, Rush recommended a gentle purge, and during the menstrual flow Maria Campbell was instructed to bathe her bowels with turpentine and sweet oil. Ten drops of laudanum per hour were to be administered if she was in pain.[18] If nothing else, the doctor provided his patient with a fairly full schedule and the hope of restored health and fertility. Maria Campbell's letters indeed indicate improved health during the period following her treatment, though she remained childless. Before, during, and after this consultation with Rush, however, Maria Campbell never mentioned her gynecological disorders in personal correspondence, demonstrating the extreme delicacy women felt about such matters.

Women labored under the handicap of modesty, and were loath to expose themselves to male physicians, even in cases of extreme discomfort. One ailing woman confided to a friend about her physician: "I disliked to show it [her leg] to him but when he found it out he said I was wrong in not telling him for he always set such bones through the clothes. He examined my knee through my clothes and in a moment put it right."[19] Nervous symptoms were common. A woman complained to her aunt: "I feel a little indisposed today and my eyes are so sore and week that I use green spectacles."[20] A planter described his wife's debilitated state during the week before Christmas: "Her nervous system is so affected that she cannot set in a room while a person walks across the floor. I am now proposing to convey her out of town in order to escape the noisy rejoicings of the season which is approaching."[21] But the physical causes of these disorders are difficult to separate from the prolonged psychological stresses that must at least have compounded them.

The female head of the household acted as doctor or nurse more often than she did patient, for it was her task to supervise the medical care of her families, white and black. She oversaw the daily dispensation of medicine and tended all the slaves' ailments; physicians called only when the white family's needs had exhausted the plantation mistress's curative powers. Medical treatments were much the same for blacks and whites, with the exception of bleeding, which was executed commonly but only on whites and only by physicians. As women often witnessed, family members could be struck by disease and be dead within hours. Letters filled with warnings about "drafts" and exhortations to "exercise" take on a deeper meaning under these circumstances. On occasion, plantation mistresses triumphed over unusual medical problems. One concerned mother wrote of her infant's ailment—after a bout with worms, the baby had refused to suck and his throat had begun to swell. Fearing for her child's life, she took matters into her own hands and lanced his neck. The amazed mother pulled out a feather, which had apparently entered her son's body through his ear or throat; she poulticed the surgical wound, and once his neck healed, the boy returned to good health.[22] But planter wives, isolated on their plantations, had reason to worry about their medical responsibilities and their distance from doctors.

Most women found their nursing tasks burdensome. A plantation mistress wrote to a friend in 1784: "I really have nothing but the Dismal to write about—I hear of nothing but sickness and Death— our Kitchen is absolutely a perfect Hospital—no less than seven sitting shivering round the fire with agues."[23] Another described her vigil at her uncle's sickbed: "I sat by his bed side from three o'clock on monday untill sunrise tuesday morning without quiting him except to go up stairs, to see how the sick children were, for I thought that every hour would be his last untill about two o'clock in the morning, I discovered a change for the better."[24] This degree of devotion was not unusual. A planter wife wrote to her husband in the autumn of 1835 about her taxing ministrations to his bedridden mother. She sought a female relative or paid nurse to relieve her of a portion of this charge, explaining, "I never feel the least impatient in your Mother's sick room, the only thing disagreeable to me is the smell of the Opium poultices which she has to apply to relieve her pain, it makes me sick and giddy."[25]

Plantation mistresses commonly kept recipe books wherein cures and remedies were mixed with common cookbook items. North Carolinian Ann Blount Pettigrew's recipe book included a cure for cancer (press the juice of sheep sorrel on a pewter plate; let it stand in the sun until it comes to a consistence), an antidote for snakebite (turpentine and wild indigo), a remedy for lightning (throw cold water over the person: if pulse is slow and extremities cold, bleed in the arm), and an insecticide for cockroaches (sprinkle black "helebone" root where they frequent). She also listed remedies for poison and a cure for opium overdose.[26]

Planter wives administered laudanum so widely that they kept careful lists of prescribed dosages. Mothers were especially careful with recommended dosages for infants. An 1833 guide suggested the following quantities:

for a child 10 days old: one-half drop
10 days to one month old: 1 drop
1 month to three months: 2 drops
3 months to 9 months: 2 drops
9 months to 18 months: 4 drops
18 months to 3 years: 5 or 6 drops[27]

Such frequent usage of this potentially dangerous drug provided for numerous mishaps. A mother described one such accident involving her daughter in 1834. After she had mistakenly given the child 500 drops of opium (instead of rhubarb), the alarmed mother poured ice over the girl, got her daughter on her feet, and rubbed her to try to increase her circulation. Next the frantic woman put a feather down her daughter's throat, which induced her to vomit. After several doses of castor oil, the young girl survived her accidental overdose.[28]

Most medicines were a combination of several ingredients, often with opium forming a base. Some recipe books contained "cures for gonnorrhea." One such remedy was a mixture of 30 drops of opium, one-half ounce of sulpher nitre, 1 ounce of Balsam Capini, and one-half dram of oil of turpentine. A recipe book recommended 20 drops of this medicine morning, noon, and night. If this remedy failed, the book also provided three others.[29] Plantation mistresses spent a great deal of time and effort keeping their medicine cabinets supplied with, for example, the following medicine to cure dysentery: "Boil one teacup of logwood chips in a pint of sweet milk, add one teacup of sugar and boil another ten minutes then cool and strain. Take four tablespoons full of brandy, put it into a saucer and set it on fire. After burning what it will, stir it into the mixture. One tablespoon three times a day. Reduce as necessary."[30]

Throughout the year women were obliged to tend to the chills and fevers, agues, and colds of the plantation population, and to keep careful watch for more serious disease. Smallpox inoculations protected most children, but this preventive measure sometimes failed. One Southerner wrote in 1795 of an unsuccessful inoculation: "Poor Betsey! was inoculated and from every appearance her arm had taken the infection and thinking herself secure, she went imprudently among the Negroes tho' cautioned against it. . . . she was seized in a most violent manner with no symptoms. . . . her recovery has been very slow."[31] Whooping cough—sometimes referred to as "putrid sore throat"—was another disease that often proved fatal; mothers were especially alarmed to discover any outbreak in the neighborhood.[32] But the two major epidemic threats to health on the plantation remained yellow fever and cholera.

In 1796, yellow fever swept through New Orleans. Ventura Morales reported: "An epidemic which broke out in the latter part of August, and which is still prevalent has terrified and still keeps in a state of consternation the whole population of this Town. Some of the medical faculty call it malignant fever; some say it is the disease known in America as 'black vomit,' and others that it is the 'yellow fever' which proved so fatal in Philadelphia." Morales goes on to add that 200 out of a white population of 2,500 had perished.[33] But urban areas were not the only environment where this disease struck. Maria Campbell, on her plantation in western Virginia, was distressed by an epidemic in 1808: "During the latter part of last summer a fever prevailed through this country very considerable and at one time three of my family were lying very low with it being all then about the house, but myself and my little negro boy Sam. In this situation I remained several nights when Mr. Campbell was so low that I hardly sometimes expected him to live, sitting by his bedside through the night. . . ." She goes on: "I attended Mr. Campbell and the two negroes for about five or six weeks and administered all the medicine to them."[34] Many plantation mistresses armed themselves with vinegar and quinine to ward off the "black vomit," but the disease was persistent and deadly. One woman wrote to a friend in 1820 of the 130 who had died of it in New Orleans in a single week.[35]

When cholera struck, Southerners fared no better. M. E. Cheves reported in 1834: "The *Cholera* broke out upon our plantation on the 10th! on the *first* day 6 were taken and in a few hours 3 *died*. 10 more

died soon after and how many are attacked have not been specified. . . ."[36] The death and desolation on plague-ridden plantations
was enormous. Epidemics took their toll both in lives and in the
mental health of the survivors; overwork and worry subjected women
to fretful exhaustion if not actual disease. In 1833 a young woman
reported to her cousin of the affliction within her home: "We have
had three sick rooms for the last three weeks and had not our friends
been untiring in their attentions we must have all died. My own health
is better than common though I have not taken off my clothes for the
last month except to change. I was so completely undone one night
that Mr. Morrow had to come up and sit with sister. Mr. Tilford [her
husband] gave up as soon as the first case appeared in town and has
starved and laid abed ever since." She concludes with the fact that
fifty had died of cholera.[37] Mr. Tilford's attitude of resignation was
not uncommon. But most women, forced to tend to the sick and
needy, were unable to lie abed and bemoan their fate. Planter families
could only avoid the disease by means of escape to a better climate.
One mistress counseled in 1829: "I do not think there will be much
danger of the cholera if you travel pretty well north and have with you
some remedy to use in the case of the slightest attack of diar-
rhea. . . ." The specific remedy recommended was the ever-popular
opium.[38]

Plantation dwellers recognized as the sickly season "the four months
commencing with the 21st of June, the whole of July, August and
September terminating with the 21st of October."[39] Travel to escape
the unhealthy climate during this period was a common practice on
most plantations. William Couper, a Sea Island planter, wrote to his
family in Scotland: "There are three months in the year that is unhealthy
here, that is Agust, Sptr. and Octobr and against that time I am in
mind to go out to the country."[40] Another southern planter described
his family's annual migrations: "My parents moved into the country,
spending the winters at Dock on from about November 1st to May
15th and the summers in the pineland."[41] While mosquitoes plagued
Southerners during summer months, planters during the ante-bellum
era perceived this as more of an annoyance than a danger. Doctors
failed to make the connection between insects and the spread of disease
until later in the century.

At times women found these routines trying. One planter wife

complained to her son in 1817: "I have not been to town for a week.
. . . Your Papa is unwilling to let me go again before a frost. I do not
feel at all afraid, and still hope I shall be able to prevail on him to let
me visit our friends there occasionally, it is quite a trial to be only six
miles from them and not be able to see them."[42] She was summering
at Sullivan's Island, a popular resort for South Carolinians located
outside Charleston. Edisto Island, John's Island, Cedar Island, and
North Island all attracted summer visitors, as did the Carolina pine
barrens.[43] Despite the trouble involved in annually shifting a large
household, most women welcomed the opportunity to escape the
plantation. In 1833 a woman wrote to a friend: "We moved to our
summer retreat about two weeks ago—the house is really a delightful
one—so very large and commodious—and the plan I think an excellent one both for coolness, comfort and convenience."[44]

Many planters sought "comfort and convenience" at the various
spas established to cater to the "finer folk." Some of the wealthier
landowners journeyed as far north as Saratoga Springs, New York,
fashionable for the rich as well as offering the most popular waters for
ailing aristocrats. But most Southerners strayed no farther north than
Virginia. Along the Blue Ridge Mountains, resorts sprang up around
the several celebrated springs of the central Virginia region. Salt Springs
was an immensely popular spot for slaveowners. "The Salt" attracted
a large crowd of South Carolinians. The White Sulphur Springs and
the Red Sulphur Springs competed for planter clientele. Each resort
maintained a variety of cabins surrounding a complex of central buildings that included a dining hall, a ballroom, and a drawing room at
the least. The splendor and luxury of these establishments varied, but
most innkeepers attempted to lure planters with lavish public rooms.
By the 1830s, many wealthy Southerners were building their own
cabins at the springs, in rows that earned nicknames like Bachelor's
Row and Paradise Row. One planter described a visit to White Sulphur
Springs in July 1839, noting that over two hundred people had gathered there from all over the country. He described one cabin as "handsomely fitted up with carpets, painting, sofas, lounges, Borking chairs
and every comfort that man can devise," and went on to lavish praise
on the "magnificent Sulphur Bath House," where one could enjoy the
waters both internally and externally.[45]

The conventional rationale for attendance at the springs was "for reasons of health." A planter wrote to his wife from Saratoga Springs: "My health is sensibly improved. It is my present intention to remain here ten days at least after which I should be ready and willing to turn my face homewards."[46] Some Southerners thought springs were a cure-all. Indeed one planter playfully described White Sulphur Springs: "The water has the pleasant flavor of a half-boiled-half-spoiled egg and according to popular belief cures the following diseases. Yellow jaundice, white swelling, blue devils and black plague, scarlet fever, yellow fever, spotted fever and fever of every kind and colour; Hydro-cephalas, Hydrothoras, Hydrocele and Hydrophobia, Hypochondria and Hypocrisy; Dispepsia, Diabetes, and die-of-anything, Gout and Grogging."[47]

Trips to the springs were sociable, however, as well as therapeutic. Maria Campbell wrote to a friend in 1809 about her stay: "We drank the water and bathed and eat and eat and bathed and drank the water—was this not fine?—We had two old canoes tied together and with two or three persons to pole and Jim in the stern with his violin we sailed most merrily up and down the river."[48] A planter described the accommodations in Bath, Virginia: "There is a fine drawing room there, in which the ladies meet to chat or work, and play at chess or devise some pleasant excursion."[49] Charles Cotton met a woman "on her way to Virginia springs not as I can perceive for the benefit of her health but to be fashionably employed during the summer."[50]

The popularity of White Sulphur Springs was widespread. A woman reported to her husband in 1838 that she could not get lodgings at the White Sulphur—"it was so crowded"—so she was unhappily settled at Salt Springs.[51] Planter St. George Coalter confided to his wife in 1833 that 270 persons were in attendance at White Sulphur, with almost a hundred servants in addition. He described the entertainment that kept the crowds so numerous: "Today we are to have an exhibition of boxing and fencing for the amusement of the Ladies, something in the style of a Tournament."[52]

Life at the springs was frivolous and relaxed. A gentleman lyrically depicted a scene at sunset: "On a little greensward, skirting along the foot of a steep mountain, at least a hundred gay people of both sexes were rambling among the trees, just in the twilight of a mild summer evening."[53] Among numerous pastimes, perhaps none was more pop-ular than gambling;[54] this might have been accounted for by the fact

that men outnumbered women at the springs.[55] Planters strictly forbade
the discussion of political topics at these springs, doubtless to provide
less opportunity for violent disagreement and to prevent duels.
Discussions remained lively nonetheless. Men especially speculated
about the young ladies who circulated at the spas. John Goldsborough
described two of the females at Sulphur Springs: "The most interesting single lady is a Miss Lawrence of New York worth half a million.
She appears to have taken a great fancy to me although I have never
been presented to her. . . . then again there's a widow lady from New
Orleans living in Bachelor's Row estimated at three million."[56] Plantation mistresses found their visits to the springs a pleasant escape
from the confines of the plantation and a welcome change from their
dull household routines. Sometimes the diversions were totally unexpected. Louise Holmes recorded the following incident in her diary
while at the Salt Springs:

> About two o'clock this morning my young companion Miss Pea-
> cham and myself who occupy a cabin to ourselves were awakened
> by a storm of rain, which occasioned a very great noise on the top
> of our house. We were a good deal alarmed at hearing the thunder
> which accompanied it. But our fright was greatly encreased by the
> shaking of our cabin and a strange noise wich proceeded from be-
> neath it. I verily believed it must have been an earthquake and that
> the hill on which we were situated might open and close us in
> forever. At length to our unspeakable pleasure we distinguished the
> squealing and grunting of a number of hogs, which had taken shel-
> ter under our habitation. We enjoyed no little mirth at our uneces-
> sary fright.[57]

Mirth was precious indeed to women in the plantation South.

But such respite came too little and too late to support the functioning of many a plantation mistress. As Harriet Martineau commented
in her *Society in America*, she had met no more hard-working nor
industrious women than those on southern plantations. But she found
a higher rate of invalidism in the South, as well: the pressures were

more pronounced, and were exacerbated by the added strain of enforced pretence to the part of "ladies of leisure."

Ironically, those whose task it was to tend to the health of the household endured poorer health themselves, particularly by virtue of their reproductive roles. Yet they had relatively little opportunity for relief. Restorative visits to springs were in fact rare and radical solutions to the problems of women's fatigue and ill-health, despite cultural prescriptions that built frailty into the female ideal. Men thronged the springs, outnumbering women five to one. The "vapors" might be real or imagined, but plantation mistresses suffered multiple assaults—direct and indirect—on their physical well-being, and no hazard was more unrelenting or more ambivalent in its implications for women than pregnancy. The dutiful southern matron, exhorted to "be fruitful and multiply," was never more vulnerable to her fears than at this time. Apprehension clouded the joy of expectancy, for whenever a plantation mistress faced childbirth, she literally prepared to die.

The long months of pregnancy caused both physical discomfort and anxiety. One woman confessed in her journal: "My personal situation is at present critical and extremely uncomfortable, yet when there is peace *within*, I without vanity can say that I bear bodily pain with some patience and fortitude."[58] One southern woman confided the reaction of a pregnant friend: "She had been living in the hope of visiting her Mother in the Spring, and . . . she found greatly to her surprise, by some symptoms which she could not misunderstand, that she was considerably advanced in pregnancy. The disappointment was so great that it actually made her sick and she was obliged to go to bed, and she expects to be confined in April."[59] When Virginian Elizabeth Gibson became pregnant in the autumn of 1813, apprehensions overwhelmed her. Gisbon's cousin, Elizabeth Fitzgerald, wrote to reassure her in February 1814: "Whatever you may say to the contrary, I am sure your affectionate Heart cannot but receive pleasure. . . . I hope my dearest Elizabeth, you have not given way to any fears which may suggest themselves to you as your family have been unfortunate in similar circumstances. Trust in the Almighty. . . ."[60] Shortly before her child was due, Elizabeth Gibson wrote to her aunt, Martha Jones, about her feelings: "I cannot say that I do not anticipate it without a considerable degree of apprehension—a feeling I believe natural to all," but went on to assert: "My reliance is placed in Heaven which has hitherto protected me and I have every reason to believe that as far as regards professional skill and proper attendance I shall be most fortunate."[61]

Christian fortitude brought occasional comfort, if only through the prospect of martyrdom. An expectant mother wrote to her mother in July 1817: "Yes, dear Momma, the time of my trial is drawing near but *I do* not dread it as I once thought I should. I believe I have suffered as much as my constitution was able to bear and when I reflect how very low I have been it appears almost a miracle that I am now able to stand alone and since that time have suffered a great deal." She goes on to affirm: "In my most severe sufferings I was supported by the consolations of religion and I have a firm belief that if I put my whole trust in Christ he will never leave nor forsake me."[62] Another plantation mistress confided to her sister: "I could not but regret that the happiness of the conjugal relation was obliged to be bought at so dear a price."[63]

In order to ensure safe and healthy pregnancies, some plantation mistresses continued to exercise, especially during the early months— a not uncommon medical practice during the early nineteenth century. Planter John Haywood advised his wife Sally during her pregnancy: "I have to ask, my love, that you will continue to ride much, and more particularly to walk much: if you will daily do so as far as your strength will permit. I am convinced you will find it of the greatest consequence."[64] Her mother agreed with this prescription: "Exercise is essentially necessary to your Health, at all times and in all situations, walk or ride every day and do not give way to any sluggish inclinations."[65] Perhaps most important, keeping to a busy but not overactive schedule helped women through their difficult periods. Indeed, some southern matrons socialized without reserve during their pregnancies.[66] Considering the amount of time many women spent being pregnant, this was not surprising.

The lack of effective birth control contributed to a high birth rate for the planter class.* Thomas Brown recorded in an account of his lineage that his ancestor Margaret Templeman "married young, was a

*See Appendix A, Table 4.

grandmother before she was 40 years old, the mother of ten sons and three daughters, eleven of whom were living."[67] Dr. George Hasell reported in his "Lectures on Midwifery" that southern women bore children late into middle age, even citing an instance of motherhood at age fifty-four.[68]

Cultural as well as medical factors affected the birth rate. Patriarchy exacted the frequent birth of heirs as a kind of tribute from planter wives.[69] Thomas Jefferson wrote to his daughter upon her announcement of his impending grandfatherhood: "Your two last letters are those which have given me the greatest pleasure of any I ever received from you. The one announced that you were become a notable housewife, the other a mother. This last is undoubtedly the keystone of the arch of matrimonial happiness. . . ."[70] A mother of six was less elated by her fertility: "Old brother Gwiner shortly after our marriage prophesied that we were to have thirteen children, and I begin to fear he is not far wrong. Is this enough to frighten our sex from the altar of hymen?"[71] Men were clearly more concerned with the result of reproduction than with its origin, being quick to claim credit for a desired heir and equally quick to lay the blame elsewhere for an unwanted pregnancy or child. As one man complained: "I am sorry to add that my very prolific wife is again in a way to add to our already numerous family."[72] Matrons like Cary Ann Nicholas realized the mixed blessings of fecundity: "John will not be satisfied to go until he has his own carriage . . . but that is a kind of pride that we find convenient to lay aside for the present, and forever if we are so imprudent as to have a child every year."[73]

Confinement was a time of crisis for husband and wife alike. While women went through the pain and anxiety of delivery, expectant fathers feared the death of their spouses. Although a husband did not attend at the actual birth, he commonly tried to be at home for his wife's lying-in. Many planters believed their presence offered essential support for wives during childbirth. South Carolinian William Elliott fell ill while away from his plantation in 1818. He wrote home to his wife: "The dread I have of being absent from you at your confinement. . . . Pray now, my dear, keep yourself quiet and do not hurry the stranger into the world, before I am down to welcome him."[74] When planter Joseph Habersham heard of the birth of a daughter via his brother, he wrote to his wife: "You may be assured that I am relieved from a load of anxiety on your account, which was considerably increased by the disagreeable necessity I found myself under of leaving you at the time I did."[75]

Female relatives gathered round the expectant mother during the final weeks of pregnancy.[76] Their presence was more for moral support than any technical assistance. Plantation mistresses were attended by doctors or midwives while giving birth. A matron reported medical advice to her sister: "A very eminent physician says a woman should not change a horisontal position for at least three days after delivery owing to the weight of the womb being so much greater at that time than any other it causes what is called a falling of that part which makes a person more weakly until the birth of another child which sometimes by propper care afterwards restores it to its propper place. . . ."[77] The doctor, of course, was referring to prolapse of the uterus. Modern medicine has determined that nursing causes natural and restorative convulsions of the uterus. The nursing mother thus did not have to fear a fallen womb, but with the increase in wet nursing during the early republican era, many southern matrons did not breast-feed their babies themselves. Ironically, both the prolapsed uterus and the lack of natural birth spacing could have contributed to an increased rate of death in childbirth.*

Death in childbirth was no idle fear, and each individual woman faced its threat.† Long and painful deliveries were not uncommon. Georgian Charles Jones described his wife's ordeal: "My dear Ruth has for the past fifty-three hours suffered intensely, and as a consequence, now that relief and reaction have supervened, is exceedingly feeble." She died shortly thereafter.[78] The Biblical injunction "in sorrow thou shalt bring forth children" was enacted literally until 1847, when chloroform finally began to be used to relieve the pain of childbirth. Even after delivery, however, a mother might still be in danger. One of the severe complications of childbirth was puerperal or "childbed" fever. If the afterbirth was not antiseptically and completely removed, the mother might become infected. Doctors were generally helpless in these cases. Sometimes a woman would linger on

*See Appendix B, Table 6.
†See Appendix A, Table 7.

for weeks, but the fever almost always proved fatal. A plantation mistress who survived the ordeal declared that "she does not think she could or would undergo the same pain that brought it to save its life, it so far exceeded her beliefs or expectation."[79]

Maria Bryan recounted the untimely demise of a friend: "She gave birth to a child on Thursday last and the instant it was born said, 'I shall die,' and expired immediately. She had been in a very critical situation some time before and to use Ma's expression, literally flooded to death. Gallons seemed to come from her without the possibility of stopping it and this produced such faintness and exhaustion that soul and body could remain together no longer."[80] Mary Elizabeth Cheves was a victim of her frequent deliveries: "In her youth, she had been a beautiful, petite woman but she had never been strong. The strain of giving birth to fourteen children in twenty-two years and of rearing them had been too much for her delicate body."[81]

Nursing, too, was a major physical strain. During the eighteenth century, plantation mistresses nursed their own babies. Chastellux remarks in his travel book of 1780 that southern women "always have a great number of slaves at hand to wait on them and on their children: they themselves suckle their infants, but that is all."[82] But although mothers nursed according to their personal inclination, by the mid-nineteenth century, many southern upper-class women had turned over the task of suckling infants to white wet nurses or slaves. Those plantation mistresses who did nurse their babies complained of exhaustion.[83] A new mother described her schedule to her own mother: "Fabius keeps me awake what few hours I have to sleep by getting up so often to Suck, for I am up every night till twelve or one o'clock at Night, preparing for the next day's dinner and then when I go to bed he disturbs me so often I can't sleep and the other Boys wake me by day break, and you know that when I am once waked in the Morning I can't go to sleep again, so that I am almost worn out. . . ."[84] Another concerned mother wrote to her husband: "A weary time I have had in nursing her. Many a night I have lain awake, fearing if I closed my eyes she would suffocate."[85]

Many plantation mistresses would gladly have relinquished their suckling duties,[86] but suitable help was surprisingly scarce, judging from contemporary newspapers filled with advertisements seeking wet nurses. One plantation mistress complained of her fruitless search on her own plantation: "I have now three children to work for and it keeps me quite busy. Cinthea's nursing well but there is not a girl on the farm that is large enough to nurse except one that is too bad for any purpose and the women all have young children so I can't make nurses of them."[87] Unfortunately, many young southern mothers waited until ill-health drove them to engage a wet nurse. A matron wrote advising her stepdaughter in 1803: "I am persuaded, my dear Fanny (and the same is the opinion of all who speak of you) that you will not be better till you call in the aid of a nurse for your little ravenous puss—you cannot spare as much sustenance as she requires."[88]

Most infants nursed for a year or longer. Southern mothers preferred not to wean their children between December and February because of the cold, nor between July and September because of the heat; nursing thus often extended into a second year.[89] Extreme care was taken with the precarious health of infants. Upper-floor nurseries were sunlit with access to fresh air; high ceilings, dry walls, and shuttered windows were considered essential. Mothers observed the adage: "A warm nursery makes a cold graveyard."[90] Plantation mothers were aware of the higher rate of infant mortality in the South. A comparative survey indicates that while infant mortality among northern planters was 12 percent, the rate for the southern planter class was 14 percent.* In 1860, District II (North) recorded 7,267 deaths of children aged 0 to 5 years, with 17,619 deaths in the same category in the southern region (District VII).[91] A sampling of a single Virginia county between 1787 and 1796 confirms this pattern: of the 452 burial permits issued during these nine years, 198 were for children.[92]

Infant mortality was so common that many plantation couples referred to their "living children," the assumption being that some were always lost in infancy or childhood.[93] A matron lamented in 1832: "The order of nature seems strangely *reversed*. Those who should have followed me to my long home have gone before. The Lord has taken faster than he gave them to me. I have lost 4 in less than nine years, and such children as promised as much health and length of life as any of the human families ever did."[94] Another bereaved woman wrote to her son in 1820: "The 18th of January, dear James, I was the mother of one of the sweetest babes . . . he is gone to a better world.

*See Appendix A, Table 5.

. . . God has endowed me with such passions or feelings, that I can't easily control them. . . . I do not wish to live out this year."[95] A Southerner wrote to his sister: "As death with his scythe at once strew along—the young, the old, the feeble and the strong."[96]

The stoical faced the loss of their kinsmen by reflecting that the departed had merely "paid their debt to nature."[97] Yet many times these "debts" seemed to exceed what the living could withstand, especially when they accumulated rapidly. E. T. Bryan described one tragic period to her friend: "Two short years stripped me of my dearly loved Grandmother, my best of Fathers, my only Brother and a lovely child; taken Bryan's sister Virginia (who was a sister to me) and her two children were all lost in the *Pulaski*."[98] (The *Pulaski* had sailed from Savannah to Charleston on June 13, 1838. When the boiler exploded, the ship sank and 160 lives were lost.)

Death among the young was doubly devastating. One planter reported in his memoirs: "The Sunday after Mrs. Claiborne was married she was taken with the scarlet fever and Died the Friday following. She was a bride one Friday and a corpse the next."[99] A grieving woman wrote her sister in 1796: "Alas! there is no such thing as human happiness; in this world of darkness, misery and Error! 'Our only Lesson is to learn to Suffer and he who knows not that was born for nothing.' "[100] Another plantation mistress described a mourning mother: "She screams out for her [the dead child] untill exhausted with convulsions and then beckons her to come to her."[101]

But most mothers of the planter class learned to cope with their grief in a more moderate manner, combatting it with a combination of spiritual strength and family support, and returning to their household routines. Martha Richardson described her sister's recovery to a nephew: "Your Mother bears the loss of her infant much better than I expected—Emily was so ill at the time and after that no doubt operated to engage her mind—and then Elizabeth's illness occupied her—she had no time for useless grief—fears and anxiety for the living nearly crazed her—she is now apparently getting over her distress."[102] A mother wrote in 1810: "In the first violence of grief I thought I would never again suffer myself to receive pleasure from *anything* but soon that idea vanished—I reflected that I still had a husband to who I owed everything, I was then roused and thank Heaven."[103]

Christian faith provided some solace, as this plantation mistress urged: "His dear little flower is not lost, but only transplanted to flourish in a more congenial soil, in the paradise above."[104] Margaret Campbell asked herself, upon the death of an infant: "Could I have detained the pure, peaceful spirit from its own congenial realm. Would I have been so cruel? the little being had not tasted of the bitter bowl of human misery before it was called to everlasting happiness."[105] Most grieving relatives made constant reference to their "trust in the Lord" and the "blessings of Heaven." A mother expressed this sentiment on the loss of her three-month-old child: "It pleased God to call him from this vale of tears, he is now, I hope, triumphing in the great Redeemer of Elect Sinners."[106]

Women—because the particular roles of nursing the ill and caring for the motherless were assigned to them by their culture—were especially close to the pain and suffering associated with death—however natural its cause.[107] Through their regular letter-writing duties, women were the couriers of death as well as of glad tidings. One plantation mistress wrote of her mixed emotions upon receiving her sister's last letter: "My feelings were overcome betwen hope and fear. I put your letter in my bosom and walked about several minutes before I ventured to open it."[108] False reports might create needless anxiety when families were separated, which reinforced the importance of frequent letter writing.[109] The mail was not merely a product of women's leisure or imagination but often a literal reassurance that all were alive and well.

The aftermath of a death was governed by ritual, custom, and tradition. Both conduct at the death scene and the reporting of the death itself reflected strict rules of decorum. With the onset of any serious illness, cousins, aunts, and uncles were called in as well as the immediate family circle. Women ministered to the needs of the sick individual, who prepared himself or herself for death by bidding farewell to the living and offering prayers to heaven. The grieving family respectfully attended the final hours and recounted the dying moments for those who, because of distance or delay, were not in attendance. A bereaved sister wrote to a friend of her regrets concerning her brother's death: "Could it have been the will of providence that he had been with us could I have heard his dying expression, I should have felt much better reconciled but this was denied."[110] Rachel Mordecai reported the plight of a recently orphaned female in 1818: "She was dreadfully shocked, the poor girl, by having the intelligence communicated in a casual manner as a piece of news at the end of a letter. . . . She has since received in more soothing language the sad confirmation of her loss."[111] The "soothing language" of the "particulars of death" followed a standard style and form. Catherine Campbell's account of her mother's death satisfied the dictates of plantation etiquette:

> The next morning she called to me in her usual way—Kitty, my dear—I wish you to be reconciled for I am: my time is come I feel willing to go for I know in whom I have put my trust. In this way she continued to talk at times until sunday morning at about 10 or 11 o'clock. I had raised her and was supporting her in my arms— when she turned her eyes and looked full in my face. I at first thought that she intended to speak to me, but soon I perceived that the organs of speach were stopt forever. . . . her lifeless clay which to me had a more majestic appearence in it than any I had ever before seen.[112]

A planter wrote to his brother of a mutual friend's death: "He was in his senses throughout the whole time and was concious that death was his portion. Before he died he professed to be willing to meet his God, this gives great satisfaction to his friends whom he left to morn for him."[113] Death was seen as a rite of passage into another world; a process rather than an event. One woman reported to a friend: "I was present when death most unexpectedly began."[114]

Funerals reflected the wealth of the deceased. The coffin and the ceremony demonstrated the rank and position of the family, and could range from simple to splendid depending upon its status.[115] Women often receded into the background during the burial; indeed, in Louisiana women were often forbidden to attend funerals.[116] They re-emerged, however, to take a prominent role in the reorganization of family affairs during the mourning period. Men charged plantation mistresses with the domestic and spiritual welfare of bereaved families, and as a planter wrote: "The forms of worship are left to the woman."[117]

· · ·

Ministers and laymen alike agreed that women's greatest influence in the South was in the spiritual realm. The Reverend Penuel Bowen suggested: "Arts & Sciences best flourish in the North; Religion most in the South . . . especially in the female part of human nature."[118] Women served as the appropriate disseminators of Christian doctrine. Author Virginia Cary advised her readers: "This is the chief end of woman—to advance the cause of the Redeemer, by exerting quietly the influence she possesses as a *woman*, over the feelings, more than the understandings of her fellow beings."[119]

Religious affiliation varied from region to region throughout the South. Episcopalians dominated the planter class in the upper and coastal regions, Catholic populations were centered in Maryland and Louisiana, and Baptists, Methodists, and Presbyterians were the major non-Anglican Protestant sects, sprinkled through the plantation South.[120] Denominational affiliation, although hotly contested by many, was of relative unimportance to most plantation mistresses. Some women switched from church to church in search of a spiritual home; others refused to participate in controversy between contesting sects. A woman asserted in 1832: "I cared nothing about *denomination* but that I could give worlds to possess that faith which triumphed over the fear of death. . . ."[121]

The competition among churches perhaps stemmed from the rivalries promoted by camp meetings and revivals in the South during this era. Both the camp meetings in rural areas and the revivals in urban centers attracted enthusiastic crowds. One Savannah resident described an 1831 revival: "The four day meeting in the Methodist church has been followed by what they call 'a powerful work'—Every afternoon and evening they have an assembly which is everything but solemn and exceeds all that I ever saw. About 80 have been converted or advanced to be prayed for, including some of all description, characters and denominations."[122] Country gatherings might not have collected as many "souls," but they were beacons for the faithful in less-populated areas. Spring and summer were the high seasons for evangelical meetings.[123] During these revival seasons, many churches vied for new members, and some plantation mistresses disapproved of the undisguised competitiveness among ministers and churchgoers. As one woman complained about the local Methodists: "I really do think their unchristian like attempts to destroy the Presbyterian church will recoil on themselves."[124]

These religious celebrations served social as well as spiritual needs. Many attendees commented that camp meetings created a festival atmosphere. One plantation mistress was ambivalent about the "carnival aspects" of religious revivals: "All kinds of things were going on back of the tents, such as trading horses, playing games and having a jolly time generally. It was hard to tell whether these meetings resulted in good or evil."[125] One "good" that came of revivals was the local prayer associations women formed on the basis of contacts made at camp meetings.[126]

Women within the formal network of church affiliation, or simply associated in Christian faith, often banded together. Sometimes these assemblies would organize a Bible class to pursue scholarly interest in Christian texts; in other instances, women focused on the Scriptures for weekly meetings but spent their time together in prayer rather than study. Both aims generated a renewed interest in religion among the planter class. Plantation mistresses also attempted to form benevolent societies to further Christian goals within plantation society.[127] Sometimes these met with resistance, either from the women themselves—who were always short of time in their hectic round of plantation chores—or from men, who frequently objected to female participation in such groups. John Randolph complained to his niece in 1828: "Our women, such is the invariable law of this disease, all of them, to the neglect of their domestic duties and many to the injury of their reputations, are running mad after popular preachers; or forming themselves into clubs of one sort or another that only serve to gratify the love of selfishness and notoriety."[128]

Perhaps some of Randolph's venom stemmed from the intuition that this sort of activity could lead to disruptive attitudes toward slavery. If women joined together to conquer the evils of society, certainly the condition of blacks within the South might come under more careful scrutiny. It was under the auspices of religious duty that plantation mistresses became involved in the tutoring of slaves. A matron described her mother's attitudes: "The Masters and Mistresses were liable not only for care of their Servants bodies, but for their Souls—She held Religious instruction a duty and on Sundays regularly assembled all who would attend and read the Scriptures."[129] Men were generally not well disposed toward female religiosity in this sphere where piety might lead to politicization: a taboo for both blacks and women.

These two groups within plantation society may well have discovered in religion an inspiration for individual advancement, even though the masters were able to maintain dominance over the collective body of the oppressed majority. Indeed, religion was an effective tool for this oppression—perhaps more so with women, trapped within the white male bastion, than with slaves, segregated into separate communities. The key to emancipation lay in the power of evangelical affiliation and religious organization. As long as women (and blacks) remained atomized within society, they presented no threat; females were considered a pliable flock, to be shepherded by male ministers. The southern clergy vigorously supported the inferior status of women and blacks, preaching submission and obedience. On the other hand, while the slaveowners and their spokesmen from the pulpits could employ religious authority to justify and bolster the status quo at the expense of slaves and plantation mistresses, these same blacks and women could in principle counter with tenets of faith derived from identical religious doctrine. But the planter patriarchy successfully promoted a noncollective approach to religion, linking it exclusively to the spiritual—never the secular—strength of believers. Thus they preserved social order in the guise of serving the spiritual order.

Most southern women were therefore preoccupied with their own souls, since young girls were encouraged to concentrate exclusively on personal salvation: to redeem themselves, accept Christ, and become faithful servants of the Lord. Southern Christians felt that conversion was the pinnacle of religious experience. One girl rejoiced to a friend: "I have relinquished that ungreatful controversy I have so long held with my Maker and that I have a heart melted down with humility and riseing with gratitude to him."[130] Of course, after the confessions of faith, Christians still faced uncertainty and temptation. Plantation mistress Margaret Campbell lamented: "For some time past many doubts have arisen in my mind whether I am really a disciple of Christ or not, I have reasoned the point and compared my heart with those rules laid down in the scripture for our guide and can find nothing in it similar to a changed heart. But all I can do is cast my unworthy self on my Savior. If I go to hell I will go pleading for mercy and for a heart to love God."[131] Mortality cast its shadow, even over the young.[132] The depravity of the human heart was a common theme in plantation letters and journals. Jeremiah 17:9 was extremely popular among antebellum women: "The heart is deceitful above all things and desperately wicked; who can know it?"[133] Diaries abound in confession and self-recrimination, while women wrote despairingly to each other of their Christian failings.[134] One plantation mistress lamented to her sister: "I know something of my own heart tho too little I fear. I must confess I find it a sink of all pollution vile and deceitful, desperately wicked. I am led to cry Lord save or I perish. O leave me not to myself."[135]

Many southern women believed that the only hope for them lay in God's mercy, and they prayed fervently for Christian deliverance.[136] Plantation mistresses faced lives of struggle, but evil was not their only adversary. These women fought against the worldly but inevitable onslaught of disease and death, on their own behalf and for the various members of their families. Constantly subjected to both aspects of this threat—above all in the process of giving birth—southern women tried to shield themselves in the armor of religious faith. Battling "sin and sorrow" in her daily life, the plantation mistress persisted bravely against the odds, and left only the record of personal documents to mark even the passing triumphs she had won.

IX

EVERY WOMAN WAS AN ISLAND

*P*lanters possessed women in almost the same way that they ruled over their vast estates—small wonder, then, that many southern women felt a powerful identification with the land. Society structured itself around the basic relationships of men and women to each other and to the land. Yet however central women were to the functioning of that society, plantation mistresses often felt unrecognized and emotionally unfulfilled. Expected almost from birth to set aside personal considerations and delay gratification, many women of the South nurtured suppressed desires that bred anxiety, vague anticipation, and an ever-increasing sense of alienation. Ellen Mordecai reflected, in a letter to her brother in 1823: "It was for me best that I yielded to the wishes of papa, our brothers and sisters—I wonder when my best will cease to be painful and when I shall begin to enjoy life instead of enduring it."[1]

The roots of alienation were several. First, the majority of women in the ante-bellum South were isolated on widely separated farms and plantations throughout the region. Most often the plantation mistress was the single white woman on the estate. She was firmly established, indeed, immured in her home by responsibilities and duties, but her status as the female head of the household brought her small reward. Besieged by domestic concerns, the white woman was cut off from society.

The plight of slaves in America has been explored extensively in the historical literature; so much recent work, in fact, has dealt with black life on the plantation that scholar John Hope Franklin has commented that American historians seem more interested in the study of blacks in slavery than after freedom. One of the salient features of this slave culture was its sense of community. Blacks were able to retain African patterns, to forge a new language, to transform Christian ideology, to both endure and transcend their status as slaves: all within the framework of community. The sense of solidarity, the flexible yet supportive interdependency of the group, the familiarity of a network of family and friends, contributed to their individual and cultural survival. Often Africans torn from their natural families could rework traditional formulas of relationship and adopt fictive kin. Thus despite the oppression of slavery, blacks failed to succumb to the dehumanization of the system. On the contrary, they proved able to affirm the very dimensions of life that their masters sought to deny them: family, pride, work, and faith. Their community evolved conditions wherein these values could flourish despite massive and determined opposition. Despite the systematic campaign of the master class to control every aspect of slave life, blacks achieved some measure of autonomy through the creation of their own subculture within plantation society.

The plantation mistress, however, had no comparable sense of community. Whereas northern women enjoyed numerous opportunities for socializing with one another and eventually succeeded in establishing communities of mutual interest, southern white women anchored on their remote estates suffered in and from solitude, rarely able to interconnect with others like themselves. The many people on the plantation were not a community for the mistress of the plantation. Kin and children, however comforting, could not provide the support of peers. Even if a husband was in constant residence, men were not an obvious source of sympathetic identity within such an oppressively patriarchal society. Slave women—likewise oppressed by white masters, sharers in such burdens of womanhood as childbearing and domestic responsibilities—were completely cut off from white females; the gulf imposed by racial discrimination was unbridgeable. Thus, as the inevitable consequence of her social definition and circumstances, the plantation mistress was compelled to spend her life alone and out of touch with her own kind. Mary Telfair wrote to her confidante, Mary Few, from her Waynesboro, Georgia plantation: "The life we lead is similar to a monastic one only that we have no nuns or confessors and are permitted to range unmolested through the gloomy pine trees. . . ."[2]

Many planters were well aware of the drawbacks life on the plantation held for women, especially during its frontier years. One cotton grower complained in 1823 that he had given up the idea of marriage because "it would be very difficult to find one who would be willing to go the wilds of Mississippi and there spend the balance of her life from her friends and relations."[3] Although it might be difficult to persuade a bride to abandon her family and follow a planter into the wilderness, once she had made that choice her place was inalterably by her husband's side, with only infrequent escapes to town (if any were accessible) or to the homes of friends and relatives. Regret could no longer be considered legitimate. The newlywed Nancy Robinson left her family home to travel to Holmes County, Mississippi, in 1833. Grieved by her departure, she wrote: "The sorrow of the whole family overpowered my feelings. I cried with them their wish to keep me made me repent leaving them, I blamed myself. I forgot my duty and wished to stay. . . ." But the bride set aside her feelings and resigned herself to her destination: "I have ended my life of folly, gaiety and amusement. I thought I will never be happy any more way from my family." Four months later, she was still melancholy: "I am sad tonight, sickness preys in my frame. I am alone and more than 150 miles from any near relative in the wild woods of an Indian nation. . . ."[4]

Unmarried girls' anticipation of such feelings meant that, in some instances, planters moved south and west without women. A southern woman remarked: "In 1836 I came to this country. It was then a dense cane brake except immediately on the Mississippi River which was at that time known as Bachelor's Bend from the fact that most of the inhabitants were unmarried men."[5] But if a planter husband's mind was set upon moving, his wife might try to convince him to migrate to a plantation near one of her recently removed siblings or to the newly settled district where cousins or friends from her home town had clustered. He, in turn, might attempt to coax a reluctant wife into transplanting their home and family. Israel Pickens wrote in this spirit to his wife, Martha, with a "message" for their daughter Julia: "Her pa is not inclined to . . . take his family away without first satisfying his good wife of the propriety of the measure. He is certain that he can do this as he is confident of the prudence, the discretion and good sense of his dear and better part and her attachment to the mutual interest and happiness of the family."[6] The Pickens family shortly thereafter settled in Alabama, despite Martha's objections.

During the early national period, frontier fever spread through the planter class. In North Carolina, Owen Holmes wrote to his sister in 1834: "I can hardly see a man but what he is fixing to move. . . . I want to leave here the first of November if I leave."[7] Women were not so restless. One young girl feared that the trend might affect her father: "I hope he will not leave Virginia. Mamma and I cannot give up the Old Dominion. Our Culpeper papers are filled with advertisements. Auburn is for sale. It is truly distressing to see many old residences that we have been accustomed to visit set up to the highest bidder."[8] Men, too, acknowledged the hardships new vistas entailed. A planter wrote back to North Carolina about his new life in Alabama: "I would advise all my young friends and relations . . . if they want fresh lands and the finest . . . let them go to new parts of Georgia and Alabama. I tell you all if you want good health, stay in North Carolina."[9] A Mississippi gentleman took a different tack in his description of the frontier: "If you wish to see splendid poverty, come to Mississippi. If you wish to see people worth millions living as they were not worth hundreds, come down here. If you wish to dine where whiskeys drank for meals, eat and dissipation carried on, come to the land of cotton and negroes."[10] Still the promise of riches pulled families into the New South region.[11]

The southwestward trek continued with little abatement during the ante-bellum era. From Virginia to Mississippi, planter families on the move dotted the roads. A planter recounted his migration from Virginia to Florida in 1827: "In true Arab style . . . my caravan consisted of my wife, six children, twenty odd young men, 144 negroes, 5 horse wagons, two carry alls and my family carriage and five saddle horses.

. . . We had large and commodious tents. . . . we travelled from 15 to 20 miles a day."[12] Mary Hatch wrote a letter to her grandmother in 1832, describing her 460-mile move from her North Carolina home to the wilds of Alabama. She and her husband traveled twenty miles a day in carriages and wagons. They stayed overnight with planters or in taverns, while their slaves camped along the way.[13]

Establishing these primitive plantations created for civilization-bred planter wives a new life of unfamiliar tasks and unexpected, often grueling challenges. A woman wrote to her sister in North Carolina: "You may think strange that I have not given you more incuragement to come to this country and not without reason. . . . We have had to beat our meal and our homeny 20 miles from eny mill. This with many other things two tedious to mention was my reason."[14] One woman confided to her grandmother after leaving her home state: "I have been low spirited but have got over it pretty much, tell Uncle Buckner that I have not had hystericks until the day before yesterday since I left him. I think then was all the time thinking about home. I thought I would have given the whole world to see my dear *grandmother*, indeed I hated to part with all my relations very much."[15] Loneliness was exacerbated by the fact that men, once arrived at these desolate sites, were as free as ever to absent themselves and move independently on and off their properties at will. A distraught Sarah Gayle wrote to her husband: "Oh, come home, for mercy sake, what can a woman do without her husband?"[16] One wife composed a doleful letter to her husband in 1801: "I think I have a little more flesh on my bones than I had when we parted but my dear do you remember when that was. Almost four weeks and am I to be depriv'd of the pleasure of seeing you for weeks to come, it makes the tears fall fast from my poor Eyes."[17] No matter how short the absence, plantation mistresses were both eager and anxious while awaiting their husbands' return.[18]

At best, life on frontier plantations proved tedious. A woman in rural Louisiana wrote to her brother, at college in Kentucky: "I wish I had some thing interesting to relate but ours is a life of monotony, and if I waited for some interesting adventure I feared you might think we neglected you."[19] Such isolation took its psychological toll on women, leaving them—despite their arduous labor for family and home—wondering about their own worth.[20] And as their letters and other personal documents testify, such feelings habitually developed even in planter wives far from the frontier. One woman confided to a friend in 1815: "I begin now to fear that the longer I live the more dejected I shall be; and alas! my dear friend I find that each day brings with it some additional sorrow or perplexity."[21] Whether she encountered them in darkest Alabama or in the heart of Virginia, the despair of loneliness colored the plantation mistress's solitary hours.

A matron wrote her sister in March 1816: "I have very little worth while writing about for I have not been off the land since some time before Christmas and I see very little company."[22] Planters, aware of the sense of entrapment their wives experienced,[23] encouraged them to visit relatives, but only occasionally; they preferred instead to receive visitors for prolonged periods of time. But by far the most common advice to a lonely plantation mistress, given by men and women alike, was—accept your exile. Martha Richardson counseled a young woman friend: "So much depends on yourself that you are bound as wife and mother to exert all your energies and determine to get rid of all disagreeable feelings—banish, my child, from your mind everything that has hitherto distressed you."[24]

Many planters hoped their wives would use work to cure their depressions. Thomas Jefferson wrote on the subject in 1787, advising his daughter: "Idleness begets ennui, ennui the hypochondria and that a diseased body. No laborious person was ever yet hysterical. . . ." He went on to warn: "If at any moment my dear you catch yourself in idleness, start from it as you would from the precipice of a gulph. . . ." Jefferson—whose own activities were prodigious in number, scope, energy, achieved excellence, and, above all, variety—could only suggest further: "Music, drawing, books, invention and exercise will be so many resources to you against ennui. But there are others which to this object add that of utility. These are the needle and domestic economy. . . . In the country life of America there are many moments when a woman can have recourse to nothing but her needle for employment."[25] Spinster Mary Telfair wrote to her most intimate friend, Mary Few, about her own desolation. She felt that the ongoing process of life weighed heavily upon her: "As our friends drop off by marriage and death and society loses all its attractions, which it has with me, we require the varied occupations of domestic life to keep us from bitterness and despondency." Yet Telfair believed that activity was a superficial solution to a deeper problem. She confessed: "I cannot take any interest in the detail of housekeeping. I could keep a house well from duty but my heart and soul could not be engaged in it."[26] So the depressed mind might be diverted by occupation, but idleness was by no means the root of misery for plantation mistresses. Melancholy often persisted simultaneously with unrelenting domestic employment.

Widowhood, of course, was especially devastating in a society so predicated upon the centrality of the male; to the loss of a husband was added the alienating loss of that central core which gave definition to everything else in a woman's life. In 1797, Judith Randolph—recently widowed, worried over the illness of her mother-in-law—responded to the letter in which her father-in-law, St. George Tucker, announced Mrs. Tucker's recovery: "Thank Heaven your better Angel averted the cruel stroke which must have consigned you, like myself, to unavailing wretchedness. Believe me, my dear Sir, that under your roof alone do I feel myself anything but a poor unprotected, desolate being, cut off from society; whose only trust is in Heaven, whose only hope for happiness lies beyond the grave."[27] Another widow expressed dismay at her daily lot: "I have so much to perplex me at times that I scarcely know how to bear all things as it comes." But this plantation mistress found a reason for living: "If I had no children . . . I would gladly leave this world."[28]

When her endurance flagged, the Christian woman turned to God for fortitude. A woman confessed her innermost feelings to her diary: "Alas! I feel that I am quite unable to resist my disposition to impatience and despondency, the effect doubtless of my pride and rebellious will. All I can do is to look to the everlasting hills whence alone my strength cometh—God of all grace, let no sin have the dominion over men, but help me to resist it and to humble myself duly under the sense of it!"[29] But religious feelings did not always relieve women of their melancholy; on the contrary, the two were often deeply intertwined. Christian humility could develop into unhealthy self-deprecation. Eleanor Douglas wrote to her sister in May 1820: "Would we spend a small part and misspent time and what worms of dust we are."[30] Four months later, she speculated: "Thirty-one years of my unprofitable life is gone. How many more months or days will be added?"[31] Along similar lines, S. Myra Smith celebrated her birthday with unhappy thoughts: "I this day upon my 30th year. For thirty years I have been the object of God's amazing love and mercy. And wherefore? For any good that is in me? Oh, no—Alas, I can do nought but fall at his feet and cry 'guilty, guilty'."[32]

Anxiety often manifested itself in the form of nightmares and forced plantation mistresses to take note of their dream life. Mary Burton wrote to a friend in 1816: "Tell me if the interpretation of your dream is likely to come to pass, but I hope it will be the reverse of what you wrote."[33] Margaret Steele described a dream about a slave to her mother: "I dreamt one night that you whipped her and unfortunately cut out her eyes—the dream woke me and I was truly happy it was but a dream."[34] Susan Hutchinson gave a graphic illustration of her emotional state in her description of a nightmare: "I thought every member of my family removed from the house and left me alone to occupy one room, all the furniture was packed away except a bed—I recollect they put away the looking glass saying I should not want it." She naïvely commented: "I do not remember to have felt the slightest dread of being left, only I wanted the time to come when we should meet at home again."[35] Susan Hutchinson may, however, have been in an unusual mood when she dreamed of her abandonment; she had taken a dose of laudanum to help her sleep.

Laudanum was commonly used throughout the ante-bellum era, prescribed with unfortunate frequency for "female complaints." To compound the problem, women were in charge of medicine on the plantation; easy access to the opiate was a constant threat and temptation. Although there are no statistics for the pre–Civil War period, a recent survey of late-nineteenth-century opium addiction has revealed interesting data. Contrary to the twentieth-century image of heroin addicts, the late-nineteenth-century profile indicates that addicts were disproportionately upper-class, southern, white, and female.[36] The women of the Jefferson Davis family, treated by a doctor liberal in his dosages, became dangerously addicted.[37] Some women used this medicine to ease pain from illness, but other plantation mistresses resorted to the drug to relieve depression or insomnia.[38]

Opium addiction was little understood during the nineteenth century. Doctors and patients alike were unaware of the degree of laudanum's addictive quality and the debilitating effect of its constant use. Plantation mistress Mary Hatch, isolated on her husband's estate in

Green County, Alabama, wrote to her grandmother in North Carolina: "Mr. Hatch has gone to Greensboro and I am all alone. . . . I have a sweet little daughter five days old. . . . I have take a great deal of Laudanum. I have been almost stupid with it."[39] Many women slipped unknowingly into addiction. In May 1827, Susan Hutchinson was despondent over her failing health, the poor state of her husband's business affairs, and her general malaise. On May 1 she wrote: "How many years have passed away and in each a rural Queen [May Queen] has been crowned under my direction—now these scenes of childish mirth are gone and soberer hours succeed." By May 10, she was in deeper despair: "Last night I took nearly one hundred drops of laudanum without benefit." Two weeks later she was still morose: "All day much indisposed—I drank mint tea—brandy toddy, cold lemonade, parched meal. . . ." But at the end of that day Susan Hutchinson, turning to her one reliable source of relief, "at last took a dose of laudanum."[40] Even if the addicted women themselves failed to realize their weakness, concerned friends saw the perils of repeated use. Martha Richardson wrote to her nephew in 1821 of the case of a female friend: "She had written for a fresh supply of black drops (two dozen bottles) under present circumstances the Doctor said in his letter it was impossible for her to exist without it—here we behold the fatal consequences of a bad habit—when she first commenced the use of it to relieve her mind after the loss of her son little did she think future existence and tolerable comfort would render its use absolutely necessary."[41]

Opportunities to "relieve the mind" existed, of course, that were not so dangerous. Love of reading, common among women, was one. The routine of a plantation mistress afforded few leisure hours, but women made time in their busy schedules for literature because of the value they set on mental improvement, as well as for the pleasure they derived from reading.[42] Charles Manigault described in his memoir: "My mother was devoted to Literature and poss'ed a fine Library, constantly added to by receiving interesting works from Paris and London. She had not many idle moments to read during the Day. But read a great deal at Night when others were in bed and the house quiet. . . ."[43] But this 1828 diary entry of another matron is doubtless more representative: "This has been a day of much hurry and trouble to me so that I have not had much time for reading and reflection."[44] These were among the few forms of entertainment for women on plantations, and matrons enjoyed reading aloud with husbands or friends.[45]

The libraries and letters of ante-bellum women demonstrate their wide-ranging appreciation of literature: from Brown's *Moral Philosophy* to *The French Revolution*, from Robert Burns to William Godwin, from Kotzebue to Hume to the ever-popular Sir Walter Scott.[46] Many planter wives sent money to friends in towns or cities to purchase books for them; more commonly, women applied to friends and relatives to borrow unavailable volumes, and routinely traded and exchanged literary finds.[47] In some areas, circulating libraries sprang up to supply the constant demand for new reading material. Virginian Maria Campbell was diligent in her search: "I have indulged my imagination by exhausting the circulating library and also the libraries of some of the neighbors in town. Among a vast quantity of trash, I have found some of the products of genius."[48] William Elliott praised his wife Ann's abilities in a letter to his sister: "She is an excessive reader and without exaggeration reads more in a month that I do in a year."[49]

Controversy raged within plantation society, as in all of America, over the subject of novel reading. Although plantation mistresses generally professed disapproval, popular novels found an increasingly wide audience among them. A woman counseled her cousin in 1818: "Do not read many novels. They are very pernicious in their effects. They poison the young mind and fill it with ideas of perfection in men."[50] A matron echoed this misgiving in her diatribe against "plays and romances": "Husbands . . . being taken up with their affairs, are not always in the humour of paying them [wives] those ridiculous compliments which are given to women in plays, in romances and the romantic life."[51] Even those who took a more balanced view remained guarded; a woman wrote to a young friend, lonesome on her isolated plantation: "But I think, Sarah, if the offense of novel reading was ever pardonable, it is as in your case, tho' I hope you mingle with it something more profitable . . . a habit which tho' delightfully pleasant, is, I believe, pernicious when immodestly indulged."[52]

Romantic and repetitive, the novels by Mrs. Southworth and Mrs.

Sigourney that so alarmed the reformers of the day were not considered morally improving enough for the impressionable minds of young girls. There were no regional literary markets during the ante-bellum era; fiction ordinarily sold to a national audience. The work of Sir Walter Scott, however, was noticeably popular in the southern states.

However transporting, literature was a poor substitute for a circle of friends. Many plantation mistresses, so long isolated on the land away from other female companionship, felt themselves out of touch with society. Sometimes they began to doubt their ability to socialize at all, or experienced, like Georgian Mary Telfair, a sense of active withdrawal: "You may imagine what my life must be—It is living in the world without any interest in its concerns. I have become so accustomed to solitude that I do not care for any society beyond my books and my own thoughts."[53] Another woman, feeling claustrophobic on her husband's estate in Alabama, explained to a friend: "We are so completely cooped up among these mountains that we have no personal intercourse with the world around and the letters of our friends are our chief visitors, but they are like 'angel visits'—few and far between."[54] Letters, the critical link, kept women in touch with the outside world and bound friends together. A woman in Alabama wrote to a female friend in North Carolina about the value she placed on correspondence: "Often when I feel lonely and melancholy I take it with others from my pocketbook and read them [the friend's letters] as I would converse with a friend and pour over their dear contents, a fount of tears, to ease the burden of my lonely heart."[55]

Plantation mistresses kept up assiduously with their confidantes despite obstacles of time and distance. Girlhood acquaintance blossomed into lifelong friendship for many women. Some women thought of their sisters as their first and dearest friends;[56] female cousins and schoolmates from academy days also maintained intimacy. Best friends often kept journals for each other's perusal; one of the most famous diaries of the period, Fanny Kemble's *Journal of Residence on a Georgian Plantation*, was a journal kept for Kemble's close friend Elizabeth Sedgwick. Bred according to strict rules of behavior, plantation mistresses closely observed the form and courtesies of friendship. Southern women chided their friends against neglect: "Even love, powerful as it may be, I cannot allow to come between me and friendship, so beware, my little friend when you get in love not to forget me."[57] A young unmarried woman declared to her sister: "Without friends, this world would not be desirable to me. Indeed, there are times when nothing appears desirable or rather to be obtained that is desired."[58]

Occasional visits from female friends certainly made women's lives less lonely and brought them news of the cosmopolitan world outside. Maria Campbell wrote to her husband David about her houseguest, Jane White: "She is very affectionate and particularly attentive to me, her friendship is exceedingly well timed. . . . our employment on these occasions is to read and converse as circumstances may direct, untill the hour arrives that we wish to go to bed and talk secrets for two or three hours before we feel an inclination to sleep."[59] Sarah Gayle reported her grief at parting with a beloved woman friend: "I think no woman living can be to me what Ann has been. A friend never possessed more entirely the confidence of another than she has mine. . . . My parting with Ann inflicted a pang for which I was hardly prepared. How much of love was condensed into the hour I sat with her previous to our starting, and when I held her to my bosom and bade her farewell, I felt that Providence would be kind indeed, if such another friend was in store for me."[60]

Almost every plantation mistress cherished one particular female friendship of special intimacy and mutual trust. These close and romantic attachments between married women were common during the nineteenth century throughout the United States, but women exiled to rural homes perhaps treasured their friendships more than those afforded the diversions of town life and urban activities. The diaries and letters of such women reveal the importance they attached to these sustaining emotional ties.[61]

A rare solution to the plight of the lonely plantation mistress was the radical one of travel. Although they were infrequently permitted purely social expeditions, women did on occasion undertake excursions, far or near, for reasons of health. Planter families might travel abroad or to the North, visiting a spa or resort during the summer to avoid disease and discomfort during the "sickly season." Poor roads hampered comfortable land travel in the southern states, and although a journey by water could provide more agreeable travel conditions, a sea voyage had its own drawbacks. Louisianian Margaret Howell described to her husband, William, her trip to New York by ship: "We arrived at Staten Island yesterday after a voyage of nineteen days . . .

poor me, from the moment we crossed the bar untill we left the ship, I was sick, nothing stayed on my stomach more than ten minutes, my dinner at the islands was the first meal since I left New Orleans."[62]

Southerners' visits were most commonly limited to short distances from their own plantations—for example, to a summer home or to a town house for the social season. These temporary moves were often elaborate operations: "The occupation of the town house for the summer season was no simple maneuver. Such an undertaking often involved the removal, bag and baggage of an entire plantation household consisting of the planter's own large family, varying numbers of relatives and friends and a retinue of house servants."[63] Most of the burden of supervision and management fell upon the plantation mistress, and the aggravations of transplanting a household at least somewhat offset the social benefits that rewarded such a move.

A woman was unable to travel, to move about at her own discretion; custom required a male companion as protector. Such traditional restraints on women's mobility could keep them in helpless isolation on the land if no suitable chaperone were available to them, as one woman lamented: "It is quite out of our power to travel any distance this summer as we have no gentleman to go with us."[64] With no means of escape from their lonely plantation exile, southern women suffered from a lack of freedom that was, in a certain sense, analogous to that of slaves.

Southerners were, nonetheless, famous during the nineteenth century for their hospitality. A woman on a visit in Indiana in 1837 reported: "They entertain more company than any other family in town. Mrs. Moore, you know, is a Southerner and still retains all the hospitality of the South."[65] The generosity and courtly manners of plantation owners were proverbial. One itinerant traveler commented in 1812: "The Gentlemen Planters off the road entertain their friends in princely style and strangers with hospitality; but do not choose to take pay, either for fear of becoming too much known to travellers or perhaps through pride, and they would by no means wish the trouble (apart from the expense) of keeping every kind of traveller who pays."[66]

But it was the plantation mistress who actually prepared for the reception of family, friends, and strangers in her home throughout the year. Dolley Madison, in her youth a popular Washington hostess, found the burdens of plantation hospitality distressing during her later years. She wrote to her niece in 1833: "It has seemed to me, my dearest Dolley, that I should never be able to write to you a letter on account of a stream of people coming and going until I fear I am quite nervous."[67] On a large plantation, a crowd of fifteen at breakfast was not uncommon. Planters expected their wives to provide lavish and gracious hospitality to relatives and travelers alike. One harassed matron wrote to her son in 1828 of a troublesome guest: 'He is really a bore. He comes here just as if it were a tavern Friday afternoon without any invitation and stays until Monday. It is too tiresome."[68] And another Southerner recounted a tale of extraordinary hospitality: "I have often been told of the gentleman and his wife, who, being asked to dine at a residence on St. Simon, found that during the meal a boat had been sent to Darien, fifteen miles distant for their luggage, and that so much pleased were host, hostess and guests with one another, that the stay was prolonged until two children had been born to the visiting couple."[69] The couple who came to dinner and stayed for two children is certainly an exaggerated but nevertheless a symbolic tale of planter hospitality.

Formal entertainment on the plantation, although infrequent, was extravagant and grand. Parties and balls, like other public displays, were planned to demonstrate a planter's wealth and liberality. Mary Campbell reported such an event in March 1810: "On the 22nd of February we had a ball in this place that exceeds anything for splendor of dress that has ever been here. . . ." Notwithstanding, the woman added, "few married ladies attended. I was not one of the number that did."[70] British traveler James Buckingham explained: "When ladies marry they usually give up going into company and confine themselves to nursing and household duties. . . . Married men as well as unmarried attend parties; but married women mostly stay at home."[71] Such segregation was common throughout America, but was especially enforced in the South.[72]

Most celebrations were seasonal and occasional in nature. Christmas was the most festive. Dances and tea parties kept plantation mistresses busy through the whole of December,[73] and southern matrons spent considerable time and effort on the preparation of food for the holiday season. Guests were served special alcoholic concoctions: songaree (a wine mix), sack posset (sherry, ale, eggs, and milk), and syllabub (white wine and whipped cream). Women cracked nuts, seeded raisins, cut orange peel, washed currants, and prepared fruitcakes, puddings, and mincemeat for their Christmas callers; they also made a candy called benne brittle from sesame seeds (called benne seeds by the Africans who first brought them to America). On Christmas Day the mistress of the house provided a huge feast, her home decorated with evergreen and mistletoe, her table crowded with family and friends.[74] Planters were hosts at elaborate entertainments on other special occasions as well: a molasses stewing, a Bachelor's Ball, a horse race, or the crowning of the May Queen.[75] In 1801, Ralph Izard wrote to his mother in Washington: "In Virginia they have once a fortnight what they call a fish feast or Barbicue at which all the Gentry within twenty miles round are present with all their families." He went on to comment: "I was very much surprised to see the Ladies young and old so fond of drinking Toddy before dinner."[76]

Parties on plantations were in essence extraordinary events, unlike the regular festivities that enlivened town life. An urban environment was unquestionably stimulating after the dull country routine. Plantation mistresses greeted trips to Charleston, New Orleans, Savannah, or other cities with delight. Charleston, for example, afforded a variety of diversions in addition to private parties. A matron reported the formation of a musical society in 1826.[77] Theater and concerts were common. Ladies organized "social assemblies" to provide a rotating schedule of teas and parties. A young girl ecstatically described her city visit to a friend: "I don't think in my life I ever spent a more delightful week that when I was in Town; it seemed to be the study of the whole family to make our time pass away as agreeably as possible. There were five beaux and as many belles in the house constantly; we did nothing at all while I was with them but eat, visit, romp and sleep; but we made less use of the last mentioned article than any of the former."[78] Indeed, the town often proved overexciting for girls fresh from the constraints and tedium of the plantation. A Richmond matron sketched such a case in 1822:

> I shall be silent and leave it to some uninterested historian to record the exploits of the nine Miss Simmons, *such*, I have no doubt, will be found, for it is impossible that a set of *country puts* should go tearing up and down the city in an old rattling carriage with a driver and footman incessantly quareling at the top of their voices and

now and then bawling to foot passengers to inquire the way to Mr. This or That, sometimes knocking at a dozen doors in a row before finding the right one and occasionally after finding the right one knocking so hard for the door to burst open, the footman to pitch in head foremost and a score of *pet dogs* to set on him at once. . . . If to *make a noise is to be a belle*, rely on it, they are the greatest belles in town.[79]

At least one plantation mistress likened her life to that of a caged bird. Although planters occasionally let women enjoy the invigoration of visiting or a city sojourn, they inevitably required their wives to re-enter the cage without complaint. Men were neither oblivious nor insensitive to the potential or actual melancholy of women's existence, but southern slaveowners required obedience without question; if women undermined the planters' absolute authority, the entire network of power relations might be challenged. Thus the necessity of their own position led men wholly to reject active resistance; complaint was as close as women could come to opposing their oppression.

When Maria Campbell wrote to her husband in Richmond, mourning his absence during the Christmas holidays, he replied: "For whatever you may think of the lonesomeness of your situation—I can assure you mine is much more so. The company here affords some amusement for a few days, but its novelty is soon gone—and then, to me, there is no more pleasure in it, without you, than if I were in a solitary wilderness."[80] His wife responded: "You have it in your power to enjoy company when you please. . . . But here I am shut up like a canary bird (in my dear little cot, to be sure) without the power of obtaining society."[81] David Campbell concluded their correspondence on the subject: "I know you are shut up like the canary bird, but you sing so sweetly that to make you sing seems mere justification for the tyranny exercised."[82]

In ante-bellum society, the power of southern slaveholders rendered tyranny just. And that power ensured that a woman remained as securely bound to the land as her husband's other property: shackled however enshrined, and melancholy however maintained. Every woman was an island, isolated unto herself and locked into place by the stormy and unsettling seas of plantation slavery.

X

THE CURSE OF SLAVERY

Speak then to your relatives, your friends,
your acquaintances on the subject of slavery; be not afraid if you are conscientiously convinced it is *sinful*, to say so
openly. . . . My object has been to arouse
you, as the wives and mothers, the daughters and sisters, of the South, to a sense of
your duty as women, and as Christian
women, on that great subject which has
shaken already our country, from the St.
Lawrence and the lakes, to the Gulf of
Mexico, and from the Mississippi to the
shores of the Atlantic; *and will continue to
shake it,* until the polluted temple of slavery fall and crumble into ruin.
—Angelina Grimké

*A*ngelina Grimké was a radical; the daughter of a wealthy
Carolina slaveholder, she rejected her birthright, moved
North, and became an abolitionist crusader. Her extreme opposition
to slavery forced her out of her homeland and led her onto the platform of a national reform campaign. Following her departure from

the South, she published in 1836 *An Appeal to the Christian Women of the South*. This attack on slavery was necessarily more rhetorical than realistic. In it, Grimké was propagandizing for a northern cause rather than pleading authentically to her southern sisters to overthrow their peculiar institution. Having been raised as an exalted specimen of southern womanhood herself, Angelina Grimké was all too aware of the impossibility of her task. No matter how she fashioned her argument, her views could hardly elicit favorable reaction from slaveholders. Nor, therefore, could Grimké anticipate response from those to whom she addressed her appeal. Southern women were not indifferent to contradictions of slavery, but the practical prerequisites of a slaveowning culture demanded female silence on this sensitive issue. Whether specter or substance, female antislavery activity—or merely sentiment—offended southern patriarchs.

In general it was considered unbecoming and unladylike for a female to initiate any political discussion. If a man wanted to engage a woman in conversation on a controversial topic, that was his prerogative, but the expectation that a woman be a well-educated, vivacious conversationalist did not include knowledge of political issues or opinions. As Savannah patriarch W. B. Bulloch wrote to his daughter in 1831: "I discover my dear Louisa that you have been dabbling a little in politics. . . . But as a female and a lady, be aloof."[1] Women with an interest in politics drew criticism: "She is very loquacious, much fonder of the company of Gentlemen than of ladies, is a great hand to talk on the affairs of the nation, physic, law, etc. takes no delight in a garden. . . . Thomas says she was intended for a man, but unfortunately was spoilt a little in the making."[2]

A notable exception to this silence in political expression was women's active expression of their own patriotism. During the undeclared war with France in the late 1790s, George Washington's niece Nelly Parke Custis wrote to a friend: "Although I am no politician, I can assure you yet I cannot avoid expressing my opinion of the French. Were I drowning and a straw only in sight, I would as soon think of trusting that slender support (which in fact could not save me) as place the smallest dependence upon the ability of the French Republican government."[3] Dolley Madison wrote to her husband in Washington in 1805: "I wish you would indulge me with some information respecting the war with Spain, and the disagreement with England, which is so generally expected. You know I am not much of a politician but I am extremely anxious to hear (as far as you think proper) what is going forward in the Cabinet."[4]

Women certainly felt their own exclusion. They disclaimed their legitimate interest and very often their obvious ability in the arena of political debate. Maria Campbell, wife of Virginia politician David Campbell, took an intense and spirited view of American politics. In 1814 she wrote to her cousin Jefferson: "You know we ladies are forbidden by the polite world to say much on this subject." Nevertheless, she continued, "tho it is not our province to be politicians, yet I cannot avoid looking around me, and viewing from my inaccessible mountains the important struggle in which my native and beloved Country is engaged—Her destiny is connected with the life blood of my heart. . . . I am willing to suffer more rather than see her savage and merciless foe triumph over her."[5] Nine months later when her husband was off at war, she comforted him with strong support of his participation in combat. She urged him to fight to free their country from the influence of tyrants. To counter his fear that she might feel neglected during his military service, she assured him that he was in fact attending to her needs, because "happiness can only be founded in virtue and virtue cannot exist without perfect liberty."[6] David Campbell's fighting against the British was, to his wife, a struggle for this essential liberty. Not unlike many planter couples, the Campbells throughout their many years of marriage exchanged a variety of political opinions—in the privacy of their personal correspondence.

Planters were afraid that public female expressions of political attitudes would cause embarrassment and unfortunate repercussions for their families. On the especially sensitive subject of slavery, planters demanded that women remain silent and safe; women were too likely to be "soft" on the topic. The abolitionist attack from the North and the southern evangelical emancipation movement weakened the proslavery bastion. Women's participation in the northern crusade—female antislavery societies, prayer vigils, petition campaigns, as well as outspoken leadership of such figures as Abby Kelley and Lucretia Mott—alarmed slaveowners, and may have further provoked the ban on women's participation in discussions of current events.

Women, however sheltered from the public sphere, inevitably felt the pressure of living in a biracial slave society. In December 1832, Sarah Gayle of Alabama wrote: "The year is fast drawing to a close. It has been marked by two of the strangest scourges which have ever visited our hitherto happy land, Nullification and the cholera."[7] Although secession was averted following the 1832–1833 crisis over South Carolina's threat to defy the federal government, the tensions over slavery increased rather than decreased during the post-Nullification period. A woman wrote to her uncle in 1838: "You have seen I suppose by the papers the excitement which prevails in Congress on the abolition question. The northerners do not know how dangerous it is for them to excite us on that question or what destruction they are heaping up for themselves at their interference."[8]

During the 1830s, the question of slavery began building to the division that eventually wrenched the country apart in a bloody civil war. While debates and conflicts erupted on the national scene, slave-owners dealt with daily reflections of the problem in their own lives. None felt more stress and contradiction than the plantation mistress, particularly in her capacity as spiritual guardian of the culture and "conscience" of the plantation. Whereas women in the North not only rejected slavery for blacks but challenged their own inferior status as well, southern plantation mistresses had to come to terms with their role within this complex system and the moral and practical contradictions within their plantation world.

The threat from within—evangelical antislavery—had declined during the post-Revolutionary years. But the threat from without—political abolitionism—was strengthening with each passing year. By the early decades of the nineteenth century, the impact of northern antislavery had made its mark on southern society. Organizations, petitions, and legislative activities combined to form solid phalanxes of opinion on slavery on either side of the Mason-Dixon line. The "immediate emancipation" forces of the North demonstrated remarkable growth and militancy during the ante-bellum era, and the abolitionists exerted considerable influence on Southerners by the 1830s. In 1836, Mary Telfair of Georgia wrote in anticipation of a visit to her friend Mary Few in New York: "Mrs. Jones empowered Geo. Jones to get us lodgings with her at the Astor Hotel *that will be very near you*. When we thought of being alone, we were opposed to a great Hotel for we take no Servants this year. A late law passed in the legislature prohibits both slaves and free coloured persons from being taken on. . . ."⁹

To Southerners, slaves were property, valuable and substantial investments; women in plantation society were schooled from an early age to this view of the necessity and value of slave labor in southern agriculture. The moral arguments endorsing African slavery and the growth and development of a proslavery doctrine have been dealt with extensively in the historical literature.¹⁰ Planters shifted their defense of slavery during the 1830s. Previous to the abolitionist attack on the South, slaveholders were willing to agree that slavery was a "necessary evil," at least in part confessing to the undesirability of slavery. Southerners actually complained that this system had been foisted upon them and that they had simply made the best of *their* burden. By the time antislavery organizations had gained some measure of respectability during the 1840s, slaveowners sophisticated and refined their philosophy of owning human chattel. First and foremost, slaveholders appealed to the racism entrenched in white America, North and South. They argued that Africans were a savage and backward race, lucky to be rescued by Europeans for transplantation into American civilization. Afro-Americans, held in equal contempt by these proponents of slavery, were described as docile, indolent, and in need of the strict regimen imposed by slavery if they were to become productive members of society. Trumpeting their religious mission to Christianize the heathen, statesmen and ministers alike further bolstered proslavery arguments with Biblical evidence that could be interpreted in favor of slaveholding. Indeed, slaveowners were prepared to laud their own treatment of blacks, arguing that slavery fostered positive, paternalistic relations between the races: the "plantation school" defense of slavery.

The religious defense of slavery did not solve the conflict between myth and reality in the daily lives of plantation mistresses. If slavery was indeed humane and masters dedicated to the Christianizing of "heathens," then Bible reading should have been the backbone of the system. Instead, planters were deeply divided on the issue of black literacy. Although some plantation mistresses taught their slaves to read and write,¹¹ southern legislatures passed laws punishing whites for even teaching blacks the alphabet. Black literacy remained a controversial subject about which few women were able to express their opinions without confusion and doubt.[12] Certainly if slaves did become literate and practicing Christians, planters did not emancipate them on these grounds. Biblical arguments defending the system of slavery often persisted to the point of absurdity—proslavery minister Charles Pettigrew wrote while on a preaching expedition in 1785 to complain that although his sermons were successful, he was having difficulty "selling negroes."[13]

The fact that economics won out over ethics was not lost on plantation mistresses. Southerners witnessed these victories of debt over conscience in their everyday lives. Slaves were not only valuable in and of themselves, but this human capital could generate income and ensure financial security. Southern women, like men, explicitly and openly viewed slaves as chattel and commonly associated blacks with their dollar value.[14] Planter women might receive slaves as gifts.[15] Even young children knew the cash value of this "commodity."

Attitudes also shifted over time. Young wives, recently saddled with the burdens of plantation affairs, were much more often outspoken against the evils of slavery. Matrons, many years of experience later, generally groaned over the evils of *slaves* rather than the curse of slavery. One woman experienced a dramatic transformation. In 1815, she expressed horror at the brutality to which slaves were subjected: "Awakened this morning by the screeching of a female slave who was fleeing from the whip of her enraged master. I never witnessed such a scene . . . her neck torn and bloody, her eyes swollen. . . . I live, it is said with one of the best masters." Seventeen years later, mistress of her own slaves, she was far less sympathetic, curtly remarking, "I had little servant Jim whipped for fighting." Her action spoke louder than her words, although she did express certain reservations: "Father of mercies, guard my heart and keep me from the seductions of evil. Oh how callous are the hearts of this people [blacks]"[16]. Perhaps this plantation mistress herself was the one whose heart had grown hard. Her years of plantation management had transformed her plea of mercy for the slaves into a plea of mercy for herself. But most women, as the traditional nurturers in plantation society, experienced their paradoxical role with divided feelings. Rachel O'Conner wrote to her brother, David Weeks, in 1826: "I think it would be best to sell the Plantation and stock of Horses and cattle and everything else except the poor Negroes to assist in discharging the Estate but the Negroes I wish you to keep amongst the heirs of my Dear Mother."[17] Thomas Jefferson's daughter Martha wrote to him in Paris in 1787: "I wish with all my soul that the poor negroes were all freed. It grieves my heart when I think that these our fellow creatures should be treated so terribly as they are by many of our countrymen."[18] But for the Jefferson family, as for many others of the planter aristocracy, financial concerns won out over ethical considerations. The example of Elizabeth Yates of Charleston, South Carolina, is a case in point.

In 1820 Elizabeth Yates, agitated by her antislavery sentiments, composed a lengthy treatise on these beliefs to send to Harrison G. Otis, the United States senator from Massachusetts.[19] Both Elizabeth Yates and her husband, Joseph, were from old Charleston families. Slavery was a way of life for the couple, who owned between forty and fifty slaves. But at forty-two, Elizabeth Yates was disillusioned with this ostensibly "Christian" system that so hampered her spiritual contentment. Her letter, however replete with the popular rhetoric of the day ("I am no Politician and pretend to know but Little of the Affairs of Nations, but I am a Mother of four sons and two daughters"), is full of sincere expressions of abolitionist sympathy: "I feel convinced the Day is Coming & sometimes flatter myself has come when all who feel for those oppressed wronged injured Human Beings must use every prudent exertion and Zeal in their Behalf." Elizabeth Yates expressed a firm conviction that Southerners would see the error of their ways and dissolve the oppressive system themselves. She argued against violent or sudden action, and advocated the moderate and gradual transformation of plantation life. As a staunch and patriotic Southerner, Elizabeth Yates defended her region with pride; as a strategist, she knew that the best defense is a strong offense, and angrily denounced northern hypocrisy: "Many persons from the North when they come here and find it to their convenience and interest to own them they then do so and advocate the horrid Crime of Enslaving a set of men to whom we pretend no Right but that they are a Defenceless Nation." In her letter to Otis she was evidently expressing her individual feelings, for at the death of her husband in 1822 the Yateses' slaves were not freed. Joseph Yates had specified in his will that his property, including real estate and slaves, be divided among his children. Elizabeth Yates moved away from the Charleston home her husband had left her, but after three years in Philadelphia, she returned to her family home to reunite her younger children with their elder siblings. Although she continued to preach against slavery, Elizabeth Yates was unable to abolish this evil even within her own family. Her example, though unusual in its open defiance, is typical in its ultimate effect. Despite spirited and well-reasoned antislavery arguments, plantation mistresses could rarely exert any influence outside their domestic circle. The failure of Elizabeth Yates, though in this context a double defeat for her, was no more than what many southern women experienced in their personal crusades against slavery.

Wives and daughters would often plead with planters for the humane treatment of slaves. Slaves clearly understood this role of white women on the plantation, and often a slave would appeal directly to the mistress to intercede with the master on his or her behalf. In addition, planter women might attempt to influence plans for the sale of slaves.[20] In a study of the role of plantation mistresses in the lives of slaves, Elizabeth Craven surveyed the nineteenth-century slave narratives as well as the twentieth-century WPA interviews of ex-slaves. She finds that 75 percent of the slaves who wrote nineteenth-century narratives discuss the mistress. In the twentieth-century interviews, however, only 40 percent of the slaves even mention the plantation mistress. Over all, 55 percent of the references to the mistress were positive, 35 percent were unfavorable, and 10 percent of opinions were decidedly mixed. Of the positive responses, 55 percent were from males and 45 percent from females. In general, slaves and former slaves saw the master as the source or authority on plantations; over 80 percent of these persons reported that plantation mistresses had little or no authority. Influence was all the power they could exercise.

Plantation mistresses were dedicated to preserving the health and well-being of slaves on the plantation. When sickness befell, the mistress was there to tend her husband's slaves. In 70 percent of the cases when slaves recalled an illness in the nineteenth-century narratives, they also remembered the mistress nursing them back to health. But in addition to this role, the mistress also disciplined the household slaves, and during the master's absence, took over the supervision of all the slaves on the plantation. A majority of those slaves who were not working in the household itself reported favorable treatment from the mistress. Thirty percent of the nineteenth-century slave narratives reported physical punishment ordered by the mistress. Most of these complaints were from house servants and children; punishments ranged from spanking to whipping. Of the minority of slaves who alleged cruel treatment, only 10 percent claimed that the mistress herself had whipped or beaten them. Thus mistresses were accountable for only a small portion of the punishment inflicted upon plantation slaves— whether personally administered or delegated for execution by others. The fact that they were accountable is not in question; but the nature and extent of their role in the physical abuse of slaves remains to be revealed.

Craven finds that many of the incidents demonstrating a mistresses cruelty involved a female slave allegedly intimate with the master. When slaveowners sexually harassed or exploited female slaves, mistresses sometimes directed their anger, not at their unfaithful husbands, but toward the helpless slaves. This was irrational, irresponsible, and reprehensible behavior. Perhaps the best modern analogy to this pattern is the syndrome of child abuse, whose victims often become child abusers themselves. Persons trapped within a system that psychologically handicaps them frequently strike out, not at their oppressors, but at those equally helpless. In some cases slaves stood up to their mistresses, even striking back and taking their chances of punishment when the master returned. Both the violence of mistresses against slaves and that of slaves against mistresses were more common on smaller plantations. Perhaps planter wives were more vulnerable to the inherent tensions of slave management on smaller estates, where the illicit affairs of slaveowners were also more easily discoverable by plantation mistresses.

Craven concludes, after her extensive survey of the nineteenth-century slave narratives:

> The slave generally saw the mistress of the plantation as a positive influence in the slave system. Those who were most likely to remember well of her were the house servants, the male slaves, and those who lived on large plantations. However, what influence the white mistress had was definitely in a subordinate position to the will of the master. . . . The mistress, by force of her personality and the social structure in which she lived, generally emerges in the slave narratives as a white woman who tried to live up to the responsibilities of her position. Accountable to her husband, she was

surrounded by dependents. Her cruelties could make life miserable for some of the slaves; her kindness could cheer the entire plantation.[21]

This interpretation of the mistress's role from the viewpoint of slaves matches in many ways the image projected by women in their own testimonies. The plantation mistress saw herself as the conscience of the slave South. Generally a mother herself, she opposed the breakup of families; mistresses often pleaded with planters to prevent slave sales that would destroy black families—a "soft" position, at least compared with the male norms.

Women frequently professed attachment to the blacks on their fathers' plantations as well as to the slaves their husbands owned. One woman wrote to her brother at home on the family estate: "I would be very glad to hear particularly from all the servants, if Mr. Poindexter has hired them out and if so to whom and if they are pleased and how often you see them."[22] Letters between members of white planter families often contained messages and remembrances to and from slaves,[23] and plantation mistresses routinely included news about the various members of their "black family" (as they referred to their slaves) in personal correspondence.[24] The concerns and travails of these slaves often touched the lives of plantation mistresses; one wrote: "I wish you would tell Diana her master says she may stay at Papa's till she is better and ask her also if she would have any objection to Hester's coming down here. I don't wish to send for her without she is willing as Hester is her only child."[25] Another woman wrote to her husband in 1807, reporting a master's devotion to his slaves and his fatal response to the loss of a favorite: "In the evening a letter was brought him from his son . . . he took up the letter to read, it contained an account of the fate of a favorite servant who was frozen to death which when he came to, he suddenly exclaimed 'Caesar is dead.' The letter dropped from his hand which fell nerveless to his side—a paralytic stroke instantly benumbed him—he was laid on the bed from which he never arose—but expired that night."[26] Mathilda Turner, still a slave in Texas, wrote to her former mistress Jane Gurley in North Carolina: "Dear Mistress, I have been long wishing to rite to you but had nott the oppertunity. . . . I have got a fine sun. His name is William Marcus. I named him after your little sun. I and all the

balance of our people is all wall and give their bast love to you."[27] The
bonds of womanhood could and sometimes did cement relationships
between owner and owned.

Many southern women viewed bondage as a curse, and some saw
slavery as a cruel and unjust system for blacks. Maria Bryan complained
to her sister Julia of the brutality of their "cursed system": "Today
Jenny came in crying very much, her face bloody and swelled. She
said that Fulton the overseer had beat her with his fist, because she
had not spun a sufficient quantity. It would have distressed you to
have seen her. Oh! how great an evil is slavery."[28] Yet whatever
sympathetic attitudes plantation mistresses held toward slaves and
their status in ante-bellum society, the vast majority of women were
more concerned with the practicalities of the system that extracted
their time and attention than with humanitarian ideology. Plantation
mistresses complained that slavery placed a disproportionate and unfair
burden upon them as caretakers. Here, too, the opposition to slaveowning had some moralizing basis, whether selfish or not. Virginia
Cary, in her advice book, warned mothers about the potentially negative influence of slavery on their offspring: "The child is allowed to
tyrannize over the unfortunate menial appointed to gratify its wants.
Parents allow this abuse of power without being aware of its fatal
tendency."[29] A plantation mistress railed against "the evils of slavery,
for slaves are a continual source of more trouble to housekeepers than
all other things, vexing them, and causing much sin. We are compelled
to keep them in ignorance and much responsibility rests on us."[30] The
"curse of slavery" tried white women in many ways. Southern ladies
were reared to display excessive modesty, yet plantation life could not
accommodate itself to these women's delicate sensibilities. Another
matron petulantly described to a friend her reception at another plantation: "We were received at the door by a dirty negro girl who showed
us into the parlour. . . . whilst we sat there at least a half dozen fat
dirty negroe women passed through the room for the sole purpose, I
believe, of looking at us."[31] The 1815 complaint of yet another plantation mistress would have found echoes throughout the South during
the ante-bellum era: "Oh, the indelicacy, the shocking indelicacy to
which I am every moment exposed . . . children with not even a
screen. . . . the ladies will sit in the presence of a naked child without
a single flush, even when gentlemen are in the same room."[32]

Slavery did pose problems of management that manifested themselves with considerable force in the plantation mistress's world. Women moved constantly between coercion and cajolery in their efforts to ensure plantation efficiency. Because management of slaves was so difficult, most southern women were capable of believing that the curse of slavery had been laid on *them* rather than on the enslaved population. In 1824 a woman complained to her sister: "I have had a sufficient trial of my Father's family of negroes. Surely they are the worst in the world. I wish I knew better how to do with them. If we can do our duty then we shall have done our part. But that is hard to do."[33]

Some plantation mistresses experienced difficulty in getting along with their husbands' overseers. Disagreements arose most often over the issue of authority when the master was away from home. Many plantation mistresses believed themselves to be solely in charge during a husband's absence. In general most overseers dealt directly with the planter and so regarded any order from the plantation mistress as interference. Clashes grew out of this struggle for control. A matron reported in 1799: "The management of the overseer I fear will not answer my wishes. He has been very insolent to me, nor have I enjoyed one days peace since my return."[34] Equally often the means employed by overseers displeased women, and they were loath to entrust slaves or duties to them. Rachel O'Conner informed her brother David: "I sincerely wish I could have confidence enough in an overseer to leave all under his care and visit you again. . . . Stokes behaved so bad when I went to see you that I am afraid to venture that far off a second time."[35] Another plantation mistress, Fanny Bland Tucker, wrote in distress to her husband St. George in 1787: "The overseer has driven off many of the most valuable negroes. . . . I can no longer leave the Miserable creatures prey to the worst part of mankind without endeavouring to mitigate as far as it is in my power, the pangs of their cruel situation."[36]

Society expected planters, as the heads of their families, to fulfill religious as well as civic obligations. Wives recalled husbands to their duties, and urged men to live up to their spiritual and secular ideas.[37] Margaret Coalter wrote to her husband in 1795: "My beloved is *not* arbitrary—he will not terrify me with harsh expressions to his servants. He will not treat them as if he thought they were not God's creatures as well as himself—He will speak to them civily, *not* exact from them *their* duty, unless he does *his* by them."[38]

But although women were the self-appointed conscience of the system, men were indisputably the authority figures. Sex roles on the plantation over all mirrored responsibilities within the family circle. A plantation mistress might be the surrogate authority during a slave-owner's absence, but often delayed the administration of discipline until her husband's return to the estate. Wives constantly resorted to their husbands' intervention in managing unruly slaves.

Planters insisted on a strict regimen for their slaves, and some attributed black disobedience to the want of good government. The majority agreed with a Mississippian that slaves required "scolding or whipping or both."[39] In men's eyes, women lacked the rigor needed to discipline slaves. When a runaway slave was returned to his plantation in 1837, "he came straight to my Mother," a southern lady reported, "whose gentle heart he well knew, and plead for mercy. She couldn't forgive the puppy:—but she begged hard for him."[40] The runaway was "let off with 50 lashes," apparently a light sentence for his seven-week absence. Plantation mistresses frequently induced masters and overseers to show similar leniency.

The system of slavery created a climate of violence that could quickly turn against the woman as disciplinarian. A Virginia planter described such an incident to his brother in 1814. The outburst stemmed from his wife's difficulty with a female slave: "Polly undertook to correct her—she rebelled and jerked the switch out of her hand. I was at the time from home. When I returned in the evening we determined to cool her. We went both into the kitchen, Polly with the cowhide and I with a walking stick. Sinah was ordered to lay off her clothes. Shortly after Danl [her husband] came in and I ordered him out. He went to the woodpile and got an ax and came on with it. But we discovered him in time and met him with the gun."[41] His owner had the slave Daniel jailed. Rachel Mordecai reported the imprisonment of one of her father's slaves following events along the same lines: "Frank replied with insolence, papa attempted to strike him, he turned and aimed a blow with the butt end of an axe, which he had in his hand. . . . If our united entreaties have any weight he will never be restored to liberty except to be placed in the hands of another master in another state."[42] Women, therefore, frequently refrained from corporal punishment until planters were present because they feared violence—discipline imposed without the male authority figure in command could be dangerous. An extreme example of this threat is the fate of Martha Morisett, who corrected her female slaves, Sall and Creasy, while they were in the process of plowing the fields. The two slaves turned on their mistress and killed her. They attempted to cover up their crime, but discovery of the body resulted in their confession.[43]

Plantation women were justifiably concerned about their own vulnerability in the case of slave insurrection. Planters—in alleged response to these fears but perhaps more for their own peace of mind than to calm their womenfolk—organized patrols. In addition to ensuring the protection of white families and their property against runaway slaves, these vigilantes guarded against slave disorder. Masters wanted slaves made aware that their influence extended beyond the boundaries of individual plantations. If slaves escaped locked cabins (as some did, by climbing out of chimneys), traveled the roads without passes, or assembled in numbers without white supervision, the patrol would exercise planter authority and mete out punishment. The patrol might clash, on occasion, with individual planters, but masters generally supported the decisions and certainly the authority, of these vigilantes. A southern matron in Edenton, North Carolina, wrote, approvingly to her daughter in 1783: "The Patrols have been taking up all the country negros that they find in town without Passes and whipping them in our hearing for this hour past."[44]

Rumors of slave unrest often circulated through the countryside. Masters were fearful of any disturbance, not just in their own counties but anywhere in the state. Whites suspected that even vague word of a plot could spark an outbreak of violence among their own slaves. A woman wrote to her brother in January of 1836: "How does the people's pulse beat in Mississippi with regard to the insurrection of the negroes and Murrell's plans, there was the greatest excitement up here I ever saw here before Christmas, particularly the females, Ma and Sister L. like to have had fits all the time of Christmas holiday. If I may judge from the Miss. papers, there are some scared people in Miss. I see a good deal in them on the subject."[45] This season of slave insurrection was in fact so notorious that those with Mississippian relatives in the wilds of the cotton belt feared for their safety. A matron in North Carolina wrote in 1835 to her sister in the Delta: "I should be almost afraid to live in Mississippi now there is so much fuss with the negroes, there has been a great deal of talk about them here but they have not attemped anything yet."[46] Fear bred talk and talk bred fear. A plantation mistress observed in 1831 to her confidante: "It is astonishing what a propensity people have for propagating horrible stories." She went on to describe her reaction to a false rumor: "We have scarcely yet recovered from the shock of hearing that Wilmington was in ashes and the inhabitants all massacred. We have near and dear friends in that town and you may judge what our feelings were on hearing of their destruction." But she concluded on a positive note: "This general excitement will I hope be productive of one good effect vis rouse the friends of emancipation to make effort to deliver our otherwise happy country from the curse of slavery."[47]

Besides the general terror of slave rebellion, planters particularly feared arson and poisoning. A plantation mistress reported in 1830: "Destructive fires succeeding each other so rapidly and so suspiciously have excited considerable alarm. One of Uncle Tucker's negroes is strongly suspected of setting fire to his buildings but the proof is not sufficient to try him."[48] Even more alarming but difficult to prove, slaves could easily execute poisonings. Blacks participated in almost all aspects of food preparation, giving them innumerable opportunities to tamper with their masters' meals. At times the murderer might make an individual master or mistress his or her target, but an entire family could be slated for death by a vengeful slave.[49] In 1811, a Southerner described a murder attempt in North Carolina: "I have not been able to give you any intelligence of the runaway woman Cate. Mr. Anthony informs me that she is a very worthless character. She threatened to poison her master Mr. Nicholl in this place and ultimately succeeded in giving him a dose at Raleigh by which he was sometime confined, she has children in Charleston and has probably made for that place."[50] Female slaves, because of their kitchen duties, could most easily perpetrate poisonings without detection.

As many scholars have noted, slave resistance in the southern states took distinctly nontraditional forms. Blacks on plantations rarely, in point of fact, organized armed revolts, plotted rebellions, or attempted violent individual resistance. But significantly, the actual infrequency of insurrection did little to lessen the constant threat of slave rebellion in the minds of planters—or their women. They allowed L'Ouverture's successful revolt—reinforced by the influx of white Haitian refugees following the revolution—to haunt them. Abolitionists in the North elaborated the theme of retributive rebellion in oratory calculated to strike terror into the hearts of slaveowners. Yet few such antislavery speakers personally addressed southern audiences, and needless to say, there are no reports of mass repentance or wholesale emancipation following any of these inflammatory speeches.

Women's responses remained conservative. Mary Boykin Chesnut reflected after hearing of a slave insurrection: "Hitherto, I have never thought of being afraid of negroes. I had never injured any of them; why should they want to hurt me? Two-thirds of my religion consists in trying to be good to Negroes. . . ." Following the strangulation of her cousin by house slaves on a nearby plantation, she asserted with unshaken confidence: "But nobody is afraid of their own negroes. These are horrid brutes—savages, monsters—but I find everyone, like myself, ready to trust their own yard. I would go down on the plantation tomorrow and stay there even if there were no white person in twenty miles."[51] Although horrified and bewildered by the brutality of the slaves' act, Mary Boykin Chesnut did not react with the outrage we might expect at such a crime of violence. This cannot be dismissed as an isolated instance of naïveté or bravado, but reflects attitudes generated by the role played by white women in the southern system of slavery. In her guise of guardian, the typical plantation mistress regarded her slaves as childlike, dependent, and of diminished responsibility; hence her great, self-reassuring, and patronizing faith in their innocence.

Another white woman, fond of the black maid who had been her companion since childhood, promised the slave freedom upon her own death. When, within a short while, the woman was taken ill, it was found that her medicines had been laced with arsenic. The mistress was shocked to discover that her maid had been trying to bring about her premature death. After the slave girl was found guilty, she confessed and repented. Her mistress "tender-heartedly" refused to have the murderous slave hanged (as prescribed by law), and sold her instead.[52]

The complement to this psychologically comforting denial was far more common in the minds of white women. This was the mentality that reviled the slave, assigning to this group collective guilt for every tension, deprivation, and frustration of plantation life. This attitude was so pervasive that, even after the Civil War, southern women continued to think they were victims of oppression rather than victimizers themselves. One former plantation mistress bitterly wrote in 1865 to her mother-in-law of her post-surrender circumstances: "Well, we are all down here poor as poverty can make us. . . . One of our freedwomen expects shortly to enter the holy estate of matrimony, and has therefore indulged in some extravagancies and petty fineries. The question arises: 'Whence came the filthy lucre to purchase these indulgences?' And my empty wardrobe echoes emphatically: 'Where?' " Women decried the "unprecedented robbery" of Reconstruction and, indeed, emancipation, referring to themselves as "chained witnesses."[53]

These apparently extreme and contradictory responses on the part of southern white women make more sense when we remember the place of the mistress within the plantation system. In general, these women functioned by resolving the moral dilemmas of slavery through the displacement of guilt. To escape their own implication in the slave system, wives either blamed their husbands—the primary beneficiaries of that system—or the slaves themselves. It was difficult for planter women to hold slaves, a group more powerless than themselves, responsible for the system that oppressed all blacks and all women. But most mistresses allowed themselves to be drawn into this syndrome of "blaming the victim" rather than blame their loved ones, the men they had married, reared, or been reared by—the men with whom they lived their entire lives.[54] Either of these transferences of blame freed plantation mistresses from personal responsibility, letting them believe they were onlookers at rather than instigators of inhumanity.

The Civil War proved a catalyst in codifying attitudes toward slavery. With the increasing strength of the abolitionist movement and the politicization of abolitionist activity, with the election of Lincoln in 1860, secession, and the onset of war, even the most sheltered plantation mistress was forced to come to grips with political issues and the great division that the question of slavery had brought about. Awareness of these realities often met resistance; despite the imminence of secession, one matron declared to her son: "I cannot see a shadow of reason for civil war in the event of Southern Confeder-acy."[55]

As the structures of their world slowly disintegrated during the war years, many women were confronted for the first time with the fact that whatever their personal objections to slavery, it was the central component of southern culture and economy. Whether or not women voiced heartfelt reservations about black servitude, southern men were clearly willing to withdraw their families and fortunes from the Union to form a new nation dedicated to the integrity and expansion of the slave system. It was a troubled reckoning for these women who had endured rather than endorsed a society based on chattel labor. Women as well as men were forced for the first time to consider the economic and political consequences of life without slavery. With the actual outbreak of war, "the Cause" took precedence over any lingering ambivalence. Women were pledged to support their men in war. Whatever antislavery sentiment plantation mistresses might harbor, nationalism—Confederate chauvinism—now claimed their loyalty. Despite one woman's damnation of slavery ("I saw that it teemed with injustice and shame to all womankind, and I hated it"[56]), she spent the greater part of the war making rebel uniforms and devotedly nursing at army camp hospitals for a government that hoped not only to guarantee the right to own slaves but to increase the domain of the slaveholders' power. Another woman wrote to her daughter, encour-aging her to take heart and support the war in spite of the fact that "secession was a mistake for which *you* and *I* were not responsible . . . even if our country was wrong and we knew it at the time."[57]

The majority of southern women succeeded in putting the morality of slavery out of their minds and devoted themselves to the war effort. As one female participant wrote: "It is folly to talk of the women who stood in the breach in those chaotic days. . . . the woman of the South . . . was trained to meet responsibilities."[58] Plantation mistresses were charged with fuller responsibilities on their estates as a result of the sporadic, or in many cases total, absence of male advisers. They carried on planting and strove to provide the Confederacy with the supplies necessary to continue the war. Without the capacity of women to supply the army with clothing, medical aid, and surplus food stocks, the South would not have been able to meet the demands of battle as long as it did. The women of the South repeated the patterns established by their foremothers during the American Revolution. Their human and material sacrifices were enormous. A favorite wartime ballad celebrated the plantation mistress's special brand of patriotism:

> *The Homespun Dress*
> *My homespun dress is plain, I know.*
> *My hat's palmetto, too.*
> *But then it shows what Southern girls*
> *For Southern rights will do.*
> *We have sent the bravest of our land*
> *To battle with the foe*
> *And we will lend a helping hand—*
> *We love the South you know.*[59]

As one mistress recalled when the war was over: "The women of the South realized their obligations and met them with reflective energy."[60]

Ironically, the southern plantation mistress believed herself to be as trapped by the system as the slaves in her charge. Personal reservations about slavery notwithstanding, the southern woman was a vital and inextricable part of plantation society and had no choice but to support the war effort. Northern sisters could and did rebel against slavery, but the repressive dictates of slaveholding society kept its women under a tight rein. Those Confederate women who did express resistance to slaveowners' hegemony during the Civil War era were all the more remarkable for their ability to withstand the pressures brought to bear on those who dared to defy planter rule. Women who challenged this rule were censured and silenced—or driven into exile like Angelina Grimké. Even articulation of ambivalence was considered heretical within the slaveowning South. The Civil War, only heightened the tensions, exacerbated the contradictions, and intensified the moral dilemmas that characterized the condition of the plantation mistress in slave society.

XI

THE SEXUAL DYNAMICS
OF SLAVERY

God forgive us, but ours is a monstrous system, a wrong and iniquity. Like the
patriarchs of old, our men live all in one house with their wives and their concubines; and the mulattoes one sees in every family partly resemble the white children. Any lady is ready to tell you who is the father of all the mulatto children in
everybody's household but her own. Those, she seems to think, drop from the
clouds. . . . A magnate who runs a hideous black harem with its consequences
under the same roof with his lovely white wife, and his beautiful and accomplished daughters? He holds his head as high and poses as a model of all human
virtues to these poor women whom God and laws have given him. . . . you see,
Mrs. Stowe did not hit the sorest spot. She makes Legree a bachelor.
—Mary Boykin Chesnut

*M*ary Boykin Chesnut's denouncement of these evils of
slavery still haunts us. Her charges have remained unan-
swered for over a hundred years. The sexual dynamics of slavery
continue to lie just beneath the surface of southern history as a tightly
coiled tangle of issues we must unravel.

Even a cursory survey of slavery indicates that this system fundamentally included sexual exploitation. This, like most facets of sexual
activity, receives only marginal attention, if any, from scholars study-

ing this period. Yet just as racial elements played a central role in the system—so much so that one can hardly disentangle color and class in the Old South—so sex is an essential factor for determining southern social relations. The difficulty comes in trying to separate out the complex elements that contributed to this hierarchical system. But the critical issue is not to weigh one causal element against another, to determine a paramount or subordinate status for each factor; rather, we must observe and understand how various elements interacted. History is not a static panorama from which we can select all the component forces and factors and put them "in order of importance"; it is a richly ever-changing and shifting context.

Gender is implicitly, even if unconsciously, acknowledged every time we discuss the subject of slavery. When we read—and it is commonly found in monographs on slavery—that slaveowners bedded with slaves with few or no social repercussions, we assume that the owner is male and the slave female. Although the literal statement might be read to indicate merely facts of color (any white sexually exploits a black) or class (a member of the planter class mates with a slave), its practical effect is completely different. In truth, we automatically factor gender into the statement to grasp the situation accurately, knowing that no other set of circumstances was historically possible. This example reveals in only a small way the profound implications of gender identification, for both black and white, under slavery in the plantation South.

Issues of gender are critical for the analysis of slaves as well as the owner class. The ways in which the roles of slave women paralleled or illuminated issues of gender and sexuality for white women make it valuable to consider the two histories together. Unfortunately, the literature on slave women is even more impoverished than the scholarship on plantation mistresses.[1] The study of slave women has been hampered by both racist and sexist attitudes. In the limited historical work on slave rebellions, for example, many scholars have promoted an unsubstantiated image of slave women as "collaborationists." In addition, historians have, in passing, claimed that the sex roles of slaves were blurred by the system: that the gender differential was inadvertently reduced for blacks by the "equalizing" slavery brought about.

There is no doubt that men and women were subjected to equally brutal exploitation as workers—the presence of pregnant women and nursing mothers in the cotton fields attests to this. An increased rate of miscarriage—especially associated with backbreaking work in the cane fields—was a typical product of this white-initiated "equalization." Once inside the slave cabins, however, slave women were expected to fulfill traditional female roles. Even insofar as masters attempted to lessen the sexual differential (for their own economic reasons), the slave community redressed the balance by placing value on established gender difference. Traditional sex roles represented a "normal" (and therefore better) life. Ironically, woman's domestic role represented "freedom" to blacks, inasmuch as they rightly perceived that it meant her partial exclusion from the productive realm. Productivity in this context served only the slaveholder. "Equal exploitation" is no equality at all.

At the same time, the *sexual* exploitation of black men and women by their white owners was in no way comparable. Both male and female slaves were sexually manipulated by owners; records show that slaves were forced into unwanted liaisons with each other, reflecting one aspect of the master's absolute power over his slaves. But the white owner could force any black woman who was his property to submit to his sexual wishes. To argue that the master's failure to honor a slave marriage—his sexual aggression—was equally painful to the husband who was being humiliated and to the wife who was being violated is sexist and irresponsible. Denial of sex to male slaves cannot be equated with the force of sex to which female slaves were subjected. The notion that slavery "equalized" men and women, if only negatively, is limited and fallacious.

Female slave life had direct bearing on the history of sexuality in the Old South through the significant figure of the Mammy. This familiar denizen of the Big House is not merely a stereotype, but in fact a figment of the combined romantic imaginations of the contemporary southern ideologue and the modern southern historian. Records do acknowledge the presence of female slaves who served as the "right hand" of plantation mistresses. Yet documents from the planter class during the first fifty years following the American Revolution reveal only a handful of such examples. Not until after Emancipation did black women run white households or occupy in any significant number the special positions ascribed to them in folklore and fiction. The

Mammy was created by white Southerners to redeem the relationship between black women and white men within slave society in response to the antislavery attack from the North during the ante-bellum era, and to embellish it with nostalgia in the post-bellum period. In the primary records from before the Civil War, hard evidence for her existence simply does not appear.

The Mammy was the positive emblem of familial relations between black and white. She existed as a counterpoint to the octoroon concubine, the light-skinned product of a "white man's lust" who was habitually victimized by slaveowners' sexual appetites. In addition, the Mammy was integral to the white males' emasculation of slavery, since she and she alone projected an image of power wielded by blacks— a power rendered strictly benign and maternal in its influence. Further, her importance was derived from her alleged influence over whites; in her tutelary role, she was, in fact, invented as the desired collaborator within slave society: idealized by the master class, a trumped-up, not a triumphant, figure in the mythologizing of slavery.

Southern orators who alluded to being "suckled at black breasts" were not, as they hoped, simply establishing a tender family feeling between the races with this image of interracial innocence. The vision in fact evoked far more than those spokesmen had bargained for; first and foremost, its erotic component cannot be denied. Whether intentionally or not, the constant harping upon this theme conveyed a sexual rather than a sentimental undercurrent. Second, the image reduced black women to an animal-like state of exploitation: Mammies were to be milked, warm bodies to serve white needs—an image with its own sexual subtext. The Mammy does not, by any means, validate the "closeness" of the races. After slavery and within the household, black and white women perhaps were able to forge an alliance. But a legacy of resentment as well as sexual competition remained.

The ambiguities of interpersonal relations, particularly in the volatile area of miscegenation, created conflict for both owners and slaves in the Old South. From the beginning of forced African immigration to the English colonies, the issue of sexual interaction was problematic for plantation owners. As Winthrop Jordan's research in *White Over Black* indicates, color and gender became rigid ruling classifications in Colonial America. All sexual indiscretions merited official reprimand and punishment, but Jordan discovered that color was a crucial factor in the outcome of such judgments. Interracial liaisons incurred prompt and severe response. In Virginia in 1630, for instance, Hugh Davis was sentenced "to be soundly whipped before an assembly of Negroes and others for abusing himself to the dishonor of God and shame of Christians, by defiling his body in lying with a Negro, which fault he is to acknowledge next Sabbath day."[2] This fall from grace might have been seen as identically sinful if the partner in question had been white, but the fact that the charges read "defiling his body in lying with a Negro" indicates that the issue was in large part, if not *wholly*, a question of racial rather than sexual misconduct. In 1662, a Virginia fine imposed for miscegenation was double the fee exacted for illicit intercourse.[3] The fate of Hugh Davis is an example of the swift and harsh retaliation such antisocial acts provoked before the Revolution.

The fate of the offspring of these liaisons became thorny problems. Initially, the colonists followed English custom by proclaiming that children inherited the status of their fathers. But the high incidence of bastards, both white and mulatto, and the difficulty of ascertaining paternity induced the planter elite to solve these questions of illegitimacy with a single stroke of the pen. In 1662 the Virginia assembly passed legislation which declared that slave offspring inherited the status of the mother *(partus sequitur ventrem)*. Maryland clung to a contrary principle *(partus sequitur patrem)* until 1712, when it changed its law to conform with other southern colonies. Though tracing descent through the maternal line was contrary to English common law, the British colonists, in instituting a pseudoclassical system of forced labor (chattel slavery), resorted to the "wisdom of the ancients." Bypassing the custom of the African slaveholders from whom they purchased their slaves (within Islamic culture the child of a slave mother and her owner was accorded freedom on the death of the father), they invoked Roman custom to protect their property interests. Following this precedent, they acquired a new slave every time a black woman gave birth. Over time, white America developed a unique position on racial classification: the "drop of ink" formulation. Just as a single drop of black ink colors a whole glass of clear water, so—white America decreed—one drop of black blood "pollutes" a human being. Sexual as well as social control therefore became doubly essential to slaveowning patriarchs' successful campaign to dominate their culture.

Some proslavery apologists proposed that sexual liaisons with slaves were meant beneficently—to relieve white women of the unpleasant task of serving their husbands' lust. In his 1838 *Memoir on Slavery*, one Southerner argues that slave-planter copulation provided for a "less depraving" effect of men's morals than did the imposition of their sexual desires on white women. If men were subject to uncontrollable lust—and many southern gentlemen acknowledged such imperfection—they could vent their passion "harmlessly" on black rather than white females. William Gilmore Simms alleged in his *Morals of Slavery* that the practice of interracial liaison actually safeguarded the virtue of white women—that most precious article.[4]

Southern planters divided women into two classes: ladies, always white and chaste; and whores, comprising all black women (except for the saintly Mammy) and any white woman who defied the established social constraints on her sexual behavior. For white men, upper-class women were thus sexually continent by definition. Any planter woman who transgressed sexually found herself a "whore," dumped into the lowest ranks of society in the company of "white trash" and blacks. (It must be remembered in this context that one of the marks of "white trash" was that the women were said to "associate"—sexually cohabit—with black men.) The racist sexual stereotype of the black woman protected the planters' self-image at the expense of others; they could cultivate a potent, virile stance while blaming all sexual sins on women. Ironically, while denying black women personality, white men nevertheless made them officially responsible for owner "morality" as well as their own. Yet they were absolutely powerless in this area. Women bore total sexual accountability; white men enjoyed total sexual control. This was a logical extension of the double standard governed by gender and race that the South had effectively instituted. Planter males fully exercised their will in all spheres, while both blacks and white women remained severely circumscribed. White men had their own code of ethics that prescribed their behavior toward each other, but in relative terms they were free to do whatever they wanted. This double standard had clear consequences in the realm of sexual attitudes, but affected far more than the simple act of fornication.

The white patriarch, by compelling all his subordinates—especially women—to do his bidding, could harness reproduction itself to suit his will, manipulating the force of natural selection with a dual goal. While mating with his wife to produce a string of legitimate heirs to carry on his name and inherit his wealth, the planter patriarch could endow his reproductive success with an economic component by fathering slaves. In this way planters gained an increase in capital— the dollar value of slave offspring—with a genetic dividend into the bargain. These were the powerful motives that drove patriarchs to tolerate no interference in their reproductive domain.

In the rest of the country during this century, women were seeking more and more control over their own lives. Recognizing autonomy as a prerequisite of power, they identified birth control as one of the logical first steps to achieve their end. In the late eighteenth and early nineteenth centuries, therefore, many females began a private crusade to limit their families, and the practice increased in middle-class homes throughout the nineteenth century.[5] Eventually this concern outgrew the private sphere and was publicly championed as one of the foremost of feminist demands.

The South, however, presents an anomaly in this as in many other aspects of modernization. The middle class was simply not a force for change within the ante-bellum South. Feminist ideology, nascent in the post-Revolutionary North and destined to emerge vigorously at mid-century, lay dormant throughout most of the nineteenth century in the South. In addition, the ante-bellum necessity to populate the ever-expanding slaveowning frontier made for large planter families.

The topic of abortion demonstrates the difference of southern priorities. Induced miscarriage, abortion, and infanticide among both black and white women were roundly condemned by planters. They needed their property to reproduce itself. With the closing of the slave trade in 1807, the South was dependent upon natural increase to supply plantations with their labor force. Many slaveowners from areas outside the cotton belt like Virginia and Kentucky, where field labor was not in such great demand, did a brisk trade in the raising and selling of slaves. A bounty of black infants may have partially disabled the work force in the short run; but slaveowners taking the long view were eager for black women to produce a crop of new workers, above and beyond the crop of cotton. Slave mothers who committed infanticide were judged guilty of murder, but were not put to death for their crime—for in that case the owner would lose not only his investment but his future profits from her. They paid a heavy price, however, for crossing a master on this matter, and slave midwives and medicine men were warned that abetting such activities could result in their being "sold down the river." Although pregnancies properly belonged within the closed concerns of the slave community, whites regularly monitored their charges in this area. Pregnant women were often given reduced work duties, depending upon the season, and sometimes an improved diet. The plantation mistress was generally the agent of these reforms, instituted in order to ensure that valuable slave infants would be brought to term. Any acts to impede reproduction were perceived as sabotage.

Slaveowners required an equally steady flow of legitimate heirs. White women were expected to fulfill Biblical imperative, biological destiny, and patriotic duty by embracing their role as mothers—as often and as long as their bodies could withstand the burden. Here, too, any attempt to interrupt pregnancy was greeted with shock and swift reprisal.

The attitude of southern planters toward abortion is especially significant when considered in a broader national context. Recent scholarship suggests that abortion in the ante-bellum North did not create anything like the kind of opposition it did in the South.[6] Abortion in the South was branded heinous and vile, and the sanctions against it were apparently successful. A survey of 500 manuscript collections discloses only one instance of abortion (with the exception of the complex and disputed Randolph case discussed in Chapter VI) in the thousands of personal papers of members of the planter class.

The incident is revealed in a letter written by Theodore Phelps to a kinsman in March 1821 (note that this is a communication between two men): "A most horrid thing that happened in our neighborhood two weeks since—an Abortion was committed on the boddy of Sally White by Francis Huntington and Noah D. Matoon, the child was committed to the flame by F. H. They were both arrested, had their trial . . . which lasted four or five days and finally bound over to court under bonds of $1,000 each."[7] Abortion was not a matter to be taken lightly: $1,000 was a considerable sum in those days. (Most important of all, this occurred in 1821, a full generation before the North began to move against abortion.) The practice may actually have been more widespread among the planter elite than this survey of correspondence indicates. Its forbidden nature may, of course, have distorted the evidence. Reaction in the sole case, however, reflects a pattern of extreme conservatism in the South.

Of course, sexual matters of any kind were rarely discussed or written about openly. A sequence of letters between a married woman and her husband in 1835 demonstrates the difficulty even intimates had in expressing their sexual feelings. Writing to her absent husband, Sarah Gordon of Savannah voiced her loneliness and regretted his absence from home. Her husband used "home" as a kind of code word for sexual intimacy in his subsequent letters, but this private meaning was evidently difficult for his wife to grasp. She wrote again on November 29, 1835: "With regard to the word you write about my own husband, I knew at once when reading your letter and thought that *anticipate was the word we spoke of.* . . . Let me know when you answer this if I am not right altho in several other parts of your letter I thought *I saw it,* yet in that *one word I think I find the one we meant.*" Her husband's secretive language produced uncertainty and anxiety in his wife. On November 30, 1835, still in search of mutual under-standing, she reiterated: "I hope you will not go again from home, at any rate for so long a time. and you must feel perfectly satisfied that we think alike on all subjects, but particularly the one I alluded to in my last One."[8] By the next week, fortunately, Sarah Gordon was reassured that she had successfully divined William's meaning, and employed the private reference knowingly:

> I trust, dear Husband, your loss of rest may not make you feel badly in any way, but that you may come home well and happy and prepared to enjoy all the happiness which we mutually anticipate from our home. I have used the letter you allude to again, and have now found out the meaning of the word intended. I thought I had guessed it rightly the last time but from your pointing it out to me in some measure in your letter received today, I read it attentively and it flashed across my mind in an instant what you meant. I feel even now that your anticipations of Home are not greater than mine are and you will find on your return how mutual have been our feelings.[9]

Obviously, Sarah Gordon had been initially unable to imagine why her husband would insist in his letters on her anticipation of "home," on her missing "home," when she remained "at home."

This "modesty" was, naturally, promoted as necessary in order to protect women from indelicacy. Men, especially young southern "rogues," were much more open about such matters—but only with each other and in private. Although licentiousness was not celebrated, southern gentlemen behind closed doors were notoriously boastful about their lust. A man remained a gentleman as long as he kept his transgressions within the flexible boundaries of southern propriety and did not flaunt his profligacy before the wrong company.

The charge of moral hypocrisy—most often aimed at men—was a direct hit. British commentator James Buckingham offered his indictment of plantation culture in 1840: "The men of the South especially are more indelicate in their thoughts and tastes than any European people; and exhibit a disgusting mixture of prudery and licentiousness combined, which may be regarded as one of the effects of the system of slavery, and the early familiarity with vicious intercourse to which it invariably leads."[10]

Interestingly, travelers who witnessed plantation life were voluble on the subject of planter indecency. Foremost among these complaints was the shocking immodesty that they considered to be displayed on southern plantations. One agitated observer exclaimed:

> In all the states where slavery is permitted, the women tolerate nakedness which would disconcert the least modest of European women. They declare that in the southern part of Virginia, in the two Carolinas, in Georgia and even in Charlestown, young Negroes, "absolutely naked," appear before their mistresses, serve them at table, without their suspecting that that is indecent. I have seen young girls, standing behind a paling fence, staring at the naked form of a Negro man who was being whipped.[11]

Chastellux concurred in his account, noting that southern women openly tolerated slave nudity "without any apparent embarrassment."[12] The indignation and amazement of these European travelers reveal their fundamental misreading of the situation.

White women trained themselves to respond to blacks, not as humans, but as animate property of favored status, like pets. Naked slaves, whether children or adults, were no more indelicate than livestock in the barnyard. Despite white women's exaggerated modesty, the body of an unclothed black gave the plantation mistress little offense. The relationship between plantation mistress and slave was never personal; this dehumanized naked object could present no threat to a woman's propriety. Although adolescent belles might make mention of the indelicacy of "naked Negroes," they soon outgrew this notion. If the issue ever arose, it was instantly repressed. White women had to render themselves immune—or, failing that, to present themselves as immune—to the black sexuality perceived by any outside observer. In doing so, they made themselves into stereotypes of sexlessness, and naked blacks into nonhumans.

The double standard was both apparent and acknowledged. Whereas illicit liaisons were equally condemned in the North whether a couple was interracial or not[13], the South gave special dispensation to white men involved in sexual dalliance with black women. This category of affair was not tabulated on the register of moral error in the ante-bellum South. In 1824, one observer declared: "Indeed in the Southern States, the ladies would be very angry, and turn anyone out of society, who kept a white woman for his mistress; but would not scruple even to marry him, if he had a colored one, and a whole family of children by her."[14]

The idea of white women sleeping with black men is an explosive proposition in American culture. From Colonial days onward, white men have harbored special fears of sexual interaction between "their" women and black males. Southern slaveholders went to great lengths to structure laws and mores so as to prohibit such interaction. In the pre-Revolutionary period, white women forfeited their freedom if they openly contracted liaisons with slaves. The slaveholding colonies passed a series of antimiscegenation measures to delegitimize further all interracial unions. The strictures against sexual activity between white women and black men were so severe that little evidence of its existence finds its way into the planter records of the ante-bellum South. A few such incidents are revealed in travel accounts by strangers to the South unaware of the full cultural implications of these liaisons. One foreign commentator observed: "A mile farther up, on the same bank of the Cape Fear River, is the home and estate of the American

General Howe. While he amuses himself in dissipation elsewhere, his unfortunate family lives here; the wife has the manner of a divorcee, and one lovely daughter, eighteen years old, has just had two sons by one of the Negro slaves."[15] Another account cited similar circumstance with more tragic results: "A planter's daughter having fallen in love with one of her father's slaves had actually seduced him; the result . . . was the sudden mysterious disappearance of the young lady."[16]

Despite the heavy toll exacted on women in ostracism and reprisal, records indicate that there were periods when, by choice or necessity, white women openly defied this social dictate in significant numbers. Both during the seventeenth century and during Reconstruction, white women outside the planter class sought sexual partnership with black men. Incidents during the Colonial era generally involved serving-maids or lower-class widows, and perhaps reflect fraternization within the servant class. But such cases were inexorably labeled deviant— the women involved were declared to be "sluts" indulging in a base display of lascivious depravity far outside sexual norms. Their lack of "morality and good sense" debased them to the lowest rung of the social ladder. Having forfeited the status of their color, sex, and previous rank, they remained permanent outcasts. During Reconstruction, when the male population was depleted throughout the country, the number of white marriageable men was so severely reduced in the South that many white women freely chose to contract alliances with black men. Emancipation had eliminated slavery, but the barrier of racial prejudice remained. This short-lived increase in the number of interracial marriages, mainly affecting lower-class women, did not signal a new era of racial amalgamation, or a relaxation of attitudes; it was only a temporary variant of the standard pattern. Prohibitions calculated to keep white women "pure" remained in force, socially if not legally.

Moral degeneracy was a popular explanation for miscegenation, which by the late ante-bellum era was perceived as a byproduct of slavery rather than as an abuse of the system. The Reverend J. D. Long exclaimed in 1857: "Amalgamation is increasing at a horrible rate throughout the slave states. . . . one of the reasons why wicked men in the South uphold slavery is the facility which it affords for a licentious life. Negroes tell no tales in courts of law of the violation by white men of colored females."[17]

The economic motives of miscegenation were also advanced by observers.[18] One woman went so far as to argue that mulattoes came into the world solely as products of unbridled capitalist greed: "I sincerely believe they are excited to that crime by no other desire or motive but that of adding to the number of their slaves."[19] There was, of course, no shortage of fertile black males during this era. White women, loath to admit that men sought such liaisons for pleasure, pleaded profit.

Slaveowners held divided opinions on miscegenation, often espousing creeds that contradicted their own actions. Planters went to considerable lengths to shield their white families from the scandal that public admission of their sexual union with slaves would cause; white men were expected, not to refrain from, but to conceal such affairs. One source reveals that the master of a plantation discharged a tutor, accusing him of "knocking up" one of his female slaves; the author of this account concludes that the master himself had done the deed, but "fearing the inquiries of the world on the subject, fathered it upon the tutor."[20] Conversely, a visitor to the home of a Georgia minister slept with a black maid. Although this was a common practice, the Reverend Charles Jones was an uncommonly devout and determined moralist. He pursued the matter, denouncing his former houseguest as a villain and attempting to expose the man's sin publicly. It is obvious from the correspondence that Jones was not concerned with the property aspect of the issue, nor with the "proprietary" element of the guest's indifference to gaining Jones's permission for such a liberty; he was outraged at this defilement of one of his God-given charges.[21] But the wrath of the Reverend Mr. Jones is a rare example.

Contrasting with the Christian rectitude of Charles Jones, the lack of restraint demonstrated by Leroy Pope was the more common planter phenomenon. After finishing his term as governor of Alabama, Leroy Pope retired from public office to manage his plantation. Former Governor Pope "notoriously kept a mulatto girl with whom he associated as freely as with his wife." The openness of this "association" scandalized the good people of Huntsville to such a degree that his wife was humiliated. Finding them once too often "in each others' embraces, the enraged Mrs. Pope made so much fuss about it" that her husband was forced to send his concubine to a distant plantation he owned in Mooresville. When, in her pursuit, he began spending more time at Mooresville than at home, the wrath of society allied itself to his wife's rage, and Pope was forced to sell the girl in New Orleans.[22]

The number of "fancy women" of color in ante-bellum New Orleans documents the popularity of concubines. A stranger to Louisiana commented on the practice itself in 1836:

> I had often heard of the beauty of quadroons. I found them pretty. They are a virtuous and amiable looking people, and have the appearance of being virtuous: but they are generally prostitutes and kept mistresses. Young men and single men of wealth have each a quadroon for his exclusive use. They are furnished with a Chamber and a sitting room and servants, and the comforts and elegancies of life. It generally costs from $1,500 to $2,000 a year to keep a quadroon. I am informed that the quadroon is faithful to a Proverb in these attachments. Married men in this City are frequently in the habit of keeping quadroons.[23]

In addition, slave mart records show that light-skinned girls were bid for at prices much higher than those offered for prime field hands. Some adolescent females of mixed race were sold as "virgins," obviously discounting the notion that slave women were invariably sought as proven breeders. The Swedish author Frederika Bremer damned the practice in 1853: "These white children of slavery become, for their part, victims of crime and sink into the deepest degradation."[24]

Romanticization of these planter-slave liaisons flourishes even in the scholarship of otherwise perceptive interpreters of slave culture whose understanding of racial exploitation is not matched by their sensitivity to sexual exploitation. Eugene Genovese, for example, writes:

> But most men, even most free-wheeling, gambling, whoring young aristocrats, do not readily indulge their sadistic impulses. It would be hard to live with a beautiful and submissive young woman for long and to continue to consider her mere property or a mere object

of sexual gratification, especially since the free gift of her beauty has so much more to offer than her yielding to force. . . . it would not be astonishing if many of the fancy girls, like their famous free quadroon sisters in New Orleans who entered into an institutionally structured concubinage with wealthy whites, often ended by falling in love with their men and vice versa.[25]

The sexual dynamics of southern race relations are fundamentally ignored in this speculation. Consent would never be more than a minor factor in a society where slaveowners maintained despotic rule. The slave female, for example, could not give herself "freely," for she did not have herself to give: she already belonged to the master. To imagine that "falling in love" might be a decisive element in the formula is a sentimental rather than analytical assessment of such interracial unions.

Evidence does reveal, however, that some ante-bellum planters in the South demonstrated long-term commitment to their slave partners. Rather than establishing a "harem," the planter more often would engage a particular female slave as his habitual lover. The offspring of these unions were sometimes recognized in a planter's will, perhaps by a white man making public admission of his alliance only after his death. In 1825, Philip Henshaw made a clear declaration of paternity and affection for a slave offspring:

> I give and bequeath to my daughter (for such I believe her to be) Floreal Floretta . . . her freedom. I also bequeath her one half my estate of every description whatsoever, to her and her heirs forever. It is my desire that my sister Sallie Gatewood, out of the estate I have devised to Floreal Floretta, shall board her at some decent white woman's house and have her educated . . . in the event of my sister Sallie Gatewood complying with the foregoing request, I give her and her heirs forever one-half of my estate.[26]

Henshaw not only provided for his daughter, he bribed his sister to ensure this provision—with good reason, for records indicate that manumissions and other bequests to mulatto or slave individuals owned by the deceased were often challenged if legal white heirs, especially widows or legitimate offspring, were living. Courts were full of litigation brought by morally and economically outraged widows and sons. The law was inclined to favor a widow's suit, especially if she was in debt. The wish of a testator to emancipate a slave was frequently dismissed as deathbed delirium, and the slave disposed of by the executor of the will.

The white and legitimate heirs to a planter's fortune were also often callous in their treatment of mulatto half brothers and half sisters. As one commentator observed: "I could mention the name of a lady not 100 miles from Washington who lets out as a servant her own natural brother, a good-looking Mulatto."[27] South Carolinian Henry Grimké, brother of the famous abolitionist sisters Sarah and Angelina, fathered three mulatto sons after his wife's death. Grimké left instructions in his will that both his common-law wife and his illegitimate offspring were to be taken care of by his son and legal heir, Montague. The three black Grimké brothers, however, were sold off or bound over at an early age; despite his father's wishes, the planter son made the most profitable use of his bastard brothers.

In some cases, affection triumphed. Females and mulattoes were disproportionately favored by slaveowners in this regard. In Colonial South Carolina, for example, fully a third of manumissions were of mulattoes and three-fourths of adult manumissions were of women.[28] Slaveowners could, by virtue of their absolute power, provide for their black families as well as the white; but when these interests clashed, planters were seldom allowed to sacrifice white profit for the sake of black freedom.

The following cases illustrate some of the ways in which society overruled individuals in this delicate area. They raise an interesting issue: although planter-slave liaisons were tolerated in private, white men were required in their public lives to obey the plantation culture's rigid dictates concerning race and sex. This standard insisted, above all, that they conduct themselves silently in such affairs. Scandal, which shone light on these contradictions, was perhaps worse than the deed itself. The plantation mistress's complex circumstances and mixed emotions have been dealt with extensively in this study. But what about the situation and the sentiments of the planter patriarch— sometimes equally conflicted?

Thomas Foster, Jr. was one of thirteen children born to a wealthy Mississippi planter.[29] Despite the large family, Foster senior was able to provide handsomely for his children. When in 1820 Thomas junior wed the thirteen-year-old Susan Carson, daughter of a Natchez minister recently removed from New York, he was a planter of some wealth, in possession of two plantations. During Susan Foster's confinement in December 1823, she went to her father's home. Her husband was noticeably inattentive to her during this absence. When she returned to the homestead, she found that her husband was smitten with a slave, ironically named Susy. Foster flagrantly pursued the affair, ignoring his parents' pleas to return to his senses and make peace with his wife. Soon he began to drink, threaten violence to his family, and taunt his wife with his love for a "black wench." In October 1826, Susan was forced to retire to her father's house to escape her husband's rages; she left with the blessing of her father-in-law, Thomas senior. But when she revisited her home, thinking mistakenly that her husband had summoned her and hoped for reconciliation, the couple quarreled. Foster vowed he would kill his wife Susan and slit their children's throats.

Shortly thereafter, young Foster was seriously ill. On his sickbed, he became penitent and sent for his wife. Fearing death and damnation, Foster promised to banish his concubine if Susan Foster would return to him. His wife insisted that he deed the slave over to his father in the presence of witnesses before she would come home. Following his recovery, Foster returned to his old ways and retracted his pledge to forsake his beloved Susy. But his father refused to give the girl back. Foster raged over the matter and, ignoring his heartbroken wife, spent his time trying to rejoin his concubine. By December of 1826, Foster senior had given his son an ultimatum: "Either give up this girl Susy and go home to your wife and children . . . or declare your intention to the contrary." On Christmas Day, Foster junior made his contrary intention clear: he stole away with Susy and the rest of his slaves, never to see his wife and children again. Thomas Foster, Jr. exiled himself from his family, his home, and decent society by his public abandonment of his wife. He could have remained an accepted—indeed, an upstanding—member of the plantation aristocracy, had he not made a spectacle of his passion and thus affronted southern decorum.

Richard Johnson was a politician of prominence and promise, an outstanding Kentucky statesman who rose to the office of vice-president. He achieved fame as a hero of the War of 1812, and even if he was not actually the slayer of Indian chief Tecumseh (the campaign slogan boasted "Rumpsey Dumpsey, Rumpsey Dumpsey, Colonel Johnson killed Tecumseh"), Johnson was an admired military figure.[30] He spent thirty-four years in public service in Washington, while maintaining a plantation in his native Kentucky. But as Johnson rose to power on a national level, his private life became a matter of public controversy.

Johnson was a popular and boisterous character; contemporary commentators noted his ruddy complexion and his taste for red vests. The feisty Kentucky colonel was a rising star within the Democratic party during the 1820s and 1830s. But in 1835, when his name was put forward for national office, the Kentuckian's family situation came under fire. Although many white southern politicians kept black concubines and sired mulatto offspring, they protected themselves; each could display a white wife and a brood of legitimate children. Johnson had never been married when he began living with a mulatto, Julia Chinn, who resided in his home and sat at his table.

Known as his "housekeeper," Julia Chinn was a faithful and devoted companion to Richard Johnson. She bore him two daughters, Imogene and Adaline. A Lexington journalist asserted in 1835 that Johnson was not being taken to task for his liaison with a woman of color; rather, he was being persecuted for his "scorn of secrecy."[31] Johnson refused to deny his connection; he acknowledged his daughters, educated them at proper schools, and accorded his mulatto family the privilege of white status. For this flagrant breach of propriety, Johnson was widely condemned. It was reported that as the featured Fourth of July speaker at a local festivity, he had attempted to bring his daughters with him onto the platform; self-righteous citizens—especially the ladies—refused to remain in the same pavilion with these illegitimate quadroon children. Johnson's "unsuitable" behavior proved his unforgivable lack of discretion. It was even alleged that Johnson had married Julia Chinn. When Johnson failed to deny this "monstrous rumor," the insult was too great for planter society.

In 1833, Johnson's beloved Julia died of cholera. Before their mother died, the two girls were well provided for, through their father's timely generosity: in 1832 the colonel had deeded over estates to his daughters and their white husbands—for Johnson had made respectable matches for his children. In this careful provision during his lifetime, his forethought was crucial. After Johnson's death, his brothers went to court to secure a ruling—which the courts provided—that Johnson had left no offspring.[32]

As early as April 1831, the press began to speculate on Johnson's unseemly position with respect to these matters of race. The Washington *Spectator* feared the Kentuckian's proximity to the White House: "The colored will have an Esther at the foot of the throne with Johnson's election, who may not only dictate modes and fashions to the female community, but may deliver her people from civil disabilities, break down the barrier of prejudice which separates the two races, and produce an amalgamation. . . . Such a consummation would be the means of an African jubilee throughout the country." The threatened "African jubilee" conjured up associations of the terrifying events in Haiti, to focus popular dread. In 1835, an observer commented that Johnson was living with "a young Delilah of about the complection of Shakespeare's swarthy Othello who is said to be his third wife; his second . . . he sold for her infidelity." The writer asserted in conclusion: "Neither now nor at any time would I act so in defiance of public opinion. . . ."[33]

Johnson's defiance stirred up political opinion as well as social censure. When the Democrats met in Baltimore in 1835 to select their candidates, Johnson was the undisputed "favorite of the West" for vice-president. But he was a candidate of considerable controversy in Dixie. Virginia was a stronghold of opposition; the statesmen of the Old Dominion argued that Johnson's precedent of "amalgamation" could generate a dangerous policy, and Virginians linked his stance on mulattoes with the "spirit of Nat Turner" that slaveowners had feared since 1831. Johnson's silence clearly aggravated planter paranoia. Upon his nomination at Baltimore, the Virginia delegation walked out.

With the distinguished figure of Thomas Jefferson, the vexed issue of sexual liaison between planter and slave reached its height of antebellum prominence—or notoriety. Throughout Jefferson's political career, he was smeared with charges that he kept a "sable concubine" and a brood of "mulatto bastards"; the opposition press remained nasty and vehement on the topic during his lifetime. After his wife's death in 1782, Jefferson never remarried, but devoted himself to his two motherless daughters, to public office, and to his beloved Monticello. It was rumored that while serving as a United States delegate in France, the widower initiated an affair with his daughter's mulatto maid, Sally Hemings, who according to gossip became pregnant and refused to return to Virginia until Jefferson pledged to free her child.[34] Although no such emancipation transpired, the scandal persisted and did not die with Jefferson in 1826. Recently, the controversy has been reanimated.[35]

Fourteen-year-old Sally Hemings was known as "dashing Sally" at her Monticello home. She did in fact travel with Jefferson to Paris as his daughter Maria's attendant. She became pregnant while in France; she returned to Monticello and bore a son whom she named Tom. Although there is evidence of a mulatto Tom of about the right age at Monticello, the presence of other Toms and the disappearance of this particular one from the records fail to shed light on the mystery. Jefferson retired to Monticello in 1794. The following year, the twenty-two-year-old Sally gave birth to a light-skinned daughter; she had four more children during the next thirteen years. Sally Hemings was not manumitted by Jefferson's will, although five male slaves were emancipated. Two years after Jefferson's death, however, his daughter Martha Randolph freed Sally Hemings and her two sons remaining on the plantation, Madison and Eston. Her other offspring had either run off over the years or disappeared from the records.

Joel Williamson has argued, in his *New People: Miscegenation and Mulattoes in the United States*, against the probability that Jefferson fathered Hemings' children. Although he readily admits that Jefferson might have taken a slave bedmate following his wife's death, Williamson persuasively argues that the woman was not Sally. The childbearing pattern of Sally Hemings does not show the frequency or the duration that might have been expected if she were regularly sexually active with her master. Nor does Jefferson's indifference in his will to the fate of this woman and her children suggest his paternity of her offspring. Miscegenation nevertheless plays a central role in this drama—but at another level.

Sally Hemings was indeed a privileged slave at Monticello, but her status was derived, not from hypothetical concubinage with Jefferson, but from her mother's role as the actual paramour of Jefferson's father-in-law. When Virginia widower John Wayles made Betty Hemings, a mulatto slave, his *de facto* wife, he followed common practice among

Colonial planters. Taking a woman of color as a bedmate after the death of one's wife was, in part, dictated by the relative scarcity of white women in early America. When Wayles's daughter Martha married Thomas Jefferson, five of her half brothers and half sisters were included in the dowry of 135 slaves. "Dashing Sally" was in fact half sister to Jefferson's wife. When she became maid to her white niece, Maria Jefferson, Sally too was following the prescribed southern custom. The daughters of slave maids often became maids themselves; Betty Hemings had been Mrs. Wayles's personal maid before the latter's death. And as in the same instance, a house servant, more frequently mulatto than not, was the likeliest surrogate wife for a planter after the death of her mistress. Thus if Sally Hemings had indeed become Thomas Jefferson's paramour and a mother of his children, they would have been well within a characteristic, virtually dynastic pattern of black and white sexual relations in the slave South.

Denial and refutation continue to stoke this smoldering controversy, as generations of journalists and scholars, novelists and politicians, repeat arguments to each other. The ferocity of the need some demonstrate to "prove" that Thomas Jefferson did indeed sleep with his slave and father mulattoes is matched only by the urgency of the defenders of Jefferson in maintaining his innocence. As a result, substance has been completely overshadowed by the intensity of the conflict. In effect, the argument is not about Thomas Jefferson; it is about American history itself.

Thomas Jefferson is seen, in this formulation, as the patron saint of American liberty, an icon of our democratic ideals—and the long-sought answer to the riddle within our past. In such a perspective, if Thomas Jefferson had an intimate relationship with Sally Hemings, the fact would not merely shed light on one man but illuminate the psyches of all slaveowners of the period. If Jefferson, conversely, could be cleared of the charge of illicit intercourse, it would exonerate his class and countrymen as well. The life of Thomas Jefferson thus becomes a battleground where ideologues thrash out their differences. Jefferson is painted as virtuous, deceitful, idealistic, hypocritical, callous, calculating, remorseful—whichever a given argument demands. Jefferson was, in truth, a man who mirrored the inherent tensions of the early republic. Plagued by historical contradictions, his life was a continual mediation between debt and conscience.

Williamson's final word on the subject suffices, in the context of our discussion of the sexual dynamics of slavery: "In the broad sweep of history it does not much matter whether Thomas Jefferson mixed at Monticello or not. Someone did, and the slave population on the mountain overlooking Charlottesville grew steadily whiter."[36]

The question of how common planter-slave liaisons were remains undecided. Although travel accounts by foreign observers and southern statesmen alike refer to the issue, the frequency of these sexual involvements within plantation society is impossible to pin down. Historians Robert Fogel and Stanley Engerman, in their *Time on the Cross*, demonstrate that this subject, like so many others related to slavery, cannot be fully reckoned by numbers or charted on graphs.[37] Miscegenation is a prime example of the failure of quantification.

An ante-bellum author exclaimed: "This evil has extended so far that more than one half the slave population are mixed with whites."[38] But Fogel and Engerman flatly assert: "The fact that during the twenty-three decades of contact between slaves and whites which elapsed between 1620 and 1850, only 7.7% of the slaves were mulattoes suggests that on average only a very small percentage of the slaves born in any given year were fathered by white men."[39] Even after discounting census error, the clash of interpretations is striking, but can easily be explained.

The two arguments are made from opposing didactic camps. The first author is an "eyewitness," heightening his testimony with hyperbole for polemical effect and charging it with the strident emotionalism of the day. He echoed the warning of an early critic of Jefferson who warned that if all planters followed in the footsteps of the Sage of Monticello, there would arise *"FOUR HUNDRED THOUSAND MULATTOES* in addition to the present swarm. The country would be no longer habitable, till after a civil war and a series of massacres."[40]

The second statement is made by co-authors who seek "dispassionately" and "scientifically" to refute the charge that planters frequently exploited their female slaves, using as their evidence a low rate of miscegenation. Although all mulattoes indeed might have been the result of planter-slave liaisons, the inverse proposition is patently false. All sexual exploitation of black by white cannot possibly be included within the subset of miscegenation. To argue that sexual exploitation can be gauged on some sort of flow chart is as absurd as the assertion that a head count of mulattoes will accurately measure interracial copulation. On questions of color and sexuality, attitudes rather than numbers elucidate the subject. Statistical evidence only partially advances our understanding of racial and sexual dynamics.

Fogel and Engerman postulate that more white planters were "put off by racist aversions" from sleeping with black women than were "tempted by the myth of black sexuality." They present the following data to support this conjecture: in 1860 only 4.3 percent of the prostitutes in Nashville were black, although 20 percent of the population in Nashville was black. They argue that there were no pure black or slave prostitutes. Finally they conclude: "The substantial underrepresentation of Negroes, as well as the complete absence of dark-skinned Negroes, indicates that white men who desired illicit sex had a strong preference for white women."[41] The weakness of this argument is self-evident in its own terms. But more important is the major ideological flaw: the failure to recognize that within the slave South, all black women were potentially surrogate prostitutes.

The racial dynamics of sexuality, so long repressed in the scholarly literature although perennially a favored topic in the popular imagination, designate a new and promising area for research in American history.[42]

In the South, that most contradiction-ridden region, race ineradicably influenced patterns of sexual expression. Complex impulses, impossible to plot by means of demographic records, entangled white with black from the Colonial period onward. The imperatives of slavery shaped planter ideology so powerfully that, by the nineteenth century, southern slaveowners were equally prepared to countenance their economic exploitation of blacks for profit and their sexual exploitation of blacks for pleasure. Because the slave South was obsessed with color and gender, the fate of individuals was drastically influenced by their particular classification. Using this rigid grid to establish a hierarchy of social interaction, white men wielded the power within society, and made all blacks, all slaves, and all women their victims.

This social constellation had certain psychological consequences. White men in the Old South were compulsively preoccupied with deference and authority. Their egos were poised on a precarious pinnacle of honor. Sex in this context, much as in Victorian England, had melodramatic elements; force, potential if not explicit, took center stage.[43] Within the complex sexual scenario of plantation society, power eclipsed other themes. It is not excessive to speculate that domination shaped erotic imagination, arousal, objects of desire, and modes of gratification. Slaveowners incorporated violence, actual or implied, into their patterns of sexual satisfaction. White masters fell prey to the ambivalent myths they themselves had promoted about blacks: their sensuality, their bestial vitality, their promiscuous desire. The "black buck" and similar sensationalist images agitated the white planter's deep-seated fears about his own virility; the "slave wench" and associated stereotypes demeaned black women by equating them with animal sexuality—and projecting onto them the sensuality denied to the plantation mistress. As a result, ante-bellum patriarchs simultaneously emasculated male slaves, dehumanized female slaves, and desexualized their own wives. The imposition of this difficult and twisted balance had become the indispensable counterpoint to a racial dynamic of sexuality that was of the white masters' own creation.

XII

FOUCAULT MEETS MANDINGO

Sex became a matter that required the social body as a whole,
and virtually all of its individuals, to place themselves under
surveillance. . . . the first figure to be invested by the deploy-
ment of sexuality, one of the first to be "sexualized," was the
"idle" woman. She inhabited the outer edge of the "world,"
in which she always had to appear as a value, and of the
family, where she was assigned a new destiny charged with
conjugal and parental obligations. Thus there emerged the
"nervous" woman, the woman afflicted with vapors. . . .
—Michel Foucault, *The History of Sexuality*

*T*he southern lady indeed suffered along the lines sketched by
Foucault in the passage above. Despite our deeper understanding of the realities of plantation culture and regardless of the historical
evidence, we cling to the comfortable familiarity of stereotypes. The
actual experience of men and women, black or white, under southern
slavery bears small relation to either the idyllic or the torrid tales of
life on the plantation as it has been projected in myth, legend, and
folklore. The American popular imagination has proved tenaciously
fond of its failed stepchild, the Old South.

Contemporary America remains haunted as well by the actual legacy of slavery, which manifests itself not only in areas of class and race but in certain aspects of sexuality and sexual ideology. This is not surprising, since slavery dominated the American economy during the first half of the nineteenth century, became a political issue that divided the nation in its bloodiest war, and created an ideological conflict that reflected the fundamental challenge of the oppressed to modern proclamations of "liberty" and "equality." Although the political economy of slavery has been demolished, patterns of exploitation that were developed and refined under the system remain. As Afro-Americans and others continue to underscore the horrors of slavery in an attempt to confront and explore these patterns, however, the repeated cataloguing of atrocities has in some degree had the tragic and profoundly ironic effect of intensifying perverse mythic images of white power over blacks. The litany of brutality reinforces the spurious strength of the oppressor as well as reveals the genuine suffering of the victim. The process of examining the past focuses attention on the fact of bondage as a persistent theme in relationships between black and white.

Foucault reminds us that we cannot merely read what is said, but must consider the context and tone of the discourse, often rich in irony. In racial and sexual matters, such irony plays havoc with the literal interpretation of attitudes. The subtexts of sexuality added to dynamics of race render almost any surface reading of social postures a distortion of circumstantial reality. In the case of the Old South, the cumulative effect of the transformation of historical event into popular mythology has been spectacular.

The extreme elements of contradiction within a biracial slave society have proved irresistible to perpetrators of lurid romanticization, dealers in intrigue and forbidden lust. Vivid modern "portraits" of the sordid subculture coexisting with the splendor and pageantry of the chivalric South reveal more about today's sexual attitudes than they do about sexual activity in the ante-bellum era. While it would be easy to dismiss the invented image as pure fantasy, it is valuable to explore what it suggests about the way we today *prefer* to "remember" the past. When we indulge in this image, we are not in fact invoking memory, but projecting; we enhance and embellish the plantation past to suit our contemporary needs. We accept the belief that planters not only lived the rich and aristocratic life briefly glimpsed in the prewar scenes of *Gone with the Wind* (1939) but that they enjoyed as well the sexual delights depicted in the likes of *Mandingo* (1975).

Mandingo, a film intended as an updated version of the plantation myth, provides a vehicle for sensational "erotic" themes: incest, flagellation, interracial sex. It is no coincidence that *Mandingo* is set in the Old South, not on the Colorado frontier, on the shores of Cape Cod, or in an anonymous geographical vacuum. The film's sexual and racial postures demand this particular place and time. Just as *Gone with the Wind* reflected the yearning romanticism of the Depression years, so *Mandingo* reveals current "sexploitation" sensibilities.

The lurid and brutal aspects of the film pander to hyperbolic distortions of attitudes that evolved during the civil rights and sexual liberation movements of the sixties. In this sense, the film presents a counterpoint to the submissive and desexualized black and female stereotypes of previous cinematic depictions of the ante-bellum South. Although *Mandingo* creates new and equally demeaning stereotypes, analysis of this celluoid portrait of plantation life allows a certain demystification of contemporary attitudes toward race and sex. The term "Mandingo" has acquired a "pop" recognition factor, involving a complex collage of images including furtive planter-slave romance, thwarted personal drives, but above all, the quenching of forbidden desires—satisfaction through interracial sex.

The best-seller list now regularly includes a novel set in the steamy emotional jungles of the Old South. The film *Mandingo* is based on one of the "Falconhurst" novels, a popular paperback "sexploitation" series. For over two decades, since his 1958 publication of *Mandingo*, author Kyle Onstott has churned out formulaic novels for an eager audience. Other fiction has capitalized on this demand as well: Eric Corder's *Slave* (1968), George McNeill's *Plantation* (1975), William Lavendar's *Chinaberry* (1976), Rachel Delauncy's *Fleur* (1979), and Dorothy Daniels's *The Sisters of Valcour* (1981), to name a few. One of the most successful of these ventures was Lonnie Coleman's *Beulah Land* (1973) which—with its sequel, *Look Away, Beulah Land* (1977)—became the basis for a television mini-series.

None of these works is distinguished; indeed, it is difficult to distinguish one from the other. The covers of the paperbacks are sensational and interchangeable, trumpeting almost identical blurbs:

She was beauty and innocence unguarded on a plantation where men know only greed, cruelty, and lust. . . .

The unforgettable novel of a shocking portion of our American heritage. . . .

The depravity and brutality of slavery—of men and women sold at auction—of young girls forced to gratify their master's lust. . . .

He was her slave, a man she owned, a man she burned to possess—but could not have. . . .

A sprawling plantation on the Mississippi . . . lush with prosperity . . . grand in hospitality . . . smoldering with forbidden desire and scandalous family secrets . . . until the night of the party, the night the master's daughter is discovered out back with her personal slaveboy. . . .

Such language is, of course, a trademark of the pulp novel. The fact of these hackneyed formulas is not as important as the way in which they underscore what might be called the "Mandingoization" of plantation history, replacing the earlier, prim and whitewashed version of the plantation with an equally distorted notion of the Old South as a swamp of sin. Although this production does provide some relatively authentic elements (the homestead in *Mandingo* is much more realistic than the mansions in *Gone with the Wind*, for example), the movie was made to exploit, not to document.

Mandingo is set during the late ante-bellum era, in an unspecified year after Nat Turner's 1831 rebellion. On a Mississippi Delta plantation, Colonel Warren Maxwell, a widower left with only one son and heir, Hammond, is anxious to continue the fame and prosperity of his family estate, Falconhurst. Since that enterprise includes the notorious commercial breeding of members of a noble African tribe, the Mandingoes, Maxwell even mates slave brother and sister when no other "purebred" match is available. The Colonel is equally zealous for a white heir, a grandson to take over Falconhurst in the years to come. Son Hammond, therefore, is sent off on a mission to needy cousins, trading a financial loan from Falconhurst for their daughter—

inevitably named Blanche—whom he marries. Eugenics and the pursuit of pleasure dominate the film.

In addition to the central drama of providing Falconhurst with a white heir, several slave subplots develop. Blacks on the plantation are divided into predictable stereotypical categories. House servants play classic "trickster" roles; they perform for the master, but make it clear to the audience that these are only masks that they must don. The character Agamemnon ("Mem") plays "Uncle Tom" to the hilt in front of his master, but when among other blacks reveals his defiant scorn. The rebel, or "bad nigger," is re-created in the person of a field slave, Cicero; a lynching party puts a noose around his neck when his bid for freedom fails. At this point, he proves quite a speechmaker, and his crude contempt for whites and agitation on behalf of violence symbolize the "Nat Turner" spirit among southern slaves. Then there are "sensitive" blacks who form attachments to their young white master. Both his concubine, Ellen, and his prize Mandingo, Mede (short for Ganymede, and like his mythological namesake, this character gains favor because of his physical allure), believe Hammond to be kinder and more reasonable than other slaveowners. Ellen and Mede are cruelly deceived and consequently betrayed by this misplaced trust.

The plot rolls along, contrived and complex. Ellen becomes pregnant and exacts a promise from Hammond that he will free their child. Mede becomes a valued trophy for Falconhurst when he wins a bout in which his master pits him against another black "buck." But while Hammond is at the fight in New Orleans, his jealous and drunken wife Blanche pushes Ellen down a staircase, causing her to lose her baby.

To soothe Blanche's rage, Hammond eventually decides to build his wife a more magnificent mansion. Blanche is portrayed as a petulant "sex kitten" who was deflowered by her brother at an early age. Her yowling she-cat routine strains the form. When Hammond suspects after their wedding night that she was not a virgin bride, he refuses to sleep with her. Blanche takes to drink, nagging her husband with toddy-soaked pleas for her conjugal rights. Hammond goes off again, this time taking Ellen with him, to sell some of his slaves—ironically, the cash is to finance his wife's "dream house." But Blanche seeks revenge for Hammond's sexual neglect of her and his continued affection for his concubine. She calls for Mede—the Maxwell prize, the Mandingo stud—and seduces him in her bedroom, in broad daylight, with the servants well in earshot. Mede cooperates only because of his mistress's threat to falsely accuse him of attacking her should *he* resist.

Melodrama increases. Blanche gives birth to a mulatto baby; her doctor allows it to bleed to death. In a move solidly endorsed by southern custom and Victorian morality, Hammond, his father the Colonel, and the doctor silently agree that Blanche must die. Still weak from her delivery, Blanche lies stricken in bed, begging her husband to forgive her. He coldly pours poison down her throat. (In the midst of all this cinematic exaggeration, her demise rings oddly true.) Hammond now stalks from the house, shotgun in hand, to hunt down Mede. When Ellen, the only woman for whom he has professed tender feelings, attempts to intercede on Mede's behalf, he knocks her down and reminds her that she is "just a nigger." In one cruel stroke their entire relationship of affection and trust is demolished. Grabbing the white man's gun, Mem attempts to thwart Hammond's execution of Mede. In response, Colonel Maxwell bellows at his steward, calling him a "loon." The insult triggers an explosion within the old slave's mind; decades of anger defy years of restraint, and Mem turns and fires on his master.

The film ends with Blanche dead upstairs, the Colonel blown to pieces on the veranda, and Hammond sprawled on the porch, surveying the ruins. Despite this bloody finale, Hammond Maxwell still has his slaves, his plantation, and fresh breeding stock in the shape of one of Mede's Mandingo babies. He can start afresh: marry a new wife, select a new black concubine, and continue as before.

Mandingo, for all its triteness and vulgarity, presents a fable of the inherent evils of slavery from the white planter's perspective, collapsing the most violent and extreme aspects of slaveowners' paranoia into one rousing disaster. From its fatalistic viewpoint, the twin threats of slave violence and white women's miscegenation could descend upon the planter at any time. The historical evils of slavery in *Mandingo,* insofar as they are implied at all in the "moral" of the story, are completely overshadowed and in some cases even inverted by the "immoral" themes of force and sexual prowess. Every white character embodies some peculiarity or excess. Perhaps the worst is Blanche's brother, Charles; not only does he seduce his sister and try to prevent her from marrying, but he makes his film appearance in a scene designed to charm only the most stalwart of sadists. Charles rides up to the Falconhurst barn just as a naked slave is gagged and strung up upside-down for a whipping. Charles leaps off his horse and takes over the punishment, obviously relishing the opportunity to draw blood. In another scene, he lashes the exposed buttocks of a young slave girl with his belt as a prelude to coitus.

Whips and chains are ornaments of subjection: political, physical, social, and psychological. They remain sexually charged objects today. Bondage has not only shed its taboo status as sexual bent but has generated a thriving subculture of modern sexuality. The persistent attraction of these artifacts of slavery for authors of pornography is undeniable. The paddle, the whip, the collar, the handcuffs and ankle cuffs, reflect a preoccupation with dominance and submission that has chosen to embody the metaphor of master and slave. Today's "equipment" of sexual domination derives in part from America's legacy of slavery.

Force and frenzy are implicit elements of sexuality in our popular depictions of the slaveowning South. Television programs, fiction, and films depict raw and violent conditions on the ante-bellum plantation. Conflicts are heated, passions inflamed; the rising steam of sexuality and rage clouds our vision of southern life. In much the same way that the indignation of abolitionists aroused as well as appalled the public during the ante-bellum era, modern campaigns to reveal the "shocking truth" about the Old South may cater on some level to lascivious appetites as well as to loftier moral aims. Ironically, these elaborate re-creations of the plantation past replace one set of stereotypes with another.

Both the traditional and the current characterizations of the plantation mistress portray gross exaggerations of sexual behavior. Historically, southern womanhood has been represented by models of purity and innocence. Plantation mistresses were supposedly chaste, fragile, and above all asexual. Recent fictional treatments emphasize the deep sexual ambivalence of white women in the Old South. In one sense, these two images seem compatible. The classic image of southern ladies ascribed their asexuality to the white female's lack of libido, whereas interpreters today see plantation mistresses as victims of repression, women with pent-up emotions and suppressed desires.

The "sexploitation" formula translates this buried passion into erratic sexual frenzy. The white woman's unfulfilled sex drive becomes an explosive element within southern culture.

The truth is that women's sexual impropriety was met, in fact and fiction, with severe reprisal in the ante-bellum South. The notion that women indulged their "forbidden passions" simply contradicts the social realities of plantation life. This is not to deny that women might have wanted to break taboos, to possess power and choice in their sexual lives. But southern women rarely seized control within any of their severely restricted spheres, and most plantation mistresses never escaped the literal or behavioral confines of their circumscribed world.

This poignant actuality makes characters like Blanche Maxwell all the more unbelievable. Her cardboard character is the ludicrous cinematic extreme of the popular fictional plantation mistress—from her self-dramatizing manner and childish grammar to her very name, with its connotations of racial purity, social status, and sensuality. Blanche's behavior turns melodrama into surrealistic fantasy. A real-life Blanche, whatever she might have been by nature, would never have defied social dictates with such abandon. The mischief of Scarlett O'Hara is tepid compared with the boiling cauldron of Blanche Maxwell's intrigues. The haughty screen heroine of *Jezebel* (1938) scandalized New Orleans by wearing red instead of the customary white to a society ball, a gesture that pales by comparison with Blanche's misdeed. This uncontrollable plantation mistress is more a product of Tennessee Williams than of the ante-bellum era. Fiction and illusion combine, as historical considerations vanish, to create a new myth: the plantation mistress as a seductress of slaves, the nagging nymphomaniac of the Old South. This "improved" model of white womanhood is hardly sympathetic and, though updated, no more authentic than previous versions.

The current popular portrait of the southern woman may have transformed her from the idle, afflicted creature of our romantic imagination, but she remains sexually stereotyped nonetheless. By conjuring up images of torn bodices and riding crops rather than exploring her unique psychosexual dilemma, by projecting our own sexual fantasies on her, we perpetuate her victimization. Whether thrust into the shadows or the limelight, the plantation mistress continues to be a prisoner of myth.

American slavery bred many strong and sturdy monsters. Racism, class oppression, and sexual exploitation remain indestructible among us; they have outgrown their parent and prowl without restraint. The victims and those who take pity on their prey ransack the past, seeking some key to ridding us of them. Facing our problems, in the past as well as the present, will not be enough unless we guard ourselves vigilantly against the prospect of an even greater failure: self-deceit.

Modern society is riddled with such deception. We flatter ourselves that we have slain the dragons, conquered the devils, defeated the deadly relics of our past. Yet we are haunted by the rattling of the chains. Despite our projections, all our debates, our countless investigations, we have still to transcend the legacy of slavery. We continue enthralled, surrounded by monsters and masks, condemned perhaps not to repeat history but certainly to rewrite it.

APPENDIX A

Comparison of Southern Sample Group (750 members of the planter elite born between 1765 and 1815) and Northern Sample Group (100 members of the Hudson Valley Dutch planter elite born between 1765 and 1815).

1. NUMBER OF MARRIAGES

2. COUSIN MARRIAGE

3. AGE AT FIRST MARRIAGE

4. NUMBER OF CHILDREN

5. NUMBER OF CHILDREN TO SURVIVE PAST INFANCY (2 YEARS) AND TO MATURITY (18 YEARS)

6. AGE AT DEATH

7. DEATH/DEATH OF SPOUSE IN CHILDBIRTH

8. BIRTHPLACE

9. PLACE OF MARITAL RESIDENCE

Note: Not all totals in these tables equal 100 percent, owing to missing data for sample members.

1. NUMBER OF MARRIAGES

Southern	0	1	2	3	4	5
Females	2.1%	90.4%	7.2%	0.3%	0%	0%
Males	3.7	76.6	15.7	3.5	0.5	0

Northern	0	1	2	3	4	5
Females	0%	98.0%	2.0%	0%	0%	0%
Males	0	89.8	8.2	0	0	2.0

2. COUSIN MARRIAGE

Southern	No	Yes
Females.......	87.7%	12.3%
Males	87.6	12.4

Northern	No	Yes
Females.......	100.0%	0
Males.........	100.0	0

3. AGE AT FIRST MARRIAGE

Southern	13	14	15	16	17	18	19	20	21–25	26–30	31–35	36–40	Over 40
Females.......	0.6%	0.5%	1.9%	7.0%	9.9%	10.2%	9.9%	11.8%	22.5%	4.3%	2.7%	0.8%	16.8%
Males.........	0	0	0	0	0.8	0.8	1.1	4.0	36.2	21.8	8.2	2.1	23.7

Northern	13	14	15	16	17	18	19	20	21–25	26–30	31–35	36–40	Over 40
Females.......	0%	0%	2.0%	2.0%	3.9%	7.8%	7.8%	3.9%	37.3%	17.6%	7.8%	2.0%	7.8%
Males.........	0	0	0	0	2.0	0	2.0	2.0	40.3	26.5	14.3	2.0	10.2

4. NUMBER OF CHILDREN

Southern	0	1	2	3	4	5	6	7	8	9	10	11	12	13	14	15	16	17
Females	15.9%	7.3%	9.6%	8.0%	7.6%	6.0%	7.3%	10.0%	5.3%	5.6%	5.6%	3.0%	6.6%	1.0%	0%	0.7%	0.3%	0%
Males	7.7	4.8	7.0	6.4	9.6	5.1	8.0	12.1	7.7	8.6	6.7	4.8	7.0	1.6	1.6	0.6	0.3	0.3

Northern	0	1	2	3	4	5	6	7	8	9	10	11	12	13	14	15	16	17
Females	3.9%	7.8%	9.8%	9.8%	11.8%	13.7%	9.8%	9.8%	13.7%	5.9%	2.0%	2.0%	0%	0%	0%	0%	0%	0%
Males	0	8.2	8.2	4.1	8.2	12.2	18.4	10.2	6.1	14.3	6.1	2.0	0	2.0	0	0	0	0

5. NUMBER OF CHILDREN TO SURVIVE

Southern	0	1	2	3	4	5	6	7	8	9	10	11	12	13	14	15	16
Past Infancy (2 years)	12.5%	5.9%	9.5%	6.7%	9.5%	6.4%	10.3%	8.7%	8.0%	5.9%	8.7%	3.0%	2.5%	1.3%	0.5%	0.3%	0.2%
To Maturity (18 years)	12.6	6.9	9.0	8.9	8.7	9.7	9.2	10.2	7.4	6.9	4.7	3.0	1.3	0.8	0.2	0.3	0.2

Northern	0	1	2	3	4	5	6	7	8	9	10	11	12	13	14	15	16
Past Infancy (2 years)	2.0%	12.0%	4.0%	14.0%	15.0%	11.0%	12.0%	10.0%	10.0%	9.0%	1.0%	0%	0%	0%	0%	0%	0%
To Maturity (18 years)	2.0	14.0	4.0	21.0	7.0	18.0	11.0	13.0	8.0	2.0	0	0	0	0	0	0	0

6. AGE AT DEATH

Southern	Under 20	21–25	26–30	31–35	36–40	41–50	51–60	61–70	71–80	Over 80
Females......	2.4%	2.7%	2.9%	6.4%	4.3%	9.9%	8.8%	12.8%	13.9%	35.8%
Males.........	0.5	1.4	1.4	3.2	3.7	10.1	14.4	22.6	17.6	25.0

Northern	Under 20	21–25	26–30	31–35	36–40	41–50	51–60	61–70	71–80	
Females.......	0%	0%	5.9%	2.0%	7.8%	11.8%	19.6%	21.6%	23.5%	
Males	0	0	0	4.1	12.2	12.2	20.4	38.8	12.2	

7. DEATH/DEATH OF SPOUSE IN CHILDBIRTH

Southern	No	Yes	Northern	No	Yes
Females	95.1%	4.9%	Females	96.0%	4.0%
Males	93.9	6.1	Males	97.9	2.1

8. BIRTHPLACE

Southern	Foreign Country	North	Border States	Maryland	Virginia	North Carolina	South Carolina	Georgia	Alabama	Mississippi
Females	2.5%	0.8%	5.5%	6.9%	59.5%	5.2%	13.2%	5.0%	0.6%	0.6%
Males	0.3	0.5	8.0	3.8	64.6	3.2	11.8	3.2	1.9	0.3

Northern	New York	New England	Middle Atlantic
Females	90.2%	7.8%	2.0%
Males	85.7	12.2	2.0

9. PLACE OF MARITAL RESIDENCE

Southern	Foreign Country	North	Border States	Maryland	Virginia	North Carolina	South Carolina	Georgia	Alabama	Mississippi	Louisiana	Texas
Females........	0.9%	1.7%	13.7%	5.1%	49.5%	3.1%	14.8%	5.7%	3.7%	0.9%	0.3%	0.6%
Males..........	0	1.1	17.5	3.9	49.3	2.5	10.9	5.6	7.0	1.4	0	0.8

Northern	New York	New England	Middle Atlantic
Females........	90.2%	7.8%	2.0%
Males..........	85.4	12.5	2.1

APPENDIX B

Comparison of Southern Sample Group members born before 1795 and those born after 1795.

1. AGE AT FIRST MARRIAGE

2. NUMBER OF MARRIAGES

3. COUSIN MARRIAGE

4. FEMALE COUSIN MARRIAGES BY AGE OF MARRIAGE

5. FEMALE AGE AT DEATH

6. DEATH/DEATH OF SPOUSE IN CHILDBIRTH

7. NUMBER OF CHILDREN FOR FEMALES

8. NUMBER OF CHILDREN TO SURVIVE PAST INFANCY (2 YEARS) AND TO MATURITY (18 YEARS)

Note: Not all totals in these tables equal 100 percent, owing to missing data for sample members.

I. AGE AT FIRST MARRIAGE

Females	13	14	15	16	17	18	19	20	21–25	26–30	31–35	36–40	Over 40
Before 1795..	1.0%	0.5%	2.2%	9.3%	9.8%	10.4%	8.7%	12.0%	20.2%	3.3%	1.6%	0%	19.1%
After 1795....	0	0.5	1.6	4.7	1.2	9.9	11.0	11.5	24.6	5.2	3.7	1.6	14.7

Males	13	14	15	16	17	18	19	20	21–25	26–30	31–35	36–40	Over 40
Before 1795..	0%	0%	0%	0%	0.5%	1.0%	0%	4.8%	34.4%	20.1%	9.1%	1.9%	27.8%
After 1795....	0	0	0	0	0.6	2.4	3.0	3.0	38.3	24.0	7.2	2.4	18.6

2. NUMBER OF MARRIAGES

Females	0	1	2	3	4
Before 1795 ...	3.3%	89.1%	7.1%	0.5%	0%
After 1795......	1.0	91.6	7.3	0	0

Males	0	1	2	3	4
Before 1795 ...	3.8%	76.6%	15.3%	4.3%	0%
After 1795......	3.6	76.6	16.2	2.4	1.2

3. COUSIN MARRIAGE

Females	Yes	No
Before 1795	11.3%	88.7%
After 1795......	13.2	86.8

Males	Yes	No
Before 1795	13.1%	86.9%
After 1795......	11.6	88.4

4. FEMALE COUSIN MARRIAGES BY AGE OF MARRIAGE

	13	14	15	16	17	18	19	20	21–25	26–30	31–35	36–40	Over 40
Before 1795	0%	0%	0%	0%	50.0%	25.0%	0%	0%	25.0%	0%	0%	0%	0%
After 1795......	0	0	10.0	20.0	30.0	0	0	10.0	0	10.0	0	0	0

5. FEMALE AGE AT DEATH

	Under 20	21–25	26–30	31–35	36–40	41–50	51–60	61–70	71–80	Over 40
Before 1795	2.2%	3.3%	1.6%	5.5%	4.9%	9.8%	7.7%	11.5%	16.4%	35.2%
After 1795......	2.6	2.1	4.2	7.3	3.7	9.9	9.9	14.1	11.5	34.6

6. DEATH/DEATH OF SPOUSE IN CHILDBIRTH

Females	Yes	No
Before 1795	3.0%	97.0%
After 1795......	6.5	93.5

Males	Yes	No
Before 1795 ...	5.3%	94.7%
After 1795......	7.0	93.0

7. NUMBER OF CHILDREN FOR FEMALES

	0	1	2	3	4	5	6	7	8	9	10	11	12	13	14	15	16
Before 1795	21.4%	6.4%	7.1%	7.1%	6.4%	3.6%	8.6%	9.3%	7.1%	7.1%	4.3%	1.4%	7.1%	1.4%	0%	1.4%	0%
After 1795	11.2	8.1	11.2	8.7	8.7	8.1	6.2	10.6	3.7	5.0	6.8	4.3	6.2	0.6	0	0	0.6

8. NUMBER OF CHILDREN TO SURVIVE

Past Infancy (2 years)	0	1	2	3	4	5	6	7	8	9	10	11	12	13	14	15	16
Before 1795	15.7%	5.9%	8.5%	4.6%	10.1%	5.6%	8 2%	10.5%	8.5%	5.6%	7.8%	2.9%	2.6%	1.3%	1.0%	0.7%	0.3%
After 1795	9.2	5.9	10.2	8.9	7.2	12.5	7.2	7.6	6.3	9.5	3.0	2.3	1.3	0	0	0	

To Maturity (18 years)	0	1	2	3	4	5	6	7	8	9	10	11	12	13	14	15	16
Before 1795	15.7%	6.2%	8.8%	7.2%	8.5%	8.5%	7.8%	11.1%	6.9%	7.8%	4.3%	2.9%	1.6%	1.3%	0.3%	0.7%	0.3%
After 1795	9.5	7.6	9.2	10.5	8.9	10.9	10.5	9.2	7.9	5.9	5.6	3.0	1.0	0.3	0	0	0

ABBREVIATIONS OF ARCHIVES REFERRED TO IN NOTES AND BIBLIOGRAPHY

ASA   Alabama State Archives, Montgomery

CW   Colonial Williamsburg Foundation, Williamsburg, Virginia

DLC   Library of Congress, Washington, D.C.

DU   Manuscript Department, William R. Perkins Library, Duke University, Durham, North Carolina

GEU   Special Collections, Woodruff Library, Emory University, Atlanta, Georgia

GHS   Georgia Historical Society, Savannah

GSA   Georgia State Archives, Atlanta

HL   Huntington Library, Pasadena, California

HNO   Historic New Orleans Collection, New Orleans, Louisiana

LSA   Louisiana State Archives, Baton Rouge

LSU   Manuscript Division, Louisiana State University Library, Baton Rouge

MSA   Mississippi State Archives, Jackson

NCA   North Carolina State Archives, Raleigh

PHS   Historical Society of Pennsylvania, Philadelphia

RC   Schlesinger Library, Radcliffe College, Cambridge, Massachusetts

SCA   South Carolina State Archives, Columbia

SCHS   South Carolina Historical Society, Charleston

SHC   Southern Historical Collection, Wilson Library, University of North Carolina, Chapel Hill

TU   Manuscripts Section, Tulane University Library, New Orleans, Louisiana

USC   Caroliniana Library, University of South Carolina, Columbia

UVA   Manuscript Department, University of Virginia Library, Charlottesville

VHS   Virginia Historical Society, Richmond

VSL   Virginia State Library, Richmond

WMC   Manuscripts Division, Swem Library, College of William and Mary, Williamsburg, Virginia

NOTES

Abbreviated citations for some collections have been used. For full title of the collection, please refer to the Bibliography.

CHAPTER I. *WOMEN IN THE LAND OF COTTON*

1. Julia Cherry Spruill, *Women's Life and Work in the Southern Colonies* (1938: reprint ed., New York: W. W. Norton & Co., 1972), p. 9.

2. The status of women in the American colonies is still a subject of debate. See Mary Beth Norton, "The Myth of the Golden Age," in Carol Berkin and Mary Beth Norton, *Women and America: A History* (Boston: Houghton Mifflin Co., 1979).

3. Spruill, *Women's Life and Work*, p. 9.

4. Clement Eaton, *The Growth of Southern Civilization, 1790–1860* (New York: Harper & Row, 1961), p. 25.

5. Carl Degler, *Place over Time: The Continuity of Southern Distinctiveness* (Baton Rouge: Louisiana State University Press, 1977), pp. 29–30.

6. *Southern Literary Messenger*, vol. 33, no. 1 (July 1861).

7. Eli Zaretsky, *Capitalism, the Family and Personal Life* (New York: Harper & Row, 1976).

8. Elizabeth Hampton to Edmund Bryan, 25 January 1836, Bryan-Leventhorpe Papers, SHC.

9. Nancy Cott, *The Bonds of Womanhood: Woman's Sphere in New England* (New Haven, Conn.: Yale University Press, 1978).

10. L. H. Butterfield, Marc Friedlander, and Mary Jo Kline, eds., *The Book of Abigail and John* (Cambridge, Mass.: Harvard University Press, 1975), p. 121.

11. Ann Douglas, *The Feminization of American Culture* (New York: Alfred A. Knopf, 1977).

12. Carl Degler, *At Odds: Women and the Family in America from the Revolution to the Present* (New York: Oxford University Press, 1980), pp. 377, 378–379.

13. See Keith Melder, "Ladies Bountiful: Organized Women's Benevolence in Early 19th Century America," *New York History* 58 (1967): 231–54; Carroll Smith-Rosenberg, "Beauty, the Beast and the Militant Woman: A Case Study in Sex Roles and Social Stress in Jacksonian America," *American Quarterly* 23 (October 1971): 562–84.

14. David Campbell to Maria Campbell, 3 January 1823, Campbell Collection, DU.

15. Mary Telfair to Mary Few, 1 December n.a., Few Collection, GSA. See also Eleanor Douglas to Mary Hall, 8 January 1820, Eleanor Douglas Collection, DU.

CHAPTER II. *SLAVE OF SLAVES*

1. See Robert Fogel and Stanley Engerman, *Time on the Cross: The Economics of American Negro Slavery* (Boston: Little, Brown & Co., 1974), and Eugene D. Genovese, *Roll, Jordan, Roll: The World the Slaves Made* (New York: Pantheon Books, 1976).

2. See David Bertelson, *The Lazy South* (New York: Oxford University Press, 1967).

3. Erasmus Darwin, *A Plan for the Conduct of Female Education in Boarding Schools, Private Families and Public Seminaries* (1798; reprint ed., New York, Johnson Reprint Corp., 1968), p. 95.

4. William T. Barry to Susan _____ 1 August 1824, Barry Papers, UVA. See also H. D. Conrad to Elizabeth Conrad, 10 April 1823, Weeks Collection, LSU.

5. See Frederick Dabney to Mildred Dabney, 1 July 1815, Dabney Papers, SHC.

6. Mary Withers to Ann Eliza Withers, 25 June 1831, Levert Papers, SHC.

7. Ann Cocke to Ann Barraud, 16 April 1807, Cocke Papers, UVA.

8. Ann Cocke to Ann Barraud, n.d. 1811, Cocke Papers, UVA.

9. Amelia Collection, MSA.

10. Elizabeth Heyward Manigault to Charles Manigault, 23 February 1826, Manigault Collection, SCHS.

11. Susan McDowell to James McDowell, 7 December 1835, James McDowell Papers, SHC.

12. Mary Withers to Ann Eliza Withers, 25 June 1831, Levert Papers, SHC. See also Ann Cleland Kinloch, 1 April 1799, Kinloch Collection, SCHS.

13. Sarah Gayle Diary, 29 June 1832, Bayne-Gayle Papers, SHC.

14. J. P. V. D. Balsdon, *Roman Women: Their History and Habits* (1962; reprint ed., Westport, Conn.: Greenwood Press, 1975), pp. 270, 272.

15. Harriott P. Rutledge to Harriott P. Horry, 20 September 1815, Ravenel Collection, SCHS.

16. See Edward Harden to Marian Harden, 28 November 1816, Harden Collection, DU.

17. Eleanor Douglas to Sally Hall, 1 May 1820, Eleanor Douglas Collection, DU.

18. David Campbell to _____, 1 January 1834, Campbell Collection, DU.

19. Eliza Person Mitchell Diary, Person Papers, SHC.

20. Susanna Clay to Clement Clay, 24 January 1833, Clay Collection, DU.

21. Rebecca Wyche to Thomas Wyche, 15 January 1836, Wyche-Otley Papers, SHC.

22. Mary Poindexter to Jane Poindexter, 25 December 1825, Clingman-Puryear Papers, SHC. See also Lucy Winn to John Winn, January 1830, Winn Collection, DU; Maria Campbell to David Campbell, 8 January 1822, Campbell Collection, DU.

23. Virginia Campbell to Catherine Campbell, 18 March 1832, Campbell Collection, DU.

24. Sarah Gayle Diary, 4 December 1829, Bayne-Gayle Papers, SHC.

25. Mary Braxton to Margaret Barnes, 15 September 1838, Barnes Collection, WMC.

26. Peggy Nicholas Cary to Jane Nicholas, 25 July 1816, Edgehill-Randolph Collection, UVA.

27. M. Manigault to Gabriel Henry Manigault, 3 January 1809, Manigault Collection, DU.

28. Undated inventory, McBee Papers, SHC.

29. I. F. Leinbach to cousin Annie, 18 June n.a., Leinbach Collection, DU. See also Louisa _____ to Mary Houston, 20 February 1837, Hannah-Barksdale Collection, VSL.

30. _____ to Charlotte Hannah, 2 April 1837, Hannah-Barksdale Collection, VSL.

31. Mary Elizabeth Eve Carmichael, 20 October 1837, Carmichael Family Books, SHC.

32. Tarmesian Scot to Nancy Graham, 22 January 1821, Graham Collection, DU.

33. Louisa _____ to Mary Houston, 20 February 1837, Houston Collection, DU. See also Lucy Ambler to Sarah Massie, 3 August 1822, Massie Collection, VHS; Sally Screven to Delia Bryan, 13 November 1822, Arnold-Screven Papers, SHC.

34. Ann Cocke to Ann Barraud, 20 October 1811, Cocke Papers, UVA.

35. Jane Cary Randolph to Mary Harrison, 11 November 1813, Harrison Collection, VHS.

36. Ann Lovell to aunt, 28 November 1833, Lovell Collection, DU.

37. See Account Books of Sarah B. Evans, Evans Collection, LSU, and Elizabeth Manigault, Manigault Collection, USC. See also Sarah Gordon to William Gordon, 9 November 1836, Gordon Collection, GHS.

38. Maria Campbell to David Campbell, 17 May 1801, Campbell Collection, DU. See also Maria Bryan Harford to Julia Cumming, 11 March 1839, Hammond-Bryan-Cumming Collection, USC; Judith Coalter to Elizabeth Bryan, 22 January 1832, Brown-Tucker-Coalter Collection, WMC.

39. Mary Telfair to Mary Few, 4 January 1833, Few Collection, GSA.

40. Walker Diary, 25 May 1835, John Williams Walker Collection, ASA.

41. Edward Harden to Marian Harden, 12 November 1816, Harden Collection, DU.

42. Ann Cocke to Ann Barraud, 20 October 1811, Cocke Papers, UVA.

43. Jane Carson, *Plantation Housekeeping in Colonial Virginia* (Williamsburg, Va.: Colonial Williamsburg, 1975), p. 75.

44. Ann Cocke to Ann Barraud, 20 October 1811, Cocke Papers, UVA. See also Jane Randolph to Mary Harrison, 11 November 1813, Harrison Collection, VHS.

45. Martha B. Eppes Recipe Book, Hubbard Papers, SHC.

46. Eliza Person Mitchell Diary, Person Papers, SHC.

47. Ann Blount Pettigrew, Pettigrew Papers, SHC; Susanna Clay to C. C. Clay, 14 July 1826, Clay Collection, DU.

48. Margaret Brashear to Thomas Tilton Burr, 19 June 1824, Brashear-Lawrence Papers, SHC; S. W. Ferguson Memoir, pp. 1–16, Heyward-Ferguson Papers, SHC; Martha Richardson to James Screven, 19 December 1818, Arnold-Screven Papers, SHC; Sarah Gordon to William Gordon, 12 April 1835, Gordon Collection, GHS; Charlotte Weeks to Mary Weeks, 14 July 1824, Weeks Collection, LSU.

49. Fanny Bland Tucker to St. George Tucker, 14 July 1781, Brown-Tucker-Coalter Collection, WMC.

50. John Steele to Mary Steele, 3 July 1796, Steele Papers, SHC. See also William Lenoir, 1824, Lenoir Papers, SHC.

51. James Gillespie to D. Gillespie, 7 May 1790, Gillespie-Wright Papers, SHC. See also William Elliott to Ann Elliott, 28 November 1827, Elliott Papers, SHC.

52. Fogel and Engerman, *Time on the Cross*, pp. 109–26, 212.

53. Bolling Hall to Polly Hall, 9 November 1814, Hall Collection, ASA. See also Bolling Hall to Polly Hall, 12 February 1816, Hall Collection, ASA; D. W. Witherspoon to his wife, 1 December 1790, Nash Collection, NCA.

54. Fanny Coalter to John Coalter, 12 September 1810, Brown-Tucker-Coalter Collection, WMC. See also Fanny Coalter to John Coalter, 25 September 1810, Brown-Tucker-Coalter Collection, WMC.

55. Sarah Gordon to William Gordon, 7 November 1836, Gordon Collection, GHS.

56. Diana Dunbar to William Dunbar, 1 August 1789, Dunbar Collection, MSA.

57. See Elizabeth Caroline Tait to Charles Tait, January–March 1818, Tait Collection, ASA.

58. William Munford to Sally Munford, 11 January 1806, Munford-Ellis Collection, DU.

59. Catherine Ambler to John Ambler, 30 October 1838, Ambler Papers, UVA.

60. John Steele to Mary Steele, 25 November 1792, Steele Papers, SHC.

61. Anne Newport Royall, 25 December 1817, in *Letters from Alabama, 1817–1822* (Birmingham: University of Alabama Press, 1969), p. 116.

62. Sarah G. Haig, 21 March 1837 and January 1838, Telfair Collection, GHS.

63. Rachel O'Conner to David Weeks, 11 November 1823, Weeks Collection, LSU.

64. Rachel O'Conner to Mary Weeks, 13 June 1824, Weeks Collection, LSU. See also Rachel O'Conner to David Weeks, 14 October 1824 and 7 March 1828, Weeks Collection, LSU.

65. See Eliza Bull, Plantation Accounts 1819–1823, Bull-Morrow Collection, GHS.

66. Mary Brown to Margaret Steele, 7 July 1808, Steele Papers, SHC.

67. Mrs. Lund Washington, 1789, Washington Collection, DLC.

68. Frances Randolph Tucker to Theodorick Bland, 4 June 1781, Tucker-Coleman Collection, WMC.

69. Dolley Madison to Payne Todd, 20 July 1834, in Lucia B. Cutts, ed., *Memoirs and Letters of Dolley Madison* (Boston: Houghton Mifflin Co., 1886), p. 191.

70. Delia Bryan to John Randolph, 7 May 1824, Bryan-Leventhorpe Papers, SHC.

71. See Mary W. Braxton to Charles Carter, 10 February 1803, Carter Collection, WMC; Jane Lees to David Lees, 14 October 1828, Lees Papers, SHC.

CHAPTER III. *CIRCLE OF KIN*

1. Michael Greenberg, "Gentleman Slaveholders: The Social Outlook of the Virginia Planter Class," unpublished Ph.D. dissertation, Rutgers University, 1972.

2. Timothy Ford, "South Carolina Travel Diary, 1785–86," 4 November 1785, *South Carolina Historical and Genealogical Magazine* 13 (1912), p. 139.

3. Thomas N. Holmes to Elizabeth Holmes Blanks, 11 January 1835, Blanks Collection, DU.

4. Nancy Turner to Agnes Alexander, 26 October 1810, Graham Collection, DU.

5. Nancy Graham to William Graham, 23 February 1821, Graham Collection, DU.

6. Anne Steele to her aunt, 12 March 1802, Steele Papers, SHC. See also Elmira Henry to Maria Campbell, 2 June 1825, Campbell Collection, DU.

7. Martha B. Eppes Recipe Book, p. 24, Hubbard Papers, SHC.

8. David Campbell to his sister, 18 July 1830, Campbell Collection, DU.

9. Nancy Cary Randolph to St. George Tucker, 9 November 1800, Tucker-Coleman Collection, WMC.

10. Littleton Tazewell Memoir, p. 214, Tazewell Papers, VSL.

11. John Ball to Thomas Slater, 28 February 1811, Ball Collection, DU.

12. Commonplace Book, Burroughs Collection, GHS. See also David Meade to Susan Meade, 13 July 1811, Funsten Papers, SHC; David M. Lees to his mother, 7 May 1825, Lees Papers, SHC.

13. William Henry Holcombe Books, 1:11, SHC.

14. See *Statistics of the United States in 1860* (Washington, D.C.: Government Printing Office, 1866); see also pp. 139–140 and Appendix B, Table 6.

15. Larkin Newby Autobiography, Newby Papers, SHC.

16. Maria Bryan Harford to Julia Cumming, 7 June 1837, Hammond-Bryan-Cumming Collection, USC.

17. Lucy Randolph to Robert Beverley, 13 April 1796, 29 March 1798, and 16 July 1815, Beverley Collection, WMC.

18. Jane Beverley to Robert Beverley, 19 January and 24 July 1811, and 30 November 1813, Beverley Collection, VHS.

19. Euphrasie Beverley to Robert Beverley, 5 February and 17 June 1834, and 19 December 1835, Beverley Collection, VHS.

20. Rebecca Beverley to Robert Beverley, 8 March 1819, Beverley Collection, VHS.

21. Rebecca Beverley to Robert Beverley, 15 March 1821, Beverley Collection, VHS.

22. Thomas Jefferson to Martha Jefferson, 6 March 1786 and 28 March 1787, in Edwin Morris Betts and James Adams Bear, eds., *The Family Letters of Thomas Jefferson* (Columbia: University of Missouri Press, 1966), pp. 30, 34.

23. Ann Ruffin to Thomas Ruffin, 29 November 1815, Ruffin-Meade Papers, SHC.

24. Thomas Jefferson to Martha J. Randolph, 4 April 1790, in Betts and Bear, *Family Letters*, p. 51.

25. John Haywood, Elizabeth Haywood, and Jane Williams, correspondence 1798–1799, Haywood Collection, SHC.

26. John Coalter to St. George Tucker, 11 January 1816, Tucker-Coleman Collection, WMC.

27. Dr. W. Kron to Adele Boulanger, 1835, Littleton Collection, NCA. See also Ellen Bankhead to Septima Randolph, 24 November 1828, Edgehill-Randolph Collection, UVA; 28 December 1806, Haywood Collection, SHC.

28. Jane Gay Robertson to John Robertson, 23 February 1819, Robb-Bernard Collection, WMC.

29. William Elliott to Mrs. Thomas Smith, 7 August 1829, Elliott Papers, SHC. See also correspondence of John Steele to Mary Steele, 25 November 1792, 2 December 1792, 1 January 1793, and 31 January 1793, Steele Papers, SHC.

30. Martha Richardson to James Screven, 15 November 1817, Arnold-Screven Papers, SHC.

31. "Various Duties Connected with Social Life," Carmichael Family Books, SHC.

32. Sarah Scott to Elizabeth Lewis, 2 May n.a., Scott Papers, VSL. See also Mary Poindexter to Jane Poindexter, 25 December 1825, Clingman-Puryear Papers, SHC.

33. William Elliott to Ann Elliott, 17 August 1828, Elliott Papers, SHC.

34. Fanny Bland Tucker to St. George Tucker, April 1787, Brown-Tucker-Coalter Collection, WMC.

35. Elizabeth Haywood to her mother, 21 January 1808, Haywood Collection, SHC. See also Amelia Montgomery to Rev. James Smythe, 2 March 1839, Montgomery Collection, LSU.

36. Sally Lacy to William Graham, 7 February 1819, Graham Collection, DU.

37. John Douglas to Eleanor Douglas, 2 January 1823, Eleanor Douglas Collection, DU. See also James Douglas to Eleanor Douglas, 17 January 1834, James Douglas Collection, DU.

38. Rachel Mordecai Lazarus to Caroline Plunkett, 23 February 1823, Mordecai Collection, DU. See also Rachel M. Lazarus to Caroline Plunkett, 9 March 1823, Mordecai Collection, DU.

39. Delia Bryan to John Randolph, 23 April 1820, Randolph Papers, UVA.

40. Jane Williams to Eliza Haywood, 30 January 1804, Haywood Collection, SHC.

41. Martha Richardson to Georgia Bryan Screven, 30 June 1833, Forman-Bryan-Screven Collection, GHS.

42. Maria Miller to _____ Bedinger, 2 August 1818, Bedinger-Dandridge Collection, DU.

43. Frances Smith to Mary Owen, 23 April 1824, Campbell Collection, DU.

44. M. W. Allen to Honoria O'Grady, 21 August 1807, Barraud Collection, WMC.

45. Delia Bryan to Joseph Bryan, 12 June 1825, Forman-Bryan-Screven Collection, GHS.

46. Sarah Gayle Diary, 16 May 1832, Bayne-Gayle Papers, SHC.

47. Ann L. Welch to Charles Tait, 19 January 1816, Tait Collection, ASA.

48. Martha Low Fannin to Tomlinson Fort, 26 September 1824, Fort Collection, GEU.

49. See Lucy Oliver to N. Williamson Barnes, 18 September 1821, Barnes Collection, WMC; Thomas Brown Memoir, 1:83, Brown Collection, DU.

50. Maria Campbell to Ann Roane, 1 January 1819, Campbell Collection, DU.

51. Martha Jones to Elizabeth Gibson, 14 March 1814, Gibson Papers, VSL.

52. Martha Jones to Patrick Gibson, 20 January 1813, Gibson Papers, VSL.

53. R. Fitzgerald to Martha Jones, 10 February 1813, Gibson Papers, VSL.

54. Elizabeth Fitzgerald to Elizabeth Gibson, 16 April 1813, Gibson Papers, VSL.

55. Martha Jones to Elizabeth Gibson, 14 March and 25 April 1814, Gibson Papers, VSL.

56. O. J. Browner to Mrs. King, 2 February 1809, Bedinger-Dandridge Collection, DU.

57. Elizabeth Ambler Carrington to Ann Ambler Fisher, January 1807, Elizabeth Jaquelin Ambler Collection, CW.

58. David Campbell to Maria Campbell, 7 August 1835, Campbell Collection, DU.

59. Cornelia Barksdale to Fanny Barksdale, 1 October 1836, Barksdale Collection, DU.

60. Maria Bryan to Julia Cumming, 7 March 1824, Hammond-Bryan-Cumming Collection, USC. See also Catharine Holmes to Elizabeth Blanks, 16 July 1833, Blanks Collection, DU.

61. Anne Daniel to Jane Daniel, 29 September 1807, and 13 July 1808, Lewis-Scott-Daniel-Greenhow Papers, VSL.

62. Anne Daniel to Jane Lewis, 4 December 1808, Lewis-Scott-Daniel-Greenhow Papers, VSL.

63. Frances Goodwin to Mary Owen, 7 October 1813, Campbell Collection, DU.

64. Frances Smith to Mary Owen, 29 October 1814, Campbell Collection, DU. See also Tarmesian Scot to Nancy Graham, 22 January 1821, Graham Collection, DU.

65. Maria Carr Memoir, p. 19, DU.

66. Catharine Smith to John Faber, 20 November 1838, Faber Collection, DU.

67. See the various Mordecai Collections: VSL, DU, NCA, and SHC.

68. F. R. Gregory to Martha Gregory, 22 November 1824, Bacon Collection, DU.

69. Nancy Carr to Elizabeth Coalter, 1 April 1822, Carr-Cary Papers, UVA.

70. Martha Randolph Triplett to Marian Harden, 2 April 1826, Harden Collection, DU. See also E. A. Spragins to Fanny Barksdale, 25 November 1836, Barksdale Collection, DU.

71. See John Steele to Mary Steele, 31 January 1793, Steele Papers, SHC. See also Elizabeth T. Stribling to _____, n.d. 1810, Bedinger-Dandridge Collection, DU.

CHAPTER IV. *THE DAY TO FIX MY FATE*

1. Anne Izard to Mary Manigault, n.d., n.a., Manigault Collection, USC. See also Mary Burton to Myra Lenoir, 13 December 1814, Lenoir Papers, SHC; Rebecca Martin to Caroline Patterson, 16 April 1825, Jones-Patterson Papers, SHC.

2. J. S. Buckingham, *The Slave States of America* (London: Fisher, Son & Co., 1842), 2:13. See also Sarah Bedinger to Elizabeth Bedinger, 8 May 1820, Bedinger-Dandridge Collection, DU. See also Ellen Mordecai to George Mordecai, Little-Mordecai Collection, NCA; S. W. Ferguson Memoir, pp. 1–14, Heyward-Ferguson Papers, SHC.

3. William Blair to Helen Blair, 25 July 1784, Iredell Collection, DU. See also Martha Richardson to James Screven, 2 December 1821, Arnold-Screven Papers, SHC; Mary Burton to Margaret Steele, 1 March 1810, Steele Papers, SHC; Mary Telfair to Mary Few, 14 January n.a., Few Collection, GSA.

4. B. L. King to Joel King, 10 June 1812, King Collection, DU. See also James McFarland to Catharine McFarland, 12 April 1834, McFarland Papers, SHC.

5. W. N. Todd to Elizabeth Todd, 14 February 1829, Miscellaneous Letters, SHC. See also Maria Bryan to Julia Cumming, 3 April 1829, Hammond-Bryan-Cumming Collection, USC; H. Georgia Screven to Thomas Forman, 8 August 1833, Arnold-Screven Papers, SHC.

6. John Dabney to Mildred Dabney, 3 January 1819, Dabney Papers, SHC.

7. William Smith to his parents, 23 June 1809, Smith Collection, DU. See also Charles Floyd to his father, 13 July 1822, Floyd Collection, GHS.

8. John Bernard, *Retrospectives of America, 1787–1811* (New York: Harper & Brothers, 1887), p. 150.

9. See Elizabeth Pinckney to Harriott Pinckney, Pinckney Collection, USC. See also William Elliott to Ann Smith, 13 May 1816, Elliott Papers, SHC.

10. Jenny Holmes to Isabella Bailey, 8 February n.a., Bailey Collection, GHS. See also Betty Dunn to her cousin Mary, 12 August 1802, Dunlop Collection, DU; _____ Withers to Ann Withers, 19 December 1834, Levert Papers, SHC.

11. See correspondence of Mildred Smith and Elizabeth Jaquelin Ambler, Elizabeth Jaquelin Ambler Collection, CW, and of Maria Bryan and Julia Cumming, Hammond-Bryan-Cumming Collection, USC.

12. _____ to Elizabeth MacKay, 20 March 1829, MacKay Collection, GHS. See also Elizabeth _____ to Elizabeth Fitzhugh, 20 April 1835, Fitzhugh Collection, DU.

13. Elizabeth Kennon to _____ , n.d., n.a., Whittle Collection, UVA.

14. Charles McDonald to Anne Brantley, 6 September 1816, McDonald-Lawrence Collection, GHS.

15. R. Fitzgerald to Betsy Fitzgerald, n.d., n.a., Gibson Papers, VSL.

16. Francis Gregory to Martha Gregory, 7 March 1825, Bacon Collection, DU. See also Virginia Smith to Ann Smith, 28 April 1835, Smith Collection, DU.

17. Arthur W. Calhoun, *A Social History of the American Family from Colonial Times to the Present* (Cleveland, Ohio: Arthur Clarke & Co., 1918), 2: 313.

18. See R. H. Trimbull to F. Gregory, 11 December 1827, Ferebee-Gregory-McPherson Papers, SHC.

19. See Caleb Blanchard to Sarah Killock, 5 May 1802, Nash Collection, NCA.

20. Charles McDonald to Anne Brantley, 6 September 1816, McDonald-Lawrence Collection, GHS. See also Miss Newman to Mrs. Campbell, 15 November 1816, Campbell Collection, DU; Sarah Nicholas to Jane Randolph, 31 December 1818, Edgehill-Randolph Collection, UVA.

21. George Bassett to N. Williamson Barnes, 23 March 1822, Barnes Collection, WMC.

22. Franklin Dabney to Harriet Dixon, 8 September 1835, Armistead-Cocke Collection, WMC. See also E. N. Bulloch to Louisa Bulloch, 4 July 1831, Bulloch Papers, SHC.

23. See T. W. Brevard to Alexander Brevard, 1–14 June 1825, Brevard Collection, NCA.

24. Maria Bryan to Julia Cumming, 19 April 1830, Hammond-Bryan-Cumming Collection, USC. See also Mary S. Harris to Amanda Edney, 12 December 1833, Gardner Collection, DU; Ann Arrington to Martha Fort, 3 February 1822, Clay Collection, DU; Maria Campbell to Jefferson _____ , 20 January 1815, Campbell Collection, DU; H. A. Lide to William Potter, 17 March 1829, Lide-Coker-Stuart Collection, USC; Mary L. Sides to J. Malloy, 13 April 1835, Lide-Coker-Stuart Collection, USC.

25. Richard Spaight to John Bryan, 19 February 1817, Bryan Collection, DU.

26. Jenny Stuart to John Coalter, January–June 1794, Brown-Tucker-Coalter Collection, WMC.

27. Edward Harden to Maryann Randolph, 1 June 1820, Harden Collection, DU; Roderick Murchison to _____ , 7 September 1815, Bruce-Jones-Murchison Collection, USC.

28. Joel Battle to _____ Johnston, 24 January 1801, Battle Papers, SHC.

29. David R. Williams to James Chesnut, 10 October 1820, Williams Collection, USC.

30. Anne Couper to John Fraser, 25 February and 18 May 1815, Fraser-Couper Collection, GHS.

31. See Sally Bedinger to Nancy _____ , 11 February 1831 and 11 March 1828, Bedinger-Dandridge Collection, DU; Maria Carr Memoir, p. 21, DU; David Campbell to _____ , 3 January 1823, Campbell Collection, DU; Martha Richardson to James Screven, 16 April 1819, Arnold-Screven Papers, SHC.

32. Jane Bruce to Samuel Jones, 20 August and 8 November 1786, Bruce-Jones-Murchison Collection, USC.

33. Mary Roane to Maria Campbell, 27 November 1814, Campbell Collection, DU.

34. Harriet Clifton to Eliza Manigault Morris, 4 August 1815, Manigault Collection, SCHS. See also Mary _____ to Frances _____ , 25 April 1835, John Beauchamp Jones Papers, SHC.

35. Commonplace Book, Forman-Bryan-Screven Collection, GHS.

36. Hiram Haines to Mary Ann Phillpotts, 17 June 1826, Haines Collection, DU; Charles Thiot to Anna Charleton, n.d., Thiot Collection, GEU; J. Lee to Louisa Lee, 12 October 1808, Teagle-Lee Collection, CW.

37. John Quitman to Eliza Turner, 17 November 1824, Quitman Papers, SHC. See also Evelina _____ to Walter Lenoir, 6 October 1819, Lenoir Papers, SHC; Augustine Smith to Alice Page, 2 July 1791, Smith-Digges Collection, CW; Maria Bryan to Julia Cumming, n.d. 1829, Hammond-Bryan-Cumming Collection, USC.

38. E. V. Lindsey to Augusta Myers, 11 May 1820, Lewis Collection, DU. See also Nancy McDougall, 31 December 1832, Robinson Collection, MSA.

39. S. C. Stevenson to her brother, 5 April 1825, Singleton-Deveaux Collection, USC. See also Amaryllis Sitgreaves to William Attmore, December 1790, Attmore Papers, SHC.

40. John Quitman to Eliza Turner, 17 November 1824, Quitman Papers, SHC.

41. Virginia Campbell to William Campbell, 16 November 1832, Campbell Collection, DU. See also Sarah Lenoir to Myra Lenoir, 2 July 1817, Lenoir Papers, SHC; Sally Sinclair to Ellen Mordecai, 24 February 1810, Whittle Collection, UVA; Eliza Kennon to Rachel Mordecai, 4 February 1810, Whittle Collection, UVA.

42. Nelly Parke Custis to Elizabeth Gibson, 3 February 1799 and n.d. 1799, Lewis Collection, PHS.

43. See Maria F. Clopton to John Clopton, 16 September 1807, Clopton Collection, DU.

44. Mary Brown to Margaret Steele, 16 April 1807, Steele Papers, SHC.

45. John Crittenden to Ann Coleman, 18 November 1831, Crittenden Collection, DU.

46. Nancy Thomas to Sally Gillet, 5 December 1824, Fuller-Thomas Collection, DU. See also M. H. Garnett to Mary Brown, 8 June 1830, Brown-Tucker-Coalter Collection, WMC; Ann Pettigrew to Mary Shepherd, n.d., n.a., Pettigrew Papers, SHC.

47. C. Snow to Elizabeth Snow, 6 November 1826, Hooker Collection, SHC.

48. Mary Grace, 9 July 1831, Cooper Diary, Cooper Collection, ASA.

49. Elizabeth H. Manigault to Charles Manigault, 31 August 1827, Manigault Collection, SCHS.

50. Joseph Habersham to John Habersham, 21 October 1787, Jones Family Collection, GHS. See also E. B. Kennon to Rachel Mordecai, 14 August 1813, Whittle Collection, UVA; Anne Bannister to Elizabeth Whiting, 10 July 1813, Blair-Bannister-Braxton-Horner-Whiting Collection, WMC.

51. St. George Tucker to Fanny Tucker, n.d., n.a., Tucker-Coleman Collection, WMC. See also John Steele to Mary Steele, 12 December 1791, Steele Papers, SHC; William Yates to Sally Yates, n.d., n.a., Randolph-Yates Papers, SHC; David Campbell to Mary Campbell, 15 May 1825, Campbell Collection, DU.

52. William T. Barry to Catherine Barry, 17 November 1819, Barry Papers, UVA.

53. John Gayle to Sarah Gayle, 25 November 1830, Bayne-Gayle Papers, SHC.

54. William Dunbar to Diana Dunbar, 23 June 1792, Dunbar Collection, MSA. See also Sarah Gordon to William Gordon, 29 November 1835, 30 November 1835 and 6 December 1835, Gordon Collection, GHS.

55. Israel Pickens to Martha Pickens, 30 October 1814, Pickens Collection, ASA. See also William Elliott to Ann Elliott, 17 September 1823, Elliott Papers, SHC; John B. Clopton to Maria Clopton, 31 August 1834, Clopton Collection, DU.

56. Ebenezer Pendleton to Ann Pendleton, 24 August 1822, Pendleton Papers, SHC. See also John Haywood to Betsy Haywood, 13 June 1798, Haywood Collection, SHC.

57. Sarah Gayle Diary, p. 176, Bayne-Gayle Papers, SHC.

58. Nelly Parke Custis to Elizabeth Gibson, 3 January 1815, Lewis Collection, PHS.

59. Martha Richardson to James Screven, 21 January 1821, Arnold-Screven Papers, SHC.

60. Jane Wood to Jane Lewis, 13 July 1809, Lewis-Scott-Daniels-Greenhow Papers, VSL. See also Maria Bryan to Julia Cumming, 13 November 1830, Hammond-Bryan-Cumming Collection, USC; Ann Fraser to John Couper, 31 January 1820, Fraser-Couper Collection, GHS; Ann Inge to Sally Gillet, 30 January 1825, Fuller-Thomas Collection, DU.

61. Eleanor Custis to Elizabeth Gibson, n.d. 1796, Lewis Collection, PHS.

62. Mary Telfair to Mary Few, 3 November n.a., Few Collection, GSA. See also John Brevard to Alexander Brevard, 3 April 1810, Brevard Collection, NCA.

63. Charles Rinaldo Floyd Diary, 15 July 1828, Floyd Collection, GHS.

64. Stephen Barnwell, *The Story of an American Family* (Marquette, Mich.: n.p., 1969), p. 44.

65. See Fanny Carter to Robert Carter, 30 January 1825, Carter Collection, WMC.

66. Lucy Randolph to Robert Beverley, 16 July 1815, Beverley Collection, WMC.

67. _____ to _____ , 2 September 1831, Hutchinson Collection, SHC. See also Mary Garland to Jane Garland, 24 January 1836, Garland Collection, DU.

68. Timothy Ford, "South Carolina Travel Diary, 1785–86," *South Carolina Historical and Genealogical Magazine* 13 (1912):198. See also Eleanor Custis Lewis to Mrs. Pinckney, 9 May 1808, Pinckney Collection, SCHS.

69. Mary Brown to Margaret Steele, 11 September 1807, Steele Papers, SHC.

70. Elizabeth Coltart to St. George Tucker, 15 October 1779, Tucker-Coleman Collection, WMC. Coltart was writing from a plantation not within the region examined by this study, but I have included her most descriptive and telling plea for aid because it eloquently reveals the distress and despair women felt when at the mercy of irresponsible or brutal husbands.

71. Ebenezer Pettigrew to Ann Pettigrew, 31 July 1819, Pettigrew Papers, SHC.

72. William Baskerville to Mary Baskerville, 17 May 1803, Baskerville Collection, DU. See also William Elliott to Ann Elliott, 12 December 1826, Elliott Papers, SHC.

73. Diana Dunbar to William Dunbar, 6 April 1790, Dunbar Collection, MSA.

74. Roderick Murchison to Elizabeth Murchison, 30 December 1816, Bruce-Jones-Murchison Collection, USC.

75. Sarah Gayle Diary, 26 January 1834, Bayne-Gayle Papers, SHC.

76. _____ Itinerant Physician's Diary, 3 November 1812, SHC.

77. Ann Coleman, n.d., n.a., Coleman Collection, DU.

78. James Iredell to Hannah Iredell, 2 and 8 December 1779, 16 and 19 April 1780, 18 May 1780, Iredell Collection, DU.

79. Fanny Bland Tucker to St. George Tucker, n.d., n.a., Tucker-Coleman Collection, WMC. See also R. M. Rutledge to Edward Rutledge, 14 June 1833, Rutledge Collection, USC; Fanny Bland Tucker to St. George Tucker, 10 July 1781, Tucker-Coleman Collection, WMC; William Campbell to Susanna Campbell, 19 November 1794 and 10 April 1800, Campbell Papers, VSL.

80. Maria Beverley to Robert Beverley, 4 April 1813, Beverley Collection, VHS.

81. See John and Sarah Gayle correspondence, 6 April 1825, 25 November 1830, 25 November 1831, 8 December 1831, and 10 January 1832, Bayne-Gayle Papers, SHC. See also Sarah and William Gordon correspondence, 5 and 23 November 1835 and 7 November 1836, Gordon Collection, GHS.

82. Eliza Quitman to John Quitman, 14 February 1836, Quitman Papers, SHC; James McDowell to Susan McDowell, 8 December 1834, James McDowell Papers, SHC.

83. Lucy Winn to John Winn, 26 January 1829, Winn Collection, DU. See also Sarah Gordon to William Gordon, 16 December 1835, Gordon Collection, GHS.

84. John Steele to Mary Steele, 31 January 1793 and 1 September 1796, Steele Papers, SHC.

85. Diana Dunbar to William Dunbar, 25 October 1789 and 6 October 1791, Dunbar Collection, MSA.

86. William Dunbar to Diana Dunbar, 9 June 1792 and 12 April 1793, Dunbar Collection, MSA.

87. Maria Campbell to David Campbell, 25 February 1813, Campbell Collection, DU.

88. James Lee to Louisa Lee, 12 October 1808, Teagle-Lee Collection, CW.

89. John Haywood to Elizabeth Haywood, 9 March 1799, Haywood Collection, SHC. See also William Munford to Sally Munford, 6 December 1805, Munford-Ellis Collection, DU; Charles Cotton, 30 August 1833, Cotton Collection, GEU.

90. John Clopton to Maria Clopton, 9 September 1832 and 31 August 1834, Clopton Collection, DU; John Quitman to Eliza Quitman, 8 January 1828, Quitman Papers, SHC; Margaret Coalter to John Coalter, 10 May 1795, Brown-Tucker-Coalter Collection, WMC.

91. Mary Manigault to Gabriel Manigault, 7 December 1791, Manigault Collection, SCHS.

92. See Hall Collection, ASA; Sally Haywood to John Haywood, 26 November 1790, Haywood Collection, SHC; Hannah Coker to Caleb Coker, 19 July 1831, Lide-Coker-Stuart Collection, USC.

93. Judith Randolph to Mary Harrison, n.d. 1806, Harrison Collection, VHS.

94. A. L. to R. Motte, 11 June 1840, George Coffin Taylor Papers, SHC.

95. Martha Richardson to James Screven, 29 November and 16 April 1819, Arnold-Screven Papers, SHC.

96. Ann Gray to Ann Thomas, 22 April 1835, Fuller-Thomas Collection, DU.

97. Ferdinand Bayard, *Travels of a Frenchman in Maryland and Virginia, with a Description of Philadelphia and Baltimore in 1791*, trans. and ed. Ben McCary (Ann Arbor: University of Michigan Press, 1950), p. 45.

98. Sarah Gayle Diary, 11 October 1832, Bayne-Gayle Papers, SHC.

99. _____ to _____ , 19 November 1845, Elizabeth Hairston Papers, SHC.

100. Jane Finely to Samuel Patterson, 28 December 1819, Jones-Patterson Collection, SHC, and Edwin A. Davis, ed., *Plantation Life in the Florida Parishes of Louisiana as Reflected in the Diary of Bennet H. Barrow* (New York: Columbia University Press, 1943), pp. 352–53.

101. D. Witherspoon to _____ Witherspoon, 1 December 1790, Nash Collection, NCA.

102. _____ to _____ , 18 November 1791, John Devereux Books, SHC.

103. Maria Clopton to John Clopton, 8 September 1834, Clopton Collection, DU.

104. D. Kron Diary, n.d., n.a., Littleton Collection, NCA.

105. Dobyns v. Dobyns, Bedford County, 16 December 1817, VSL.

106. Ball v. Ball, Culpeper County, 9 December 1806, VSL.

107. See, for example, Pannell v. Pannell, King William County, 5 May 1837, VSL.

108. See Haywood Roebuck, "North Carolina Divorce and Alimony Petitions: 1813," *North Carolina Genealogical Society Journal* (April 1975).

109. Gambell v. Gambell, 1810, SCA.

110. Wilson v. Wilson, 1821, SCA.

111. Winget v. Winget, 1830, SCA.

112. See McCindless v. McCindless, MSA, and McClelland v. McClelland, 1830, MSA.

113. Ann Cocke to Judy Applewaite, 19 December 1815, Cocke Papers UVA. See also Sarah Gayle Diary, 23 May 1833, Bayne-Gayle Papers, SHC.

114. See 5 January 1830, Weeks Collection, LSU.

115. Nelly Parke Custis to Elizabeth Gibson, 25 August 1811, Lewis Collection, PHS.

116. Julia Ellis to Richard Ellis, 3 February 1818, Ellis-Farrar Collection, LSU.

117. Thomas Carson to Thomas Butler, 1 September 1817, Ellis-Farrar Collection, LSU.

118. E. B. Kennon to Rachel Mordecai, 15 September 1816, Whittle Collection, UVA.

119. Edith Duncan Johnston, ed., "Kollock Letters," *Georgia Historical Quarterly* 31 (1900): 62.

120. Mary Burton to Myra Lenoir, 28 October 1814, Lenoir Papers, SHC.

121. Judith Tomlin to Virginia Savage, n.d., n.a., Brown-Tucker-Coalter Collection, WMC.

122. Nancy Walton to Jane Gurley, 9 September 1836, Gurley Papers, SHC.

123. Ann Daniels to Jane Lewis, 5 March 1816, Lewis-Scott-Daniels-Greenhow Papers, VSL.

124. Mary Telfair to Mary Few, 28 October 1814 and 15 December 1838, Few Collection, GSA. See also Nancy Randolph to St. George Tucker, 15 June 1790, Tucker-Coleman Collection, WMC.

125. M. Means to Sally Thomas, January 1820, Fuller-Thomas Collection, DU. See also Ellen Mordecai to Samuel Mordecai, 20 June 1824, Mordecai Papers, SHC.

126. Maria Clopton to John Clopton, 10 September 1832, Clopton Collection, DU.

127. Rachel Mordecai to Samuel Mordecai, 8 February 1821, Mordecai Collection, DU. See also H. D. Conrad to Sidney Conrad, 28 January 1825, Weeks Collection, LSU; Nancy McDougall, December 1832, Robinson Collection, MSA.

CHAPTER V. *THE MORAL BIND*

1. See Joel Kovel, *White Racism: A Psychohistory* (New York: Pantheon Books, 1970).

2. Bolling Hall to Polly Hall, 22 June 1813, Hall Collection, ASA.

3. David Campbell to Margaret Campbell, 26 September 1831, Campbell Collection, DU.

4. J. H. Jeffreys, Commonplace Book, 1828, Amelia Jeffreys Collection, DU.

5. A. M., n.d., n.a., Cohen-Hunter Collection, GHS.

6. See Anne Firor Scott, *The Southern Lady: From Pedestal to Politics, 1830–1930* (Chicago: University of Chicago Press, 1970), chap. 2.

7. Sarah Gayle Diary, 26 January 1834, Bayne-Gayle Papers, SHC.

8. Calhoun, *American Family*, 2: 295.

9. 6 September 1829, Susan Nye Hutchinson Diary, SHC.

10. Virginia Cary, *Letters on Female Character* (Richmond, Va.: A. Works, 1830), p. 176.

11. Margaret MacKay Jones, ed., *The Journal of Catherine Devereux Edmondston: 1860–1866* (Mebane, N.C.: privately published, 1956), p. 14.

12. 12 January 1821, Richard Jones Collection, DU.

13. Martha Richardson to James Screven, 22 July 1821, Arnold-Screven Papers, SHC.

14. John Henry Campbell to Margaret Campbell, 1 September 1827, Campbell Collection, DU.

15. H. D. Conrad to his sister Elizabeth, n.d., n.a., Weeks Collection, LSU. Conrad did go on to maintain that "although amiable and feminine manners are absolutely necessary in a female, dignity, firmness and spirit are just as necessary."

16. Mary Telfair to Mary Few, 20 October n.a., Few Collection, GSA.

17. Toasts, 1830–1835, Brown-Tucker-Coalter Collection, WMC.

18. 4 July 1803, Steele Papers, SHC, and Buckingham, *Slave States of America*, 2: 229.

19. Jesse Siler Books, 1814, SHC.

20. Buckingham, *Slave States of America*, 2: 278.

21. Elisha Mitchell, *North Carolina, 1827–1828*, James Sprunt Historical Monograph no. 6 (Chapel Hill: University of North Carolina, 1905).

22. Calhoun, *American Family*, 2: 327.

23. "No man was ever blessed with a purer, better wife." Thomas Brown Memoir, 1:92, Brown Collection, DU.

24. 29 June 1815, Susan Nye Hutchinson Diary, SHC.

25. Harriet Meade to Sarah Ross, 22 December 1834, Whitaker-Meade Papers, SHC.

26. See Barbara Welter, "The Feminization of American Religion: 1800–1860," *Dimity Convictions: The American Woman in the Nineteenth Century* (Columbus: University of Ohio Press, 1976).

27. See Douglas, *Feminization of American Culture*.

28. See Grace Barnett Hunter Journal, Hunter-Garnett Collection, UVA.

29. See Elizabeth Ambler Carrington to Ann Ambler Fisher, 1 January 1807, Elizabeth Jaquelin Ambler Collection, CW, and also Bumpas Papers, SHC.

30. Eleanor Douglas to Sally Hall, August 1821, Eleanor Douglas Collection, DU.

31. Jane Norwood to Sarah Lenoir, 4 January 1829, Lenoir Papers, SHC.

32. Cary, *Letters on Female Character*, p. 173. See also Martha Richardson to James Screven, 18 November 1818, Arnold-Screven Papers, SHC.

33. Bolling Hall to Polly Hall, 25 February 1814, Hall Collection, ASA.

34. Virginia Terrell to Edward Graham, 12 March 1812, Graham Collection, DU.

35. Martha Richardson to James Screven, 18 November 1818, Arnold-Screven Papers, SHC.

36. William O. Gregory to Martha Gregory, 6 February 1825, Jackson-Prince Papers, SHC.

37. Bolling Hall to Polly Hall, 30 June 1813, Hall Collection, ASA.

38. Thomas Jefferson to Martha Jefferson, 22 December 1783, Betts and Bear, eds., *Family Letters*, p. 22.

39. Maria Campbell to David Campbell, 1 December 1822, Campbell Collection, DU.

40. David Campbell to Maria Campbell, 12 December 1822, Campbell Collection, DU.

41. Charlotte Cross to Helen Blair, 13 July 1784, Iredell Collection, DU.

42. Mary Roane to Maria Campbell, 24 May 1815, Campbell Collection, DU.

43. See Elizabeth Haske to Helen Blair, 30 January 1786, Iredell Collection, DU.

44. Peggy Nicholas to Jane Randolph, 23 May 1818, Edgehill-Randolph Collection, UVA.

45. Jeannie Long to her father, 12 June 1811, Bedinger-Dandridge Collection, DU.

46. E. Chalmers to Hester Van Bibber, 10 October 1816, Tabb Collection, DU. See also Ellen Mordecai, "Fading Scenes Recalled," p. 88, Mordecai Collection, SHC.

47. *Magnolia,* January 1842, p. 42.

48. Sarah Gayle Diary, 25 October 1832, Bayne-Gayle Papers, SHC.

49. Thomas Jefferson to Martha Jefferson, 20 September 1786, in Betts and Bear, eds., *Family Letters,* p. 30.

50. Eleanor Douglas to Sally Hall, 1 May 1820, Eleanor Douglas Collection, DU.

51. John Steele to Mary Steele, 15 May 1790, Steele Papers, SHC.

52. Bolling Hall to Polly Hall, 10 July 1813, Hall Collection, ASA.

53. James Norcom to Mary Norcom, 28 February 1837, Norcom Collection, NCA.

54. Thomas Jefferson to Martha Jefferson, 11 December 1783, in Betts and Bear, eds., *Family Letters,* p. 21. See also Bolling Hall to Polly Hall, 3 July 1817, Hall Collection, ASA.

55. David Campbell to Virginia Campbell, 18 April 1828, Campbell Collection, DU.

56. John Steele to Margaret Steele, 12 March 1807, Steele Papers, SHC.

57. David Campbell to Maria Campbell, 11 October 1800, Campbell Collection, DU. See also Elizabeth Ambler Carrington to Ann Ambler Fisher, 1807, Elizabeth Jaquelin Ambler Collection, CW.

58. Bolling Hall to Martha Hall, 26 July 1819, Hall Collection, ASA.

59. Bolling Hall to Polly Hall, 3 July 1817, Hall Collection, ASA.

60. John Steele to Mary Steele, 7 August 1796, Steele Papers, SHC.

61. J. E. N. Bacon to F. Rogers Gregory, 4 July 1828, Ferebee-Gregory-McPherson Papers, SHC.

62. George Davis to William Clark, 6 August 1831, Clark Collection, DU.

63. Calhoun, *American Family*, 2: 288.

64. Maria Bryan to Julia Cumming, Hammond-Bryan-Cumming Collection, USC.

65. E. Pegram to R. Gregory, 7 September 1827, Ferebee-Gregory-McPherson Papers, SHC.

66. William D. Valentine Diary (Bethel, N.C.), 26 March 1837, SHC.

67. For valuable studies dealing with masculinity in the Old South see Dickson Bruce, *Violence and Culture in the Antebellum South* (Memphis: University of Tennessee Press, 1979), and the more recent Bertram Wyatt-Brown, *Southern Honor* (New York: Oxford University Press, 1982).

68. Martha Richardson to James Screven, 3 February 1819, Arnold-Screven Papers, SHC.

69. Susanna Clay to C. C. Clay, Jr., 1 April 1834, Clay Collection, DU.

70. Jane Gay Robertson Bernard Journal, September 1835, Robb-Bernard Collection, WMC.

71. Sarah Gayle Diary, 23 May 1833, Bayne-Gayle Papers, SHC.

72. C. Snow to Elizabeth Snow, 6 November 1826, Hooker Collection, SHC.

73. Daniel Mulford to Betsy Crane, 22 July 1809, Mulford Collection, GHS.

74. Ellen Mordecai to Solomon Mordecai, 28 March 1823, Mordecai Collection, DU.

75. Maria Bryan to Julia Cumming, 7 April 1827, Hammond-Bryan-Cumming Collection, USC.

76. Ann Mordecai to Ellen Mordecai, 13 December 1832, Mordecai Papers, SHC.

77. C. Snow to Elizabeth Snow, 6 November 1826, Hooker Collection, SHC. See also Boynton Merrill, Jr., *Jefferson's Nephews: A Frontier Tragedy* (Princeton, N.J.: Princeton University Press, 1976).

78. Rachel O'Conner to David Weeks, 7 March 1828, Weeks Collection, LSU.

79. Rachel O'Conner to Mary Weeks, 7 May 1826, Weeks Collection, LSU.

80. John Quitman to Elizabeth Quitman, 9 December 1830, Quitman Papers, SHC.

81. William O. Stevens, *Pistols at Ten Paces: The Story of the Code of Honor in America* (Boston: Houghton Mifflin Co., 1940), pp. 4–31.

82. Ibid., p. 78.

83. Sarah Screven to James Screven, 22 July 1821, Arnold-Screven Papers, HC. See also Henry B. Davenport to _____ , 19 October 1823, Bedinger-Dandridge Collection, DU.

84. Martha Richardson to James Screven, 22 July 1818, Arnold-Screven Papers, SHC.

85. Joseph Manigault to Gabriel Manigault, 24 January 1807, Manigault Collection, SCHS.

86. _____ to _____ , n.d., n.a., Weeks Collection, LSU.

87. B. C. Franklin to Catherine McDonald, n.d., n.a., McDonald-Lawrence Collection, GHS.

88. Ann McDonald to J. L. Lamar, 22 November 1828, McDonald-Lawrence Collection, GHS.

CHAPTER VI. *THE FALLEN WOMAN*

1. C. A. Hull to Sarah Thomas, 10 September 1817, Fuller-Thomas Collection, DU.

2. Anne Cleland Commonplace Book, 1785, Cheves Collection, SCHS.

3. For a fuller treatment see G. J. Barker-Benfield, *The Horrors of the Half-Known Life: Male Attitudes Toward Women and Sexuality in 19th Century America* (New York: W. W. Norton & Co., 1976).

4. George Skinner, *Practical Compendium of Midwifery*, 3rd ed. (Philadelphia: Haswell, Barrington & Haswell, 1840), pp. 47–48.

5. James Iredell to Hannah Iredell, 16 January 1779, Iredell Collection, SHC.

6. Rachel O'Conner to Mary Weeks, 11 July 1825, Weeks Collection, LSU.

7. Jane Garland to Thomas Garland, 14 March 1833, Garland Collection, DU.

8. Sarah Nicholas to Jane Randolph, 4 April 1819, Edgehill-Randolph Collection, UVA.

9. Charlotte Sweyse to Mary Weeks, 3 August 1824, Weeks Collection, LSU.

10. Dolley Madison to her niece Mary, 3 December 1834, in Cutts, ed., *Memoirs and Letters of Dolley Madison*, p. 190.

11. See correspondence of Mildred Smith and Elizabeth Jaquelin Ambler, 1780–1782, Elizabeth Jaquelin Ambler Collection, CW.

12. See "Editorial Note: Commonwealth v. Randolph," in Charles Cullen and Herbert Johnson, eds., *The Papers of John Marshall* (Chapel Hill: University of North Carolina Press for the Institute of Early American History and Culture, 1977), vol. 2; Francis Biddle, "Scandal at Bizarre," *American Heritage* 12 (August 1961): 10–13, 79–82.

13. Nancy Cary Randolph to St. George Tucker, 16 December 1808, Tucker-Coleman Collection, WMC.

14. Ibid.

15. Nancy Cary Randolph to Joseph C. Cabell, October 1808, Tucker-Coleman Collection, WMC.

16. See Loren J. Kallsen, *The Kentucky Tragedy: A Problem in Romantic Attitudes* (Indianapolis: Bobbs-Merrill Co., 1963), p. 8.

17. Ibid., p. 4.

18. Ibid., p. 156.

19. Ibid., p. 97.

20. Ibid., p. 113.

CHAPTER VII. *EQUALLY THEIR DUE*

1. Maria Campbell to Mary Hume, 21 September 1819, Campbell Collection, DU. See also Mary G. Franklin to her daughters, 1 May 1838, McDonald-Lawrence Collection, SHC.

2. See Linda Kerber, *Women of the Republic: Intellect and Ideology in Revolutionary America* (Chapel Hill: University of North Carolina Press for the Institute of Early American History and Culture, 1980).

3. Alice Felt Tyler, "The Rights of Women," in Barbara Welter, ed., *The Woman Question in American History* (Hinsdale, Ill.: Dryden Press, 1973).

4. Bolling Hall to Polly Hall, 30 June 1813, Hall Collection, ASA.

5. Samuel Bowles, "Unequal Education and the Reproduction of the Social Division of Labor," in Martin Carnoy, ed., *Schooling in a Corporate Society* (New York: David McKay Co., 1972).

6. Elijah Fletcher, 1 October 1810, in Martha von Briesen, ed., *The Letters of Elijah Fletcher* (Charlottesville: University of Virginia Press, 1965). See also Merrill, *Jefferson's Nephews*, pp. 167–68; Sarah Cutler, 4 August 1821, Bulloch Papers, SHC.

7. Delia Bryan to John Randolph, 23 April 1810, Randolph Papers, UVA.

8. Hannah More, *Strictures on the Modern System of Female Education* (Philadelphia: Budd & Bartram, 1800), 1: 1.

9. Mary Wollstonecraft, *A Vindication of the Rights of Woman* (1792; reprint ed., New York: W. W. Norton & Co., 1975), p. 145.

10. William T. Barry to Susan Barry, 21 May 1826, Barry Papers, UVA.

11. Dr. Augustine Smith to Graham Frank, 17 August 1791, Smith-Digges Collection, CW.

12. Mrs. E. T. Bryan, 14 April 1842, Edmund Bryan Papers, SHC.

13. Mrs. S. E. Van Bibber to Georgia Screven, 3 November 1833, Forman-Bryan-Screven Collection, GHS. See also Ann Cocke to Ann Barraud, 2 March 1811, Cocke Papers, UVA.

14. Bolling Hall to Polly Hall, 12 February 1816, Hall Collection, ASA.

15. William Dunbar to Diana Dunbar, 5 May 1794, Dunbar Collection, MSA.

16. Eliza Robertson to Mildred Campbell, 15 March 1820, Campbell Collection, WMC. Robertson had thirteen pupils. See also Robert Lewis to Lawrence Lewis, 1 February 1816, Lewis Collection, VHS.

17. Delia Bryan to John Randolph, 23 April 1819, Randolph Papers, UVA.

18. See Florence Davis, "The Education of Southern Girls from 1750 to 1860," unpublished Ph.D. dissertation, University of Chicago, 1951, pp. 211–13. Davis concerns herself not only with the education of the planter daughters but also with education for the middle and lower classes.

19. Ann Mary Crittenden to John J. Crittenden, 5 May 1828, Crittenden Collection, DU.

20. Cynthia Jelks to her aunt, n.d., n.a., Sills Collection, DU.

21. American Traveler, SCHS.

22. Margaret Page to John Page, 19 January 1820, Page-Saunders Collection, WMC. See also John Smith to Edward Campbell, 10 July 1804, Campbell Collection, DU; Archibald Alexander to Margaret Graham, 9 November 1813, Graham Collection, DU.

23. Amanda Hall to Martha Bailey, 6 June 1830, Hall Collection, ASA.

24. William Elliott to Ann Smith, 6 January 1817, Elliott Papers, SHC.

25. Maria Foster Clopton to John Clopton, 3 September 1832, Clopton Collection, DU.

26. Raleigh Academy Collection, NCA.

27. James Campbell to David Campbell, 27 January 1819, Campbell Collection, DU.

28. See Petitions to the State Legislature, 1823, MSA.

29. Published in London by J. Johnson, 1797.

30. Rachel Mordecai to Samuel Mordecai, 18 April 1812, Mordecai Papers, SHC.

31. Haynsworth Collection, p. 166, ASA. See also Anna Calhoun to Patrick Calhoun, 27 August 1837, Calhoun Collection, USC.

32. Rebecca Beverley to Robert Beverley, Beverley Collection, VHS.

33. William T. Barry to Susan Barry, 19 November 1819, Barry Papers, UVA.

34. Frances Barksdale to M. Spragins, 18 January 1832, Barksdale Collection, DU. See also Balsora Barnes to Williamson Barnes, 30 January 1822, Barnes Collection, WMC.

35. William Gregory, 3 March 1822, Robert Jackson Papers, SHC.

36. _____ to Lucy, 21 June 1805, Lyons Papers, SHC. See also Delia Bryan to Georgia Bryan, Forman-Bryan-Screven Collection, GHS; Charlotte Chisholm to Robert McKay, 20 February 1827, MacKay Collection, USC.

37. John Randolph to Elizabeth Tucker Coalter, 19 January 1822, Randolph Papers, UVA. See also John Lyle to Edward Graham, 17 April 1810, Graham Collection, DU.

38. _____ to Lucy, 21 June 1805, Lyons Papers, SHC.

39. Edward Rutledge to his daughter, 1795, Rutledge Collection, SCHS. See also Lucy Nelson to William Nelson, 1810, Byrd Collection, VHS.

40. Charles Cotton to Eliza Cotton, 29 August 1838, Cotton Collection, GEU.

41. *Telemachus,* published by Fénélon in 1699, was one of the most widely read and translated works of eighteenth- and nineteenth-century children's texts. The *Catalogue Général des Livres Imprimés de la Bibliothèque Nationale* lists 730 editions.

42. John Randolph to Elizabeth Tucker Coalter, 19 January 1822, Randolph Papers, UVA. See also Susanna Bowdoin to Joseph Prentis, 20 December 1825, Bowdoin-Prentis Collection, UVA; Jonathan Smith to Edward Campbell, 10 July 1804, Campbell Collection, DU; Lucy Barnes to Williamson Barnes, 17 November 1825, Barnes Collection, WMC; Sally Lacy to William Graham, 7 February 1819, Graham Collection, DU; Monthly Report, September 1839, Bedford Female Seminary, Barksdale Collection, DU.

43. Journal of Grace Garnett Hunter, 1838, Hunter-Garnett Collection, UVA. See also John Randolph to Elizabeth Tucker Coalter, 21 March 1822, Randolph Papers, UVA.

44. Charlotte Chisholm to Robert McKay, 20 February 1827, MacKay Collection, USC. See also Mary Jackson to Martha Jackson, 25 October 1821, Jackson-Prince Papers, SHC.

45. Thomas Jefferson to Martha Jefferson, 28 November 1783, Jefferson Collection, VHS.

46. Journal of Mary Ann Hunt, 1 October 1834, Stockwell Collection, MSA.

47. Euphradian Academy Collection, DU.

48. Lincolnton Academy Collection, DU.

49. Maria Carr Memoir, p. 29, DU.

50. M. I. Manigault to Charles Manigault, 25 November 1811, Manigault Collection, USC.

51. Rachel Mordecai to Samuel Mordecai, n.d. and 11 March 1816, Mordecai Collection, NCA.

52. 3 November 1820, Harden Collection, DU. See also September 1839, Barksdale Collection, DU.

53. David Campbell to Margaret Campbell, 10 November 1828, Campbell Collection, DU.

54. Patsy Lenoir to Eliza Lenoir, 27 September 1811, Pickens Collection, ASA.

55. Elisha Barksdale to Fanny Barksdale, 26 April 1834, Barksdale Collection, DU.

56. Charles Macmurdo to Elizabeth Macmurdo, 4 July 1805, Gibson Papers, VSL.

57. See 9 May 1800, Woolfolk Collection, VHS; Catherine H. Lyon, "The Development of Secondary Education for Women in the United States," unpublished M.A. thesis, Duke University, 1936, p. 21; 27 April 1810, Brevard Collection, NCA; 3 January 1816, McDonald-Lawrence Collection, GHS; and Susanna Bowdoin to Joseph Prentis, 20 December 1825, Bowdoin-Prentis Collection, UVA.

58. 1811, Fraser-Couper Collection, GHS. These figures may be exaggerated owing to inflation, but despite fluctuations in currency rates, they are nonetheless significantly high.

59. Susanna Bowdoin to Joseph Prentis, 20 December 1825, Bowdoin-Prentis Collection, UVA.

60. Cornelia Barksdale to Frances Barksdale, 1 October 1836, Barksdale Collection, DU.

61. Mary Howard to Georgia Bryan, January 1823, Forman-Bryan-Screven Collection, GHS.

62. _____ to Laura Rootes, 9 December 1815, Jackson-Prince Papers, SHC. See also Maria Winn to Mary Jane Winn, 20 April 1831, Winn Collection, DU; William T. Barry to Susan Barry, 19 November 1819, Barry Papers, UVA; Carolina Pinckney to Charles Pinckney, 5 December 1833, Pinckney Collection, GEU; Anne Caroline Lessesne Diary, 26 March 1836, Lessesne Collection, SCHS; Mary Telfair to Mary Few, 26 May 1820, 30 January 1835, and 5 March 1836, Few Collection, GSA.

63. Virginia Terrell to Edward Graham, 12 March 1812, Graham Collection, DU. See also Maria Campbell to Elizabeth Russell, 19 August 1809, Campbell Collection, DU.

64. Mary E. G. Harden, 15 February 1826, Harden Collection, DU.

65. Mary Howard to Georgia Bryan, 24 July 1823, Forman-Bryan-Screven Collection, GHS. This is a perplexing passage, for although Mary Howard indicates that she is preparing for college, no higher institution in the North or South admitted women at this time.

66. Anonymous Booklet, 1786, GHS.

67. Delia Hurd to Ann Cocke, 3 February 1832, Cocke Papers, UVA.

68. Israel Pickens to General Lenoir, 31 May 1826, Pickens Collection, ASA.

69. Maria Campbell to David Campbell, 4 June 1825, Campbell Collection, DU.

70. Maria Campbell to Elizabeth Russell, 19 August 1809, Campbell Collection, DU.

CHAPTER VIII. *PRECIOUS AND PRECARIOUS IN BODY AND SOUL*

1. See *Statistics of the United States in 1860*.

2. Buckingham, *Slave States of America*, 1: 12–13.

3. Darwin, *A Plan for Female Education*, p. 97.

4. Sally Rutherfoord to John Rutherfoord, 8 July 1836, Rutherfoord Collection, DU.

5. John Quitman to Eliza Quitman, 2 February 1828, Quitman Papers, SHC; St. George Tucker to Fanny Tucker, 16 May 1786, Tucker-Coleman

Collection, WMC; Roderick Murchison to Elizabeth Murchison, 1 November 1816, Bruce-Jones-Murchison Collection, USC.

6. Maria Campbell to Elizabeth Russell, 19 August 1809, Campbell Collection, DU. See also John Steele to Margaret Steele, 29 January 1807, Steele Papers, SHC; John Bernard, *Retrospectives of America, 1797–1811* (New York: Harper & Brothers, 1887), p. 189.

7. Bayard, *Travels in Maryland and Virginia*, p. 40.

8. 19 June 1827, Juliana Conner Diary, SHC.

9. See E. Van Bibber to Thomas Forman, 22 April 1823, Arnold-Screven Papers, SHC.

10. Nelly Parke Custis to Elizabeth Gibson, 6 September 1796, Lewis Collection, PHS.

11. Caroline Howard to Anne White, 20 January 1819, Gilman Collection, SCHS.

12. M. Wood to Mrs. Wm. Lacy, 17 May 1834, Lacy Papers, SHC.

13. John J. Crittenden to Ann Coleman, 18 November 1831, Crittenden Collection, DU.

14. Marquis de Chastellux, *Travels in North America in the Years 1780, 1781 and 1782*, trans. Howard C. Rice, (Chapel Hill: University of North Carolina Press for the Institute of Early American History and Culture, 1963), 2: 297.

15. Rachel O'Conner to Mary Weeks, 27 November 1832, Weeks Collection, LSU.

16. George Bryan to _____ Forman, 10 September 1818, Arnold-Screven Papers, SHC.

17. David Campbell to Benjamin Rush, 7 December 1806, Campbell Collection, DU.

18. Benjamin Rush to David Campbell, 7 February 1807, Campbell Collection, DU.

19. Ann Cox to Sally Cranberry, 23 July 1833, Bailey Papers, SHC.

20. Amelia Jones to Elizabeth Alston, 29 April 1835, Alston-DeGraffenreid Collection, NCA.

21. _____ to _____ , 23 December 1816, Marshall Papers, SHC.

22. Mary C. Poindexter to Jane Poindexter, 25 December 1825, Clingman-Puryear Papers, SHC.

23. Penelope Dawson to Helen Blair, 22 October 1784, Iredell Collection, DU. See also E. A. Smith to her daughter, 3 October 1815, Hawes Collection, VHS.

24. _____ to _____ , 28 February 1835, Clopton Collection, DU.

25. Sarah Gordon to William Gordon, 15 November 1835, Gordon Collection, GHS.

26. Vol. 14, Pettigrew Papers, SHC.

27. 1833–1834, Miscellaneous Letters, SHC.

28. A. J. Bingham to Mary Lynch, 2 January 1834, Lynch Collection, DU.

29. See Edwards Collection, NCA.

30. See McDonald-Lawrence Collection, GHS.

31. S. C. to Eliza Whiting, 11 July 1795, Blair Bannister-Braxton-Horner-Whiting Collection, WMC.

32. _____ to _____ , 24 March 1820, Jackson-Prince Papers, SHC.

33. Ventura Morales, 31 October 1796, Copeland Collection, TU.

34. Maria Campbell to _____ , 4 January 1808, Campbell Collection, DU. See also Martha Richardson to James Screven, 16 September 1820, Arnold-Screven Papers, SHC.

35. Eleanor _____ to Elizabeth Timberlake, 9 September 1820, Ker-Texada Collection, TU.

36. M. E. Cheves to Ann Lovell, 20 September 1834, Lovell Collection, DU.

37. Amanda Dougherty to Jane Vance, n.d. 1833, Worthington Collection, MSA.

38. Mary C. Betts to _____ , 22 April 1829, Ramsey Collection, DU.

39. John L. E. W. Shecut, *Medical and Philosophical Essays* (Charleston, S.C.: A. E. Miller, 1819), p. 58.

40. William Couper to _____ , 12 April 1802, Fraser-Couper Collection, GHS.

41. W. Ferguson, 1900, Heyward-Ferguson Papers, SHC. See also Abraham Baldwin to Clara Kennedy, 17 June 1806, Baldwin Collection, HL.

42. Alicia Middleton to Nathaniel Middleton, 29 September 1817, Middleton Collection, USC.

43. Lawrence Fay Brewster, *The Summer Migrations and Resorts of South Carolina Lowcountry Planters* (Durham, N.C.: Duke University Press, 1947), pp. 15–24.

44. Emma Bond to Georgia Screven, 12 June 1833, Forman-Bryan-Screven Collection, GHS.

45. John Goldsborough to Louis Goldsborough, 14 July 1839, Goldsborough Collection, DU.

46. Charles Cotton to Eliza Cotton, 30 August 1833, Cotton Collection, GEU. See also _____ to his father, 30 May 1835, Hill Papers, SHC; Anne Bannister to Eliza Whiting, 12 September 1810, Blair Bannister-Braxton-Horner-Whiting Collection, WMC.

47. Caleb Coker to Hannah Coker, 26 July 1835, Lide-Coker-Stuart Collection, USC.

48. Maria Campbell to Elizabeth Russell, 19 August 1809, Campbell Collection, DU. See also Sarah Rutherfoord to John Rutherfoord, 12 July 1811, Rutherfoord Collection, DU.

49. James K. Spaulding (1817), in Percival Reniers, *The Springs of Virginia: Life, Love and Death at the Waters, 1775–1900* (Chapel Hill: University of North Carolina Press, 1941), p. 37.

50. Charles Cotton to Eliza Cotton, 9 August 1833, Cotton Collection, GEU.

51. Lucy Baytop to James Baytop, 6 September 1838, Baytop Collection, WMC. See also Caroline Jones to Selina Lenoir, 12 August 1829, Pickens Collection, ASA.

52. St. George Coalter to Judith Coalter, 18 and 21 July 1833, Brown-Tucker-Coalter Collection, WMC.

53. James K. Spaulding, in Reniers, *Springs of Virginia*, p. 37.

54. Henry Massie to Sarah Massie, n.d., n.a., Massie Collection, VHS.

55. Reniers, *Springs of Virginia*, pp. 55, 72.

56. John Goldsborough to Louis M. Goldsborough, 14 July 1839, Goldsborough Collection, DU. See also ibid., 24 July 1839.

57. Louise Holmes Diary, 31 July 1816, Cocke Papers, UVA.

58. Jane Bernard Journal, November 1825, Robb-Bernard Collection, WMC.

59. Maria Bryan to Julia Cumming, 14 January 1827, Hammond-Bryan-Cumming Collection, USC.

60. Elizabeth Fitzgerald to Elizabeth Gibson, 16 February 1814, Gibson Papers, VSL.

61. Elizabeth Gibson to Martha Jones, 12 May 1814, Gibson Papers, VSL.

62. Sally Lacy to Margaret Graham, 21 July 1817, Graham Collection, DU.

63. Maria Bryan to Julia Cumming, 3 April 1828, Hammond-Bryan-Cumming Collection, USC. See also 6 February and 18 March 1844, Bumpas Papers, SHC.

64. John Haywood to Sally Haywood, 14 November 1790, Haywood Collection, SHC.

65. Jane Williams to Elizabeth Haywood, November 1790, Haywood Collection, SHC.

66. Eleanor Custis Lewis to _____ Pinckney, 3 January 1803, Pinckney Collection, SCHS.

67. Thomas Brown Memoir, 1:10, Brown Collection, DU.

68. Dr. George Hasell, "Lectures on Midwifery," p. 39, SCHS.

69. H. S. Ball to John Ball, 15 January 1830, Ball Collection, DU.

70. Thomas Jefferson to Martha Jefferson, 9 February 1791 in Betts and Bear, eds., *Family Letters*, p. 71.

71. Maria Boddie to Elizabeth Hilliard, 3 August 1830, Pittman Collection, NCA.

72. Grey Skipwith to John Randolph, 9 October 1823, Randolph Papers, UVA.

73. Cary Ann Nicholas to Jane Randolph, 23 February 1817, Edgehill-Randolph Collection, UVA.

74. William Elliott to Ann Elliott, 23 April 1818, Elliott Papers SHC.

75. Joseph Habersham to Bella Habersham, 5 January 1788, Jones Collection, GHS. For other descriptions of men's attitudes toward childbirth, see J. E. Henry to Caroline Patterson, 28 June 1833, Jones-Patterson Papers, SHC; William Munford to Mary Preston, 6 January 1803, Munford-Ellis Collection, DU; David Andersen to Kitty Lee, 25 July 1824, Clark Collection, DU. For women's views, see Ann Cocke to Judy Applewaite, 15 December 1815, Cocke Papers, UVA; and Mary Pemberton to Amanda Edney, n.d. 1836, Gordon Collection, GHS.

76. Ann Daniel to Jane Lewis, 20 May 1810, Lewis-Scott-Daniel-Greenhow Papers, VSL.

77. Sarah Bagwell to Charlotte Hannah, 6 December 1837, Hannah-Barksdale Collection, VSL.

78. Robert Manson Myers, ed., *The Children of Pride: A True Story of Georgia and the Civil War* (New Haven, Conn.: Yale University Press, 1972), p. 454.

79. Jane Williams to Elizabeth Haywood, 30 January 1804, Haywood Collection, SHC.

80. Maria Bryan to Julia Cumming, 12 May 1828, Hammond-Bryan-Cumming Collection, USC.

81. Archie Vernon Huff, *Langdon Cheves of South Carolina* (Columbia: University of South Carolina Press, 1977), p. 206.

82. Chastellux, *Travels in North America*, 2: 442.

83. Eliza Quitman to John Quitman, 3 January 1836, Quitman Papers, SHC.

84. Elizabeth Haywood to _____ , 20 December 1803, Haywood Collection, SHC.

85. Julia Betts to Charles Betts, 15 April 1827, McClenaghan Collection, USC.

86. For complaints about sore nipples, see _____ to Martin Gash, 5 July 1832, Gash Collection, NCA; Peggy Nicholas to Margaret Nicholas, 29 June 1816, Edgehill-Randolph Collection, UVA; Sally Munford to William Munford, 22 February 1803, Munford-Ellis Collection, DU; Sarah Bagwell to Samuel Hannah, 3 December 1838, Hannah-Barksdale Collection, VSL; 1833–1834, Miscellaneous Letters, SHC.

87. Lucy Ambler to Sarah Massie, 18 April 1823, Massie Collection, VHS.

88. Leila Tucker to Fanny Coalter, 5 June 1803, Brown-Tucker-Coalter Collection, WMC. See also Cary Ann Smith to Peggy Nicholas, 6 June 1819, Edgehill-Randolph Collection, UVA.

89. See Rachel Lazarus to Carolina Plunkett, 9 March 1823, Mordecai Collection, DU; Martha Randolph to Thomas Jefferson, 20 February 1792, in Betts and Bear, eds., *Family Letters*, p. 94; Sarah Lyle to Margaret Graham, 28 July 1802, Graham Collection, DU; Fanny Coalter to John Coalter, 25 September 1810, Brown-Tucker-Coalter Collection, WMC.

90. Elizabeth Andrews Wilson, "Hygenic Care and Management of the Child in the American Family Prior to 1860," unpublished M.A. thesis, Duke University, 1940, p. 70.

91. See *Statistics of the United States in 1860*.

92. Wyndham Blanton, *Medicine in Virginia in the Eighteenth Century* (Richmond, Va.: Garrett & Massie, 1931), p. 69.

93. Benjamin Covington to Samuel Clark, 25 June 1831, Scarborough Collection, DU. See also Louisa McAllister to Sarah Cutler, 27 December 1822, Bulloch Papers, SHC.

94. Margaret Brashear to Frances Brashear, 10 July 1832, Brashear-Lawrence Papers, SHC.

95. Sarah Screven to James Screven, 16 March 1820, Arnold-Screven Papers, SHC. See also Martha Richardson to James Screven, 3 February 1819, Arnold-Screven Papers, SHC; M. H. Crozier to Mary Brashear, 26 July 1822, Brashear-Lawrence Papers, SHC.

96. Robert Steptoe to Sarah Steptoe, 26 October 1828, Andrew Collection, GEU.

97. Martha Richardson to James Screven, 16 September 1822, Arnold-Screven Papers, SHC.

98. E. T. Bryan to Rebecca Meade, 14 April 1842, Whitaker-Meade Papers, SHC. See also Mary Burton to Myra Lenoir, 7 September 1816, Lenoir Papers, SHC; John Norwood to Myra Lenoir, 5 September 1823, Lenoir Papers, SHC.

99. William Bolling Memoirs, p. 53, Bolling Collection, VHS. See also Milly Jones, 12 January 1821, Richard Jones Collection, DU; H. Georgia Screven to Thomas Forman, 11 April 1834, Arnold-Screven Papers, SHC.

100. Margaret Page to _____ McLaine, 22 February 1796, Page-Saunders Collection, WMC. See also Mary Long to Mary Nash, 5 February 1820, Nash Collection, NCA.

101. Julia Mitford to S. Randolph, 8 July 1821, Randolph-Yates Papers, SHC.

102. Martha Richardson to James Screven, 2 December 1821, Arnold-Screven Papers, SHC.

103. Mary Ann Johnson to Fanny Coalter, 27 May 1810, Brown-Tucker-Coalter Collection, WMC.

104. Mary Fraser to Mary Davie, 3 August 1833, Fraser-Couper Collection, DU. See also Ann Andrew to Mary Andrew, 25 October 1828, Andrew Collection, GEU.

105. Margaret Campbell to Margaret Campbell, 11 June 1831, Campbell Collection, DU. See also E. Chalmers to Esther Van Bibber, 29 March n.a., Tabb Collection, DU.

106. Mary McDonald to _____ Hart, 13 July 1784, McDonald-Lawrence Collection, GHS. See also W. Brown to _____ , 21 February 1809, Bedinger-Dandridge Collection, DU; John B. _____ to Neill Brown, 20 December 1825, Brown Collection, DU.

107. Fanny Watts to _____ Lee, 2 February 1822, Clark Collection, DU. See also Mary Howard to Georgia Bryan, 26 September 1822, Forman-Bryan-Screven Collection, GHS; A. I. Deas to M. Manigault, 14 May 1813, Manigault Collection, USC.

108. Rachel O'Conner to Mary Weeks, 9 April 1833, Weeks Collection, LSU.

109. Susanna Clay to Clement Clay, 24 September 1824, Clay Collection, DU. See also John Brookes to Iveson Brookes, September n.a., Brookes Collection, SHC; Frances Smith to Mary Owen, 29 October 1814, Campbell Collection, DU.

110. Catherine _____ to Lucy Young, August 1819, Simpson Papers, SHC.

111. Rachel Mordecai to Ellen Mordecai, 8 February 1818, Mordecai Papers, SHC. See also Mary Peck to John Gayle, 20 August 1815, Bayne-Gayle Papers, SHC; Sidney Goode to _____ , 10 January 1837, Tait Collection, ASA; Mary Davie to Mary Fraser, 12 October 1833, Fraser-Couper Collection, DU; Esther Lowry to Mary Swain, 19 June 1832, Gash Collection, NCA.

112. Catherine Campbell to William Campbell, 11 June 1827, Campbell Collection, DU.

113. G. J. Clarke to Samuel Clarke, 18 May 1832, Scarborough Collection, DU.

114. Amanda Deaderick to Hester Van Bibber, 2 January 1816, Tabb Collection, DU.

115. "Recollections of Rocktown," Maria Carr Memoir, pp. 26–27, DU.

116. Amelia Watts, "Reminiscences on a Louisiana Plantation in 1832," p. 5, Watts Collection, MSA.

117. John Eppes to Frances Eppes, n.d., n.a., Eppes Collection, DU.

118. Penuel Brown to _____ , n.d., n.a., Eppes Collection, DU.

119. Cary, *Letters on Female Character*, p. 50.

120. See Donald G. Mathews, *Religion in the Old South* (Chicago: University of Chicago Press, 1977).

121. Sarah Gayle Diary, 28 October 1832, Bayne-Gayle Papers, SHC. See also Mary Withers to Ann Withers, 28 April 1832, Levert Papers, SHC;

Maria Carr Memoir, p. 34, DU; Harriet Simons to James Simons, 26 November 1811, Simons Collection, USC; A. J. Bingham to Mary Lynch, 11 October 1834, Lynch Collection, DU; Susanna Knox to _____ , 20 April 1799, Lynch Collection, DU.

122. E. N. Bulloch to Louisa Bulloch, 4 July 1831, Bulloch Papers, SHC.

123. Amarilla T. Baugh to Gustavas Pope, 22 November 1833, Pope-Carter Collection, DU; Catharine McNon to Mary Lynch, 3 November 1832, Lynch Collection, DU; A. T. Beale to J. H. Davis, 11 August 1836, Beale-Davis Papers, SHC; Lucy Andersen to Susan _____ , March 1815, Clark Collection, DU.

124. Martha Triplett to Marian Harden, 17 July 1826, Harden Collection, DU.

125. See Maria Carr Memoir, DU. See also 4 August 1827, Juliana Conner Diary, SHC.

126. Catharine McNon to Mary Lynch, 3 November 1832, Lynch Collection, DU.

127. See Margaret Graham to Nancy Graham, 9 June 1817, Graham Collection, DU; Louisa Foster to Amanda Edney, 20 July 1833, Graham Collection, DU; 9 June 1817, Graham Collection, DU; Eleanor Douglas to Mary Hall, 26 September 1820, Eleanor Douglas Collection, DU; Mary Howard to Georgia Bryan, January 1823, Forman-Bryan-Screven Collection, GHS; Susan Moore to Hannah Lide, 20 July 1830, Lide-Coker-Stuart Collection, USC; Mary Turner to James Douglas, 23 May 1835, James Douglas Collection, DU; Elam Morrison to James Morrison, 4 June 1823, Morrison Collection, DU.

128. J. R. Randolph to Betsy Coalter, 25 December 1828, John Randolph Papers, UVA. See also David Campbell to Maria Campbell, 3 January 1823, Campbell Collection, DU.

129. Eliza Clitherall, Clitherall Collection, SHC. See also Thomas Brown Memoir, 1: 89, Brown Collection, DU; Louisa Cocke Diary, 14 January 1828, Cocke Papers, UVA.

130. Nancy to Elmire, 14 May 1823, Winn Collection, DU.

131. Margaret Campbell to John Campbell, 10 November 1828, Campbell Collection, DU.

132. Catherine Holmes to Elizabeth Blanks, 9 September 1837, Blanks Collection, DU. See also _____ to John Oliver, 14 October 1816, Campbell Collection, DU; Mary Howard to Georgia Bryan, 1 November 1823, Forman-Bryan-Screven Collection, GHS; R. M. Rutledge, 10 October 1832, Rutledge Collection, USC.

133. See Scott, *Southern Lady*, p. 11.

134. Martha Triplett to Maria Harden, 17 July 1826, Harden Collection, DU. See also Judith Ann Smith, 24 July 1824, Hawes Collection, VHS.

135. Frances Smith to Mary Owen, 7 June 1824, Campbell Collection, DU.

136. Jane Wright to Maria Campbell, 15 December 1814, Campbell Collection, DU. See also Margaret Campbell to Margaret Campbell, 20 June 1828, Campbell Collection, DU; Mary McDonald to _____ Hart, 13 July 1784, McDonald-Lawrence Collection, GHS.

CHAPTER IX. *EVERY WOMAN WAS AN ISLAND*

1. Ellen Mordecai to Solomon Mordecai, 22 January 1823, Mordecai Collection, DU.

2. Mary Telfair to Mary Few, 19 October 1814, Few Collection, GSA.

3. William B. Dabney to Williamson Barnes, 4 September 1823, Barnes Collection, WMC.

4. Nancy Robinson, January and April 1833, Robinson Collection, MSA. See also Mary Cocke to Jane Rapelye, 9 March 1822, Ellis-Farrar Collection, LSU.

5. Grandma Finley, n.d., n.a., Archer Collection, NCA.

6. Israel Pickens to Martha Pickens, 18 March 1816, Lenoir Papers, SHC.

7. Owen Holmes to Elizabeth Banks, 23 September 1834, Blanks Collection, DU.

8. Eliza Fitzhugh to Elizabeth Fitzhugh, 20 April 1835, Fitzhugh Collection, DU.

9. A. M. Graham to _____, n.d., n.a., Miscellaneous Letters, SHC.

10. W. N. Todd to Elizabeth Todd, 14 February 1839, Miscellaneous Letters, SHC.

11. B. Nicholls to Mary Pettigrew, 5 October 1822, Pettigrew Collection, NCA.

12. Thomas Brown Memoir, 2: 61, Brown Collection, DU.

13. Mary Hatch to _____, 8 December 1832, Hatch Collection, NCA. See also _____ to Ann Glass, 17 November 1818, Joseph Glass Collecton, DU; Ann Coleman Memoirs, part II, p. 13, Coleman Collection, DU; Sally Lacy to William Graham, 9 February 1821, Graham Collection, DU; Margaret Roane to Maria Campbell, 30 October 1817, Campbell Collection, DU; Catherine Goldsborough to Elizabeth Goldsborough, 20 March 1834, Goldsborough Collection, DU.

14. Nancy Gillespie to Mary Murphy, 8 September 1827, Brown Collection, DU. See also Nancy Walton to Jane Gurley, 16 January 1836, Gurley Papers, SHC.

15. Mary Hatch to Frances Hill, 9 February 1833, Hatch Collection, NCA.

16. Sarah Gayle to John Gayle, 10 January 1832, Bayne-Gayle Papers, SHC. See also Sarah Gordon to William Gordon, 15 November 1835, Gordon Collection, GHS.

17. Margaret Prentis to Joseph Prentis, 6 May 1801, Bowdoin-Prentis Collection, UVA. See also Sarah Gordon to William Gordon, 15 November 1835, Gordon Collection, GHS.

18. Jane Gay Robertson, Journal, 1825, Robb-Bernard Collection, WMC. See also Rebecca Brashear to Walter Brashear, 18 January 1830, Brashear-Lawrence Papers, SHC.

19. Nancy McDougall, July 1832, Robinson Collection, MSA. See also Catherine P. Chevalie to John Chevalie, February 1803, Brock Collection, HL.

20. Sarah Gayle to John Gayle, November 1829, Bayne-Gayle Papers, SHC.

21. R. Lorrain to Sarah Yates, 11 January 1815, Randolph-Yates Papers, SHC.

22. Ann Daniel to Jane Lewis, 5 March 1816, Lewis-Scott-Daniel-Greenhow Papers, VSL.

23. William Elliott to Ann Elliott, 4 December 1818, Elliott Papers, SHC.

24. Martha Richardson to Georgia Screven, 24 May 1833, Forman-Bryan-Screven Collection, GHS.

25. Thomas Jefferson to Martha Jefferson, 28 March 1787, Betts and Bear, eds., *Family Letters*, p. 35.

26. Mary Telfair to Mary Few, 6 April 1837, Few Collection, GSA.

27. Judith Randolph to St. George Tucker, 5 November 1797, Tucker-Coleman Collection, WMC.

28. Mary Poindexter to Jane Clingman, 10 February 1831, Clingman-Puryear Papers, SHC.

29. Mary Moragne Diary, 6 June 1837, in Mary E. Davis, ed., *The Neglected Thread: A Journal from the Calhoun Community, 1836–1842* (Columbia: University of South Carolina Press, 1951), p. 39. See also Eliza Howe to Helen Blair, 25 May 1783, Iredell Collection, DU.

30. Eleanor Douglas to Sally Hall, 1 May 1820, Eleanor Douglas Collection, DU.

31. Eleanor Douglas to Mary Hall, 26 September 1820, Eleanor Douglas Collection, DU.

32. S. Myra Smith Diary, 31 August 1852, Somerville-Howorth Collection, RC.

33. Mary Burton to Myra Lenoir, 7 September 1816, Lenoir Papers, SHC.

34. Margaret Steele to Mary _____ , 7 September 1818, Steele Papers, SHC.

35. 14 June 1827, Susan Nye Hutchinson Diary, SHC.

36. I would like to thank David Courtwright for making available a copy of his paper presented at the 1978 meeting of the American Association for the History of Medicine, "The Nineteenth-Century Opiate Addict and What She Has to Tell Us About the Nature of Opiate Addiction." For a fuller treatment of the subject see his study, *Dark Paradise: Opiates in America Before 1940* (Cambridge, Mass.: Harvard University Press, 1982). For a comparative perspective, see Virginia Berridge, "Opium on the Fens in Nineteenth-Century England," *Journal of the History of Medicine* 34 (1979): 293–313.

37. See Mitchell Bradford to Lucinda Bradford, 9 February 1845, Mitchell Collection, TU.

38. James Iredell to Hannah Iredell, 19 October 1785, Iredell Collection, DU.

39. Mary Hatch to _____ , 9 February 1833, Hatch Collection, NCA.

40. May 1837, Susan Nye Hutchinson Diary, SHC.

41. Martha Richardson to James Screven, 22 July 1821, Arnold-Screven Papers, SHC.

42. Maria Campbell to David Campbell, 4 June 1825, Campbell Collection, DU; Mary Carter to Mary Lee, 22 February 1833, Custis-Lee-Mason Papers, VSL; Martha Randolph to Septima _____ , 30 July 1832, Edgehill-Randolph Collection, UVA; Ann Steele to John Steele, 11 February 1801, Steele Papers, SHC; J. L. Bailey to _____ , 13 July 1820, Bailey Papers, SHC; Martha Fannin to Tomlinson Fort, n.d., n.a., Fort Papers, SHC.

43. Charles Manigault Memoir, Manigault Collection, USC.

44. Louisa Cocke, 1 January 1828, Cocke Papers, UVA. See also Grace Garnett Hunter, 28 November 1838, Hunter-Garnett Collection, UVA.

45. 11 January 1847, James H. Greenlee Diary, SHC. See also Mrs. R. E. Lee to Mrs. Lee, n.d. 1831, Lee Collection, VHS.

46. See Ann Crittenden to John Crittenden, 4 January 1828, Crittenden Collection, DU; Margaret Tomlin to Williamson Barnes, 24 February n.a., Barnes Collection, WMC; Mary Telfair to Mary Few, 28 October 1814 and 17 February 1817, Few Collection, GSA; Rachel Mordecai to Samuel Mordecai, 13 July 1808, Mordecai Collection, DU; Maria W. Wilson to Delia Hayes, 9 November 1813, Claiborne Collection, VHS; _____ to _____, 17 May 1810, Hillhouse Collection, GEU; Martha Triplett to Marian Harden, 2 April 1826, Harden Collection, DU.

47. Ann Daniel to Jane Daniel, 22 March 1809, Lewis-Scott-Daniel-Greenhow Papers, VSL. See also Mary Claiborne to Herbert Claiborne, 7 January 1804, Claiborne Collection, VHS; Eliza Johnston to Sarah Massie, 11 February 1818, Massie Collection, VHS.

48. Maria Campbell to David Campbell, 22 December 1822, Campbell Collection, DU.

49. William Elliott to Mary Elliott, 16 July 1817, Elliott Papers, SHC.

50. Sarah Brown to Priscilla Brownrigg, 28 September 1818, Bailey Papers, SHC. See also Maria Campbell to David Campbell, 22 December 1822, Campbell Collection, DU.

51. Susannah Quince, 1803, Quince Collection, SCHS.

52. Harriet Meade to Sarah Lightfoot, 7 May 1836, Whitaker-Meade Papers, SHC.

53. Mary Telfair to Mary Few, 30 January 1835, Few Collection, GSA. See also Ann Nicholas to Judith Applewaite, 5 October 1807, Cocke Papers, UVA; Mary Telfair to Mary Few, Few Collection, GSA.

54. E. Goffe to Carolina Ferguson, 14 February 1835, Edmond Collection, DU.

55. Margaret Taylor to Sally Thomas, 1 October 1822, Fuller-Thomas Collection, DU.

56. See Maria Bryan to Julia Cumming, 13 May 1824, Hammond-Bryan-Cumming Collection, USC; Francis Gordon to Mary Owen, 13 October 1813, Campbell Collection, DU.

57. Mary Harris to Amanda Edney, 12 September 1833, Gardner Collection, DU.

58. Francis Goodwin to Mary Owen, 7 October 1813, Campbell Collection, DU.

59. Maria Campbell to David Campbell, 20 January 1822, Campbell Collection, DU.

60. Sarah Gayle, 13 January 1833 and 6 March 1833, Bayne-Gayle Papers, SHC. See also Mary Meade to Harriet Meade, 1 May 1837, Whitaker-Meade Papers, SHC; Jane Allison to Caroline Patterson, August 1824, Jones-Patterson Papers, SHC.

61. Carroll Smith-Rosenberg, "The Female World of Love and Ritual: Relations Between Women in Nineteenth-Century America," *Signs* 1 (Autumn 1975): 1–29. See also Louisa Mercer to Fanny Coalter, February–October 1810, Brown-Tucker-Coalter Collection, WMC; Mary Telfair to Mary Few, Few Collection, GSA.

62. Margaret Howell to William Howell, 1 August 1836, Howell Collection, MSA.

63. Brewster, *Summer Migrations*, p. 17. See also Amanda Norvell to Louisa Brown, 13 October 1824, Worthington Collection, MSA; Sarah Screven to James Screven, 24 August 1819, Arnold-Screven Papers, SHC; Martha Pickens to Ann Jones, 10 January 1815, Pickens Collection, ASA; Nelly Parke Custis to Elizabeth Gibson, 3 February 1799, Lewis Collection, PHS.

64. Rebecca Martin to Caroline Patterson, 16 April 1825, Jones-Patterson Papers, SHC. See also Sarah Bedinger to her mother, 15 November 1839, Bedinger-Dandridge Collection, DU.

65. Mary Meade, to ———— , 1 May 1837, Whitaker-Meade Papers, SHC. See also 16 June 1827, Juliana Conner Diary, SHC.

66. Itinerant Physician's Diary, 2 December 1812, SHC.

67. See Mary Gordon to Sarah Lenoir, 11 April 1819, Lenoir Papers, SHC. See also Dolley Madison to her niece, 1 August 1833, in Cutts, ed., *Memoirs and Letters*, p. 187.

68. Alicia Middleton to her son, 27 February 1828, Middleton Papers, SHC. See also Caroline Adams to Elizabeth Blanks, 2 January 1839, Blanks Collection, DU.

69. Calhoun, *American Family*, 2: 336.

70. Mary Campbell to Mary ———— , 12 March 1810, Campbell Collection, DU.

71. Buckingham, *Slave States*, 2: 124.

72. Eleanor Armistead to Jane Cocke, 26 May 1797, Armistead-Cocke Collection, WMC. See also Peggy Nicholas to Jane Randolph, 3 January 1819, Edgehill-Randolph Collection, UVA; Ann Pettigrew to Ebenezer Pettigrew, 30 December 1824, Pettigrew Papers, SHC.

73. Margaret Steele to John and Mary Steele, 25 December 1814, Steele Papers, SHC.

74. Adelaide Hechtlinger, *The Seasonal Hearth: The Woman at Home in Early America* (Woodstock, N.Y.: Overlook Press, 1977), pp. 250–51.

75. Eliza Richardson to Ann Smith, 10 January 1826, Smith Collection, DU. See also Margaret Steele to Mary _____ , n.d., 1807, Steele Papers, SHC; Charlotte Chisholm to Robert Mackay, 20 February 1827, MacKay Collection, USC; Mary Ferrand to Mary Steele, 30 April 1834, Steele Papers, SHC; Louisa Lenoir to Louisa Lenoir, 3 May 1828, Lenoir Papers, SHC.

76. Ralph Izard to Alice Izard, 28 May 1801, Cheves Collection, SCHS.

77. Harriet Chisholm to Georgia Mackay, 13 July 1826, MacKay Collection, USC.

78. Sally Kennon to Ellen Mordecai, 6 December 1807, Whittle Collection, UVA.

79. Elizabeth Randolph to Jane Randolph, 10 January 1822, Edgehill-Randolph Collection, UVA.

80. David Campbell to Maria Campbell, 11 December 1822, Campbell Collection, DU.

81. Maria Campbell to David Campbell, 22 December 1822, Campbell Collection, DU.

82. David Campbell to Maria Campbell, 1 January 1823, Campbell Collection, DU.

CHAPTER X. *THE CURSE OF SLAVERY*

1. W. B. Bulloch to Louisa Bulloch, 5 August 1831, Bulloch Papers, SHC. See also John Steele to Ann Steele, n.d., n.a., Steele Papers, SHC.

2. Sarah Lenoir to Myra Lenoir, 2 July 1817, Lenoir Papers, SHC. See also Susanna Clay to Clement Clay, Jr., 1 April 1834, Clay Collection, DU; Sarah Gayle Diary, 30 October 1832, Bayne-Gayle Papers, SHC; Maria Campbell to David Campbell, 8 January 1828, Campbell Collection, DU; Amanda Dougherty to Mary Ann Tilford, 11 December 1820,Worthington Collection, MSA; Mary Telfair to Mary Few, 19 October 1814, Few Collection, GSA.

3. Nelly Parke Custis to Elizabeth Gibson, 23 November 1798, Lewis Collection, PHS. See also William Lenoir, 1824, Lenoir Papers, SHC.

4. Dolley Madison to James Madison, 1 November 1805, in Cutts, ed., *Memoirs and Letters,* p. 60.

5. Maria Campbell to Jefferson _____ , 20 January 1815, Campbell Collection, DU.

6. Maria Campbell to David Campbell, 1 September 1812, Campbell Collection, DU.

7. Sarah Gayle Diary, 1 December 1832, Bayne-Gayle Papers, SHC. See also Susanna Clay to Ann Withers, 24 January 1833, Levert Papers, SHC.

8. Anna Calhoun to James Calhoun, 10 January 1838, Calhoun Collection, USC.

9. Mary Telfair to Mary Few, 18 June 1836, Few Collection, GSA.

10. See especially Drew Gilpin Faust, *The Ideology of Slavery: Proslavery Thought in the Antebellum South* (Baton Rouge: Louisiana State University Press, 1981).

11. See Eleanor Douglas to Mary Hall, 8 January 1820, Eleanor Douglas Collection, DU. See also Mary Boyd to Jane ———— , 8 February 1825, Boyd Collection, USC.

12. See Harriet Martineau, *Society in America* (London: Saunders & Otley, 1837).

13. Charles Pettigrew to Mary Pettigrew, 11 March 1785, Pettigrew Papers, SHC.

14. Margaret Brashear to Caroline B., 19 February 1823, Brashear-Lawrence Papers, SHC. See also Margaret Steele to Mary Steele, January 1815, Steele Papers, SHC; Jane Robertson to Robert Beverley, 10 October 1820, Beverley Collection, VHS; Maria Bryan Harford to Julia Cumming, Hammond-Bryan-Cumming Collection, USC; Nancy Cary Randolph to St. George Tucker, 30 January 1803, Tucker-Coleman Collection, WMC; A. J. Bingham to Mary Lynch, 2 January 1834, Lynch Collection, DU.

15. Mary C. Poindexter to Jane Poindexter, 25 December 1825, Clingman-Puryear Papers, SHC.

16. 29 July 1815 and 3 January 1832, Susan Nye Hutchinson Diary, SHC.

17. Rachel O'Conner to David Weeks, 13 July 1826, Weeks Collection, LSU. See also Will of Mary Houston, 27 April 1833, Houston Collection, DU.

18. Martha Jefferson to Thomas Jefferson, 3 May 1787, Betts and Bear, eds., *Family Letters*, p. 38. See also Martha Jefferson Randolph to Ellen Coolidge, n.d., 1809, Martha Randolph Collection, VHS.

19. Elizabeth Yates to Harrison G. Otis, 30 September 1820, Yates Collection, SCHS.

20. See Frances A. Kemble, *Journal of Residence on a Georgian Plantation in 1838–39* (1863; reprint ed., New York: Alfred A. Knopf, 1961); Alfred

Steele to Mary Steele, 15 November 1835, Steele Papers, SHC; Maria Campbell to David Campbell, 10 February 1818, Campbell Collection, DU.

21. I wish to thank Elizabeth Craven, Princeton University, for making her unpublished manuscript available to me. Her generosity and scholarship are greatly appreciated.

22. Sarah Bagwell to Claiborne Barksdale, 1 January 1837, Hannah-Barksdale Collection, VSL.

23. Caleb Coker to Hannah Coker, 7 September 1835, Lide-Coker-Stuart Collection, USC; Rachel Mordecai to Samuel Mordecai, 28 July 1828, Mordecai Collection, DU; John Coalter to Fanny Coalter, 25 May 1810, Brown-Tucker-Coalter Collection, WMC; Elizabeth Gibson to Patrick Gibson, 13 September 1821, Gibson Papers, VSL.

24. See Maria Campbell to David Campbell, 20 January 1822, Campbell Collection, DU.

25. Anne Butler to Margaret Duncan, n.d. 1815, Ellis-Farr Collection, LSU.

26. Mary Nash to Frederick Nash, 14 March 1807, Nash Collection, NCA. See also Maria Bryan Harford to Julia Cumming, 11 December 1835, Hammond-Bryan-Cumming Collection, USC.

27. Mathilda Turner to Jane Gurley, 9 September 1836, Gurley Papers, SHC.

28. Maria Bryan to Julia Cumming, 27 January 1827, Hammond-Bryan-Cumming Collection, USC.

29. Cary, *Letters on Female Character*, p. 174.

30. 15 August 1844, Bumpas Papers, SHC.

31. Sarah Nicholas to Jane Randolph, 4 December 1818, Edgehill-Randolph Collection, UVA.

32. 29 July 1815, Susan Nye Hutchinson Diary, SHC.

33. Frances Smith to Mary Owen, 23 April 1824, Campbell Collection, DU. See also Sarah Gordon to William Gordon, 18 November 1836, Gordon Collection, GHS; Sarah Pickens to her sister, 4 March 1818, Patterson Collection, DU; Eliza Gould Memoir, 1823, p. 28, Gould Collection, ASA.

34. Lucy Thornton to Martha Rootes, 15 November 1799, Jackson-Prince Papers, SHC.

35. Rachel O'Conner to David Weeks, 4 June 1832, Weeks Collection, LSU.

36. Fanny Bland Tucker to St. George Tucker, November 1787, Tucker-Coleman Collection, WMC.

37. Martha Washington to Elizabeth Powell, 20 May 1797, George and Martha Washington Letters, VSL.

38. Margaret Coalter to John Coalter, 10 May 1795, Brown-Tucker-Coalter Collection, WMC.

39. James Smythe to Amelia Montgomery, 1 June 1829, Montgomery Collection, LSU. See also Anne Butler to Margaret Duncan, n.d. 1815, Ellis-Farr Collection, LSU; Maria Campbell to David Campbell, 9 and 23 August 1812, Campbell Collection, DU; 24 March 1837, Whitaker-Meade Papers, SHC; and Catherine Hammond to J. H. Hammond, 14 August and 4 October 1829, Hammond Collection, USC.

40. Sarah G. Haig, 1837, Telfair Collection, GHS. See also Delia Bryan to Georgia Bryan, 23 January 1823, Arnold-Screven Papers, SHC.

41. Samuel Brown to Henry Brown, 30 December 1814, Brown-Tucker-Coalter Collection, WMC.

42. Rachel Mordecai to Samuel Mordecai, 11 February 1810, Mordecai Collection, NCA.

43. James H. Johnston, *Race Relations in Virginia and Miscegenation in the South* (1937; reprint ed., Amherst: University of Massachusetts Press, 1970), pp. 20–22.

44. Mrs. J. Blair to Nelly Blair, 29 June 1783, Iredell Collection, DU.

45. Rebecca Wyche to Thomas Wyche, 15 January 1836, Wyche-Otley Papers, SHC.

46. Martha Goodson to Elizabeth Blanks, 13 October 1835, Blanks Collection, DU.

47. Caroline Jones to Selina Lenoir, 18 September 1831, Pickens Collection, ASA.

48. Sarah Carter to John Rutherfoord, 26 March 1830, Rutherfoord Collection, DU.

49. Louisa Lenoir to Louisa Lenoir, 19 April 1830, Lenoir Papers, SHC.

50. 1 October 1811, Pettigrew Collection, NCA. See also 4 September 1847 in "Schirmer Diary," *South Carolina Historical and Genealogical Magazine*, vol. 79, no. 1 (1978).

51. C. Vann Woodward, ed., *Mary Chesnut's Civil War* (New Haven, Conn.: Yale University Press, 1981), pp. 199, 211–12.

52. Harriet Martineau, *Views on Slavery and Emancipation* (New York: Pierce & Reed, 1837), pp. 5–6.

53. Myers, *Children of Pride*, pp. 1280, 1274.

54. There were few exceptions to this rule. But see, for example, Mary Boykin Chesnut (Woodward, *Mary Chesnut's Civil War*; Elisabeth Muhlenfeld, *Mary Boykin Chesnut: A Biography* [Baton Rouge: Louisiana State University Press, 1981]); and Mary Berkeley Minor Blackford (L. Minor Blackford, *Mine Eyes Have Seen the Glory: The Story of a Virginian Lady* [Cambridge, Mass.: Harvard University Press, 1954]).

55. Myers, ed., *Children of Pride*, p. 627.

56. Elizabeth Lyle Saxon, *A Southern Woman's Wartime Reminiscences* (Memphis, Tenn.: Pilcher Printing Co., 1905), p. 14.

57. Caroline E. Merrick, *Old Times in Dixie Land: A Southern Matron's Memories* (New York: Grafton Press, 1901), p. 81.

58. Ibid., p. 76.

59. Clarence Poe, ed., *True Tales of the South at War* (Chapel Hill: University of North Carolina Press, 1961), p. 55.

60. Belle Kearney, *A Slaveholder's Daughter* (1900; reprint ed., Westport, Conn.: Greenwood Press, 1981); Earl Schenck Miers, *When the World Ended: Diary of Emma LeConte* (New York: Oxford University Press, 1957), p. 90; Sarah Morgan Dawson, *A Confederate Girl's Diary* (Boston: Houghton Mifflin Co., 1913), p. 24.

CHAPTER XI. *THE SEXUAL DYNAMICS OF SLAVERY*

1. See Deborah G. White, "Ain't I A Woman? Female Slaves in the Antebellum South," unpublished Ph.D. dissertation, University of Illinois at Chicago Circle, 1979; Barbara Bush, "The Role of Slave Women in British West Indian Slave Society, 1650–1832," unpublished M.Phil. thesis, Sheffield University, 1979; and, for a theoretical discussion, Angela Davis, *Women, Race, and Class* (New York: Random House, 1981).

2. Joel Williamson, *New People: Miscegenation and Mulattoes in the United States* (New York: Free Press, 1980), p. 7.

3. John G. Mencke, *Mulattoes and Race Mixture: American Attitudes and Images, 1865–1918* (Ann Arbor: University of Michigan Research Press, 1979), p. 7.

4. See Rosser H. Taylor, *Antebellum South Carolina: A Social and Cultural History* (Chapel Hill: University of North Carolina Press, 1926), p. 22.

5. See Robert Wells, *Revolutions in Americans' Lives: A Demographic Perspective on Americans, the Families and Society* (Westport, Conn.: Green-

wood Press, 1982). See also Linda Gordon, *Woman's Body, Woman's Right: A Social History of Birth Control in America* (New York: Viking Press, 1976).

6. James Mohr, *Abortion in America: The Origins and Evolution of National Policy* (New York, Oxford University Press, 1978). Taking a case study of Philadelphia will illustrate the transformation of the issue in the mid-nineteenth-century North. Roger Lane's excellent *Violent Death in the City: Suicide, Accident and Murder in Nineteenth Century Philadelphia* (Cambridge, Mass.: Harvard University Press, 1979) reveals that change began late in the crucial decade of the 1850s. During the ante-bellum era, abortions were relatively easy to obtain in this city, where the cost was approximately $100. Lane pinpoints the first incident of prosecution for "a 'simple' abortion—inducement of miscarriage" in 1857. Despite the toughening of the law, Lane reports that society was slow to respond. He finds only one case of prosecution for abortion per year between 1869 and 1873. However, after this period there was a definite escalation: 1874–1880, 29 indictments; 1881–1887, 38 prosecutions; 1888–1894, 36 cases; and 1895–1901, 30 cases. Of the 151 persons indicted in post-bellum Philadelphia, 127 were brought to verdict. Twenty-two pleaded guilty and 25 others were convicted, giving a 31 percent conviction rate (although factoring out the guilty pleas lowers the rate to 19 percent). One must conclude that abortion was "acceptable" in the North.

7. Theodore Phelps to Edwin Phelps, 10 March 1821, Phelps Collection, HNO.

8. Sarah Gordon to William Gordon, 29 and 30 November 1835, Gordon Collection, GHS.

9. Ibid., 6 December 1835.

10. Buckingham, *Slave States of America*, 2: 241.

11. Bayard, *Travels in Maryland and Virginia*, p. 20.

12. Chastellux, *Travels in North America*, p. 245.

13. Bayard, *Travels in Maryland and Virginia*, p. 20.

14. William N. Blane, *An Excursion Through the United States and Canada During the Years 1822–1823* (1824; reprint ed., New York: Negro University Press, 1969), p. 204. See also Calhoun, *American Family*, 2: 300.

15. Francisco de Miranda, *The New Democracy in America: Travels of Francisco de Miranda in the United States, 1783–84,* trans. Judson P. Wood, ed. John S. Ezell, (Norman: University of Oklahoma Press, 1963), p. 14.

16. Calhoun, *American Family*, 2: 305.

17. Ibid., 2: 295.

18. Buckingham, *Slave States of America*, 2: 214. See also Blane, *Excursion*, p. 205.

19. Evangeline Andrews, *Journal of a Lady of Quality: Being the Narrative of a Journey from Scotland to the West Indies, North Carolina and Portugal in the years 1774–1776*, ed. Janet Schaw (New Haven, Conn.: Yale University Press, 1939), p. 154.

20. John Davis, *Travels of Four Years and a Half in the United States of America during 1798, 1799, 1800, 1801 and 1802* (1803; reprint ed., New York: Henry Holt & Co., 1909), p. 56.

21. Myers, ed., *Children of Pride*, pp. 741–42, 752–54, and 799–800.

22. Lucius Verus Bierce, *Travels in the Southland, 1822–23*, ed. George W. Knepper (Columbus: Ohio State University Press, 1966), p. 100.

23. Herbert A. Kellar, ed., "Diary of James D. Davidson," *Journal of Southern History* 1 (1935): 348.

24. Quoted in Williamson, *New People*, p. 69.

25. Genovese, *Roll, Jordan, Roll*, p. 417.

26. Cited in Johnston, *Race Relations in Virginia*, p. 221.

27. Blane, *Excursion*, p. 204. See also Thomas Hamilton, *Men and Manners in America* (Edinburgh: William Blackwood, 1833), 2: 223.

28. Mencke, *Mulattoes and Race Mixture*, p. 7.

29. I am indebted to Bertram Wyatt-Brown both for introducing me to the Foster family through his own work *Southern Honor* and for referring me to Terry Alford's *Prince Among Slaves* (New York: Harcourt Brace Jovanovich, 1977). I derive my information on Foster from Alford's account.

30. I am indebted to my former colleague Perry Blatz, who first drew my attention to Johnson's celebrity.

31. Leland Meyer, *The Life and Times of Colonel Richard M. Johnson of Kentucky* (New York: Columbia University Press, 1932), p. 317.

32. Ibid., pp. 322–23.

33. Ibid., pp. 422, 341.

34. Williamson, *New People*, p. 44.

35. Fawn Brodie, *Thomas Jefferson: An Intimate History* (New York: W. W. Norton & Co., 1974); Barbara Chase-Riboud, *Sally Hemings* (New York: Viking Press, 1979); Virginius Dabney, *The Jefferson Scandals: A Rebuttal* (New York: Dodd, Mead & Co., 1981). See also *New York Times*, 2 June 1981.

36. Williamson, *New People*, p. 47.

37. Their discussion of planter-slave sexuality has been critiqued by Susan Brownmiller; see *Against Our Will: Men, Women and Rape* (New York: Simon & Schuster, 1975), pp. 170–73.

38. Bierce, *Travels in the Southland*, p. 78.

39. Fogel and Engerman, *Time on the Cross*, p. 132.

40. Quoted in Ron Takaki, *Iron Cages: Race and Culture in Nineteenth Century America* (New York: Alfred A. Knopf, 1979), p. 53.

41. Fogel and Engerman, *Time on the Cross*, p. 135.

42. Much of the sociological literature on the subject is wholly inadequate and clustered at two poles: either a jumble of jargon and tables or, at the opposite extreme, completely impressionistic studies. Calvin Hernton's *Sex and Racism* (London: André Deutsch, 1969) falls into this latter category. However, a recent theoretical tackling of the subject offers some hope for the future: Charles H. Stember's *Sexual Racism: The Emotional Barrier to an Integrated Society* (New York: Harper & Row, 1978). Psychological studies have proven erratic, but the works of Frantz Fanon (see *Wretched of the Earth* [New York: Grove Press, 1968], and *Black Skin, White Masks* [London: MacGibbon & Kee, 1968]) and Joel Kovel (*White Racism*) are valuable. Another absorbing approach to the subject is O. Mannoni's *Prospero and Caliban: The Psychology of Colonization*, trans. P. Powesland (New York: Frederick A. Praeger, 1956). Only a handful of historical studies of America tackle this subject: Wilbur Cash's *Mind of the South* (New York: Alfred A. Knopf, 1941), Lillian Smith's *Killers of the Dream* (New York: W. W. Norton & Co., 1949), the repeatedly cited Winthrop Jordan's *White Over Black*, and Jaqueline Dowd Hall's *Revolt Against Chivalry: Jessie Daniel Ames and the Women's Campaign Against Lynching* (New York: Columbia University Press, 1979). One hopes that this dearth of literature will be amended by an explosion of scholarly interest in the coming decades.

   Now that Michel Foucault has pioneered the history of sexuality with the initial installment of a proposed multivolume study, *The History of Sexuality: An Introduction* (New York: Pantheon Books, 1979), scholars are afforded his theoretical groundwork, much in the same way Philippe Ariès' *Centuries of Childhood* paved the way for numerous studies on the family with its publication in 1962.

   Work on sexuality in England provides American historians with some profitable examples, most notably Lawrence Stone's monumental study *The Family, Sex and Marriage in England, 1500–1800* (New York: Oxford University Press, 1977) and Judith Walkowitz's *Prostitution and Victorian Society: Women, Class and the State* (New York: Cambridge University Press, 1981).

   Lillian Faderman's *Surpassing the Love of Men: Romantic Friendship and*

Love Between Women from the Renaissance to the Present (New York: William Morrow & Co., 1981) is a pathbreaking study.

On a subject so multifaceted as the history of sexuality, scholars have a challenging opportunity to make use of some of the valuable work being done on sex and gender in the fields of literature, psychology, and anthropology as well as other disciplines ripe for cross-pollination.

43. I would like to thank Mary Ryan for a written copy of her comments at the Fourth Annual Social History and Theory Seminar (Irvine, Calif., March 1981).

BIBLIOGRAPHY

MANUSCRIPT COLLECTIONS

I wish to thank all the archives listed below for permission to use material from their manuscript collections. Their collective generosity and individual assistance have been invaluable in the completion of this book.

For those interested in further pursuing the study of plantation mistresses, the family papers named below are especially valuable in that the "voice" and the contents of the letters and diaries afford significant insights into the lives of ante-bellum southern white women:

The letters of MARIA CAMPBELL, especially those to her husband, DAVID, Campbell Family Collection, DU.

The letters of MARIA BRYAN, Hammond-Bryan-Cumming Collection, USC.

The MORDECAI Family Collections at VSL, NCA, DU, and SHC.

The letters of DIANA DUNBAR to her husband, WILLIAM, Dunbar Collection, MSA.

For an interesting and reflective observer of life, see MARTHA RICHARDSON's correspondence, Arnold-Screven Family Papers, SHC.

For an excellent example of patriarchal interest in female offspring, see the letters of BOLLING HALL to his daughters MARTHA (PATSY) and MARIA (POLLY), Bolling Hall Family Collection, ASA.

The archives and manuscript collections consulted include:

Alabama State Archives (Montgomery)

Mary Grace Cooper Collection
Eliza Gould Collection
Bolling Hall Family Collection
Sarah Gayle Haynesworth Collection
Israel Pickens Collection
Tait Family Collection
George Augustus Beverley Walker Collection
John Williams Walker Collection

Huntington Library (Pasadena, California)

Baldwin Family Collection
Brock Collection
Postlethwaite Collection

Library of Congress (Washington, D.C.)

Brodeau Collection
Clinch Collection
Stephens Collection
Washington Collection
Wilson Collection

Special Collections, Woodruff Library, Emory University (Atlanta, Georgia)

Andrew Collection
Cotton Collection
Fort Collection
Hillhouse Collection
North Six-Mile Baptist Church Record Book
Pinckney Family Collection
Stephens Collection
Thiot Family Collection

Georgia State Archives (Atlanta)

Martha Baldwin Collection
Boulware Family Collection
Butner Family Collection
Chunn-Land Family Collection
Few Collection
Lee Collection
McCall Collection

Georgia Historical Society (Savannah)

Allen Collection
Anonymous Booklet
John Bailey Collection
Berrien Collection
Blanche Collection
Bull-Morrow Collection

Burroughs Collection
Cohen-Hunter Collection
Floyd Collection
Forman-Bryan-Screven Collection
Fraser-Couper Collection
Gilbert Collection
Gordon Family Collection
Greene Collection
Harris Collection
Houston Collection
Seaborn Jones Collection
Jones Family Collection
Keith Collection
Lebey-Courtney Collection
McDonald-Lawrence Collection
Mackay Collection
Mackay Family Collection
Morgan Collection
Mulford Collection
Potter Collection
Rogers Collection
Savannah Free School Collection
Telfair Collection

Louisiana State Archives (Baton Rouge)

Manuscript Division, Louisiana State University Library (Baton Rouge)

Anonymous Diary
Bowman Collection
Ellis-Farrar Collection
Evans Collection
Marston Collection
Montgomery Collection
Reynes Collection
Weeks Collection
Williams Collection

Historic New Orleans Collection (New Orleans, Lousiana)

Phelps Collection
Boze Diary, Henri de Ste. Geme Collection

Manuscripts Section, Tulane University Library (New Orleans, Louisiana)

    Brenan Family Collection
    Cochran Family Collection
    Colcock Family Collection
    Copeland Collection
    Eliza Gould Memoir
    Gurley Family Collection
    Charles Colcock Jones Collection
    Ker-Texada Collection
    McConnel Family Collection
    Lise Mitchell Collection
    Slave Manuscripts
    Weeks Collection

Schlesinger Library, Radcliffe College (Cambridge, Massachusetts)

    Hooker Collection
    Somerville-Howorth Collection

Mississippi State Archives (Jackson)

    Amelia Collection
    Archer-Finlay-Moore Collection
    Burrus Collection
    Dunbar Collection
    Howell Collection
    Hunt Collection
    Montgomery Collection
    Pride Collection
    Robinson Collection
    Eunice Stockwell Collection
    Wade Collection
    Watts Collection
    Wilson Collection
    Worthington Collection

Southern Historical Collection, Wilson Library, University of North Carolina (Chapel Hill)

    David Aiken Autobiography
    Lysander Amsden Letters
    Arnold-Screven Family Papers
    Archibald Arrington Papers
    William Attmore Papers

John Lancaster Bailey Papers
Barrow Family Papers
Battle Family Papers
Bayne-Gayle Family Papers
Beale-Davis Family Papers
Edmund Ruffin Beckwith Papers
James Baylor Blackford Papers
Brashear-Lawrence Family Papers
Iveson Brookes Papers
John Peter Broun Papers
Edmund Bryan Papers
Bryan-Leventhorpe Family Papers
Mrs. W. R. Buffington Papers
Bulloch Family Papers
Bumpas Family Papers
Cameron Family Papers
Carmichael Family Books
Carter-Farish Papers
Magdalene Claiborne Papers
Clingman-Puryear Family Papers
Eliza Clitherall Books
John Ewing Colhoun Papers
Juliana Margaret Conner Diary
Henry Connor Papers
Miriam Cox Papers
Mariane Cozens Diary
Charles Dabney Papers
Hannah Day Collection
John Devereux Books
F. A. Dickins Papers
Habersham Elliott Papers
Ferebee-Gregory-McPherson Family Papers
Susan Fisher Papers
Letitia Floyd Memoirs
Fort Family Papers
David Funsten Papers
Gillespie-Wright Family Papers
Graves Family Papers
James H. Greenlee Diary
John B. Grimball Diary
Guion Family Papers
Jane Gurley Papers
Peter Hagner Papers
Elizabeth Hairston Papers

Peter W. Hairston Papers
W. S. Hamilton Papers
James H. Hammond Letters
Harding-Jackson Family Papers
Henry William Harrington Papers
James T. Harrison Papers
Hawkins Family Papers
Ernest Haywood Collection
Heartt-Wilson Family Papers
Heyward-Ferguson Family Papers
William Hill Papers
William Henry Holcombe Books
Richard James Hooker Collection
Hubbard Family Papers
B. R. Huske Collection
Susan Nye Hutchinson Diary
Itinerant Physician's Diary
Robert A. Jackson Papers
Jackson-Prince Papers
Bartlett Jones Papers
Edmund W. Jones Papers
John Beauchamp Jones Papers
Joseph Seawell Jones Papers
Thomas Jones Papers
Jones Family Papers and Books
Jones-Patterson Papers
Roger Kelsall Letters
Mary Hunter Kennedy Papers
Kollock Plantation Books
Drury Lacy Papers
Levin Lane Papers
Caroline O. Laurens Diary
David M. Lees Papers
Lenoir Family Papers
Levert Family Papers
James Lyons Papers
Alexander McAllister Papers
Macay-McNeely Family Papers
McBee Family Papers
William P. McCorkle Papers
Charles Harper McDowell Collection
James McDowell Papers
Catharine McFarland Papers
Louis Marshall Papers

Matrimony Creek Baptist Church Records
N. R. Middleton Papers
Milligan Family Papers
Miscellaneous Cures and Recipes
Miscellaneous Letters
William C. Moore Papers
Mordecai Family Papers
Columbus Morrison Papers
Miriam G. Moses Papers
Mount Prospect Papers
Mehetable Mumford Letters
Murdock-Wright Family Papers
John Nevitt Diary
Larkin Newby Papers
Norton-Chilton-Dameron Family Papers
John Osbourn Diary
James W. Patton Papers
William Nelson Pendleton Papers
Person Family Papers
Pettigrew Family Papers
Pickens-Dugas Family Papers
Charlotte Porcher Papers
Quitman Family Papers
John Randolph Papers
Randolph-Yates Family Papers
Roach-Eggleston Family Papers
Elijah F. Rockwell Papers
Louisa H. Rogers Letters
William Royall Papers
F. G. Ruffin Papers
Thomas Ruffin Papers
Ruffin-Meade Family Papers
John Rutledge Papers
James Shackelford Papers
Jesse Siler Books
William D. Simpson Papers
Simpson-Bryan Family Papers
Slack Family Papers
Thomas B. Slade Papers
William R. Smith Papers
Sparkman Family Papers
John Steele Papers
Rebecca Street Sketch
Strudwick Family Papers

James Stuart Papers
Mary Stubblefield Letters
Francis Taylor Diary
George Coffin Taylor Papers
William D. Valentine Diary
Whitaker-Meade Family Papers
Edmonia C. Wilkins Papers
Witherspoon-McDowall Family Papers
Wyche-Otley Family Papers

Manuscript Department, William R. Perkins Library, Duke University (Durham, North Carolina)

Herbert Bacon Collection
John Ball Collection
Peter Barksdale Collection
William Baskerville Collection
Bedinger-Dandridge Family Collection
Ebeneezer Bell Collection
Samuel Biddle Collection
Elizabeth Blackwell Collection
Elizabeth Blanks Collection
James Boardman Collection
Neill Brown Collection
Bryan Family Collection
Samuel Bryarly Collection
Campbell Family Collection
Maria Carr Memoir
Eli Washington Caruthers Collection
Samuel Clark Collection
C. C. Clay Collection
John Clopton Collection
Ann Coleman Collection
John Jordan Crittenden Collection
Matthew Dickinson Collection
Eleanor Douglas Collection
James Douglas Collection
Samuel Downing Collection
George Coke Drumgoole and Richard B. Robinson Collection
Adam Dunlop Collection
Kate Edmond Collection
John Wayle Eppes Collection
Euphradian Academy Collection
John C. Faber Collection

Elizabeth D. Fitzhugh Collection
Mary D. Fraser Collection
Fuller-Thomas Family Collection
Amanda E. Gardner Collection
Thomas Garland Collection
Joseph Glass Collection
Louis Goldsborough Collection
William Graham Collection
Hiram Haines Collection
Edward Harden Collection
Placebo Houston Collection
James Iredell, Sr. and James Iredell, Jr. Collection
Amelia High Jeffreys Collection
Mrs. James M. Jeffreys Collection
Mrs. Christopher C. Jenkins Collection
Richard Jones Collection
Seaborn Jones Collection
Thomas Thweatt Jones Collection
Joel King Collection
Edward Leinbach Collection
Thomas Lenoir Collection
Lewis Family Collection
Lincolnton Female Academy Collection
Louisburg Female Academy Collection
Ann Reid Lovell Collection
Thomas Lynch Collection
Duncan and Dugal McCall Collection
Louis Manigault Collection
Jacob Mordecai Collection
Munford-Ellis Family Collection
Elizabeth Page Collection
Samuel Patterson Collection
Pope-Carter Family Collection
William and John Preston Collection
George Junkin Ramsey Collection
John G. Rutherfoord Collection
Harriott Horry Rutledge Collection
Scarborough Family Collection
Daniel Shine Collection
Louisa Sills Collection
Humberston Skipwith Collection
Ann M. Smith Collection
Elizabeth M. Smithson Collection
Cornelia Storrs Collection

Hester E. Van Bibber Tabb Collection
Anne A. Turner Collection
Winn Family Collection
Sophia and Augustus Zeveley Collection

North Carolina Archives (Raleigh)

Albright-Dixon Collection
Alston-DeGraffenried Family Collection
Alexander Brevard Collection
Archer Collection
Weldon Edwards Collection
Gales Collection
Mary A. Gash Collection
Mary D. Hardin Collection
Cullen B. Hatch Collection
William A. Jeffreys Collection
Little-Mordecai Collection
W. K. Littleton Collection
Michaux-Randolph Collection
Mordecai Collection
Frederick Nash Collection
James Norcom Collection
Pettigrew Collection
Thomas M. Pittman Collection
Raleigh Academy Collection
Zollicoffer Collection

Historical Society of Pennsylvania (Philadelphia)

Butler Family Collection
Lewis Collection

South Carolina Historical Society (Charleston)

Allston Collection
Bowen-Cocke Collection
Cheves Collection
DeSaussure Collection
Gilman Collection
Kinloch Collection
Lessesne Collection
Manigault Family Collection

Pinckney Family Collection
Quince Collection
Ravenel Collection
Rutledge Collection
Vanderhorst Collection
Yates Family Collection

Caroliniana Library, University of South Carolina (Columbia)

Ball Family Collection
Boyd Collection
Bruce-Jones-Murchison Collection
Calhoun Collection
Charles Family Collection
Chesnut Collection
Gaston-Crawford Family Collection
Guignard Family Collection
Hammond Collection
Hammond-Bryan-Cumming Collection
Hampton Collection
Hart Collection
Hort Collection
Huger Collection
Izard Collection
Johnson Collection
Lide-Coker-Stuart Collection
MacKay Collection
McClenaghan Collection
Manigault Family Collection
Middleton Family Collection
Noble Family Collection
Pinckney Family Collection
Reid Collection
Rutledge Family Collection
Screven-Edwards-Clarkson-Heriot Family Collection
Seibels Family Collection
Simons Family Collection
Singleton-Deveaux Family Collection
Smith Collection
Springs Family Collection
Williams Collection

South Carolina State Archives (Columbia)

Manuscript Department, University of Virginia Library (Charlottesville)

Elizabeth Barbour Ambler Collection
Ambler Family Papers
Barry Family Papers
Bowdoin-Prentis Collection
Bryan Family Papers
Cabell Papers
Cabell-Carrington Papers
Carr-Cary Papers
Cocke Family Papers
Martha Dyer Papers
Edgehill-Randolph Collection
Fernando Fairfax Papers
Hunter-Garnett Collection
Jefferson-Coolidge Collection
Lewis Family Papers
Maury Papers
Maury Family Papers
Meade Family Papers
Minor-Carr-Terrell Papers
John Randolph of Roanoke Papers
Philip Slaughter Diary
Creed Taylor Papers
Tucker-Harrison-Smith Papers
Whittle Family Collection

Virginia Historical Society (Richmond)

Adams Collection
Allmand Collection
Eliza Lavalette Barksdale Collection
Beverley Collection
William Bolling Collection
Byrd Collection
Claiborne Collection
Cocke Family Collection
Couper Collection
Early Family Collection
Hammond Collection
Harrison Collection
Hawes Collection
Holladay Collection
Jefferson Collection

Lee Collection
Robert Lewis Collection
Lomax Family Collection
Marshall Collection
Massie Family Collection
John Randolph Collection
Martha Jefferson Randolph Collection
Richard Randolph Collection
Taylor Collection
Trist Collection
Woolfolk Collection
Wormley Collection

Virginia State Library (Richmond)

Ball Family Papers
Berry Family Papers
Campbell Family Papers
Sarah Chandler Diary
Coalter-Tucker Correspondence
Custis-Lee-Mason Papers
Daniel Family Papers
Andrew Dunscomb Correspondence
Martha B. Eppes Collection
Fitzhugh-Taliaferro-Catlett Family Papers
Gannaway Family Papers
Gibson Family Papers
Francis Walker Gilmer Papers
Katherine Haigler Letter
Hannah-Barksdale Collection
Henry Family Papers
Jones Family Papers
Lansley Papers
Lewis-Scott-Daniel-Greenhow Family Papers
Madison Collection
Madison Family Collection
Mitchell Papers
Ellen Mordecai Papers
Page Family Correspondence
Francis Bouldin Raine Reminiscences
John Randolph Collection
Thomas Mann Randolph Papers
Rutherford Family Papers
Scott Family Papers

Taylor Family Papers
Tazewell Family Papers
Waller Family Papers
George and Martha Washington Letters

Manuscripts Division, Swem Library, College of William and Mary (Williamsburg, Virginia)

Armistead-Cocke Collection
Barnes Family Collection
Barraud Collection
Baytop Family Collection
Berkeley-Thweatt Collection
Beverley Collection
Blair-Bannister-Braxton-Horner-Whiting Collection
Blow Collection
Brown-Tucker-Coalter Collection
Burwell-Catlett Collection
Campbell Collection
Carter Collection
Garland Collection
Homassel Collection
Lewis Collection
Page-Saunders Collection
Nancy Randolph Collection
Robb-Bernard Collection
Augustine Smith Collection
Tucker-Coleman Collection

Colonial Williamsburg Foundation (Williamsburg, Virginia)

Elizabeth Jacquelin Ambler Collection
Smith-Digges Collection
Teagle-Lee Collection

TRAVEL ACCOUNTS

Abdy, Edward Strutt. *Journal of Residence and a Tour of the United States of North America from April, 1833, to October, 1834.* London: John Murray, 1835. 3 vols.

Andrews, Evangeline. *Journal of a Lady of Quality: Being the Narrative of a Journey from Scotland to the West Indies, North Carolina and Portugal in the Years 1774–1776.* Ed. Janet Schaw. New Haven, Conn.: Yale University Press, 1939.

Bayard, Ferdinand. *Travels of a Frenchman in Maryland and Virginia, with a Description of Philadelphia and Baltimore in 1791.* Trans. and ed. Ben C. McCary. Ann Arbor: University of Michigan Press, 1950.

Bernard, John. *Retrospectives of America, 1797–1811.* New York: Harper & Brothers, 1887.

Bernhard, Duke of Saxe-Weimar-Eisenach. *Travels Through North America During the Years 1825 and 1826.* Philadelphia: Carey, Lea & Carey, 1828.

Bierce, Lucius Verus. *Travels in the Southland, 1822–1823.* Ed. George W. Knepper. Columbus: Ohio State University Press, 1966.

Blane, William N. *An Excursion Through the United States and Canada During the Years 1822–1823.* 1824. Reprint ed. New York: Negro University Press, 1969.

Buckingham, J. S. *The Slave States of America.* London: Fisher, Son & Co., 1842. 2 vols.

Chastellux, Marquis de. *Travels in North America in the Years 1780, 1781, and 1782.* Trans. Howard C. Rice. Chapel Hill: University of North Carolina Press for the Institute of Early American History and Culture, 1963.

Darusmont, Frances Wright. *Views of Society and Manners in America.* London: Longman, Hurst, Rees, Orme & Brown, 1821.

Davis, John. *Travels of Four Years and a Half in the United States of America during 1798, 1799, 1800, 1801 and 1802.* 1803. Reprint ed. New York: Henry Holt & Co., 1909.

De Miranda, Francisco. *The New Democracy in America: Travels of Francisco de Miranda in the United States, 1783–84.* Trans. Judson P. Wood. Ed. John S. Ezell. Norman: University of Oklahoma Press, 1963.

Featherstonough, G. W. *Excursion Through the Slave States.* London: John Murray, 1844. 2 vols.

Ford, Timothy. "South Carolina Travel Diary, 1785–86." *South Carolina Historical and Genealogical Magazine* 13 (1912): 132–204.

Hall, Mrs. Basil. *The Aristocratic Journey and the Outspoken Letters of Mrs. Basil Hall, written during a fourteen months' sojourn in America, 1827–28.* Ed. Una Pope-Hennessy. New York: G. P. Putnam's Sons, 1931.

Hamilton, Thomas. *Men and Manners in America.* Edinburgh: William Blackwood, 1833. 2 vols.

Janson, Charles W. *The Stranger in America: Containing Observations Made During a Long Residence in That Country.* London: J. Cundee, 1807.

Mason, Jonathan. "Travel Diary." *Massachusetts Historical Society Proceedings, 1885–86.* 2nd ser. 2.

Newsome, A. R. "John Brown's Journal of Travel in Western North Carolina in 1795." *North Carolina Historical Review* 11 (1934): 284–313.

Olmsted, Frederick Law. *A Journey in the Seaboard Slave States in the Years 1853–1854.* New York: G. P. Putnam's Sons, 1904. 2 vols.

Owen, John, "Journal of Removal from Virginia to Alabama in 1818." *Publications of the Southern Historical Association,* 1:2.

Robertson, Powhatan. "Williamsburg." *William and Mary Quarterly,* 2nd ser., vol. 11 (1931).

Royall, Anne Newport. *Letters From Alabama, 1817–1822.* Ed. Lucille Griffith. (Birmingham: University of Alabama Press, 1969).

Smith, William L. "Travel Diary." *Proceedings of the Massachusetts Historical Society* 51 (1917–18).

Steiner, Bernard C., ed. "The South Atlantic States in 1833." *Maryland Historical Magazine* 13 (1918): 267–386.

Stirling, James. *Letters from the Slave States.* London: J. W. Parker & Son, 1857.

PRIMARY LITERATURE

Aime, Valcour. *Plantation Diary of the Late Mr. Valcour Aime.* New Orleans, La.: Clark & Hofeline, 1878.

Ambler, Charles H. *Life and Diary of John Floyd.* Richmond, Va.: Richmond Press, 1918.

Anderson, John Q., ed. *Brokenburn: The Journal of Kate Stone, 1861–1868.* Baton Rouge: Louisiana State University Press, 1955.

Andrews, Eliza Frances. *The War-Time Journal of a Georgia Girl: 1864–1865.* New York: D. Appleton & Co., 1908.

Betts, Edwin Morris, and James Adam Bear, eds. *The Family Letters of Thomas Jefferson.* Columbia: University of Missouri Press, 1966.

"The Black Race in North America." *Southern Literary Messenger,* vol. 21 (November 1855).

Blackford, L. Minor. *Mine Eyes Have Seen the Glory: The Story of a Virginian Lady.* Cambridge, Mass.: Harvard University Press, 1954.

Blanton, Wyndham. *Medicine in Virginia in the Eighteenth Century.* Richmond, Va.: Garrett & Massie, 1931.

Bleser, Carol, ed. *The Hammonds of Redcliffe*. New York: Oxford University Press, 1981.

Boggs, Marion Alexander. *The Alexander Letters, 1787–1900*. Savannah, Ga.: G. J. Baldwin, 1910.

Bonner, James C. "Plantation Experiences of a New York Woman." *North Carolina Historical Review* 33 (1956): 384–412, 529–47.

Bottorff, William K., and Roy Flannagan. "*The Diary of Frances Baylor Hill* of 'Hillsborough,' King and Queen County, Virginia (1797)." *Early American Literature* 2 (1967): 4–53.

Boyd, Julian, ed. *The Papers of Thomas Jefferson*. Princeton, N.J.: Princeton University Press, 1947.

Brooks, Robert Preston, ed. "Letters of James Hamilton Couper to His Wife, 1833–36." *Georgia Historical Quarterly* 14 (1930): 150–73.

Brown, William Wells. *Clotel, Or, The President's Daughter*. 1853. Reprint ed. New York: Macmillan Co., 1970.

Burke, Emily P. *Reminiscences of Georgia*. New York: James M. Fitch, 1850.

Burwell, Letitia. *A Girl's Life in Virginia Before the War*. New York: Frederick A. Stokes Co., 1895.

Carroll, Bartholomew R., comp. *Historical Collections of South Carolina: Embracing Many Rare and Valuable Pamphlets, and Many Other Documents, Relating to the History of That State, from Its First Discovery to Its Independence in the Year 1776*. 1836. Reprint ed. New York: AMS Press, 1972. 2 vols.

Cary, Virginia. *Letters on Female Character*. Richmond, Va.: A. Works, 1830.

Charleston News and Courier, 1803–1822.

Clayton, Virginia V. *White and Black Under the Old Regime*. Milwaukee, Wis.: Young Churchman Co., 1899.

Clift, G. Glenn, ed. *The Private War of Lizzie Harden*. Frankfort: Kentucky Historical Society, 1963.

Copland, Charles. "Diary." *William and Mary Quarterly*, 1st ser., vol. 14 (1904).

Cutts, Lucia B., ed. *Memoirs and Letters of Dolley Madison*. Boston: Houghton Mifflin Co., 1886.

Darwin, Erasmus. *A Plan for the Conduct of Female Education in Boarding Schools, Private Families and Public Seminaries*. 1798. Reprint ed. New York: Johnson Reprint Corp., 1968.

Davis, Edwin A., ed. *Plantation Life in the Florida Parishes of Louisiana as Reflected in the Diary of Bennet H. Barrow*. New York: Columbia University Press, 1943.

Davis, Mary E., ed. *The Neglected Thread: A Journal from the Calhoun Community, 1836–42*. Columbia: University of South Carolina Press, 1951.

Dawson, Sarah Morgan. *A Confederate Girl's Diary*. Boston: Houghton Mifflin Co., 1913.

Dew, Thomas Roderick. "Dissertation on the Characteristic Differences Between the Sexes." *Southern Literary Messenger*, vol. 1, no. 9 (May 1835).

"Divorce." *DeBow's Review*, vol. 2 (September 1846).

Douglass, Frederick. *My Bondage and My Freedom*. New York: Auburn, Miller, Orton & Mulligan, 1855.

Easterby, J. H., ed. *The South Carolina Rice Plantation as Revealed in the Papers of Robert F. W. Allston*. Chicago: University of Chicago Press, 1945.

————— . "Charles Cotesworth Pinckney's Plantation Diary, 1818." *South Carolina Historical and Genealogical Magazine* 41 (1940): 135–50.

Eastman, Mary. *Aunt Phyllis' Cabin or Southern Life as It Is*. Philadelphia: Lippincott, Brambo & Co., 1852.

Elliott, Charles. *Sinfulness of American Slavery*. Cincinnati, Ohio: L. Swormsted & G. H. Power, 1850, 2 vols.

Eppes, Susan Bradford. *Through Some Eventful Years*. Macon, Ga.: J. W. Burke Co., 1926.

Fearne, Frances. *Diary of a Refugee*. New York: Moffat, 1910.

"Female Education." *Southern Literary Messenger*, vol. 6 (1840).

Fithian, Philip V. *Journals and Letters*. Ed. Julia Rogers Williams. Princeton, N.J.: Princeton University Press, 1900–34.

Fitzhugh, George, and Hinton R. Helper. *Antebellum: Three Classic Works on Slavery in the Old South*. Ed. Harvey Wish. New York: Capricorn Books, 1960. Includes *Sociology for the South or the Failure of Free Society* (1854) and *Cannibals All! Or, Slaves Without Masters* (1857) by George Fitzhugh; and *The Impending Crisis of the South: How to Meet It* (1857) by Hinton R. Helper.

Fletcher, John. *Studies on Slavery*. Natchez, Miss.: Jackson Warner, 1852.

Gara, Larry. "A New Englander's View of Plantation Life: Letters of Edwin Hall to Cyrus Woodman, 1837," *Journal of Southern History* 18 (August 1952): 343–54.

Garnett, James M. *Lectures on Female Education*. Richmond, Va.: T. W. White, 1825.

Gass, W. Conrad. "A Felicitous Life: Lucy Martin Battle, 1805–1874." *North Carolina Historical Review* 52 (1975): 367–93.

Gayle, Sarah. "Journal of Mrs. Governor John Gayle." *Alabama Historical Quarterly* 5 (1943): 159–87.

Gilman, Caroline. *Recollections of a Southern Matron.* New York: G. P. Putnam & Co., 1852.

Green, Fletcher M., ed. *Ferry Hill Plantation Journal.* Chapel Hill: University of North Carolina Press, 1961.

Grimké, Angelina. *An Appeal to the Christian Women of the South.* New York: American Anti-Slavery Society, 1836.

Hopley, Catherine Cooper. *Life in the South.* London: Chapman & Hall, 1963. 2 vols.

Horry, Peter. "South Carolina Diary." *South Carolina Historical and Genealogical Magazine,* vols. 38–45 (1937–1945).

House, Albert Virgil. *Planter Management and Capitalism in Ante-bellum Georgia: The Journal of Hugh Fraser Grant, Ricegrower.* New York: Columbia University Press, 1954.

Hunter, John. "Washington at Mount Vernon." *Pennsylvania Magazine of History and Biography* 17 (1893): 76–82.

Ingraham, Joseph Holt. *The Sunny South.* Philadelphia: G. G. Evans, 1860.

Iredell, James, and François-Xavier Martin. *The Public Acts of the General Assembly of North Carolina.* Newbern: Martin & Ogden, 1804.

Johnston, Edith Duncan, ed. "Kollock Letters." *Georgia History Quarterly,* vols. 30–32 (1900).

Jones, Margaret Mackay, ed. *The Journal of Catherine Devereux Edmondston, 1860–1866.* Mebane, N.C.: privately published, 1956.

Jones, Virginia K., ed. "The Bowie Letters." *Alabama Historical Quarterly* 22 (1960): 231–43.

Kearney, Belle. *A Slaveholder's Daughter.* 1900. Reprint ed. Westport, Conn.: Greenwood Press, 1981.

Keith, Alice Barnwell. "William MacLeans's Travel Journal." *North Carolina Historical Review* 15 (1938): 378–88.

Kellar, Herbert A., ed. "Diary of James D. Davidson." *Journal of Southern History* 1 (1935): 345–77.

Kemble, Frances A. *Journal of Residence on a Georgian Plantation in 1838–1839.* 1863. Reprint ed. New York: Alfred A. Knopf, 1961.

King, Spencer Bidwell, Jr., ed. *Ebb Tide: As Seen Through the Diary of Josephine Clay Habersham.* Athens: University of Georgia Press, 1958.

Knight, Edgar W. *A Documentary History of Education in the South Before 1860.* Chapel Hill: University of North Carolina Press, 1949–53. 5 vols.

Lee, Rev. Jesse. *Memoir of Rev. Jesse Lee.* New York: N. Bangs & T. Mason, 1823.

LeGrand, Julia. *The Journal of Julia LeGrand: New Orleans, 1862–63.* Richmond, Va.: Everett Waddey Co., 1911.

Lemmon, Sarah McCulloch, ed. *The Pettigrew Papers.* Raleigh, N.C.: State Department of Archives and History, 1971.

Macaulay, Alexander. "Diary." *William and Mary College Quarterly*, 1st ser., vol. 11 (1902).

Magnolia, 1841–1843.

Mallard, Robert O. *Plantation Life Before Emancipation.* Richmond, Va.: Whitlet & Shepperson, 1892.

Manigault, Ann. "Journal." *South Carolina Historical and Genealogical Magazine* 20 (1919): 128–46, 204–12.

"Marriage and Divorce." *Southern Quarterly Review*, vol. 26 (1854).

Martineau, Harriet. *Society in America.* London: Saunders & Otley, 1837.

———— . *Views on Slavery and Emancipation.* New York: Pierce & Reed, 1837.

Mason, Emily V. *Journal of a Young Lady of Virginia, 1782.* Ed. Lucinda Orr. Baltimore: J. Murphy & Co., 1871.

McCrady, Edward. *The History of South Carolina Under the Royal Government 1719–1776.* New York: Macmillan Co., 1901.

McIntosh, Maria J. *Woman in America: Her Work and Her Reward.* New York: D. Appleton & Co., 1850.

Merrick, Caroline E. *Old Times in Dixie Land: A Southern Matron's Memories.* New York: Grafton Press, 1901.

Miers, Earl Schenck. *When the World Ended: Diary of Emma LeConte.* New York: Oxford University Press, 1957.

Mitchell, Elisha. *North Carolina, 1827–1828.* James Sprunt Historical Monograph no. 6. Chapel Hill: University of North Carolina, 1905.

Montgomery, Cora. *Eagle Pass or Life on the Border.* New York: G. P. Putnam & Co., 1852.

Myers, Robert Manson, ed. *The Children of Pride: A True Story of Georgia and the Civil War.* New Haven, Conn.: Yale University Press, 1972.

Newman, Frances William. *Characters of the Southern States of America.* Manchester, Eng.: Manchester Union and Emancipation Society, 1863.

Newsome, Alfred R. "Twelve Counties." *North Carolina Historical Review* 5–6 (1928–29): 413–46, 67–99, 171–89, 281–309.

Noel, Baptist W. *Freedom and Slavery in the United States of America.* London: J. Nisbet & Co., 1863.

"Northern and Southern Slavery." *Southern Literary Messenger,* vol. 7, no. 4 (April 1841).

Orr, Lucinda. *Journal of a Young Lady of Virginia, 1782.* Ed. Emily Virginia Mason. Baltimore: J. Murphy & Co., 1871.

Padgett, James A., ed. "A Yankee Schoolteacher in Louisiana." *Louisiana Historical Quarterly* 20 (1937): 651–79.

Page, Thomas Nelson. *Social Life in Old Virginia Before the War.* New York: Charles Scribner's, Sons 1898.

Pennington, Patience. *A Woman Rice Planter.* Cambridge, Mass.: Harvard University Press, Belknap Press, 1961.

Poe, Clarence, ed. *True Tales of the South at War, 1861–65.* Chapel Hill: University of North Carolina Press, 1961.

Presley, Delma Eugene. *"Dr. Bullie's" Notes: Reminiscenes of Early Georgia and of Philadelphia and New Haven in the 1800's.* Ed. James Holmes. Atlanta, Ga.: Cherokee Publishing Co., 1976.

Preston, Mrs. William. *The Land We Love.* Charlotte, N.C.: J. P. Irwin & D. H. Hill, 1867–69.

Pringle, Elizabeth Allson. *Chronicles of Chicora Wood.* New York: Charles Scribner's Sons, 1922.

Robertson, Mary D., ed. *Lucy Breckenridge of Grove Hill: The Journal of a Virginia Girl, 1862–1864.* Kent, Ohio: Kent State University Press, 1979.

Roebuck, Haywood. "North Carolina Divorce and Alimony Petitions: 1813." *North Carolina Genealogical Society Journal,* vol. 1 (April 1975).

Rowland, Mrs. Dunbar. *Life, Letters and Papers of William Dunbar.* Jackson: Press of the Mississippi Historical Society, 1930.

Russell, Sir William Howard. *My Diary North and South.* Boston: T. O. H. P. Burnham, 1863.

Salls, H. Harriet, ed. "Pamela Savage Diary, 1825–27." *North Carolina Historical Review* 29 (1952): 540–68.

Saxon, Elizabeth Lyle. *A Southern Woman's Wartime Reminiscences.* Memphis, Tenn.: Pilcher Printing Co., 1905.

Scott, Edwin J. *Random Recollections of a Long Life, 1806–76.* Columbia, S.C.: C. A. Calvo, 1884.

Sharon, James. *The Adventures of James Sharon.* Baltimore, 1808.

Shecut, John L. E. W. *Medical and Philosophical Essays.* Charleston, S.C.: A. E. Miller, 1819.

Sherrill, Charles H. *French Memories of Eighteenth Century America.* New York: Charles Scribner's Sons, 1915.

Skinner, George. *Practical Compendium of Midwifery.* 3rd ed. Philadelphia: Haswell, Barrington & Haswell, 1840.

Slade, Jeremiah. *North Carolina Diary, 1819.* Trinity College Historical Papers, no. 6. 1966.

Smedes, Susan Dabney. *Memorials of a Southern Planter.* New York: Alfred A. Knopf, 1965.

Smith, Daniel E., Alice R. Huger Smith, and Arney R. Childs, eds. *Mason Smith Family Letters, 1860–68.* Columbia: University of South Carolina Press, 1950.

Smith, Josiah. "Prison Diary." *South Carolina Historical and Genealogical Magazine* 33 (1933): 31–39, 67–84, 138–48, 194–210.

Southern Review, 1828–1833.

Statistics of the United States in 1860. Washington, D.C.: Government Printing Office, 1866.

Sterling, Ada, ed. *A Belle of the Fifties: Memoirs of Mrs. Clay of Alabama.* New York: Doubleday, Page & Co., 1904.

Tarboro Free Press, 1829.

Taylor, Mrs. *Practical Hints to Young Females.* Boston: 1816.

Thornton, Anna M. "Diary of Mrs. William Thornton, 1800–63." *Columbia Historical Society Records,* 10, 19.

Tower, Philo. *Slavery Unmasked, Being a Truthful Narrative of a Three Years' Residence and Journeying in Eleven Southern States.* 1856. Reprint ed. Westport, Conn.: Greenwood Press, 1969.

Von Briesen, Martha, ed. *The Letters of Elijah Fletcher*. Charlottesville: University of Virginia Press, 1965.

Weld, Theodore, ed. *American Slavery as It Is*. New York: American Anti-Slavery Society, 1839.

Wood, Virginia, and Ralph Wood, eds. *Ruben King Journal, 1800–06*. Collections of the Georgia Historical Society, no. 15. Savannah, 1971.

Woodward, C. Vann, ed. *Mary Chesnut's Civil War*. New Haven, Conn.: Yale University Press, 1981.

Woolsey, T. D. *Divorce and Divorce Legislation*. New York: Charles Scribner's Sons, 1882.

SECONDARY SOURCES

Alford, Terry. *Prince Among Slaves*. New York: Harcourt Brace Jovanovich, 1977.

Bailey, Hugh C., and William P. Dale. "Missus Alone in de Big House." *Alabama Review* 8 (1955): 43–54.

Barker-Benfield, G. J. *The Horrors of the Half-Known Life: Male Attitudes Toward Women and Sexuality in Nineteenth-Century America* (New York: W. W. Norton & Co., 1976).

Barnwell, Stephen B. *The Story of an American Family*. Marquette, Mich.: n.p. 1969.

Berkin, Carol, and Mary Beth Norton. *Women and America: A History*. Boston: Houghton Mifflin Co., 1979.

Biddle, Francis. "Scandal at Bizarre." *American Heritage* 12 (August 1961): 10–13, 79–82.

Blake, John B. "Women and Medicine in Ante-Bellum America." *Bulletin of the History of Medicine* 39 (March –April 1965): 99–123.

Blassingame, John. *The Slave Community: Plantation Life in the Antebellum South*. New York: Oxford University Press, 1972.

Brewster, Lawrence Fay. *Summer Migrations and Resorts of South Carolina Lowcountry Planters*. Durham, N.C.: Duke University Press, 1947.

Bruce, Dickson. *Violence and Culture in the Antebellum South*. Memphis: University of Tennessee Press, 1979.

Calhoun, Arthur W. *A Social History of the American Family from Colonial Times to the Present*. Cleveland, Ohio: Arthur Clarke & Co., 1918. 3 vols.

Carroll, Berenice. *Liberating Women's History: Theoretical and Critical Essays.* Urbana: University of Illinois Press, 1976.

Carson, Jane. *Plantation Housekeeping in Colonial Virginia.* Williamsburg, Va.: Colonial Williamsburg, 1975.

Cash, Wilbur J. *The Mind of the South.* New York: Alfred A. Knopf, 1941.

Clissold, Stephen. *The Barbary Slaves.* Totowa, N.J.: Rowman & Littlefield, 1977.

Coleman, Mary H. *St. George Tucker: Citizen of No Mean City.* Richmond, Va.: Dietz Press, 1938.

Cooper, Frederick. *Plantation Slavery on the East Coast of Africa.* New Haven, Conn.: Yale University Press, 1977.

Cooper, William J., Jr. *The South and the Politics of Slavery, 1826–1856.* Baton Rouge: Louisiana State University Press, 1978.

Cowden, G. S. "The Randolphs of Turkey Island: A Prosopography of the First Three Generations, 1650–1806." Unpublished Ph.D. dissertation, William and Mary College, 1977.

Cott, Nancy. *The Bonds of Womanhood: Woman's Sphere in New England.* New Haven, Conn.: Yale University Press, 1978.

Courtwright, David. *Dark Paradise: Opiates in America Before 1940.* Cambridge, Mass.: Harvard University Press, 1982.

Davis, David Brion. *The Problem of Slavery in Western Culture.* Ithaca, N.Y.: Cornell University Press, 1966.

Degler, Carl. *At Odds: Women and the Family in America from the Revolution to the Present.* New York: Oxford University Press, 1980.

——— . *Place Over Time: The Continuity of Southern Distinctiveness.* Baton Rouge: Louisiana State University Press, 1977.

Dollard, John. *Caste and Class in a Southern Town.* New Haven, Conn.: Yale University Press, 1937.

Douglas, Ann. *The Feminization of American Culture.* New York: Alfred A. Knopf, 1977.

DuBois, Ellen. *Feminism and Suffrage: The Emergence of an Independent Women's Movement in America, 1848–1869.* Ithaca, N.Y.: Cornell University Press, 1968.

Eaton, Clement. *The Growth of Southern Civilization, 1790–1860.* New York: Harper & Row, 1961.

Elkins, Stanley. *Slavery: A Problem in American Institutional and Intellectual Life*. Chicago: University of Chicago Press, 1962.

Faderman, Lillian. *Surpassing the Love of Men: Romantic Friendship and Love Between Women from the Renaissance to the Present*. New York: William Morrow & Co., 1981.

Faust, Drew Gilpin. *The Ideology of Slavery: Proslavery Thought in the Ante-bellum South*. Baton Rouge: Louisiana State University Press, 1981.

_____ . *The Sacred Circle: The Dilemma of the Intellectual in the Old South*. Baltimore: Johns Hopkins University Press, 1978.

Finley, M. I. *Ancient Slavery and Modern Ideology*. New York: Viking Press, 1980.

Firestone, Shulamith. *The Dialectic of Sex: The Case for Feminist Revolution*. New York: Bantam Books, 1971.

Fletcher, Susan Bradford. "Certain Phases of the Social History of Savannah Before 1860." Unpublished M.A. thesis, Duke University, 1938.

Fogel, Robert, and Stanley Engerman. *Time on the Cross: The Economics of American Negro Slavery*. Boston: Little, Brown & Co., 1974.

Foner, Eric. *Free Soil, Free Labor, Free Men: The Ideology of the Republican Party Before the Civil War*. New York: Oxford University Press, 1971.

Foucault, Michel. *The History of Sexuality: An Introduction*. New York: Pantheon Books, 1979.

Gaines, Francis Pendleton. *The Southern Plantation: A Study in the Development and Accuracy of a Tradition*. New York: Columbia University Press, 1925.

Galloway, Charles B. *Elizabeth Female Academy: The Mother of Female Colleges*. Publications of the Mississippi Historical Society, no. 3. Jackson, 1899.

Gamble, Thomas. *Savannah Duels and Duelists, 1733–1877*. Savannah, Ga.: Review Publishing and Printing Co., 1923.

Gay, Dorothy Ann. "The Tangled Skein of Romanticism and Violence in the Old South: The Southern Response to Abolitionism and Feminism, 1830–1861." Unpublished Ph.D. dissertation, University of North Carolina at Chapel Hill, 1975.

Genovese, Eugene D. *The Political Economy of Slavery: Studies in the Economy and Society of the Slave South*. New York: Pantheon Books, 1969.

_____ . *Roll, Jordan, Roll: The World the Slaves Made*. New York: Pantheon Books, 1976.

Greenberg, Michael. "Gentlemen Slaveholders: The Social Outlook of the Virginia Planter Class." Unpublished Ph.D. dissertation, Rutgers University, 1972.

Gutman, Herbert. *The Black Family in Slavery and Freedom, 1750–1925*. New York: Pantheon Books, 1976.

Hall, Jaqueline Dowd. *Revolt Against Chivalry: Jesse Daniel Ames and the Women's Campaign Against Lynching*. New York: Columbia University Press, 1979.

Holliday, Carl. *Woman's Life in Colonial Days*. Williamstown, Mass.: Corner House Publishers, 1968.

Howard, George Elliott. *A History of Matrimonial Institutions*. Chicago: University of Chicago Press, 1904.

Huff, Archie Vernon. *Langdon Cheves of South Carolina*. Columbia: University of South Carolina Press, 1977.

Jennings, Francis. *The Invasion of America: Indians, Colonialism and the Cant of Conquest*. Chapel Hill: University of North Carolina Press for the Institute of Early American History and Culture, 1975.

Johnson, Guion Griffis. *Ante-Bellum North Carolina: A Social History*. Chapel Hill: University of North Carolina Press, 1937.

Johnston, James H. *Race Relations in Virginia and Miscegenation in the South, 1776–1860*. 1937. Reprint ed. Amherst: University of Massachusetts Press, 1970.

Jordan, Winthrop. *White Over Black: American Attitudes Towards the Negro, 1550–1812*. Chapel Hill: University of North Carolina Press, 1968.

Kallsen, Loren J. *The Kentucky Tragedy: A Problem in Romantic Attitudes*. Indianapolis: Bobbs-Merrill Co., 1963.

Kerber, Linda. *Women of the Republic: Intellect and Ideology in Revolutionary America*. Chapel Hill: University of North Carolina Press for the Institute of Early American History and Culture, 1980.

Kovel, Joel. *White Racism: A Psychohistory*. New York: Pantheon Books, 1970.

Lane, Ann, ed. *The Debate over Slavery: Stanley Elkins and His Critics*. Chicago: University of Chicago Press, 1971.

Lerner, Gerda. *Black Women in White America*. New York: Pantheon Books, 1972.

_____ . *The Grimké Sisters from South Carolina: Rebels Against Slavery*. Boston: Houghton Mifflin Co., 1967.

Levine, Lawrence. *Black Culture and Black Consciousness: Afro-American Folk Thought from Slavery to Freedom*. New York: Oxford University Press, 1977.

Lyon, Catherine Hill. "The Development of Secondary Education for Women in the United States." Unpublished M.A. thesis, Duke University, 1936.

Lyon, Ralph M. "The Early Years of Livingston Female Academy." *Alabama Historical Quarterly* 37 (1975): 192–205.

MacLeod, Duncan. *Slavery, Race and the American Revolution*. London: Cambridge University Press, 1974.

Mannoni, Octave. *Prospero and Caliban: A Study of the Psychology of Colonization*. Trans. P. Powesland. New York: Frederick A. Praeger, 1956.

Mathews, Donald G. *Religion in the Old South*. Chicago: University of Chicago Press, 1977.

Melder, Keith. "Ladies Bountiful: Organized Women's Benevolence in Early 19th-Century America." *New York History* 58 (July 1967): 231–54.

Mencke, John G. *Mulattoes and Race Mixture: American Attitudes and Images, 1865–1918*. Ann Arbor: University of Michigan Research Press, 1979.

Merrill, Boynton, Jr. *Jefferson's Nephews: A Frontier Tragedy*. Princeton, N.J.: Princeton University Press, 1976.

Meyer, Leland. *The Life and Times of Colonel Richard M. Johnson of Kentucky*. New York: Columbia University Press, 1932.

Mohr, James. *Abortion in America: The Origins and Evolution of National Policy*. New York: Oxford University Press, 1978.

Muhlenfeld, Elisabeth. *Mary Boykin Chesnut: A Biography*. Baton Rouge: Louisiana State University Press, 1981.

Norton, Mary Beth. *Liberty's Daughters: The Revolutionary Experience of American Women, 1750–1800*. Boston: Little, Brown & Co., 1980.

Oakes. James. *The Ruling Race: A History of American Slaveholders*. New York: Alfred A. Knopf, 1982.

Osterweis, Rollin G. *Romanticism and Nationalism in the Old South*. Boston: Little, Brown & Co., 1929.

Phillips, U. B. *American Negro Slavery: A Survey of the Supply, Employment and Control of Negro Labor As Determined by Plantation Returns*. New York: D. Appleton & Co., 1918.

————. *Life and Labor in the Old South*. Boston: Little, Brown & Co., 1929.

Ravenal, Harriott H. *Eliza Pinckney*. New York: Charles Scribner's Sons, 1896.

Reniers, Percival. *The Springs of Virginia: Life, Love and Death at the Waters, 1775–1900*. Chapel Hill: University of North Carolina Press, 1941.

Robateau, Albert. *Slave Religion: The Invisible Institution in the Antebellum South*. New York: Oxford University Press, 1978.

Robinson, Donald L. *Slavery in the Structure of American Politics, 1765–1820*. New York: Harcourt Brace Jovanovich, 1971.

Rogers, Lou. *Tar Heel Women*. Raleigh, N.C.: Warren Publishing Co., 1949.

Ruoff, John C. "Frivolity to Consumption: Or, Southern Womanhood in Antebellum Literature." *Civil War History* 18 (1972): 213–29.

Scott, Anne Firor. *The Southern Lady: From Pedestal to Politics, 1830–1930*. Chicago: University of Chicago Press, 1970.

Sides, Sudie Duncan. "Southern Women and Slavery." *History Today* 20 (1970): 54–60, 124–30.

Simkins, Frances Butler, and James Welch Patterson. *The Women of the Confederacy*. Richmond, Va.: Garrett & Massie, 1936.

Smith, Lillian. *Killers of the Dream*. New York: W. W. Norton & Co., 1949.

Smith-Rosenberg, Carroll. "Beauty, the Beast, and the Militant Woman: A Case Study in Sex Roles and Social Stress in Jacksonian America." *American Quarterly* 23 (October 1971): 562–84.

———. "The Female World of Love and Ritual: Relations Between Women in Nineteenth Century America." *Signs* 1 (Autumn 1975): 1–29.

Spruill, Julia Cherry. *Woman's Life and Work in the Southern Colonies*. 1938. Reprint ed. New York: W. W. Norton & Co., 1972.

Stampp, Kenneth. *The Peculiar Institution: Slavery in the Ante-Bellum South*. New York: Alfred A. Knopf, 1956.

Stanard, Mary. *Colonial Virginia, Its People and Customs*. Philadelphia, J. B. Lippincott Co., 1917.

Stephenson, Wendell Holmes. *Isaac Franklin: Slave Trader and Planter of the Old South*. Baton Rouge: Louisiana State University Press, 1938.

Stevens, William O. *Pistols at Ten Paces: The Story of the Code of Honor in America*. Boston: Houghton Mifflin Co., 1940.

Stone, Lawrence. *The Family, Sex and Marriage in England, 1500–1800*. New York: Oxford University Press, 1977.

Takaki, Ron. *Iron Cages: Race and Culture in Nineteenth Century America*. New York: Alfred A. Knopf, 1979.

Taylor, Rosser H. *Antebellum South Carolina: A Social and Cultural History*. Chapel Hill: University of North Carolina Press, 1926.

Taylor, William R. *Cavalier and Yankee: The Old South and American National Character*. New York: George Braziller, 1961.

Waring, Martha G. "Savannah's Earliest Private Schools." *Georgia Historical Quarterly* 14 (1930): 324–34.

Wells, Robert. *Revolutions in Americans' Lives: A Demographic Perspective on Americans, the Families and Society*. Westport, Conn.: Greenwood Press, 1982.

Welter, Barbara. *Dimity Convictions: The American Woman in the Nineteenth Century*. Columbus: University of Ohio Press, 1976.

Williamson, Joel. *New People: Miscegenation and Mulattoes in the United States*. New York: Free Press, 1980.

Wilson, Elizabeth Andrews. "Hygienic Care and Management of the Child in the American Family Prior to 1860." Unpublished M.A. thesis, Duke University, 1940.

Wood, Peter. *Black Majority: Negroes in Colonial South Carolina From 1670 Through the Stono Rebellion*. New York: Alfred A. Knopf, 1974.

Woodson, Carter G. *Absentee Ownership of Slaves in the United States in 1830*. Washington, D.C.: Association for the Study of Negro Life and History, 1924.

Woody, Thomas. *A History of Women's Education in the United States*. New York: Science Press, 1929.

Wyatt-Brown, Bertram. *Southern Honor*. New York: Oxford University Press, 1982.

Zaretsky, Eli. *Capitalism, the Family and Personal Life*. New York: Harper & Row, 1976.

INDEX

fashion, 99
fathers, 40–4
Fayette (North Carolina), 128
female academies, 12–13, 54; costs, 135, 271;
    curriculum, 130–3; discipline, 133–4
female culture, 11, 174–5
female friendships, 12, 54, 62, 174–5
feminism, 205
Feminism and Suffrage (Dubois), 13
Feminization of American Culture, The
    (Douglas), 9
Fénélon, François, 132
Few, Mary, 27, 93, 166, 169, 183
films, 225, 226, 228, 229
Fisher, Ann Ambler, 53
Fisher, Janetta, 53
Fitzgerald, Elizabeth, 151
Fitzhugh, George, 13
Fleur (Delauncy), 225
Floretta, Floreal, 213
Floyd, Charles Rinaldo, 71
Fogel, Robert, 29–30, 220–1
food: holiday, 177; preparation, 19–21, 23–4
Ford, Timothy, 37, 72
Foster, Hannah Webster, 10
Foster, Susan (Carson), 215
Foster, Thomas, junior, 214–15
Foster, Thomas, senior, 214–15
Foster, Thomas F., 64
Foucault, Michel, 223, 224, 293
France (Sismondi), 132
Frank (slave), 192
Franklin, John Hope, 165
Fraser, John, 65
freckles, 100
French Revolution, The (Carlyle), 173
frontier fever, 166–8

Galloway, Grace, 10
Gambell, Henry and Nancy, 82
gambling, 105–6
gardening, 23
Gatewood, Sallie, 213
Gayle, Sarah, 73, 168, 175, 183
Genovese, Eugene D., xii, 212
Gibson, Elizabeth (Macmurdo), 51–2, 67, 70,
    71, 151
Gibson, Patrick, 51–2
Godwin, William, 173
Goldsborough, John, 150
Goldsmith, Oliver, 120
Gone with the Wind (1939), 4, 225, 226
gonorrhea. *See* venereal diseases
Gordon, Sarah and William, 207–8

governesses, 47, 126–7
Great Awakening, Second, 11
Gregory, William O., 97
Grimké, Angelina, 10, 180–1, 189, 198
Grimké, Henry, 214
Grimké, Montague, 214
Grimké, Sarah, 214
Gurley, Jane, 189

Habersham, Joseph, 153
Haig, Sarah G., 32
Haitian Revolution, 127, 195, 217
Hall, Bolling, 30, 89, 98, 102
Hall, Maria (Polly), 98, 102
Hall, Martha, 98, 102
Hamilton, Elizabeth, 82
Hammond, James, 5
Harden, Marian, 57
Harrison, Randolph, 115
Hasell, Dr. George, 153
Hatch, Mary, 168, 171
Haywood, Elizabeth, 44
Haywood, John, 44, 152
Haywood, Sally, 152
health, 139, 152; exercise, 140–1. *See also*
    death; medicine; nervous disorders;
    opium; springs and resorts
Hemings, Betty, 218–9
Hemings, Madison and Eston, 218
Hemings, Sally, 218–9
Henshaw, Philip, 213
Herodotus, 132
Hester (slave), 189
History of America (Smith), 132
History of Greece (Gille), 132
hogs. *See* pork
Holmes, Louise, 150
Holmes, Margaret, 38
Holmes, Owen, 167
Holmes, Thomas N., 37
"Homespun Dress, The," 198
honor. *See* Code of Honor
horseback riding, 140–1
hospitality, 176–7
House of Burgesses (Virginia), 4
housekeeping, 18–21, 26
Howard, Caroline, 141
Howell, Margaret, 175
Hull, C. A., 110
Hume, Mary, 123
Hunt, Mary Ann, 133
Huntington, Francis, 206
Huntsville (Alabama), 211
Hutchinson, Susan, 171, 172

ABOUT THE AUTHOR

Catherine Clinton was born in Seattle and grew up in Kansas City. She was educated at Harvard, the University of Sussex, and Princeton University, where she received her Ph.D. in American history. She now teaches history at Union College in Schenectady, N.Y. She and her husband live in New York City.